BERLITZ®

DISCOVER
LOIRE VALLEY

Pat and Hazel Constance

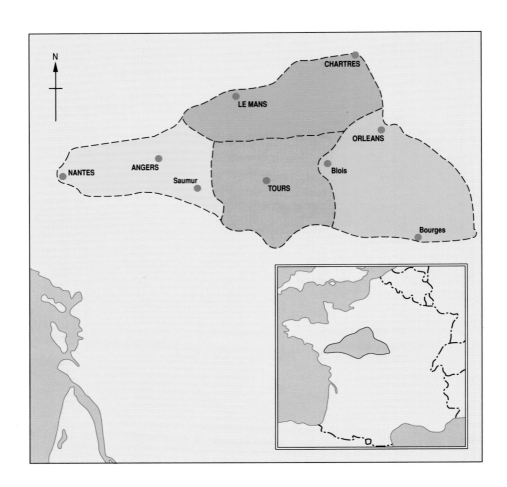

BERLITZ®

DISCOVER
LOIRE VALLEY

Edited and Designed by
D & N Publishing,
Lambourn, Berkshire.

Cartography by
Hardlines, Charlbury, Oxfordshire.

Phototypeset by FIDO Imagesetting, Witney, Oxfordshire.

Printed by Butler and Tanner Ltd., Frome, Somerset.

Although we have made every effort to ensure the accuracy of all the information in this book, changes occur incessantly. We cannot therefore take responsibility for facts, addresses and circumstances in general that are constantly subject to alteration.

Acknowledgements

The authors would like to thank: Pauline Hallam and Marc Humphries of the French Government Tourist Office, London; The Departmental Tourist Offices in France, especially Martine Pagliocca in Le Mans, Hélène Pouleau in Angers, Catherine Petit-Jouvet in Chartres, Pascal Ferrare in Blois and Jean-Paul Dorié in Nantes; and Campanile Hotels, Confortel Louisiane, Select Site Reservations, Unicorn Holidays Ltd., Eurocamp and Brittany Ferries, for their help and assistance during the preparation of this book.

Cover photographs by the authors.

Photographic Acknowledgements

All photographs by the authors except the following which is courtesy of the Comité Départemental du Tourisme de l'Anjou: p 314. The following photographs © Berlitz Publishing Co. Ltd: pp6, 13, 19, 20, 29, 31, 33, 38, 50, 118, 150, 151, 162, 164, 171, 214, 215, 237, 241, 243, 247, 273, 274, 281 (lower), 285, 286, 298, 299, 324.

 The Berlitz tick is used to indicate places or events of particular interest.

Contents

Loire—Garden of France, Birthplace of the French Renaissance

In this introduction on how best to travel to and enjoy the Valley of the Loire we ask that you do not come as a "tourist", but come to visit this fascinating part of France, to seek out some of the lesser known villages, to relax and enjoy the peaceful countryside and savour the delights of good food and wine. While in the Loire marvel at the buildings, great and small, which have evolved over the centuries, and read from them the story of how this land has played its part in France's history and its neighbours.

"Valley of the Loire". The very words are likely to conjure up thoughts of a stately river lined with fantastic castles and romantic châteaux set in beautiful formal gardens. The truth does include such features, but much more besides.

The whole of the area covered by this book abounds in places of interest—châteaux and country houses which are not on the usual "tourist routes", hidden gems of villages set in peaceful and pleasant rural landscapes, historic towns and cities. The towns are full of surprises—behind the rather

The 14th-century feudal fortress of Sully-sur-Loire was built to command a crossing-point of the river.

neglected shuttered windows with peeling paintwork, one can often gain a glimpse of delightful courtyards and gardens hidden behind gates which are usually closed. Another delight lies in the *villages fleuris* with window boxes, flower beds and ornamental trees and shrubs along the streets. These villages are hoping to win a prize for the best effort but, win or lose, the overall effect is still most attractive.

In the early summer countryside (late May and June) the eye is struck by masses of colour, where whole fields are filled with sunflowers (*tournesols*) grown for the oil used in margarine manufacture. By contrast, autumn brings its own visual feast as the many trees change their colours. Added to all this splendour is a long

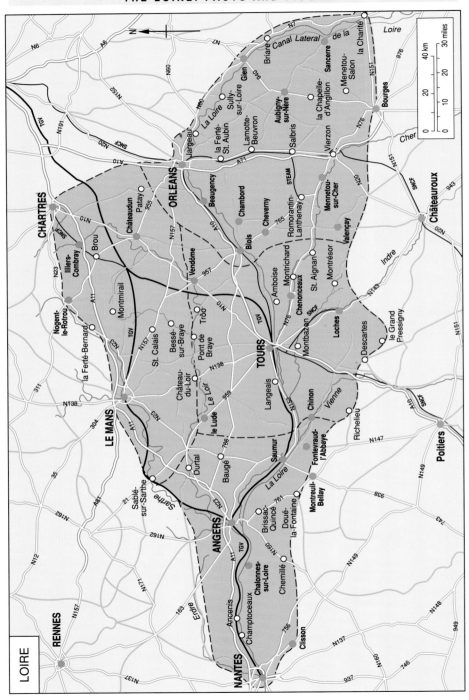

and fascinating history, and wines and gastronomic delights to please all tastes. Enjoy the Valley of the Loire at your leisure.

To be strictly accurate, it is *La Loire*, the longest river in France, that dominates the area of interest. Starting as a mountain stream among the spectacular peaks of the Cévennes in the Massif Central, less than 160km (100 miles) from the Mediterranean coast, it first flows north through gorges to more level country and on to Orléans where it turns in a wide sweep westwards towards Tours, Angers and Nantes, eventually reaching the Atlantic, over 965km (600 miles) away at St Nazaire.

The *Val de Loire* is usually assumed to mean the country bordering the section of the river from around Gien, through the châteaux area, downstream to between Angers and Nantes. To limit one's travelling in such a way is to ignore much delightful country and breathtaking scenery, with beautiful old towns steeped in history, interesting museums both large and small, quiet roads ideal for exploring by car or bicycle through old villages which seem to have remained unchanged for many centuries. Plenty of opportunities exist for gentle or arduous walks, or for fishing or canoeing. Even hot-air balloon trips can be taken: an unusual but fascinating way to see some of the incredible châteaux. In this book the area of interest has

A map of the general area of the Loire valley.

been extended to cover the country bounded roughly by the A11 Autoroute from Nantes to Chartres, the Chartres to Orléans road and the river Loire to La Charité-sur-Loire. From here, the triangle is completed by the road to Bourges and, from there, back to Nantes. The towns of Chartres and Nantes are included, both of which are too good to miss.

Although dominated by the main river of la Loire, the area also includes a number of tributary river valleys. To the south of la Loire the main tributaries are the Cher, the Indre and the Vienne, and to the north are the Authion and the Maine. The Maine takes its water from the Mayenne, the Sarthe and le Loir before it joins the main river. Le Loir (spelt without an 'e') contributes much to the varied and beautiful scenery of the area.

How To Get There

Almost anywhere in the Loire area can be reached within a day by driving from the French Channel ports, or if you don't have a car you could take advantage of one of the fly–drive or rail-plus-car-hire arrangements.

By Air
Services to Paris (Orly or Charles de Gaulle) fly from major airports around the world and from most of the UK airports. Domestic flights connect to Nantes from both Paris terminals. Additionally, there are direct services from London Heathrow to Nantes and an infrequent service from London Gatwick to Tours. Air France operates an inclusive air/rail service from most

major UK airports to Paris (Charles de Gaulle) airport, and from there by rail to Chartres, Le Mans, Nantes, Orléans, Tours or Saumur.

By Sea

A number of UK cross-Channel ferry services take passengers with or without cars, the shortest sea routes being from Dover to Calais (P & O European Ferries and Sealink Stena Line) and from Dover to Boulogne (P & O European Ferries). Fast services between Dover and Calais or Boulogne are provided by Hoverspeed, operating hovercraft or catamarans, although these schedules are more subject to weather conditions. Other routes include Newhaven to Dieppe (Sealink Stena Line), Poole to Cherbourg (Truckline Ferries), Portsmouth to Caen (Brittany Ferries), Portsmouth to Cherbourg (P & O European Ferries), Portsmouth to Le Havre (P & O European Ferries), Portsmouth to St Malo (Brittany Ferries) and Southampton to Cherbourg (Sealink Stena Line). A number of other ferry services are available which, although involving longer road or rail journeys on the Continent to reach the Loire valley, may be more convenient from the north of England or from Scotland. These include North Sea Ferries routes from Hull to either Rotterdam or Zeebrugge, P & O European Ferries service from Felixstowe to Zeebrugge, and the Sealink Stena Line ferry from Harwich to Hook of Holland. Other possibilities are the Olau Line Sheerness to Vlissingen (Holland) and the Sally Line Ramsgate to Dunkerque ferries. From the south-west of England, Brittany Ferries operate from

Plymouth to Roscoff in Brittany. Finally, for travellers from Ireland, Brittany Ferries sail from Cork to Roscoff. The excellent road and rail network across the water makes any of these routes worth considering. Out of the high season it is possible to travel without booking in advance, although this is not to be recommended. Most ferry companies offer special rates depending on date and time of crossing, the age of either the driver or passengers, and whether or not a package

deal includes accommodation in France and hire of bicycles or cars. It pays to shop around.

By Train

The French rail system SNCF (*Société Nationale des Chemins de Fer*) is very well organized and is well integrated with neighbouring European railway networks. Fast services run from Paris to the main centres in the Loire valley. The most prestigious are the TGV (*Trains à Grande Vitesse*) or high-speed

A typical summer scene in Anjou, where whole fields of yellow sunflowers brighten the landscape.

trains, which can reach Le Mans, Tours, Angers or Nantes in less than 2 hours from Paris Gare Montparnasse. From Paris Gare Austerlitz, taking only slightly longer the high-speed express trains known as *Trains Corail* will take you to many more centres in the area. From further afield, *Trans Europ Expresses* (TEE) link into the French system, and for those travelling by ferry as foot passengers there are plenty of good services from all the Channel ports, either via Paris or by more local routes. SNCF offers a number of special fares. Any foreign travellers can buy a "France Vacances" rail pass from their home travel agents, allowing unlimited rail travel for the period of validity, and senior citizens and students holding the appropriate rail passes can obtain substantial reductions. It should be noted that any rail tickets bought in France must be validated (*composter*) by an orange-coloured date stamping machine sited at the station platform entrance. Combined rail and car hire and rail and cycle hire package deals are often available from travel agents.

By Coach
Eurolines operate a scheduled express coach service from London via Dover, stopping at Orléans and Tours. Within Britain, National Express coach services connect from many centres all over the country.

By Car
One of the best ways of seeing the country is by using one's own car. The choice of routes for getting to the Loire area from any area of Europe is very great. The French motorway (*autoroute*) system provides speedy access to most areas. With the exception of the Paris ring road (*périphérique*), most French motorways are toll roads (*autoroutes à péage*), but they provide speedy and well-signed roads for long journeys. The A25 from the ferry port of Dunkerque, and the A26 from Calais link with the A1 which runs south into the *Boulevard Périphérique* around Paris and so on to the A10. This leads to Orléans and the Loire towns towards Tours. From Dieppe and Le Havre, the A13 may be joined south of Rouen, and from there to the A10 south of Paris. From Le Havre, it is necessary to cross the toll bridge at Tancarville. South-west of Paris, the A11 leaves the A10 motorway to serve Chartres, Le Mans, Angers and Nantes, whereas from the A10 at Orléans the A71 continues across la Loire to Bourges. If time is not pressing, there are a number of alternative routes to the area using the excellent main roads.

Before You Go

When To Go

The western part of the area enjoys a mild climate with fresh summer breezes. Touraine and Anjou have similar climates, with mild winters, a rather wet early spring, and dry summers tempered by fresh westerly breezes. To the east beyond Orléans the winters are much colder and the summers are hotter. The open prairie-like Beauce has a much harsher and windier climate, often with snow and ice in winter and with dry summers, while the wooded regions to the south enjoy a milder, wetter, more changeable climate. The best months to visit the Loire are late May, June and July when the flowers make the countryside look most beautiful. For autumn colour, September is particularly attractive although the nights will be getting colder. The summer months tend to be hot and dusty with towns and villages crowded with visitors. Average temperatures can range from 6 °C (43 °F) in winter to 21 °C (70 °F) in summer but can frequently go much higher or lower.

The meandering River Loire is often divided by shallows and sandbanks. Many of the bridges have a long history.

Passports and Visas

Visitors to France from EC countries (and from USA and Canada for stays of up to three months) do not require visas. Those from other countries are advised to consult their nearest French Consulate. British nationals require either a full British Passport, a full EC "common format passport" or a British Visitor's Passport, valid for 1 year for western Europe only. Applications for the full passports must be sent to the appropriate Passport Office. Application forms are available from any post office, but do allow plenty of time. The British Visitor's Passport may be obtained from any main post office (ask for Form VP) but two photographs are required. Although a husband, wife and children under 16 can be included on one passport, this is not a very good idea because a wife or children cannot travel alone on the husband's passport.

Health Matters

The cost of essential medical or hospital treatment may be partly or completely refunded to EC citizens under EC rules, but you will need to obtain a form before leaving your home country to prove your entitlement. The form can be obtained free from any post office, has unlimited validity and is accompanied by an explanation of the procedure to follow if needing medical help. In the UK, leaflet T1 (formerly SA 40/41) issued by the Department of Health gives useful information on health matters for travellers going abroad, and is also available free from any post office. It is recommended that one or two photocopies of the completed form are carried. Since cover under the EC scheme is limited, visitors should ensure they have adequate additional independant insurance against accident or illness.

Motor Vehicles

Although the statutory minimum third-party insurance cover is sufficient, it is advisable to obtain fully comprehensive cover before leaving for France, confirmed by possession of a "green card" from your insurance company. Each driver, who must be over 18, must carry a full driving licence (not provisional). The original vehicle registration document or a Certificate of Registration form V379 must also be carried and, if you are not the owner of the vehicle, you must have written authority from the owner for you to use the vehicle. You will also need a warning triangle, a set of spare light bulbs, and the means to convert the headlamp beams for driving on the right. Although not a legal requirement for vehicles not registered in France, it is a good idea to paint the headlamp glasses yellow. A plate must be displayed near the rear number plate showing your country of origin. Some essential spares such as a fan belt, and any special tools, should also be carried. A sensible precaution is to have the vehicle checked before leaving home. Most garages operate a pre-holiday inspection service.

Camping and Caravanning

In addition to obtaining adequate insurance for your equipment, an International Camping Carnet issued by the Camping and Caravanning Club, the Caravan Club or any other organization of which you are a member and which is affiliated to the FICC or AIT, confirms that you hold third-party insurance cover whilst camping or caravanning. Many sites allow discount on fees to holders of the Carnet, and it may possibly be retained during your stay by site owners in place of your passport.

Money Matters

There is no limit to the amount of sterling or foreign currency that may be taken out of the UK. Obtain some French currency before you go, including some small change if possible. Traveller's cheques in French currency are probably the safest way of carrying money, but Eurocheques supported by a Eurocheque card are becoming more common and are perhaps more convenient. They will allow you to draw out French currency at most banks, the amount drawn being debited to your current account at home. Credit cards such as Visa/Barclaycard (*Carte Bleue*), Eurocard (Mastercard/Access) and Diner's Club are widely accepted.

Maps

Two major sources of maps can be recommended. The French *Institut Géographique National* (IGN) publishes detailed maps of the whole country at various scales. The Green series at 1:100,000 is probably the most useful for general use, and shows the *Sentiers de Grande Randonnée* (GRs) or long-distance walking routes, while, for route planning, the Red series (1:250,000) highlights tourist attractions, historical sites and other interesting features. Motorists will probably find the 1:200,000 scale maps by

Michelin very useful and cheaper. Each sheet has a small gazetteer listing the main towns and villages. These maps are available as a complete set bound into the *Michelin Motoring Atlas of France*, although the single sheets are revised more frequently. Michelin also produce a single sheet at a scale of 1:200,000 highlighting a number of the outstanding tourist attractions along the Loire valley. This map is entitled *"La Vallée des Rois"* and includes most of the area covered in this book. For pre-planning, these Michelin maps, together with sheet 106 of the IGN Red series, will meet most of your touring requirements. Other maps may be bought in France as required. A very good series of town plans, indexed and with tourist information, is published by Blay, and can best be bought locally.

Electrical Appliances

If taking any electrical appliances for use, remember to take a continental adaptor plug. The mains supply in France is almost universally 220 volts, 50 hertz a.c. although in a few places 110 volts may still be found.

Getting About

By Car

Documentation has already been dealt with in the *PRE-PLANNING* section. All drivers must carry a current and valid driving licence, insurance certificate (and green card) and vehicle registration document at all times. Be prepared to produce them on demand if stopped by the police.

Car Hire

Combined air/car and rail/car arrangements have been mentioned. It is also possible to hire independently through one of the international car-hire firms. The advantage of hiring is that you will have a left-hand drive vehicle. All the following points about driving in France apply whether you are using your own car or hiring.

Driving in France

French roads are generally good, with clear road signs. The fast, safe motorways or autoroutes, designated by "A", are nearly all toll roads where a card is taken at the entry point (*péage*) and payment is made when leaving the motorway. The procedure is quite simple, and payment by Visa or Access credit card is possible. Orange-coloured emergency telephones are positioned every 2 km (1.2 miles) along the route and service stations with all amenities and rest areas (*aires*) are located at intervals. Other major highways designated "N" (*Routes Nationales*) are also excellent, while secondary roads or *Routes Départementales* (D) provide an interesting network for exploring the country. Road designations can be confusing as there appears to be a scheme for changing them which has not yet been completed! Be prepared for discrepancies between your road maps and what you find on the ground. Also, the number of a "D" road can change as it crosses a *départemental* boundary. Where road numbers are quoted in route descriptions, these are what were found at the time, so be warned! Minor roads, marked "V" (*Chemins Vicinaux*) are shown uncoloured on the road maps and provide interesting routes for local exploration. Many French N and D roads run as straight as an arrow across country for long distances, with perhaps a sharp kink at a stream or river crossing. As they are lined very often with trees, these roads can lull a tired driver into forgetting that there are blind spots where the road runs over the top of a rise, just where a tractor may be coming out of a hidden side turning.

Direction Signs on motorways are white on blue, and for other main roads are white on green. *Itinéraire Bis* signs with yellow lettering on a green background, and bearing the word "Bis" on yellow, indicate less congested alternative routes, and yellow signs with black lettering show temporary routes or diversions (*déviations*). On secondary and minor roads, signs are black on white. It can be confusing sometimes when you approach a junction, because a direction arrow to a destination pointing to the left means, in fact, that you go straight on! Also it seems as if you are only intended to approach villages from the direction the road planners wish. It is not uncommon to see the blank back of a sign, with the name of your intended destination on the reverse side, visible when coming in the opposite direction. It all makes for an interesting drive!

Seat belts must be worn by drivers and by all passengers including those in rear seats. Children under the age of 10 years are not allowed in front seats.

Traffic drives on the right in common with the rest of continental Europe. If you are driving your own (right-hand drive) car, take extra care when starting out, overtaking or at roundabouts. The rule of giving way to all vehicles approaching from your right no longer applies. Traffic on major roads has priority, but at crossroads the sign *Danger. Priorité à Droite* indicates that you must give way to vehicles coming from the right. The international sign of a yellow diamond denotes a major road which has priority. Traffic on a roundabout always has priority. Where there are no signs take extra care when approaching side turnings.

Use of headlights is compulsory at night, but they must be dipped in built-up areas. They should also be used in poor visibility. If an oncoming driver flashes you, pull over and let him pass.

Overtaking is prohibited where the road has one or two continuous unbroken lines, or when another vehicle is already being overtaken. Processions, funerals or marching troops must not be overtaken at more than 30 kph (18 mph). Where lines are broken, signal and overtake if your way is clear, but you must return immediately to the right after passing.

Speed limits are as follows:
50 kph (31 mph) within city areas
60 kph (37 mph) in towns/villages or as indicated
90 kph (56 mph) outside built-up areas on normal roads
110 kph (68 mph) on dual carriageway roads
130 kph (81 mph) on toll motorways (autoroutes)
In rain or bad weather the above limits are lowered to:
110 kph (68 mph) on motorways
100 kph (62 mph) on dual carriageway roads

80 kph (50 mph) on other roads outside built-up areas.

A minimum speed limit of 80 kph (50 mph) applies to the outside lane of motorways during daylight in good visibility, and a driver must not exceed 90 kph (56 mph) during the first year after passing the test.

Traffic Lights

There is no amber light after the red light. Flashing amber means proceed with caution and flashing red means no entry. A flashing yellow arrow shows you may go in the direction indicated, but you must give way to pedestrians and to the traffic flow you are joining.

Drinking and Driving

Do not drink and drive. Drivers exceeding the limit of 0.08 per cent alcohol level will be prosecuted.

Parking

Parking meters are often installed in town centres. Alternatively, Blue Zones permit parking for a stated time, usually for 1 hour, provided a parking disc (*disque de stationnement*) is displayed inside the car. These discs may be obtained free from police stations, tourist offices and from some shops. When parking, set the disc to show the time of arrival, and the time when the space will be free. Do not park where the kerbs are marked with yellow paint. Away from towns, you must pull off the road to park. There may be signs which indicate the side of the road where parking is allowed, for example, on odd or even days, or they may tell you times during which parking is, or is not, allowed.

Fuel

Most major international petrol companies have filling stations in France, and many are self service (*libre service*). Premium (*super*) and regular (*essence*) grades of leaded petrol are available. Unleaded (*sans plomb*) is also available although not as common as one would think. This situation is improving. Diesel oil (*gas-oil*) is cheap. A list of filling stations supplying LPG (*Gepel/ GPL*) is obtainable free from the French Government Tourist Office. Many petrol stations accept credit cards. The cheapest petrol is likely to be from supermarket or hypermarket pumps, although not all of them stock lead-free petrol.

Traffic police (*Garde Mobile*) patrol the roads and motorways in cars or on motor cycles. They can be helpful in an emergency but they can also impose heavy on-the-spot fines for traffic offences such as speeding, or driving after drinking.

By Motorcycle or Moped

This is a wonderful way of exploring the region. Generally, the same rules of the road apply as for cars, except that an approved helmet must be worn by the rider. Speed limits and minimum ages are as follows:

Light motorcycles (51cc–80cc): 75 kph (46 mph). Minimum age 16.

Medium (81cc–400cc): Limits as for cars. Minimum age 18.

Heavy (over 400cc): as for cars but a heavy motorcycle licence required. Otherwise, all riders must hold full licences.

Registration plates, country identification plate and third-party insurance cover are required and dipped headlights are to be used at all times when moving. Motorcycles are allowed on motorways.

Mopeds up to 50cc, designed not to exceed 45 kph (28 mph) require no licence, but the rider must be over 14 and must be covered by insurance. Approved helmets must be worn. Mopeds are forbidden on motorways and must use cycle paths where they exist.

Passengers may only be carried where a separate passenger seat is fitted. Only one passenger is allowed on a solo machine and not more than two when a side-car is fitted. Approved helmets must be worn by all passengers and all must be covered by insurance.

Moped hire is an economical alternative to car hire and most towns have a hire centre, often in conjunction with bicycle hire. Legal requirements are that the rider must be over 21 and have held a full driving licence for more than 1 year.

By Bicycle

The Loire valley is particularly suitable for exploring by bicycle as there are no very steep hills to climb. You can either tour with full camping kit or just with personal clothing if sleeping in fixed accommodation, or you can use the bicycle for day trips. Ride on the right, and use cycle paths where they exist. Cycles may be hired at many places, including railway stations. Insurance is recommended.

By Train

Local train services are good and are backed up by SNCF-operated buses which will take you to outlying destinations. A number of special concessionary fares are available: *France-*

Vacances gives unlimited 1st or 2nd class travel on any 4 days during a period of 15 days or for any 9 days during 1 month. The pass must be purchased before arriving in France, from SNCF or from travel agents. Other special fare passes are available for senior citizens, families or for young people under 26. Certain trains will carry bicycles as hand luggage. Details of these, and any other services, as well as times of trains, can be obtained from any SNCF station. A number of stations operate a bicycle hire service which enables you to hire the cycle at one station and return it to another.

By Bus

Bus terminals are usually close to railway stations, and some services are run by SNCF in conjunction with the trains. Bus stations in the main towns are known as *gares routières,* and a bus or coach is a *car* in French. Details of routes and service times may be obtained locally.

By Taxi

In larger towns, taxi stands are to be found at the railway stations and in town centres. In small towns and villages, a taxi will usually be located at a hotel or garage. Fares vary and for longer journeys it is advisable to check the price before you start out. A tip of 10 to 15 per cent is usual.

Where to Stay

Accommodation is easy to find with the help of the local *Office de Tourisme* or *Syndicat d'Initiative.* A number of larger towns have *"Accueil de France"* tourist offices which, in addition to having information on all types of accommodation in the town and in the surrounding area, can make bookings, for personal callers only, for the same day or for up to eight days in advance. A small fee is charged to cover telephone or telex costs. *Accueil de France* offices may be found in Angers, Blois, Nantes, Orléans and Tours, and are open every day.

Hotels

Many of the larger towns have a good selection of hotels which have been classified as one-star to four-star, on the basis of their facilities, by the Ministry of Tourism. Rates are normally quoted per night for two persons, with continental breakfast charged extra. Many hotels have their own restaurant and would normally expect you to take dinner there at night. They will often quote for room and all meals (full board or *pension*) or for room, breakfast and main meal (half board or *demi-pension*). Prices must be displayed in each room, but check if these prices include taxes and service. Many hotels, particularly in smaller towns and villages, are family managed and often offer extremely good value. In and near larger towns, and in popular tourist areas, a number of chains of hotels have been established. Some of these are very good, providing a known and consistent standard, and often have very good restaurants. In general, prices for accommodation vary with the grading but are very reasonable. The hotel is

Dominating the river, a castle has stood at Saumur for hundreds of years, surviving the ups and downs of war and political intrigue.

only allowed to charge what the government regards as a fair and reasonable price for the services provided. An increasing number of motels now exist, classified in the same way as other hotels but designated in hotel guides by the letter "M".

Château Hotels

A number of châteaux and country houses have been converted into luxury hotels with commensurately higher prices. In addition, a number of privately owned châteaux offer accommodation for paying guests who may enjoy the luxury of a stately home and may take meals with the owners. One must expect to pay more than in an ordinary hotel, although it must be stressed that these are private homes and not hotels.

Logis and Auberges de France

Logis and *auberges* are small- or medium-sized family-run hotels and inns, located away from large towns and providing accommodation with good cooking. Although they are in the lower categories of the Ministry of Tourism classification, they meet high standards of quality and comfort and are grouped in a voluntary organization which sees that these standards are maintained. An annual guide to the *Logis* and *Auberges* is published covering the whole country, but local regions often publish extracts from the

*T*he river mirrors an open rowing boat typical of the region. During periods of flood it is not always so placid!

main guide. Before leaving the subject of hotels, it is worth remembering that *Hôtel de Ville* is the Town Hall!

Bed and Breakfast

Chambres d'hôtes or bed and breakfast accommodation is becoming increasingly popular in France and can provide very good value, normally for stays of a week or more. Some owners provide main meals in addition to breakfast, and this is a very good way of meeting people and learning about the local way of life.

Gîtes de France

The word *gîte* means shelter or lodging, and is usually taken to mean self-catering holiday accommodation. It can take the form of a converted farm cottage, a flat, a chalet or a house in a village. Owners belong to a non-profitmaking organization, the *Fédération Nationale des Gîtes Ruraux de France*, which lays down standards and helps country people convert redundant properties into holiday accommodation. This type of accommodation is extremely popular with the French themselves so it is necessary to book early in the year. Guides in English are available which list the *gîtes* with full details of facilities available and how to book, together with a specimen booking letter or booking form. Visitors should, however, bear in mind that these *gîtes* are often rather isolated and away from public transport, so a car will be virtually essential. The same organization covers *gîtes d'étapes* which provide simple self-catering hostel-type accommodation for individuals, or for groups of walkers, cyclists or other travellers.

Youth Hostels

Auberges de la Jeunesse provide simple accommodation for members of national Youth Hostels organizations affiliated to the International Youth Hostel Federation (IYHF). Hostels in France are under the control of either the *Fédération Unie des Auberges de Jeunesse* (FUAJ) or the *Ligue Française pour les Auberges de la Jeunesse* (LFAJ). The FUAJ is affiliated to the IYHF but the LFAJ appears not to be. Both hostel chains accept overseas visitors. Hostels are classified in three categories according to the services provided and the level of comfort. Sleeping accommodation is in either dormitories or family rooms. Most hostels have facilities for self-catering, or, alternatively, meals may be available. Details of FUAJ hostels are available from national Youth Hostels organizations. LFAJ information is available from LFAJ, 38 bd Raspail, 75007 Paris. Tel: 45-48-69-84.

Camping and Caravanning

There are many officially approved campsites which are graded with one to four stars according to the amenities. Minimum facilities include fresh water and toilets, while luxury sites may have heated swimming pools, restaurants, television rooms and other such amenities. Many towns and villages have a *camping municipal* or public campsite which can be cheap but very good. Simple small sites in the country known as *Aires naturelles de camping* offer quiet uncrowded pitches with limited accommodation and basic facilities (water and toilet), while *Camping à la ferme* sites can be even smaller, but still with the minimum provision of water and toilet. Larger sites may accept touring caravans and there are also approved "caravan only" sites. Details of local camp and caravan sites of all categories are available from the local tourist office or *Syndicat d'Initiative*. A very complete guide listing nearly 10,000 sites of all categories over the whole of France is published by the *Fédération Française de Camping et de Caravaning*. An International Camping Carnet is almost essential, as mentioned in the section BEFORE YOU GO. As an alternative to camping with your own equipment, a number of firms provide ready-pitched and fully equipped tents, mobile homes or chalets on carefully selected sites, chosen for their location and amenities.

Money and Other Matters

Currency

The French *franc* (F) is divided into 100 *centimes* (cts). Banknotes are issued in denominations of 20F, 50F, 100F, 200F and 500F. Bronze-coloured coins are valued at 5, 10 and 20 cts, with silver coins to the values of 50cts, 1F, 2F and 5F. The 10F banknote has now been replaced by a 10F nickel and gilt coin of modern design. Smaller shops may be reluctant to accept banknotes of 200F or 500F, so try to obtain smaller denominations when drawing cash or exchanging traveller's cheques. Do not be confused if you see marked prices which appear to be very high. Often the decimal point is omitted before the centimes, so just

22

divide the amount by 100 and all will be well! You may see the last two figures for the centimes written in smaller figures, but still without the decimal point.

Traveller's Cheques
These are a safe way of carrying money when travelling. Available from high street banks or from Thomas Cook, they are typically issued in denominations of £10, £20, £50 and £100 sterling or in equivalent values in US dollars or French francs. They may either be cashed, or used to pay for goods or services. Security is assured by signing each cheque when it is issued and countersigning it again when you cash it. When purchasing, ask for a selection of different values. Unused traveller's cheques may be cashed in when you return home. There are arrangements for replacing lost or stolen traveller's cheques, as explained in the booklet issued with the cheques.

Eurocheques
Holders of current accounts at most of the high street banks can apply for Eurocheques. Together with the Eurocheque card issued for a small annual fee, these are accepted as payment by many larger shops, hotels and other establishments which bear the blue and red 'ec' symbol. The amount is written in the local currency, i.e. French francs, and the amount is debited from your current account at the exchange rate applying at the time of debiting your account. An additional fixed commission and service charge are added, but Eurocheques are probably one of the most effective ways of paying for goods and services when

abroad. Additional advantages are that all the major banks bearing the blue and red "ec" symbol will issue cash against a Eurocheque, and a growing network of automatic cash dispensers, also bearing the symbol, can be used in conjunction with your own personal identification number (PIN).

Credit Cards
Holders of Access or Visa credit cards may use them to pay for goods or services at establishments bearing the Access, Visa, Mastercard or Eurocard signs. Keep the transaction slips to check your account when you return home. It may be 2 months before the entry appears on your monthly account, which will show the actual amount in French francs and the converted equivalent at the exchange rate applying at the time of entry.

The Visa "carte bleue" is used very widely in France, even in many supermarkets and hypermarkets. Access and Visa cards may also be used for drawing cash from a wide network of automatic dispensers which are indicated by the familiar Mastercard and Eurocard signs, provided you remember your PIN. Note that interest is charged to your account immediately in respect of cash withdrawals using Access or Visa cards , so cashing a Eurocheque is probably cheaper. Diner's Club and American Express cards are accepted by many hotels and by the larger shops.

Girobank
Holders of British Girobank accounts may cash postcheques at French post offices, which are normally open at more convenient times than the banks.

Banks

The major French banks are usually open from 8.30 a.m. to noon and from 2– 5.30 p.m. on Monday to Friday. In some provincial towns banks may open on Saturdays but are then closed on Mondays. These times may vary and all banks are closed on public holidays (q.v.). Savings banks (*caisses d'épargne*) do not provide exchange facilities.

Exchange Facilities

Many hotels, stores or restaurants will exchange cash or traveller's cheques but you are likely to be charged an unfavourable rate and higher commission than if you go to a bank or official *bureau de change* which will display the sign "Change". These may be found in major towns and cities, at main railway stations and at airports. Some tourist offices will exchange currency at the official bank rate outside banking hours. Take your passport when changing money or traveller's cheques. When returning from France, spare cash may be used on ferries to pay for meals or for other goods but the rate of exchange may not be favourable. Coins are not usually changed, so unless you plan to return to France try to spend your loose change and retain notes for exchange.

Security

Never carry large amounts of cash. Keep Eurocheque cards and traveller's cheque purchase receipts and serial number records separate from the actual cheques, and never write down your credit card or Eurocheque card PIN where it can be recognized. In case of loss or theft, follow the instructions given by the issuing bank or agent, and report the matter to the local police immediately. Try to obtain a signed statement from the police to say that you have reported the occurrence.

Tipping and Taxes

A tip is a *"pourboire"*. Hotel and restaurant bills usually include a 10–15 per cent service charge (*service compris*) automatically, and if you are satisfied with the service, you might like to leave behind any coins in the change. Approximately the same amount may be added to the meter price as a tip for taxi drivers. For other services, about 2 to 10 francs, depending on the effort involved, is adequate. Lavatory attendants will expect between 50cts and 1 franc and cinema usherettes 1 franc per seat. Guides taking visitors around monuments or museums may expect 1 to 2 francs per person. TVA (*Taxe sur la valeur ajoutée* or Value Added Tax) is imposed on almost all goods and services but visitors from countries other than EC countries may claim exemption from TVA on expensive items purchased for their own use and which are to be taken out of the country when they return home. Major shops will be able to supply the forms necessary for reclaiming the tax. A copy of the form must be given to customs on leaving the country. Tourist tax is normally included in hotel, campsite and other accommodation charges.

Help

In an emergency, dial 17 from any telephone for the local police, and 18 for the fire service. For an ambulance, phone the police. Motorists who break down on major roads or motorways can use the orange-coloured emergency telephones to contact police or re-pair/rescue services. Note that the word for breakdown is *"panne"*, as distinct from *"accident"* which is self-explanatory. For minor ailments which do not justify seeing a doctor, most *pharmacies* (marked with a green cross sign) will be able to help. Otherwise they can direct patients to the nearest doctor who is *"conventionné"*, which means he works within the French sickness insurance scheme. Take your E111 (and copies) with you as well as your passport. Full instructions are included with your E111. Some areas operate a "Doctor on Call" service, (*Médecin de garde*), or a "Flying Squad" for emergency medical help, known as SAMU (*Service d'assistance médicale d'urgences*).

Postal Services

Post offices are identified by a sign with a stylized blue bird on a white ground with or without the word *Poste* or the letters PTT. Main post offices are open from 8 a.m. to 7 p.m. Mondays to Fridays and from 8 a.m. to 12 noon on Saturdays. One useful service available in major post offices is *Minitel*, where you can dial up local information and have it displayed on a video screen. *Post Restante* is also available at main offices. Letter boxes are yellow in colour and are usually fixed to walls. Stamps can be bought from post offices, from yellow coin-op-erated machines in the street or from tobacconists (*tabac*). You should always include the five-digit postal code when you address letters. The code is written in front of the name of the town, and the first two digits represent the *département* in which the town is situated.

Public Holidays (*Jours fériés*)

The following are national holidays:
January 1 *Jour de l'An* New Year's Day
May 1 *Fête du Travail* Labour Day
May 8 *Fête de la Libération* Victory Day (1945)
July 14 *Fête Nationale* Bastille Day
August 15 *Assomption* Assumption
November 1 *Toussaint* All Saints' Day
November 11 *Armistice* Armistice Day
December 25 *Noël* Christmas Day

Movable holidays are:
Lundi de Pâques Easter Monday
Ascension Ascension Day
Lundi de Pentecôte Whit Monday

Children have different school holidays depending on whereabouts in France they live, the main holiday periods being winter between early February and early March, spring between early April and late April (depending upon Easter) and summer between the end of June and mid-September. Banks, services and most shops close on public holidays.

Public Toilets

Good public toilets are still not too common in France. Facilities in cafés are usually free but you should leave a tip in the plate provided (see *TIPPING AND TAXES*). The same applies to large department stores and supermarkets, which often have toilet facilities. Women's toilets are marked *Femmes*

These old lavoirs *on the river bank at Saint-Calais are typical of the old communal wash-houses, once a common feature of French towns.*

holiday. Popular tourist areas may have different arrangements, but there is no consistent rule about this. Shops have to display their times of opening on the door or window. Most hypermarkets stay open until 9 or 10 p.m. although they may be closed on Monday mornings.

Where to Shop

The larger towns such as Angers, Blois, Le Mans, Tours and Saumur have excellent shops of all kinds including branches of many national and international stores selling as wide a range of goods as can be found anywhere. For the widest choice and most sophisticated shopping, Orléans, Nantes and Chartres are probably the best. Many large towns now have shopping centres (*centres commerciaux*) on the outskirts with extensive free parking, where you will often find big hypermarkets and other large stores. Hypermarket chains include Intermarché, Mammouth, E. le Clerc, Carrefour and Euromarché. Street markets are often a source of interest, offering almost everything imaginable! If you are prepared to haggle, you can sometimes get bargains.

What to Buy

Apart from the obvious wine, which can be bought everywhere, in Orléans and in the Tours area riding gear is

or *Dames*, and the men's *Hommes* or *Messieurs*, or they may be marked with the universal symbol of a lady or man.

Shopping (see also "Eating and Drinking" page 28)

Shopping Times

Most shops and department stores open from about 9 a.m. until noon, and again from 2 p.m. to as late as 7 p.m. from Tuesdays to Saturdays. Many are closed all day or for half a day on Mondays, and during the summer many will close for two weeks' one of the best buys for those interested. Fishing tackle is also readily available but is expensive. All kinds of gifts relating to riding, hunting and fishing may be found as well as many attractive locally produced items of china and pottery made in Gien. Religious medallions and souvenir keyrings depicting famous châteaux are available everywhere, but are probably cheapest in Saumur where they are made. Saumur is famous for its carnival masks which are exported all over the world. In the Saumur–Angers region, wooden articles ranging from tables to table ornaments are made from vine branches, while, in the Sologne, decorative wrought-ironwork has taken the place of horseshoe-making. Locally made wickerwork from Thouarcé near Angers, or from Villaines-les-Rochers near Chinon is worth looking out for, and most towns have antique dealers, often located near the local château. One of the best buys could be old china plates.

Shopping Tips
Whatever you are buying, compare prices in several shops to decide a basic price for comparison. Boutiques usually charge more than chain stores but look for the sign "*Solde*" meaning "Sale". Sales are usually held in January and July. *Un rabais* is a discount, and you can try asking for one if you are making a substantial purchase in a small shop, especially if you are paying cash.

Maison de la Presse is the paper shop, where you can get newspapers, magazines, postcards, local maps and guidebooks. In larger towns English language newspapers are usually available, although they will cost more than at home and usually be at least one day out of date. In smaller towns the paper shop may hold stocks of free local information leaflets for when the tourist office or *Syndicat d'Initiative* is closed.

Prices
Basic food prices in supermarkets or in village stores, are comparable to those in Britain when averaged out, although confectionery including the products of the *pâtisserie* tends to be very expensive. Drinks, including wine, can be very reasonable in price if you shop wisely. Good cooking pans and plain glassware can be a good buy, especially if purchased from a hypermarket, and good coffee is quite cheap. Clothes of all kinds including footwear are not cheap, even in the markets. Electrical goods may often be quite cheap, but take care that they are suitable to use at home. Mains plugs will almost certainly have to be changed if they are already attached, and lamps usually have screw fittings for the bulbs.

Telephones
France Télécom operates a fully automatic system allowing direct dialling. Telephone numbers in France have eight digits. The country is divided into two zones: the Paris area and the provinces. To call a subscriber in the same zone, dial the eight digits. To call from Paris to a provincial subscriber, dial 16 followed by the required number. To call from the provinces to Paris dial 16 + 1 + the eight-digit number. For enquiries, dial 12. Cheap rates apply after 6 p.m. on weekdays, after noon on Saturdays and all day on

Sundays and holidays. Cheap rates also apply for overseas calls after 9.30 p.m. on weekdays, after 2 p.m. on Saturdays and all day on Sundays and holidays. Public call boxes or public payphones accept coins or phone cards (*Télécartes*). Phone cards may be purchased for 50 or 120 units from *France Télécom* offices, post offices, tobacconists, railway stations and any shops which carry the sign *Télécarte en vente ici*.

International calls may be made by first dialling the international code 19, followed by the required country code and the number required. In some cases credit cards may be used to make calls via the operator. "Collect calls" (PCV), otherwise known as "reverse charge" calls, can be made to other countries via the operator.

Details of all phone services are given in a booklet written in French and English issued free by *France Télécom* and entitled *How to phone from (and to) France*. Note that phone calls made from payphones in hotels or restaurants may be surcharged, but that this surcharge must not be greater than 30 per cent.

Time

French summer time starts on the last Sunday in March at 2 a.m., and ends on the last Sunday in September at 3 a.m. During this period, French time is 2 hours ahead of Greenwich Mean Time (GMT), and during the winter it is 1 hour ahead of GMT. The 24-hour clock system is normally used in France. The change over from winter to summer time and vice-versa may not be the same time as in other European countries.

Eating and Drinking

With its reputation as the "Garden of France", together with its fresh running rivers and its vineyards, it is no wonder that the valley of the Loire offers much to tempt the appetite. Whether the visitor plans on self-catering or on eating out, the rich variety of fresh fruits, vegetables, fish and meat, nuts, mushrooms and dairy products to be bought in the markets is matched by tempting local recipes and specialities, and there is always the wine. The best of both worlds can be had by combining self-catering with some measure of self-indulgence in some of the excellent restaurants to be found in the region.

Food of the Loire

Fish

Fish caught locally in the Loire or in its tributaries include salmon, pike, shad, grey mullet, perch, bream, trout and eels. Freshly caught, sautéed or poached and served with white butter sauce (*beurre blanc*), they form the basis for many a memorable meal. Trout, carp or pike *à la Chambord* is more elaborate. The fish is stuffed with fish purée and truffles and garnished with local vegetables. Other local fish dishes include *quenelles*, dumplings of pike served in a crayfish sauce, and shad served with *beurre blanc* on sorrel cooked in cream. A plateful of small deep-fried fish, a *petite friture de la Loire,* can be simple but delicious.

Meat

Meat dishes are often excellent, and a local speciality is *noisette de porc aux pruneaux* (pork cutlets with prunes). Worth trying are *rillettes*, a sort of pâté made from minced pork, and *andouillettes* which are tripe sausages grilled over charcoal or a vine branch.

Poultry

Local poultry is well worth sampling. Often served in local wine sauces accompanied by onions and mushrooms, another local speciality grown in caves in the tufa, the flavour is quite different from that of "mass-produced" birds found elsewhere. Also try *coquelet à la moutarde* or *à l'estragon* (spring chicken served with mustard or tarragon sauce). Duck and game figure prominently on menus in season.

Cheese

Locally produced goat's milk cheese may be found even on supermarket shelves, and is well worth trying. *Crottin de Chavignol* from the Sancerre district is rather strongly flavoured, but others include Ste Maure, Celles-sur-Cher and Valençay. An interesting variation is warm *crottin* on toast served with, for example, *petits lardons* (tiny pieces of fried pork) on a bed of salad. Other cheeses from the region include St Paulin and Olivet, a small round cheese matured in ashes of vine branches. A speciality is *crémet d'Angers*, a fresh white cream cheese eaten as a dessert, sprinkled with sugar.

Desserts

Desserts can be a problem, ice cream and such things tending to be very expensive. A wide range of pastries and open fruit tarts will tempt the appetite. A local speciality is *Tarte Tatin*, an apple tart baked with the crust side up. A good one can be delightful. Local almonds form the basis for macaroons originating in Cormery, and from Nançay comes *sablé* or shortbread. In season, fresh fruit of all kinds, grown locally, is freely available.

A market stall in Angers piled high with fresh fruit to tempt the shopper.

Eating Out

Where to Eat

Restaurants vary from the very expensive to the small inexpensive establishments with paper tablecloths where you are expected to use the same knife and fork for two courses. In general, the standard of food and service is high and you may be fairly certain that restaurants patronized by the locals are worth choosing.

The French tend to eat a main meal at midday, and restaurants specializing in lunch (*déjeuner*) may have a restricted menu for evening dinner (*dîner*). Most restaurants start serving dinner from around 7.30 to 8 p.m. It pays to stroll around a town studying the menus and prices displayed outside before deciding where to eat, bearing in mind the advice about watching where the French go.

It is a tradition for families to meet together for a meal at lunchtime on Sundays, so if you want to visit a particular restaurant for a Sunday lunch it may be as well to book a table in advance. Many restaurants are closed on Sunday evenings, and perhaps on Mondays. Except in very exclusive establishments, casual (but of course tidy) dress is accepted. Choosing your meal should not be hurried. Choosing various dishes *à la carte* can be expensive, so it may pay to choose one of the fixed-price *menus*. Do not hesitate to ask if you do not understand what the various dishes are.

Drinks

The question of what to drink may cause some problems. Drinking water (*eau potable*) will be supplied free if requested. It will be from the tap and probably will be all right, but many prefer to ask for mineral water (*eau minérale*). You could simply ask for the preferred variety by name. A plain non-sparkling (*non-gazeuse*) variety such as Vittel is quite refreshing. It should be brought to your table with the seal on the bottle unbroken.

Wine can often double the bill for the meal if you choose a full bottle of an expensive wine. Study the wine list and, especially if driving, order perhaps a half-bottle between two people or even a glass each. According to the experts there are rules as to which wine should be drunk with which dishes, but provided you avoid very strong red wine with lighter dishes the best way is probably to please yourself! Ask the advice of the *patron* or the wine waiter (*sommelier*) if you like. Often a *carafe* or *pichet* (jug) of the house wine will prove very acceptable. It will probably be a local wine, and no restaurant is likely to risk its reputation by recommending a poor one.

Loire wines and their production play such an important part in the local economy and provide such an enjoyable accompaniment to the local food that a more detailed account of the subject is given in the essay associated with this section.

If a non-alcoholic drink is preferred, ask for fresh orange juice (*jus d'orange*) or a bottle of Perrier or similar gaseous water. With a meal in a restaurant, children in France often drink watered-down wine.

The Wines of the Loire—From Grape to Glass

"*Bonne cuisine et bons vins—c'est le paradis sur terre*" (good cooking and good wines, that is earthly paradise) is what the French king Henri IV is supposed to have said. France deservedly has a worldwide reputation for its many fine wines, and the Loire valley is in the forefront when it comes to the growing of grapes and the production of a variety of notable wines.

Louis Pasteur, the renowned 19th-century French chemist whose research into bacteria helped the wine industry so much, is quoted as saying "Wine is the most healthful and most hygienic of beverages." Perhaps not so pedantic

Many fine sparkling wines start their life hidden underground, their bottles being carefully turned in the racks every day.

but far more encouraging was Cardinal Richelieu's query "If God forbade drinking would He have made wine so good?" One hears of the vast amounts of wine consumed by the French of all ages, but the reality is that wine is very pleasant to drink before or during a meal, or simply as a drink on its own. As with most good things, wine taken in moderation does no harm, but in the words ascribed to *Hâjî Abdû* in Richard Burton's *Kasîdah*, "Who drinks the score must e'er expect to rue the headache of the morn." Probably Rabelais suffered from "hangovers"—those headaches of the morn—but his philosophy seems to have been summed up in the words "*Fay ce que vouldras*"—Do what you wish.

A Little History

Wild vines existed in what is now France in prehistoric times, as shown by fossil remains. Around 600 years BC it is possible that Phoenician traders brought cultivated vines to the south of France. Later, Greeks settled in the south and wine became an important commodity, being not only a drink but also used medicinally and as part of a religious ritual. The greatest stimulus to viticulture in France came from the Romans, who spread their prosperity and knowledge northwards to include the Loire area, which saw the establishment of extensive vineyards. Following the overthrow of the Roman Empire in the 5th century AD, Islamic influence spread into southern Europe and France, before being defeated in 732, but although Islam outlawed wine, early Christian missionaries preserved their knowledge of viticulture. Wine formed part of the Christian ritual and wherever they built their churches wine production flourished. Throughout the Dark Ages the people of the religious orders were the only ones with the knowledge and dedication to continue to produce good wines. The abbeys and monasteries naturally became centres owning and working vineyards, many of which still exist.

During the 12th century the crowning of Henry Plantagenet as Henry II of England resulted in increased prosperity for Bordeaux and the profitable wine export trade continued through the varying shifts of power virtually to the present day. At the same time wine production increased in other areas, including the Loire valley, so that by the early 19th century France had considerable wealth invested in her vineyards.

The second half of the century, however, brought disaster to the *vignerons* when a form of mildew, followed by an infestation of an insect from America, nearly devastated the vineyards of Europe. Steps were taken to overcome these problems, and today, in spite of excise duty, consumption and export of wines from the Loire, as from the rest of France, continues to increase.

The French Wine Trade
"I often wonder what the vintners buy one half so precious as the Goods they sell", says that devotee of wine, Omar Khayyâm, as paraphrased by Edward Fitzgerald in his classic *Rubâiyât*. Basic methods of wine production have changed little over the centuries but equipment has been modernized and the industry has expanded to meet the increasing demand, both from France and elsewhere. After the Revolution many of the great estates with their vineyards were broken up, including those belonging to the Church. They were sold to the people, resulting in a multiplicity of small owners. There are still a number of large estates, together with the small growers and large companies with international markets. The growers, producers and supporting services, such as those supplying bottles, packing cases, corks, and all the machines and equipment required by this major sector of the national economy, form a thriving industry. Grape production, particularly in the Loire, is dominated by the small growers, many of whom sell their grapes to larger companies or co-operatives. Because the equipment and facilities for making and distributing wine are expensive and only in use for a limited period during the year, it is more economic for the small growers to group themselves into co-operatives. They simply supply the grapes and are paid according to the quality and quantity. The cooperative establishes a wine-making plant and marketing operation and when the wine is sold the grower receives a share of the profits. The more traditional owners of larger vineyards producing high quality grapes prefer to make their own wines.

Although today the wine industry is very competitive and efficient, there are still many traditional practices.

One way in which the growers and wine makers maintain tradition and also ensure the quality of their produce is through membership of one of the societies or *confréries*, ancient orders with ornate costumes and elaborate ceremonies for admitting new members. Such a society is that at Chinon known as the *Eutonneurs Rabelaisieurs*, an organization of wine growers and shippers who are particularly concerned with marketing methods. Perhaps meetings of the societies provide a welcome social break from the long and anxious hours spent tending the vines and watching the weather.

An important link in the chain from grape to glass is the *courtier* or wine-broker, who with his extensive knowledge and expertise acts as the middle man between the *vigneron* and the *négociant* or wine merchant, who besides maintaining stocks of quality wines from particular areas or individual vineyards will also sell his own house brands, known as *monopole* wines. *Négociants* often have agencies abroad and their reputation relies on the quality of the wines that they sell.

The final link in the chain from grape to glass is either a restaurant, a traditional wine shop or, increasingly, supermarkets and hypermarkets.

What's in a Name?

Various attempts to raise standards and protect the consumer have been made in the past. Today, EC regulations on the subject define two main categories, namely "table wine" and "quality wine produced within a designated region". The latter group, of higher quality, has additional regulations governing, for example, grape type, methods of cultivation and vinification, and maximum yield. In France, each main EC category is sub-divided, so there are four types. In terms of quality the lowest is general *vins de table*, then *vins de pays*, *Vins Délimités de Qualité Supérieure* (VDQS) and finally *Appellation d'Origine Contrôlée* (AC).

Vins de table may be produced from local grapes or from wines or *must* (freshly pressed grape juice) imported from other EC countries. The label must state either "French table wine" or "a blend of wines from different countries of the EC". If, on the other hand, the wine is made in France from imported *must* it is described as "wine made in France from grapes harvested in ..." Formerly known generally as "*vin ordinaire*", table wine can be quite pleasant and is usually sold under a brand name. *Vins de pays* will also carry the words *vin de table*. They can only be produced from approved varieties of grape grown in the designated area

Traditional wooden casks for maturing wine are hand-made by craftsmen like this tonnelier *at Saumur.*

named on the label and are subject to quality control. When buying, they probably offer better value than some of the *vins de table*.

Vins Délimités de Qualité Supérieure (VDQS) have to satisfy high quality standards laid down by the national controlling authority, and the grape variety, maximum yield per hectare, the method of cultivation and vinification and the place of origin are all specified. VDQS wines are of high quality, particularly as many of the producers are aiming at the highest quality category.

Appellation d'Origine Contrôlée (AC) denotes the highest category. Very strict requirements must be satisfied regarding all aspects of the type, planting, cultivation and pruning of the vines together with the methods used in producing, ageing and storing the wine.

The quality of the final product, including its alcohol content, is also controlled. The AC designation is awarded in respect of wine produced in a specific region, district or even an individual vineyard or estate.

Viticulture—A Long and Complicated Process

Climate and soil are two fundamental factors affecting the growing of vines. The vine requires a cool rainy winter during which the dormant plants can recover their strength, a warm spring to allow the buds to form, and a long hot summer with around 6 hours of sun each day, moderate rainfall and warm humid nights to ripen the fruits. However, we have no control over the weather and late frosts, hailstorms and strong winds can all bring disaster for the grower. As regards the soil, it is perhaps a fortunate paradox that ground which appears poor, stony and arid to the farmer is very suitable for producing good wine, provided it is well drained. For these reasons, most of the vineyards of the Loire and its tributaries are set upon sloping hillsides where they can get plenty of sun and shelter from cold northerly winds, and where the ground drains well. The soil (*le terroir*) varies from clay and marl to pebbly gravel, flint, limestone and chalk, making for considerable variety in the types of grape grown (*le cépage*).

Normally the vines are grown from cuttings, often European varieties grafted on to insect-resistant American root stock. Fruit is borne after three years but it is better to wait five years. From then on, the vine may be harvested, reaching its peak in about 15 years. Most plants are discarded after 30 years. A vital factor in the care of the plants is their pruning and training, which requires considerable effort on the part of the *vigneron* and his work-

ers. An established *vignoble* or vineyard in winter or early spring presents a strange picture of row upon row of low garlanded and twisted bushes which look half dead. This is the result of the ruthless pruning which encourages growth of a few selected shoots to bear the coming season's crop. In fact, the pruning and training of the vines is a never-ending process. During late spring the *vigneron* will be keeping a close watch for late frosts, to be combated by setting smoke burners among the rows. From this time on the crops will also be sprayed to give protection against the many pests and diseases to which the vines are prone. Many of these attack either the leaves, the flowers or the roots, but the most serious pest is the tiny bug known as *Phylloxera vastatrix*. Only a third of a millimetre long, this insect came from America in the 1870s and almost destroyed the European wine industry by the end of the century. Constant vigilance is required to guard against these pests and many vineyards use specially developed tractors with narrow bodies and high wheels which can run along between the rows of vines, the machine passing above the low bushes. They are used for ploughing and crop spraying, and also to haul the loaded trailers at harvest time. The steeper areas still make use of horse-drawn carts and ploughs and hand spraying, a very labour-intensive task.

In September and October the *vigneron* has to make the crucial decision when to commence the harvest. The grapes must be just right, but so must the weather. The *vendage* or harvest is a time of intense activity, ending usually in celebrations and festivities in which the whole community joins. It is then time for the annual cycle of work to begin again, in preparation for the next year's *vendage*.

The Grape Vines of the Loire

The grapes used for wine come from the *Vitis vinifera*, just one of a family of as many as 5,000 varieties of vine. Of these only about 50 are used for wine making. The colour of the ripe grape varies from green through amber to blue-black, but the colour of the skin does not necessarily determine what colour the finished wine will be.

The choice of grape variety to be grown depends on a number of factors, such as the micro-climate prevailing in the vineyard, the soil type, and the wine to be produced. Yield, resistance to disease and tradition all play their part in the selection. Since a planting of vines may remain in production for 30 years or more, it can be appreciated that sudden changes of type are unlikely. Considerable capital is tied up in even a small vineyard and the expertise of the *vigneron* gained over many years will show what is most likely to succeed.

Throughout the more than 200,000ha of vineyards in the Loire region, the variety of soil and climate means that many varieties of grape are grown with a correspondingly varied selection of wines. Some of the most widely grown grapes in the region are the Chasselas, Chardonnay, Chenin Blanc and Sauvignon Blanc, used to produce a variety of white wines. Red and rosé wines are made from such varieties as the Pinot Noir, Gamay, Cabernet Franc, Cabernet Sauvignon and Groslot. In Western Loire, the area south of Nantes is largely devoted to growing the Muscadet grape from which white wines are made.

Vinification or the Wine-making Process—From Grape to Bottle

In simple terms, wine is the result of yeast acting on sugars in the presence of air to produce alcohol. Carbon dioxide gas is released during the process, which is called *fermentation*. The task of the wine maker is to control this process in such a way that just the required amount of fermentation occurs to produce, for example, a sweet wine with high alcohol content, or a dry wine with lower concentration of alcohol. A sparkling or fizzy wine results if all the carbon dioxide does not escape. The two requirements of yeast and sugar exist naturally in the grape. The former is present on the skin of the grape, visible as *bloom*. The sugars, together with fruit acids, pectins and trace minerals, are present in the juice. Tannin in the skin affects the acidity and taste of the final product.

The grapes are crushed immediately after picking and the resulting *must* is allowed to ferment under conditions of controlled temperature in a vat, a process which takes from 10 to 12 days. The *must* may then be run off into barrels for a period of secondary fermentation during which time the sediment is allowed to settle before the clear wine is racked or siphoned off for bottling.

For red wine the amount of tannic acid and colour is controlled by removing the skins before completion of the fermentation. For rosé wine the skins are removed after a much shorter period of around 24 hours.

Both red and white grapes may be used to make white wine but immediately after crushing the skin and pips must be removed before the juice is run into the fermentation vat for completion of the process as before.

The degree of fermentation and residual sugar determines whether the wine will be *sec* (dry), *demi-sec* (medium dry), *moelleux* (sweet) or *doux* (very sweet). A gently sparkling wine may be described as *pétillant* while a true sparkling wine is *mousseux*. A wine described as *sur lie* has been allowed to stand on the lees or sediment before final bottling which gives a characteristic flavour and slight sparkle.

Some of the cheaper sparkling wines are made by forcing carbon dioxide gas under pressure into the still wine. However, the best quality sparkling wines are made by adding yeast and sugar and allowing a secondary fermentation to take place after bottling. The closed bottles are laid in racks with their necks pointing down. During the lengthy process each bottle must be carefully turned daily (*rémuage*) to allow the sediment or lees to settle in the neck. When fermentation is complete this sediment must be removed. The modern way is to freeze it into a plug which is then expelled (*dégorgement*). The bottles are then corked and wired. The whole process takes time and great care, which accounts for the high price demanded for such wines. Any sparkling wines made using this process may only be described as having been made by the *méthode champenoise*. By law, the name *Champagne* may only be applied to sparkling wines from the Champagne region of France.

The Last Step—From Bottle to Glass and Beyond

To attain the best results, different wines are allowed to age or mature for differing lengths of time. When it comes to buying wine, if you are a real expert on wine, you will not need to read this. If, on the other hand, you feel you know very little of the subject, then our advice is quite clear. Do not be put off by what we may call "wine snobs" who use extravagant language to describe a wine. Remember the advice of Rabelais, which we can paraphrase as "drink what you like"! One way to find out what you do like is to drink wine with a meal in a restaurant. If you like what you drink, try to buy a bottle or two of the same wine locally. Another alternative if touring around is to call at one of the vineyards or wine vaults open to visitors, where it is possible to discuss, taste and buy wine. Good bargains may often be had. Look for signs bearing the word *dégustation* for tasting or *cave ouverte* for cellars or vaults open to visitors. When tasting wine it is not necessary to spit out what you have taken into your mouth. Simply look to see if the wine is clear and has a good colour. Twirl the glass and sniff. If there is no unpleasant smell or *bouquet* take a small quantity into your mouth, hold it for a moment, swirl it around and then swallow it. If the taste and aftertaste is to your liking that is sufficient. There is simply no space here to embark on a long discussion and list of different producers, vintages, and so on. This can be found elsewhere if required.

A final word. If you have bought some wine, let it settle before attempting to open the bottle. Store bottles on their sides in a cool dark place. Do not get unduly bothered about what wine should go with what food. Rules are for guidance, not an unbreakable law, but as a general rule red wines do not go well with fish and sweet wines do not taste pleasant with main course meat or fish. With these general guidelines, again the rule is to drink what pleases you. When serving wine, open the bottle and allow it to stand for up to half an hour to "breathe". Red wine is best served at around 18°C to 21°C (64°F to 70°F). This is cooler than the average room temperature. White wine is best served chilled. This can be done by placing the bottle in the freezer for 20 to 30 minutes, but don't forget to remove the cork first, or the bottle may burst! Santé.

Snacks

If time is pressing, and if all you want is a snack, a *crêperie* or pancake house may suffice, and in the towns modern fast food chains are beginning to appear, although they are not popular with the older French citizens! A café-bar will often serve snacks such as a *Croque Monsieur* (toasted cheese sandwich) or *frites* (fried chips). Cold drinks or coffee are always available. One very useful innovation is the self-service cafeteria to be found in many of the larger supermarkets and hypermarkets. The choice of dishes available is quite wide, and drinks including wine are available. For a quiet cup of tea, French-style, with a choice of tempting cakes and pastries, try a *salon de thé*, which may often be found in a *pâtisserie* (cake and pastry shop).

Self-catering

When camping or staying in a *gîte*, you have to go shopping for food, and this can be an experience in itself. Once again, good advice is to go and do as the French do, which means shop in the local shops and market. Language need not be too big a barrier. Pointing can achieve wonders, and if you speak French, even only a few words will gain lots of friendly help. It is the custom when entering a shop to say *"bonjour"*, and on leaving to say *"au revoir"*. Before you start shopping it is as well to have a rough idea of how much ¼, ½ or 1 kilo of various items amounts to in terms of helpings, if you are buying fresh fruit, vegetables or meat. Food shops normally open from about 8 a.m., close for lunch from 12 noon to 2 or 2.30 p.m. and remain open until about 7 p.m. Many close for half or all of Monday but some open on Sunday mornings. Most hypermarkets open until 9 or even 10 p.m. Mondays to Saturdays but many close on Monday mornings. Knowing where to go is half the battle when shopping.

Boucherie

Butchers sell beef, veal and lamb, and now they also sell pork. Lamb is a luxury, but pork is the cheapest meat. The butcher also sells bacon and ham, and most sell poultry and game. Note that a *boucherie chevaline* sells horse meat, and usually has a horse's head sign.

Boulangerie

The baker usually bakes *croissants*, *brioches* and some plain cakes as well as the traditional long white French loaves (*baguettes*) freshly baked every day. It is common to see French men or women walking or cycling from the baker carrying one or more of these long loaves. As the loaves don't keep very well, this ritual continues on Sunday mornings, and in the country a car will go to the nearest village baker to collect the bread, which is awaited by groups of housewives standing gossiping, still wearing their dressing gowns! Wholemeal bread (*pain intégral* or *pain complet*) and rye bread (*pain de seigle*) are more commonly available now, and you may be able to buy round loaves of hard country bread (*pain de campagne*). If the baker does not stock this you could try the grocer or the supermarket. *Croissants* will keep several days in a plastic bag in the freezer or in the ice tray of a fridge. If you heat them up under the grill, they can replace bread for breakfast.

Charcuterie
Originally, the pork butcher sold pork in various forms: raw, cooked or cured, and in sausages or pâté. Today, the pork butcher sells prepared meat dishes and pies (freshly cooked on the premises), cooked meats, and often dishes of prepared salads.

Confiserie
Confectioners still exist in big towns and in areas where they make chocolates and other sweets on the premises. Very nice but very expensive.

In Tours, visitors may see how mouth-watering confectionery is made before buying—but don't count the calories!

Epicerie
The term *alimentation* is also used to designate the grocer, who still survives in the country, although self-service and pre-packed food has replaced the old-style grocer in most places. Local vegetables, fruit, cheese and poultry may also be sold by the country grocer.

Fromagerie
Specialist cheese shops are not so common, but are a good source of local farmhouse cheeses.

Pâtisserie
Cake shop seems an inadequate description for a shop selling all kinds of fruit tarts, flans, cream-filled éclairs, cream cakes and rich pastries together with ice cream (*glace*), sorbets and sometimes fresh cream.

Poissonnerie
The fishmonger will stock not only fresh fish from the region but also a wide variety of prepared dishes, fish pâtés and sauces in tins or jars, and salted or smoked herring and salmon.

Traiteur
Strictly speaking, this is a caterer but the term often applies to a "take-away" shop selling all kinds of cooked meats and fish, salads of many kinds and other pre-prepared foods. Look out for them in smaller provincial towns.

Volailler
The poulterer is where to go for poultry, game, and pâtés, terrines and tinned prepared duck and goose.

Supermarché

These range from small local self-service grocers to branches of national supermarket chains. Convenient for almost all household goods, for branded goods such as tea bags, coffee, sugar and for all those things which are needed in a hurry or were forgotten until the local shops were shut. They are no substitute for the small local grocers and others, though, if you want fresh produce or local dishes.

Hypermarché

Hypermarkets, like the larger supermarkets, are often sited on industrial or commercial estates on the edges of big towns. They seem to sell almost everything from electrical goods and furniture to food and drink. The big advantage is convenience, and you need to know hardly any French, because all the goods are displayed with prices and you just pick up what you want and take it in a trolley to the checkout. The exception to this is where there are delicatessen, fish, meat, cheese or wine counters where you are served by the assistants. Many hypermarkets also have good self-service restaurants and petrol stations, and provide free car parking. Names to look out for are Intermarché, Mammouth, E. le Clerc, Carrefour and Euromarché. Payment can be by credit card and all hypermarkets are well signed from the surrounding roads.

Le pique-nique

Picnics are very popular with the French, and roadside picnic areas with tables and bench seats are common. This is the ideal way to have lunch when motoring or cycling through the country.

A fresh baked *baguette* with cheese, cooked meat or pâté, fresh fruit and a can or carton of fruit juice, or even a bottle of good wine, will bridge the gap between breakfast of *croissants* and coffee, and a more substantial meal in the evening.

A Land of Contrasts, Steeped in the History of the Western World

In this chapter we look at the administrative boundaries past and present, the landscape and the rivers which form it, the people and the complex history of the region, which all contribute to the fascination of the Val de Loire.

The area described in this book lies along both sides of the river Loire but does not coincide with any one regional or administrative boundary. In general, the main part of the administrative regions of Centre Val-de-Loire and Western Loire is covered, comprising part or all of the *départements* of Cher (18), Loiret (45), Indre (36), Loir-et-Cher (41), Eure-et-Loir (28) and Indre-et-Loire (37) in the Centre region, and Sarthe (72), Maine-et-Loire

The medieval town gate spans a busy street in La Ferté Bernard—little wonder this is a pedestrianized area!

(49) and Loire-Atlantique (44) in Western Loire. The French system of local government administration gives numbers to the *départements*. These numbers form the first two digits of postal codes in the respective areas, and the last two numbers on car registration plates. A *département* is roughly equivalent to an English county. The administration, headed by the chief executive known as *le Préfet*, is centred in the *Préfecture*. Modern departmental boundaries do not always relate to natural areas or to older historical areas, some of whose names are now almost forgotten. In the 18th century, this area of interest would have taken in all or part of the old *gouvernements* of Berry (Bourges), Orléanais (Orléans), Touraine (Tours),

41

Maine (Le Mans), Saumurois (Saumur) and Anjou (Angers), the capitals of which were the towns shown in brackets. A town or city hall is known as the *mairie* or *hôtel de ville*.

The River Loire

Although large, la Loire is not a great navigable waterway. It used to carry plenty of commercial traffic, but there were always problems caused by the great difference between the flow in summer and in winter. Since very early times the river had been troubled by violent floods, changing rapidly from a placid, almost empty stream into a raging torrent. To protect the surrounding valley, dykes were built in the 9th century, and today long stretches of the river are enclosed by high *levées*, many of which carry roads along the top. Further efforts to control the water have been made by building barrages in the upper Loire, notably at Villerest, north of Roanne in the upper reaches. Here, a dam was opened in 1982 to control the flow and to regulate the supply of cooling water to a nuclear power station. Further plans have been the subject of much debate and objection, on environmental, social and economic grounds, but a controversial project to build a dam at the Serre de la Fare gorge has now been dropped. In summer, much of the river bed between the *levées* is occupied by pools and narrow channels of water running between sandbanks, and the coming of the railways at the turn of the century spelt the end of navigation above Angers. In contrast to this, many of the tributary streams, notably le Loir, provide very pleasant and peaceful scenery enhanced by picturesque villages, water mills and the ever-present *châteaux*.

The Landscape

After passing north through the gorges in the volcanic rocks of its upper reaches, the river Loire gradually opens out and flows more slowly. Beyond Nevers and Gien it swings to the west, being deflected by the harder rock of the Beauce without which the Loire would have become a tributary of the Seine.

Rising sea levels after the Ice Age made the Atlantic flood into western France as far as Touraine, forming the ancient Mer des Faluns and laying down deposits of fossil-rich limestone. These layers were then covered with sediments of clay and sand from which the chalky deposit known as tufa was derived. This is visible today along the river banks as chalk cliffs often honeycombed with caves.

The part of northern Berry lying around Bourges includes an area of clay soil, while to the north towards Orléans is the Sologne, a rather remote land formed on sandy detritus brought down from the upper reaches of the river Loire. The heathland covered with broom and heather and stretches of forest form a flat countryside scattered with small lakes or *étangs*. The acid soil once supported extensive oak forests, now largely depleted. To the east, towards the river Loire, lies the Sancerrois, an area of steep rounded hills where vines and other crops are cultivated.

Downstream past Gien the river valley opens out into the Orléanais, with meadows devoted to horticulture, south facing slopes being occupied by vineyards and orchards. The north bank here borders the limestone area of the Beauce, a high treeless plain, the granary of France; to the south of the river, alluvial sand supports the cultivation of vegetables while still bearing large areas of dense brushwood formerly used as royal hunting forests. Between Amboise and Tours the valley slopes of flinty chalk are covered with vineyards whereas the white tufa cliffs are riddled with tunnels and caves, many of which are, or have been, used as dwellings.

The low-lying river valley below Tours is known as the Garden of France. The river runs slowly between sandbanks and the soil of the alluvial plain is rich and fertile, bounded by the poorer soil of the infertile uplands

T he wooded landscape of the Sologne is dotted with fields of poppies in the spring.

known as *gâtines*. North of the Loire, between it and le Loir, lies the *gâtine* of Touraine, which was formerly a great forest, but is now mainly cultivated. However, large tracts of heath and woodland still exist.

Similar country occupies the ground south of the Loire, between the Cher and Indre. This is the Touraine *champeigne* where walnut trees are a common sight in the fields. Continuing downstream from Tours, a fertile belt of land covered with small gardens and fields lined by poplars lies between the Loire and the Vienne. Towards Saumur, market gardens along the valley are surrounded by vineyards backed by pine-covered hills. The land between the Loire and its tributary, the Authion, is occupied by more market gardens, orchards and flowers, with willows lining the banks of the Authion.

South of the Loire, the slopes of the Saumurois are covered with vineyards among woodland and plains. The steep valley sides of tufa are occupied by old caves, many of which are now used for growing mushrooms.

To the north of the Loire lies an area of sandy ground with mixed woods interspersed with arable land, known as the Baugeois In the area around Angers there are many nursery and market gardens growing flowers. Beyond them, to the south, is the Mauges: wooded farmland with small fields and banks topped by hedges, and traversed by deep lanes. The same type of landscape, known as *bocage*, also lies to the north of the river valley, extending into Maine and as far as Le Mans.

The People and the Language

The area has a moderate climate and a countryside not given to extremes, so this can perhaps give a clue to the nature of the people of the region. People from Anjou are Angevins while those from Touraine are Tourangeaux; from Blois come the Blésois, and folk from Orléans are called Orléanais. The Romans called the Loire the *Liger*, hence the collective name *Ligerians* for inhabitants of the Val de Loire, who may otherwise be known as *Vallerots*. The original inhabitants of the valley came under Celtic influence from the east in the Bronze and Iron Ages, followed by a strong Roman presence until the 5th century AD. These, together with Visigoth, Saracen, Norse and English incursions over the centuries must all have had their effect on the people and culture. As regards language, French is spoken, but, although local dialect may be heard among country folk, the people of Touraine claim, in fact, to speak the purest French. As Alfred, comte de Vigny said: "not too slow, not too fast and without accent".

Culture and Religion

Christianity may be seen really to have established itself in the region when Martin, a former soldier in the Roman army, was elected Bishop of Tours in AD 371. Through his influence country folk began to be converted, parish churches increased, and after his death Tours became a centre of learning which survived through the Dark Ages. At around the end of the 8th century, and during the 9th century, an English scholar, Alcuin of York, founded a school of philosophy and theology in Tours which, together with a school in the abbey of St Benoît at Fleury and a university at Orléans, achieved widespread fame, partly for the reform in calligraphy. In spite of setbacks caused by Norse invasions, the spread of literature and learning up to the 11th century was closely associated with the church. By the 14th century universities had been founded in Orléans (1305) and Angers (1364), attracting some of the greatest minds in Europe. With the move of the

French court to Touraine, music, literature and the fine arts flourished in the Loire valley, and a university was founded in Bourges in 1463.

From the end of the 15th century when the Renaissance came to the valley, intense rivalry among the wealthy stimulated the introduction of Italian ideas of architecture, sculpture, painting, embroidery and gardening. A leading figure in this was the king, François I, who invited Leonardo da Vinci to spend the last three years of his life at Amboise. All his imported ideas were to be modified for the French.

The 16th century saw such literary giants as Rabelais and Ronsard. René Descartes, the philosopher and mathematician, and Honoré de Balzac, the writer, were both natives of Touraine.

In 1756, the Royal School of Surgery was founded in Tours.

The 19th-century sculptor Pierre-Jean David showed his attachment to his birthplace by always signing his work "David d'Angers". Finally, 1970 saw the foundation of Tours university.

Today, a large majority of the French population are Roman Catholics, although there are also many Protestants. In general, the Loire region is no exception, Catholics being predominant in the rural areas.

Some of the most attractive examples of local traditional costume come from Anjou, and may be seen at some of the folklore festivals.

Customs, Crafts and Industry

With such a diverse area there are few customs or traditions which are typical of the region as a whole, neither are there any traditional local costumes or music. However, local museums do display examples of the old characteristic dress and artefacts from defined districts such as Sologne or Berry. A number of local festivals, mostly linked to wine making or agriculture, and traditional craft fairs and markets still survive, although many are now rather aimed at the tourist. Many local activities and industries have now disappeared, such as hemp growing and rope making, saffron cultivation in the Gâtinais, the Tours silk industry and the important fishing and water transport industries along la Loire and its tributaries. Flint knapping can only be seen in museums, but extensive slate quarries near Angers and the basket

Local custom or national pastime? Jeux de Boules *may be seen at almost any time, and when a tournament is in progress things get really serious.*

making and wickerwork centred at Villaines-les-Rochers still survive. Pottery and porcelain form an important industry, from the decorated glazed coloured porcelain of Gien and Mehun to the bricks and tiles of Sologne.

The "garden of France" is an important producer of fruit, flowers and vegetables, especially mushrooms. The Beauce is the granary of France, while the region is probably most noted for its cultivation of the vine and the resultant wine industry. In recent times, however, tourism has undoubtedly become the most important industry of the Loire area. With its long history and unique inheritance of magnificent buildings, linked to the

46

attractive scenery along the river valley, many festivals, *Son et Lumière* performances and pageants take place, and catering for holiday, sport and leisure activities provides a major source of employment. In addition, during the last two or three decades many modern industries such as electronics, aerospace, motor manufacture, chemicals and nuclear power have come into the area, but they do not detract from the region's appeal as a holiday area.

Historical Background

Why are so many great fortresses, mansions, châteaux and estates concentrated in this part of France? Much of the explanation lies in the region's history: a very complex tale of internal power struggles, battles against outside forces and struggles for freedom, interspersed with periods of relative peace. It would take a larger book than this to set out in detail the full history, but don't forget that history concerns people rather than dates. Apart from the intrigues and actions of the powerful nobles, kings and queens which fill the history books, the land has been inhabited for many centuries by people who have cultivated and formed it into what we see today. History is also the story of the thousands of men who served, maybe unwillingly, in the armies of the contenders for power, or even rebelled against their rulers.

The history of the Valley of the Loire is not only the history of France —it is also part of the history of

A lthough historically relations between England and the Loire region have been stormy, perhaps this scene in Luynes (Indre-et-Loire) represents the entente-cordiale!

England. A large part of the region was once ruled by the kings of England, and two English kings and queens are buried in Fontevraud Abbey, near Saumur. In modern times, English and American history has been closely linked with the Loire, as no doubt they will be in the future.

Joan of Arc—
Saviour of
France?

The Hundred Years War was in progress; the English and French were fighting over French territory; the French were even fighting amongst themselves. Civil war was a fact, and there was a rising tide of nationalism throughout the land.

The Background

Edward III of England had disputed the right of Philip of Valois to inherit the kingdom of France, maintaining that he had this right as the husband of the late king's sister. Thus what began as a family quarrel developed into the Hundred Years War. English possessions had once included the greater part of western France from the English Channel to the Spanish borders. By the middle of the 14th century, Edward was in control of much of northern France and Aquitaine. Civil war broke out in France between the Burgundians and the Armagnacs before the end of the century, causing many problems for the French king Charles VI, who was gradually losing his reason. The Burgundians held sway in most of the north-east, as well as in Burgundy itself. The rest of France was loyal to the Valois King.

In 1413, Henry V acceded to the throne of England, and immediately attempted to regain all the lost territory in France. After the battle of Agincourt, France was divided and an Anglo-Burgundian alliance was formed; the Dauphin Charles was disinherited by his parents, and was even called a bastard by his own mother! Catherine of Valois, daughter of Charles VI, was to marry Henry V, and he would inherit the French kingdom on the death of his father-in-law.

In 1422, only two years after his marriage, Henry V returned to France to take up arms against the Dauphin Charles, leaving behind an infant son, also named Henry. Unfortunately king Henry V caught dysentery and died, a fact which probably changed the course of history. "The best laid plans of mice and men ..."

Two Kings of France

Two months later, Charles VI died, and the Dauphin proclaimed himself King of France at Mehun-sur-Yèvre. Unfortunately, there were still many in France who were happy to give their allegiance to the young Henry VI—after all, his mother was Catherine of Valois.

For a while, Charles was left alone, partly because the English were quarrelling amongst themselves as to who should govern both England and France whilst the king was still a minor. Charles VII, being weak and indecisive, was apparently content to sit and wait for the English to go away! Eventually, his mother-in-law, Yolande of Sicily, had to push him into standing up for himself. The civil war raged on; Charles had to employ mercenary soldiers, which stretched his finances to their limits and made him even more unpopular.

Joan of Arc Arrives

Then, in 1429, Joan of Arc appeared. Joan was a normal young girl, helping about the family home in the village of Domrémy, on the Burgundian border, until she began to have "visions" at around the age of 13. She believed these visions to be St Michael, St Margaret and St Catherine, and she referred to them as her "voices". When she was about 16 years old, her voices told her that she was to save France and see the Dauphin crowned king.

Joan's voices must have spoken to her at a very opportune time for the Dauphin; he was rapidly running out of money, and the English had besieged Orléans. Joan insisted that she would raise the siege of Orléans, and that she herself would lead the army which would throw the English out. No one was prepared to believe her at first, but she was so persistent that the people of her village, perhaps sensing some miracle, were gradually won over.

To See the Dauphin
So how did this young girl even gain audience with the Dauphin? More than once she ran away from her home to see the commander of the nearest Valois garrison at Vaucouleurs, one Robert de Baudricourt. She tried several times to convince him that she could save France, but he sent her home. Eventually, she persuaded a cousin that she meant what she said, and he persuaded Baudricourt to accept her story. With an escort of six men provided by him, she set off for Chinon, where she knew the Dauphin to be. The perilous journey took eleven days, and the little party travelled mostly by night. Joan travelled dressed as a man, mainly for her own safety. From Vaucouleurs she travelled to Gien, then crossed the Sologne to Mennetou-sur-Cher. Here the party turned west and after spending a night at Chanceaux-près-Loches, went on to St Catherine-de-Fierbois. Finally, Joan came to Chinon, and managed to get across the river in a small boat. At first, the Dauphin refused to see her, but eventually a letter arrived from Baudricourt telling the Dauphin that he had sent Joan to see him, and she was allowed into the castle. Charles tried to disguise himself, and hid among his courtiers, but Joan recognized him and told him of her mission.

A Desperate Situation
The military at the time was desperate; the garrison at Orléans, under the command of Jean Dunois, the "Bastard" of Orléans, was valiantly holding out against the English. If Orléans fell, then the Anglo-Burgundian alliance would be able to gain access to the whole of the southern half of France. That would spell disaster for the Dauphin, and he was almost at the point of giving in and fleeing to Spain. Joan, however, persuaded him that at all costs he must stand his ground, and that she would raise the siege of Orléans. Some of the Churchmen and courtiers suspected witchcraft and sorcery, and Charles was afraid that Joan's voices might have come from the devil. Joan was taken to Poitiers to be examined "for her virginity and her beliefs". The priests there were apparently quite happy with her answers, and Yolande of Aragon testified to the fact that she was a virgin. It may be that those priests were only too anxious to try anything that would help save France from her troubles.

A Knight in France
Joan returned to Chinon, and was equipped as a knight of France, and fitted out with a suit of armour reputedly made for her in Tours. She already had a sword found buried in the ground by the altar of the church in St Catherine-de-Fierbois. When found it was, according to Joan herself, "rusty, and with five crosses". This marks it as a Crusader's sword, which had probably belonged to a local lord who had been

involved in the Crusades. An armourer in Chinon had sharpened it for her, and a sheath had been made for it. Whilst in Tours Joan began to gather her entourage around her, including a chaplain, squire, and pages. Her brothers Jean and Pierre are also believed to have joined her here.

An Army Gathers

During this time of preparation, Charles began to gather an army together at Blois, and Joan followed him there. Whilst in Blois, her standard was blessed by the Bishop, and she then rode towards Orléans.

Joan's army carried with it supplies of food and ammunition for the besieged city. Instead of going round to the north of the town, as she had advised, the French commanders kept to the south of the river. Joan was furious, but somehow they managed to get their supplies, and the fresh troops, across the river and into the city under the noses of the English. This gave the besieged army new heart, and the simple soldiers put their faith in Joan. After some preliminary sorties, the battle for Orléans was joined on 6th May, 1429. The English had captured a ring of forts around the city, and these had to be retrieved. After some heavy fighting, during which Joan was wounded twice, the English were driven from their forts and many of them drowned in the Loire. Orléans was relieved. The next day, she entered the city in triumph, having defeated the English very soundly.

The superb statue of Joan of Arc in place Martroi in Orléans.

The Dithering Dauphin

Joan returned to Tours immediately after the siege was lifted, to see the Dauphin and persuade him to go to Reims for his coronation. The Dauphin could not decide what to do, and was heavily influenced by Georges de la Trémouille, one of his courtiers who had no time for Joan. He decided that caution must be exercised, and instead of marching on Reims he decided to drive the English out of the Loire region first. In retrospect, this was probably a great mistake, because the English army had been routed and would not have been able to recover quickly enough to prevent a successful march on Reims. Jargeau, Beaugency and Patay were all taken, but still there was indecision. The Dauphin was at Sully, with de la Trémouille, celebrating its return to its rightful owner. The army captains were arguing about what to do, and with no firm orders they withdrew to the Loire to consolidate their positions. They might have done better to have marched on Paris.

Coronation at Reims

All Joan wanted was to persuade the Dauphin to go to Reims to be crowned. Eventually she succeeded and the army mustered at Gien. After a journey across Burgundian territory, during which many towns and villages surrendered to the King, Joan and Charles reached Reims on 16 July 1429. The following day, with Joan at his side, he was crowned in the Cathedral. Joan's main mission was accomplished.

Joan continued to lead the soldiers in her second mission, to throw the English out of France. The King was still indecisive, and having started to move towards Paris he suddenly decided he wanted to go back to Chinon! The English, meanwhile, had reinforced their positions round Paris, and cut off Charles' retreat to the south. Finally Joan and the commander of the French forces, the Duke of Alençon, took matters into their own hands and tried to capture Paris. During the battle she was wounded and had to be rescued from the trenches. The French withdrew, and some two weeks later, because he had run out of money, Charles disbanded his army at Gien.

Capture and Death

Georges de la Trémouille had arranged a peace with the Burgundians, and Henry VI was crowned in England. Charles spent the winter at Sully, but was soon to learn that the Burgundians were reneging on their truce; preparations were being made for the recapture of all the places Joan's army had succeeded in taking. Charles did not know what to do. In fact, as he had no money, he decided he could do nothing about it, and told his people so. They were appalled, as was Joan.

In April she left Sully in secret (some would say that she escaped) and led a small army of some 500 men to try and keep the Burgundians out. Things came to a head at Compiègne; during a sortie against the Burgundians she was pulled from her horse by an archer and soon was handed over to the English. Very soon political intrigue dictated that Joan was to be handed over to the church for trial in return for what was in effect a ransom and the following year she was tried for heresy.

Pierre Cauchon, Bishop of Beauvais, with a panel of 131 judges, assessors and other clergy, conducted her trial. Only eight were Englishmen and of these only two appeared to have played a very active part in the proceedings. She was convicted and was burned at the stake in Rouen on 30 May 1431. Charles VII had made no attempt to save her.

Who was She?

Just who was she, this young girl from Domrémy? There is no record of her birth in any parish register, so the date can only be approximate, based on the evidence given at her trial in 1431, when she admitted to being about 19 years old. Her father was not, as is commonly believed, a simple peasant, but a tenant farmer, who would have had rather more standing. How was it that Joan, who had never seen the Dauphin before, knew him?

There have been many theories, and most believe that she was indeed the daughter of a farmer or peasant. However, the theory has been put forward that she was the illegitimate daughter of the Duke of Orléans and Queen Isabella of Bavaria, and that a still-born infant had been substituted for her and buried as "Philippe". Apparently, the child Joan was taken to Domrémy to be brought up by the Arc family. It was also suggested that Charles VII was indeed a bastard, as his mother had denounced him, of the same parentage. This might explain the rapport between Joan and the Dauphin, and perhaps would have explained her ability to command, and to be a good horsewoman.

We shall never really know, as many of the records taken at different times during her life are missing. There were doubts about her simple origins in her own lifetime, and even William Shakespeare supports the theory that she had royal blood in her veins. Whoever she was, she is regarded as the true saviour of France, and her memory will never be dimmed.

Trade and Migration

A mild climate and long river systems such as the Loire invited migration, trade and invasion, and lying as it does on the extreme western edge of the continent of Europe, at the end of an unbroken plain extending to Siberia, France has been a highway for the movement of culture and people over many centuries. There is evidence of habitation, industry and trade dating from early Stone Age times through to the Iron Age, which saw an influx of Celtic peoples from northern and central Europe into what was to become known as Gaul.

Romans

Roman merchants settled along the Loire and in about 52 BC Julius Caesar occupied Touraine and other parts of the Celtic provinces of Gaul. During the next 200 years or so, the Roman Empire retained its importance along the Loire—various remains, including parts of the Roman city wall of Tours, are still visible. However, Roman influence was waning, leading to the capture of Tours by the Goths in the 5th century AD, later to be retaken by the Frankish king Clovis. Meanwhile, Christian monasticism was born in Tours, followed by the building of a number of monasteries, ab- beys and cathedrals in the region which became centres of culture in an emerging Europe.

Raiders

The 9th and 10th centuries saw attacks by Norse (Viking) raiders, many of whom then settled in what is now Normandie. Their destruction was equalled by that of the savage Foulques Nerra, Count of Anjou, who plundered the countryside and built chains of massive forts, many on Roman sites and often forming sites of future Loire châteaux.

In AD 987, when Hugh Capet, Count of Paris became the first true king of France, the power of the monarchy was limited to the Ile de France, but it was always the aim of the monarchs to extend France's frontiers to the natural boundaries of the Rhine, the Alps and the Pyrénées.

English Conquests

In 1154, Henry Plantagenet, Count of Anjou and Duke of Normandie, married to Eleanor Duchess of Aquitaine, became Henry II of England through his descent from William the Conqueror. His domain extended from the north of England and Ireland to the Pyrénées. Henry died in 1189 and is buried in the Abbey of Fontevraud together with his wife Eleanor. He was succeeded by his son Richard I Coeur de Lion, who on his death in 1199 was also laid to rest here, together with Isabelle of Angoulême, wife of his brother, King John of England.

The Plantagenet rulers of England and much of France spent more time in Anjou than in England, the English and French history of this period becoming inextricably mixed. Extending over three centuries, their influence had a lasting effect on the Loire Valley, but efforts by the French kings to limit the English power led to a bitter and long struggle. The series of wars and campaigns known as the Hundred Years War, lasting from 1337 to 1453, gave rise, among other things, to the building of many medieval fortresses such as the château of Angers, and the early Renaissance fortresses, built for defence but with some attempt being made at elegance and comfort. Saumur, although modified in later years, is a good example.

Further complex shifts of power led to the French throne being taken by the young Henry VI of England in 1422, against claims by the Dauphin Charles. Soon, almost the whole of France north of the Loire was under English control. It was then, in 1429, with the English forces surrounding Orléans and attempting to cross the Loire, that the legendary Jeanne d'Arc appeared on the scene, and by her strength of character persuaded the Dauphin Charles and his army to attack the English and relieve Orléans, going on from there to Reims where the Dauphin was crowned King. The rest of the story is well known, ending with the death of Joan in a way which reflects no credit on either side. By 1453 the French had regained almost the whole country but it was devastated by war and by the Black Death.

The Renaissance

The late 15th and early 16th centuries under Louis XII and Francis I saw the Renaissance, a period of internal peace and stability with an upsurge in art, literature, architecture, learning and industry. The Loire Valley started to become a place of pleasure. Many of the Loire châteaux were rebuilt and new ones were created during this period, No longer needed as uncomfortable fortresses, these new-style buildings were planned for comfort and elegance, as in the case of Azay-le-Rideau whose moat is the river Indre, planned

to enhance the appearance of the building whose interior is designed for graceful living.

Catholics and Protestants

This period of growth and development was interrupted by the "Wars of Religion" between Roman Catholics and Protestant Huguenots. The Reformation started fairly quietly in France, and the prosperous trading towns of Angers and Saumur became powerful Protestant centres. However, in 1562 the prince of Condé called for religious freedom at Orléans, leading to civil war lasting until 1598, when Henry IV of Navarre, the first Bourbon king of France, proclaimed the Edict of Nantes giving religious and political protection to Huguenots.

Louis XIV

The seat of power was shifting from the Loire to Versailles, although the valley continued to be favoured as a retreat for many nobles and notable personalities. Great changes to the system of government, advances in art, science and literature and improvements in communication took place under the influence of Cardinals Richelieu and Mazarin.

The long reign of Louis XIV, "le Roi Soleil" (1643 to 1715), saw continued progress in many ways, although his revocation of the Edict of Nantes in 1685 caused large-scale emigration of Huguenots including many highly skilled artisans from the Loire Valley. Nevertheless, during this time industry expanded within the area and many châteaux were built in the classical style, as exemplified by the château at Cheverny.

The Revolution

The reigns of Louis XV and Louis XVI continued to see much activity in the fields of science, art and industry, but increasing inflation and unemployment resulted from disputes and conflict over North American colonies and Austrian and Spanish affairs. This situation, coupled with food shortages in Paris, and opposition by the upper middle classes to absolute monarchy, led gradually to the Revolution of 1789. In fact the Loire region was surprisingly less violent than might have been expected, possibly because food shortage was not such a problem as in the cities.

Although the contents of many châteaux were damaged or destroyed, most of the buildings were preserved. Violence flared between Catholic Royalists and the Convention, spreading from St Florent-sur-Loire to Angers and south into Vendée before being suppressed in Angers.

The Republic

During the 19th century under the Republic, general prosperity returned to the Loire with the development of rural industries, drainage in the Sologne and other measures. Many châteaux were taken over by well-to-do industrialists and others, many of whom restored the buildings to something approaching their former glory. Then the Franco-Prussian War of 1870 saw German forces advancing to the Loire, and defeating French resistance at Orléans and Blois before bombarding and occupying Tours.

World Wars I and II

During World War I, Tours became a base for American troops, but World War II saw treasures from the Louvre being stored in the château of Chambord, while Tours became the temporary seat of government.

All main Loire towns from Gien and Orléans to Tours and Angers were heavily bombed by the Germans and a gallant action by cadets from Saumur held three Loire bridges in a delaying action against an armoured division. Hitler met the aged Marshal Pétain at Montoire-sur-le-Loir north of Tours and agreed the boundary between occupied France to the north and unoccupied France to the south. The boundary was along la Loire and le Cher. Resistance to the invaders resulted in a reign of terror imposed by the occupying German forces, and further damage in the region resulted from Allied bombing during the liberation of France in 1944.

Present day

Since 1945, much reconstruction has taken place and the Loire region has seen the growth of industry, agriculture and horticulture and the expansion of the major towns. Orléans has a thriving university, and a general air of prosperity pervades the area.

Strangely, all this has been achieved without la Loire being used in its old role as a trading highway. The river remains as the central decorative feature of a landscape which has seen so much change but which still retains much of its original charm.

Just the Essentials

On a first-time visit to the Loire Valley, you may be overwhelmed by the sheer wealth of choices you have wherever you start. The major landmarks and places to see and visit are proposed here to help you establish your priorities.

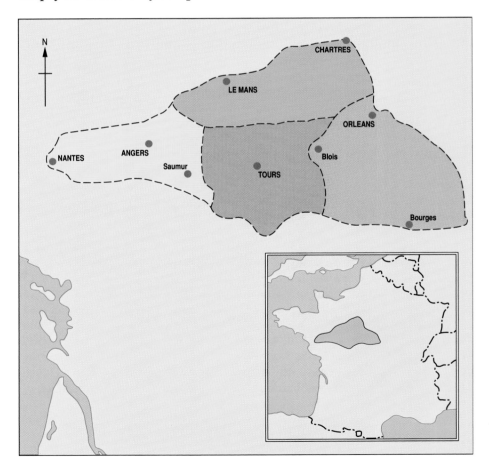

Le Mans
Musée de Tessé
l'Escalier de la Grande Poterne
Maison de la Reine Bérengère
(east) Abbaye de l'Epau
(la Ferté Bernard) Notre-Dame-
des-Marais
(further afield)—Montmirail
Chartres
Chartres Cathedral
St Pierre church
Musée des Beaux Arts (old
Bishops Palace)
Enclos de Loëns
(further afield)—Nogent-le-Rotrou
Valley of le Loir—Châteaudun
Vendôme—Abbey Church of la
Trinité
Valley of le Loir—Troo
(troglodyte dwellings)
le Lude—Son et Lumière
performances

Orléans
Maison Jeanne d'Arc
Parc Floral, la Source
(further afield)—Germigny-des-
Prés
—Sully medieval fortress
—Gien—Musée International de
la Chasse
—Briare—aqueduct
—Beaugency
The Sologne
Aubigny-sur-Nère
Souvigny-en-Sologne
Bourges
Bourges cathedral
Palais Jacques Coeur
Prés-Fichaux Gardens
(further afield)—Sancerre
—Mennetou-sur-Cher

Blois
château
Poulain Chocolate Factory
Maison des Acrobates
(further afield)—Château of
Beauregard
Amboise
château
le Clos-Lucé
(further afield)—Château of
Chenonceau
Tours
Cathédrale St Gatien
Historiale de Touraine
place Plumereau
(further afield)—Château Villandry
—Chinon
—Sunday Market at Descartes
—Loches

Saumur
Musée des Arts Décoratifs
(the surrounding area)—Musée du
Champignon (at Saint Hilaire-
Saint-Florent)
—Montreuil-Bellay
—Fontevraud abbey
—Dénizé-sous-Doué—
underground cavern with figures
Angers
château
Museum of David d'Angers
Maison Adam
(the surrounding area)—Hôpital
Saint-Jean (in la Doutre)
(further afield)—Musée de la
Vigne et du Vin d'Anjou at
Saint-Lambert du Lattay
Nantes
Château des Ducs de Bretagne
Passage Pommeraye
(further afield)—Clisson

Going Places with Something Special in Mind

The following suggestions are for leisure routes which cater for all kinds of interests. A few are given as itineraries, but most indicate where the particular interest may be followed.

Long-distance Footpaths

They are known in France as *Grandes Randonnées* and are numbered with a prefix "GR".

GR3

Follows the whole of the Loire from its source at Gerbier-de-Jonc to the Atlantic Ocean. It passes through Gien, Orléans, Chambord, Tours, Chinon, Saumur, Chalonnes-sur-Loire, Champtoceaux and Sucé-sur-Erdre.

A trip around the vineyards of the Loire is to many the ideal leisure route.

GR3C

Leaves GR3 near Chambord and crosses the northern part of the Sologne to Gien.

GR31

Leaves GR3 near Chambord and winds its way across the Sologne to Sancerre, and joins GR3 again just beyond here in the Loire Valley.

GR35

Follows the valley of Le Loir from Illiers-Combray to Seiches-sur-le-Loir.

GR36

Runs from the English Channel at Ouistreham to the Spanish border. It passes through Le Mans, Le Lude and Saumur on its way through the region.

GR41
Runs from Tours along the valley of the Cher and out of the region to finish at Evaux.

GR46
Runs from Tours to Loches and beyond, as far as Vers in the Valley of the River Lot.

GR48
Runs from Chinon along the valley of the Vienne to Ile Bouchard and beyond.

GR235
Crosses the *Perche-Gouet* from La Ferté Bernard to Les Ponts de Cé.

GR335
Runs from Montoire-sur-le-Loir to Tours.

Wine Routes

Valley of Le Loir
The vineyards here cover a very small area, but towns and villages of particular interest include:

1 VENDOME
Ancient Abbey, and the centre for VDQS Côteaux du Vendômois wines.

2 MONTOIRE
Old houses by the river. Small *caves* to visit, with wine-tasting.

3 LA CHARTRE-SUR-LE-LOIR
Centre for AOC Côteaux du Loir wines. A *Station Vert des Vacances* or country holiday centre.

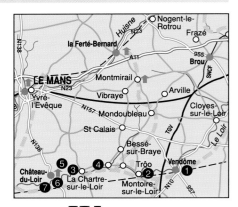

Wine routes in the Valley of Le Loir.

4 RUILLE
A tiny hamlet to the north-east of La Chartre, yet has five *vignerons* producing the famous Jasnières yellow wine.

5 L'HOMME
Another small hamlet where Jasnières wine is made. Small wine museum.

6 MARCON
Several vineyards here, but also a centre for fruit liqueurs.

7 VOUVRAY-SUR-LOIR
Has municipal *cave* offering wine tasting.

Touraine
This is the principal wine-growing area of the Loire Valley, with some 2,000 hectares of vineyards producing a wide variety of high-quality wines. Numerous small *Routes des Vins* are signed along minor roads in the area. Listed here are some of the more interesting wine towns and villages.

60

1 MESLAND
A small village north of the river which gives its name to AOC Touraine-Mesland, mainly red and rosé wines which are quite light but have a pleasant fruity taste.

2 ONZAIN
Small wine museum in the *Office de Tourisme*.

3 AMBOISE
Famous château which has links with Mary Queen of Scots. Centre for Touraine-Amboise wines.

4 MONTLOUIS
Home of still and sparkling white wines, ranging from sweet to extra dry. The wines are said to impart gaiety and happiness!

5 VOUVRAY
Known for its fine white wines, which have excellent keeping qualities. Many "troglodyte" dwellings which cling to the hillside above the river. Local wine museum.

6 TOURS
Major wine distribution centre. Museum of Wines of Touraine.

7 AZAY-LE-RIDEAU
Famous château with good *Son et Lumière*. Good white and rosé wines.

8 CHINON
Famous for excellent red wines which mature rapidly. Fascinating animated wine museum. Signed *Route du vin*.

9 BOURGEUIL
Interesting market town with imposing

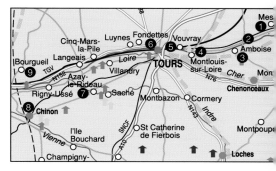

W ine routes in Touraine.

abbey. Centre of wine-growing district with two distinctive AOCs.

Upper Loire
There are many vineyards in this area, famous for Sancerre wines:

1 SANCERRE
Beautiful old town standing on a hill, surrounded by vineyards. Major wine centre, and wine festival at Whitsun. Signed wine route around town.

2 POUILLY-SUR-LOIRE
Home of the renowned *Pouilly Fumé* wine. Good wine route through steep vineyards to Les Loges and Tracy.

3 COSNE-SUR-LOIRE
Centre for Côtes du Gien wine-growing area.

4 MENETOU-SALON
Fine château and good wine. The vineyards once belonged to Jacques Coeur.

5 QUINCY
Small village near Mehun-sur-Yèvre, making a full-bodied white wine.

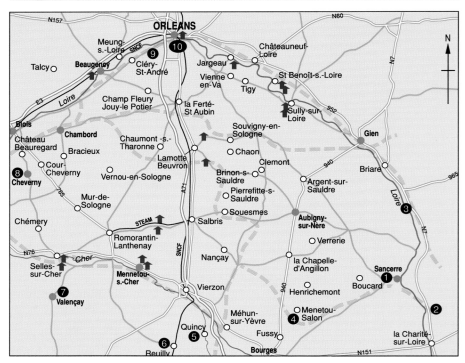

*W*ine routes in Upper Loire.

6 REUILLY
11km (6½ miles) south-west of Quincy. Rather lighter white wines.

7 VALENCAY
Elaborate château, open to the public. Produces good wines, mostly white.

8 CHEVERNY
Château renowned for its hunting trophies, but also a major producer of fine white wine.

9 MAREAUX-AUX-PRES
The centre of a small wine-growing area between Cléry-St-André and St-Hilaire-St-Mesmin, south-east of Orléans. It is said that the vineyards were founded by Charlemagne, and the wines were once famous. There is a signed *Route des Vins* to follow.

10 ORLEANS
Joan of Arc's city and centre for trade and distribution. It gives its name to Orléanais VDQS wines.

Western Loire
The wines of the Western Loire—including Saumur, Côtes du Layon and Muscadet country.

Anjou
1 SAUMUR
Famous for all kinds of wine, with no less than 6 AOC in the area. Sparkling wines are especially good. A signed *Route des Vins* may be followed.

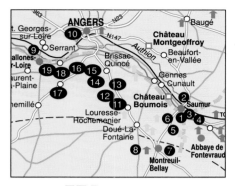

*W*ine routes in Anjou and Côteaux du Layon.

Medieval château, and town famous for equestrianism.

2 ST-HILAIRE-ST-FLORENT
Suburb of Saumur, where sparkling wines are made.

3 SOUZAY
Hamlet beside the Loire. *Tufa* caves where the wine, a light red, is stored.

4 CHAMPIGNY
Centre for Saumur-Champigny AOC.

5 ST-CYR-EN-BOURG
Wine cooperative. Tour of underground galleries. Wine tasting.

6 CHACE
Museum of Champigny wine in *cave*, including a collection of old wine bottles.

7 MONTREUIL-BELLAY
Magnificent medieval château. Vineyards.

8 LE PUY-NOTRE-DAME
Interesting 13th-century Angevin church in the centre of the wine-growing area.

9 CHALONNES-SUR-LOIRE
Petit train takes visitors through the vineyards. Wine tasting at *Maison du Vin*.

10 ANGERS
Maison des Vins with information on local wines, where they can be purchased

Côteaux du Layon
The wines from this area are very fruity white wines, which are almost like a liqueur.

11 MARTIGNE-BRIAND
Ruined château surrounded by vineyards.

12 VILLENEUVE-LA-BARRE
Benedictine monastery, with interesting chapel in converted barn.

13 BONNEZEAUX
"Twin hills rise up here; one offers nectar, the other divine water" (unnamed poet).

14 FAYE-D'ANJOU
Village among vineyards above the Layon Valley.

15 RABLAY-SUR-LAYON
Attractive, sheltered wine village with an interesting half-timbered house with overhanging upper storey.

16 BEAULIEU-SUR-LAYON
13th-century frescoes in the church, and a fine view over the neighbouring vineyards.

17 ST-LAMBERT-DU-LATTAY

Interesting wine museum and public footpath through the vineyards.

18 CHATEAU DE LA HAUTE-GUERCHE

Ruins of château destroyed in the Vendée wars. Fine views over the surrounding countryside.

19 CHAUDEFONDS-SUR-LAYON

Old lime kilns and beautiful old *lavoirs* in village.

Muscadet Country

There are two areas within the boundaries of this book, Muscadet des Côteaux de la Loire and Muscadet de Sèvre et Maine, which is the largest of the three Muscadet areas. The vineyards are mostly small, and do not normally offer guided tours.

1 NANTES

Centre for distribution. *Maison des Vins.*

2 VERTOU

Vineyards planted by monks in 11th century.

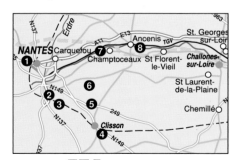

W ine routes in the *Muscadet Country of the Western Loire region.*

3 ST FIACRE

Interesting Byzantine-style church tower.

4 CLISSON

Beautiful 15th-century market hall. Ruined château in town. Vineyards.

5 VALLET

Maison de Muscadet. Wine tasting.

6 LE LOROUX-BOTTEREAU

Ancient town lived in continually since first century AD.

7 CHAMPTOCEAUX

Fine views across the river to Ancenis vineyards.

8 ANCENIS

Once a busy wine-shipping port. Produces both Muscadet (white) and Gamay (rosé) wines.

Caves and Troglodyte Dwellings

1 LES ROCHES L'EVEQUE

Some of the best troglodyte dwellings to be seen in the valley of Le Loir.

2 TROO

Beautiful troglodyte village with whole streets of troglodyte houses. Fine views from top of hill.

3 VOUVRAY

Many troglodyte dwellings in this village, famous for its wines.

4 ROCHECORBON

Cliffs are riddled with troglodyte dwellings and hermits' caves. Remains of Marmoutier Abbey.

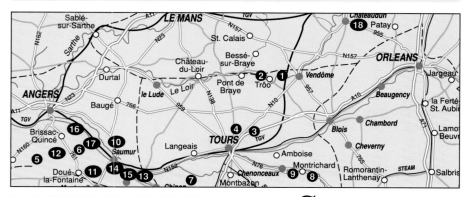

5 LOURESSE-ROCHEMENIER
Troglodyte village and museum, built in caverns below ground.

6 FORGES
Troglodyte hamlet of La Fosse.

7 VILLAINES-LES-ROCHERS
Wicker baskets made in workshops.

8 BOURRE
Troglodyte dwellings and caves where mushrooms are cultivated.

9 MONTRICHARD
Caves used for ageing sparkling Touraine wines by Taittinger.

10 ST-HILAIRE-ST-FLORENT
Mushroom museum in tufa caves beside the Loire.

11 DOUE-LA-FONTAINE
Troglodyte dwellings made in old quarries. Exhibition hall in underground cavern.

12 DENEZE-SOUS-DOUE
Underground sculpted caverns.

13 MONTSOREAU
Mushrooms cultivated in tufa caves.

Sites of caves and troglodyte dwellings.

14 SOUZAY
Remains of troglodyte houses and *ruelles* (lanes) cut into the rock.

15 TURQUANT
Troglodyte Manor House. Restaurant in another troglodyte house.

16 COUTURES
Many troglodyte dwellings here.

17 ST-GEORGES-DES-SEPT-VOIES Troglodyte *gîte d'étape*.

18 CHATEAUDUN
Grottes de Foulon—caves used as fulling sheds for the treatment of skins in the tanning process.

Links with Joan of Arc

The following is a list of some of the places visited by Joan on her way to Chinon before the battle of Orléans, and some of the places where she fought against the English.

1 GIEN

A memorial plaque, made from Gien Faïence, is situated on the outside of the Church.

2 VOUZON

Sologne village, with a *chemin de la pucelle* (path of the Maid).

3 LAMOTTE-BEUVRON

Joan passed through here, but it is today more famous for *Tarte Tatin*.

4 SELLES-ST-DENIS

Another interesting Sologne village. Church dedicated to St Genoulph (St Knee!).

5 MENNETOU-SUR-CHER

Joan spent a night here on her way to Chinon, and a plaque on the ruined gateway to the medieval town records this fact.

6 SELLES-SUR-CHER

There are two châteaux here, one medieval and one Renaissance, which are linked together by a walkway.

7 CHANCEAUX-PRES-LOCHES

Joan spent the second night of her journey here.

8 MONTFOUE

The story goes that no corn will grow along the path which Joan once trod, now known as the *chemin de Jeanne d'Arc*.

9 MEHUN-SUR-YEVRE

Joan of Arc received her *lettres de Noblesse* from Charles VII in the château here.

10 STE-CATHERINE-DE-FIERBOIS

According to another legend, Joan of Arc found her sword here.

11 CHINON

Joan first met the Dauphin here, and saw through his disguise. There is a museum to Joan in the clock tower of the château.

Sites associated with Joan of Arc.

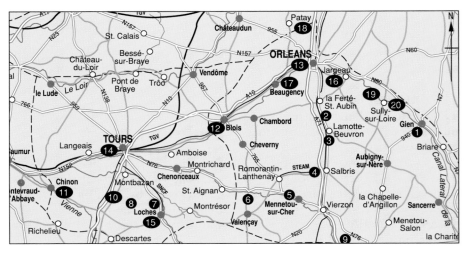

12 BLOIS

The Bishop of Reims blessed Joan's standard here before she set out for Orléans.

13 ORLEANS

Scene of her triumphal entry into the city, and where she defeated the English in May 1429.

14 TOURS

Joan returned to Tours after the battle of Orléans. It is said that a suit of armour was made for Joan in an armourer's shop which once stood on the site of the *Maison de la Pucelle armée*, or house of the armed maiden, in rue Colbert.

15 LOCHES

Another place where she stayed before further battles. It was here that she finally convinced the Dauphin to go to Reims for his coronation.

16 JARGEAU

Liberated by Joan in June 1429.

17 BEAUGENCY

Liberated a few days after Jargeau.

18 PATAY

Joan defeated the English here two days after Beaugency.

19 ST-BENOIT-SUR-LOIRE

Joan prayed here for guidance, in the company of the Dauphin.

20 SULLY-SUR-LOIRE

Joan first stayed here to persuade the Dauphin to go to Reims for his coronation. Later, she was kept a virtual prisoner here, but managed to escape.

Plantagenet Connections

The Loire Valley has many links with the Plantagenet Kings of England. Henry II was born here and died here, Richard Coeur de Lion died here.

1 LE MANS

Henry II born here in 1133. Maison Dieu de Coëffort founded by him. Abbey of Epau founded by Queen Berengaria, wife of Richard I.

2 LA FERTE-BERNARD

Scene of a fruitless dialogue between Henry II, Richard Coeur de Lion and Philippe-Auguste of France.

3 MONTMIRAL

Fine medieval château, where there was an attempt at reconciliation between Henry II and Thomas à Becket.

4 ANGERS

Henry II and his court resided here, making it a second capital of England. Built the Hospital of St Jean, the cathedral and three other churches.

5 BAUGE

Original château built by the Plantagenets.

6 FONTEVRAUD

Magnificent abbey containing the tombs of Henry II, his wife, Eleanor of Aquitaine, Richard I, Coeur de Lion, and Isabella of Angoulême, wife of King John.

7 MONTREUIL-BELLAY

The fortress was built by Foulques Nerra, ancestor of Henry II.

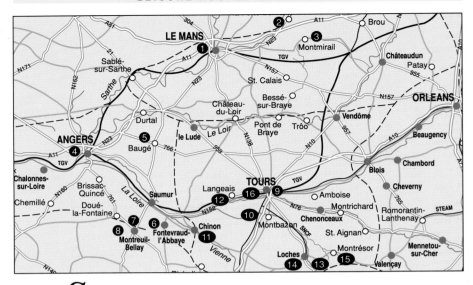

Sites with Plantagenet connections.

8 LE-PUY-NOTRE-DAME
The church is one of the better examples of Angevin architecture, introduced by Henry II.

9 TOURS
Thomas à Becket took part in the Council of Tours in 1163. The town was the cause of many battles between Henry II and Philippe-Auguste.

10 AZAY LE RIDEAU
Henry II conquered the domain, but it was later confiscated from his descendant, King John, and returned to the original family.

11 CHINON
Owned by the Counts of Anjou. Henry II made it the centre of his empire, and he died there in 1189. After Richard Coeur de Lion died, his body was taken here. His brother, John, married Isabella of Angoulême in the chapel.

12 LANGEAIS
Keep built by Foulques Nerra, and in possession of the Plantagenets until it was captured by Philippe-Auguste in 1218.

13 LE LIGET
Monastery founded by Henry II, as penance for Becket's murder.

14 LOCHES
Captured and recaptured by the Plantagenets, the fortress belonged to Berengaria, widow of Richard Coeur de Lion.

15 MONTRESOR
The keep, attributed to Foulques Nerra, belonged to Henry II.

16 VILLANDRY
Henry II and Philippe-Auguste agreed a peace treaty there in 1189.

In Search of the Famous

This route lists some of the places in the Loire Region which are associated with famous French writers and artists, scientists and engineers.

1 AMBOISE
Leonardo Da Vinci lived in the town for three years and died at his home there.

2 ANGERS
Birthplace and home of Pierre-Jean David, sculptor and medallist. Museum contains all the plastercasts for his works, which he gave to his home town. Rabelais also studied for a while in the city.

Sites associated with famous French writers, artists, scientists and engineers.

3 BLOIS
The physicist and inventor, Denis Papin was born here.

4 BOURGES
Home of contemporary painter, Maurice Estève. Museum devoted to his work.

5 LA CHAPELLE D'ANGILLON
Home of the World War I novelist, Alain-Fournier, who used the Château as the setting for his novel *Le Grand Meaulnes*.

6 CHATEAUDUN
Emile Zola used to observe the local farmers in *Le Bon Laboureur* when researching for his novel, *La Terre* (The Earth).

7 CHENONCEAU
Jean-Jacques Rousseau lived here for several years, first as tutor and then as secretary to the owners. Voltaire also stayed here.

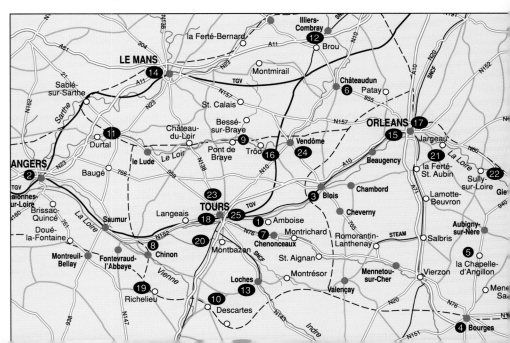

8 CHINON

Rabelais was born at La Devinière, near Chinon, where there is a museum illustrating his life and work, including a study on the origins of Gargantua, his most famous character. As a boy, he lived in Chinon itself, and there is a statue of him on the Quai Jeanne d'Arc.

9 COUTURE-SUR-LOIR

Birthplace of the poet Ronsard.

10 DESCARTES

Town named after the famous French philosopher, physicist and mathematician who was born here. Museum in his boyhood home includes many of his works.

11 LA FLECHE

Most famous of the pupils at the Jesuit College, now the Prytanée Militaire, was Descartes.

12 ILLIERS-COMBRAY

The writer Marcel Proust spent much of his childhood here, and the town is the setting for many of his books.

LIRE

A museum in this village south of Ancenis contains souvenirs of the poet, Joachim du Bellay, one of the group called the *Pléiade*, who was born here.

13 LOCHES

Birthplace of Alfred de Vigny, soldier and poet.

14 LE MANS

Ronsard was a canon of the cathedral here in 1560. Another canon was Paul Scarron, author of *Le Roman Comique*. Amedée Bollée built the first car with an engine under the bonnet here.

15 MEUNG-SUR-LOIRE

The poet François Villon was imprisoned in the château at Meung, and another poet, Jehun de Meung, was responsible for completing and publishing the *Roman de la Rose*, an early bestseller.

16 MONTOIRE-SUR-LE-LOIR

The chapel of St Gilles is all that remains of the priory of which Ronsard was once titular head.

17 ORLEANS

The poet, Charles Péguy, and the sculptor, Michel Bourdin, both lived in Orléans.

18 PLESSIS-LES-TOURS

Ronsard lived the last 20 years of his life as prior here, and is buried in the remains of the Priory of St Cosmé.

19 RICHELIEU

Named after the famous Cardinal, who also planned the layout of the town.

20 SACHE

Honoré de Balzac stayed at the 16th-century manor house and wrote some of his best work here.

21 SAINT-BENOIT-SUR-LOIRE

Max Jacob, the poet, spent the last years of his life here before he was deported in World War II.

22 SULLY

Voltaire wrote and performed several

of his plays here whilst staying at the château.

23 TOURS
Connections with many famous men from the earliest times: Gregory of Tours, Alcuin of York, Honoré de Balzac, the painters Jean Fouquet and François Clouet and the sculptor Michel Colombe.

24 VENDOME
Balzac spent his school days here at the College of Oratorians – and hated them! The college is now named Lycée Ronsard, after the poet who also had many connections with the town.

25 VOUVRAY
Beaumarchais, who wrote the original *Barber of Seville* lived at Vouvray.

Cathedrals and Churches

The Loire region has some of the most beautiful cathedrals and churches in France. They cannot all be listed but these are some of the most interesting.

1 ANGERS
St Maurice's Cathedral is a mixture of styles, but the vaulted roof is the earliest example of Angevin vaulting known.

2 BEAULIEU-LES-LOCHES
Ruins of a Romanesque Abbey where Foulques Nerra is buried.

3 BLOIS
Under the Gothic cathedral of St Louis is a 10th-century crypt.

4 BOURGUEIL
Interesting church with a small Romanesque nave but very large Gothic chancel.

5 BOURGES
One of the largest Gothic cathedrals in France, with a particularly fine west front and beautiful flying buttresses.

6 CANDES-ST-MARTIN
Beautiful vaulted porch with central supporting pillar. A chapel inside the church marks the spot where the saint is said to have died.

7 CHAMPIGNY-SUR-VERDE
Beautiful Renaissance chapel with some fine 16th-century stained glass.

8 CHARTRES
This superb Gothic cathedral is a UNESCO World Heritage Site, and is probably the finest cathedral in the world. It is a beautiful building, renowned for its fine stained glass windows.

Eglise St Pierre: a fine collection of stained-glass windows, second only to those in the cathedral.

9 CLERY-ST-ANDRE
Gothic church containing the tombs of Louis XI and Jean Dunois, Joan of Arc's companion.

10 CUNAULT
Beautiful Romanesque church with richly decorated doorway.

11 LA FERTE-BERNARD
Flamboyant Gothic church with some fine stained glass.

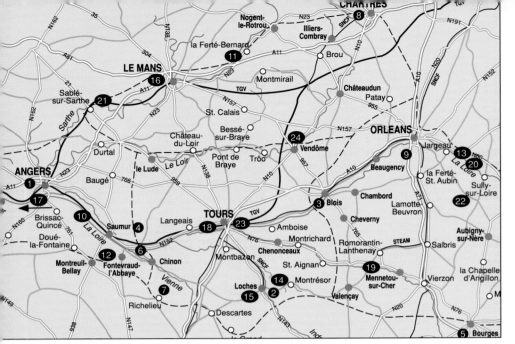

12 FONTEVRAUD
The royal abbey, where two kings of England are buried.

13 GERMIGNY-DES-PRES
One of the oldest churches in France, a fine example of Carolingian architecture, with a superb mosaic inside.

14 LE LIGET
Twelfth-century round chapel of St Jean du Liget contains some good Romanesque frescoes.

15 LOCHES
St Ours' Church, situated inside the castle walls, has unusual pyramid vaulting in the nave and a carved Romanesque west porch.

16 LE MANS
St Julien's Cathedral is a mixture of three distinct styles—Romanesque pillars, Angevin vaults, and a Gothic choir. Abbey of Epau, where Queen Berengaria, wife of Richard I is buried.

*S*ites of the main cathedrals and churches.

17 NANTES
Cathedral built in flamboyant Gothic style, the only one in France whose interior has been completely restored (after a disastrous fire in 1972).

18 PLESSIS-LES-TOURS
Priory of St Cosmé, now a ruin, where Ronsard is buried.

19 SELLES-SUR-CHER
Fifteenth-century church with fine murals, dedicated to St Genoulph (St Knee).

20 ST-BENOIT-SUR-LOIRE
Beautiful Romanesque porch with richly carved capitals.

21 SOLESMES
Massive Benedictine Abbey standing

high above the River Sarthe, where Gregorian Chant may still be heard.

22 SOUVIGNY-EN-SOLOGNE
Beautiful church with 16th-century half-timbered *caquetoire* or gossips' porch.

23 TOURS
Exceptionally fine Renaissance cloister in St Gatien's Cathedral.

24 VENDOME
Beautiful Gothic abbey church with separate Romanesque belfry.

Châteaux

There are so many châteaux in the Loire valley that it would be impracticable to try and visit them all. The lists given will help you make your own routes in the areas you wish to visit.

The Perche and Valley of Le Loir
There are not many châteaux in this area, but those that are there are worth visiting.

1 CHATEAUDUN
Medieval and Renaissance château, founded by Jean Dunois.

2 COURTANVAUX
Attractive Renaissance château with pleasant parkland.

3 LE LUDE
Medieval and Renaissance château, noted for its superb *Son et Lumière* performances.

4 MONTMIRAIL
Henry II of England attempted a reconciliation with Becket here. Fine views over surroundings of *Le Perche-Gouët*.

5 NOGENT-LE-ROTROU
Massive ruined chateau standing high above the town.

6 PONCE-SUR-LOIR
Château contains a fine Renaissance staircase.

7 VENDOME
Ruined château but with spectacular views from old ramparts.

Upper Loire and the Sologne
The most famous of all châteaux, Chambord, is included in this itinerary.

1 BEAUGENCY
Château Dunois, built as a medieval fortress, now contains the Orléans regional museum.

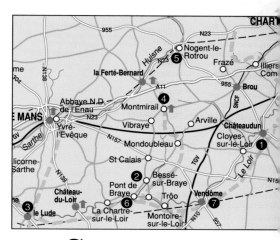

*S*ites of châteaux in the Perche and Valley of Le Loir.

2 LA BUSSIERE
The fishermans' château, with a museum of everything to do with angling.

3 BLANCAFORT
An old medieval fortified house, built in the 15th-century.

4 BOUCARD
Fourteenth-century fortress surrounded by moat.

5 BOURGES
Palais Jacques Coeur; built when he was financial advisor to Charles VII.

6 CHAMBORD
The largest of all châteaux, and not to be missed.

7 CHEMERY
Medieval moated manor house.

8 CHEVERNY
Elegant château in classical style, famous for hunting trophies.

9 GIEN
Red brick château, containing hunting museum.

10 MENETOU-SALON
Ornate Renaissance château.

11 MEUNG-SUR-LOIRE
Grim medieval château with oubliette where prisoners were left to starve.

12 LE MOULIN
Delightful brick château with some original furnishings.

Sites of châteaux in the Upper Loire and the Sologne.

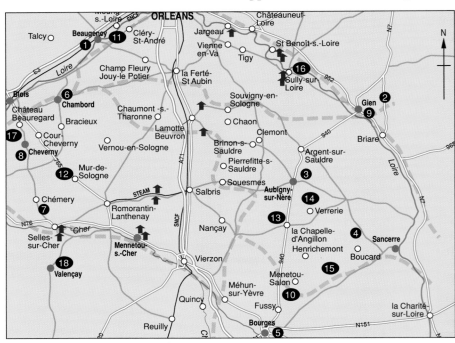

13 LA CHAPELLE D'ANGILLON
Château de Béthune, the setting for a novel by the World War I novelist Alain-Fournier.

14 LA VERRERIE
Attractive château in lakeside setting, once owned by the Stuarts and the Duchess of Portsmouth.

15 MOROGUES
Château de Maupas contains an interesting collection of china plates displayed on the staircase.

16 SULLY
Feudal fortress with a keep containing very well-preserved roof timbers.

17 TROUSSAY
Small Renaissance-style château, containing the Musée de Sologne.

18 VALENCAY
Elegant Renaissance château where Talleyrand entertained in style.

Touraine
One of the loveliest of all châteaux, Chenonceau, is in this itinerary.

1 AMBOISE
The royal apartments and chapel are all that remains of a much larger château. Fine views from battlements.

2 AZAY-LE-RIDEAU
Attractive little château built on a lake, with some fine Renaissance furnishings.

3 BEAUREGARD
Graceful small château, with a famous portrait gallery.

4 BLOIS
Built over a wide period of time, this is an interesting château to visit. English *Son et Lumière*.

5 CHAUMONT
Fifteenth-century château which Catherine de Medici gave to Diane de Poitiers in exchange for Chenonceau. Interesting 19th-century stable block.

6 CHENONCEAU
Superb château built over the river Cher, and not to be missed.

Sites of châteaux in Touraine.

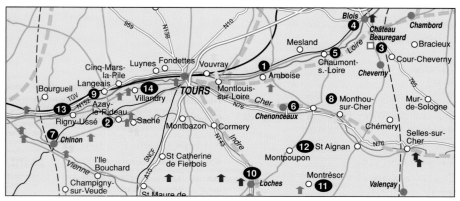

7 CHINON
Once the residence of Henry II, but now mostly in ruins. A small museum to Joan of Arc is in the clock tower.

8 GUE-PEAN
Isolated Renaissance château with unusual watch-tower with bell-shaped roof and sentry walk.

9 LANGEAIS
Medieval château, with remains of Foulques Nerra's Keep.

10 LOCHES
Massive keep built by Foulques Nerra. It was in the royal apartments here that Joan of Arc convinced the Dauphin he should go to Reims for his coronation.

11 MONTRESOR
Charming Renaissance château standing within original curtain walls built by Foulques Nerra.

12 MONTPOUPON
Fifteenth-century château with two original 13th-century towers. Interesting displays in the stables and other outbuildings explain how the estate was run during the 19th-century, including hunting costumes and horns.

13 USSE
Attractive Renaissance château on medieval foundations, believed to be the setting for Perrault's *Sleeping Beauty*.

14 VILLANDRY
Elegant Renaissance chateau renowned for its wonderful gardens.

Western Loire
An area not so well known for its châteaux, there are still several worth visiting.

1 ANGERS
Massive medieval château, containing magnificent tapestries and beautiful gardens in the moat.

2 BRISSAC
Another château founded by Foulques Nerra, but altered through the centuries. Beautifully decorated beamed ceilings and fine furnishings.

3 GOULAINE
Fifteenth-century château with tropical butterfly house.

4 MONTGEOFFROY
Lovely 18th-century château containing original furnishings.

5 MONTREUIL-BELLAY
Superb medieval castle standing high above the river Thouet. Many of the original defensive walls still remain.

6 MONTSOREAU
Attractive Renaissance château overlooking the Loire. Museum of Moroccan Goums who fought in World War II.

7 NANTES
Once the château of the Dukes of Brittany, it houses three museums and is the setting for the Nantes festival.

8 LE PLESSIS BOURRE
15th-century château whose guardroom has a particularly fine painted and coffered ceiling.

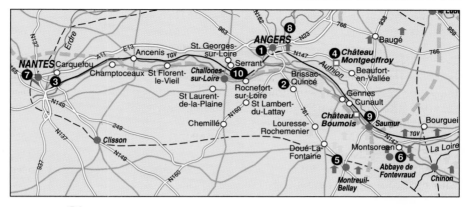

*S*ites of châteaux in Western Loire.

Secular Architecture

9 SAUMUR

Feudal castle standing high above the town, containing two museums.

10 SERRANT

Attractive Renaissance château containing some lovely coffered ceilings and a fine library. Connections with Bonnie Prince Charlie of Scotland.

Secular Architecture

Aqueducts

BRIARE

Pont-Canal or aqueduct, designed by Gustav Eiffel, carrying the *Canal Lateral de la Loire* over the River Loire.

LUYNES

Remains of a Roman aqueduct which used to supply water to Tours.

Tithe Barns

BOURGES

Small half-timbered tithe barn with outer stairway, adjoining cathedral.

BRACIEUX

Beautiful 16th-century market hall with a tithe barn built above it.

CHARTRES

Magnificent tithe barn and undercroft, used for International Stained Glass Centre.

MESLAY

One of the largest tithe barns in France, used for concerts during Touraine music festival.

Market Halls

BROU

Particularly fine roof timbers in this ancient covered market in the town square.

CHATEAUNEUF-SUR-LOIRE

Interesting old wooden market hall, where the river boats used to be stored, plus an elegant 20th-century hall with decorative wrought-iron roof supports.

CLISSON
Beautiful 16th-century covered market. It was the only building in the town to survive the destruction of the Revolution.

LA-FERTE-BERNARD
Sixteenth-century covered market hall with tiled roof supported by fine timbers.

LUYNES
Fine timber-framed market hall has a very high roof made of flat tiles.

RICHELIEU
This 17th-century market hall has a very fine timbered roof.

ST-MAURE-DE-TOURAINE
Medieval covered market in village famous for its goat cheeses.

Other Places of Interest

AMBOISE
Pagoda de Chanteloup. An example of 18th-century chinoiserie; there is a fine view from the top of the pagoda.

ANGERS
Hospital of St John. Beautiful 12th-century hospital ward with Angevin vaulting, home for the contemporary tapestries of Jean Lurçat *"Le Chant du Monde"*.

ARVILLE
Commandery of the Knights Templar.

ASNIERES-SUR-VEGRE
Cour d'Asnières, the remains of an old gothic court-house.

AVOINE
Modern visitor centre at nuclear power station near Chinon.

GENNES
Roman amphitheatre: the best-preserved half-amphitheatre in western France.

NANCAY
Giant radio-telescope.

NANTES
Passage Pomeroy; superb 19th-century shopping arcade on three levels, near the Office du Tourisme.

For Children (and Adults)

The Loire area is not specifically geared to children, but there are several places where children, and their parents and grandparents, may spend some hours of enjoyment.

Beaches and Sandy Areas
The following places all have bathing beaches, play equipment, walks and canoeing.

ANGERS
Le Lac de Maine; newly created recreation area to the west of the town.

NORTH OF ARGENT-SUR-SAULDRE
Etang des Puits, recreation area in heart of Sologne countryside.

BLOIS
Le Lac de Loire; the river is partially dammed and makes a recreation area.

Animal Parks and Zoos

DOUE-LA-FONTAINE
Zoo in old quarries, enabling animals to appear in their natural habitat.

LA-FERTE-ST-AUBIN
Animal park and children's farm in château grounds.

LA FLECHE
Zoo contains 700 animals from all over the world, including a unique reptile collection.

ORLEANS
Parc Floral La Source has a small children's zoo, plus play areas and a miniature train.

PESCHERAY
Domestic and small animals in château park, which is part of an employment scheme for handicapped adults.

ST AIGNAN
Beauval Ornithological Park. Rare breeds preservation centre, including tropical birds and water fowl.

SPAY
Tropical bird gardens.

Museums of Special Interest to Children (Mainly for Boys)

AMBOISE
Models made to Leonardo da Vinci's drawings on display in Le Close Lucé.

BRIARE
Museum of old cars in a disused lime quarry.

CHARTRES
La Compa museum of agricultural machinery.

LE MANS
Motor car museum at racing circuit.

ROMORANTIN
Museum of Matra racing cars.

SAUMUR
Museum of toy soldiers in château casemates; tank museum in the town.

VALENCAY
Museum of old cars, all in working order, in château grounds.

Steam Trains run from:
CHINON to RICHELIEU;
SALBRIS to ROMORANTIN

Museums of Special Interest to Children (Mainly for Girls)

NANTES
Museum of dolls and old toys.

TOURS
Doll museum.

USSE
Waxworks depicting the story of the *Sleeping Beauty.*

For Boys and Girls

CHATEAU DE ROUJOUX
Play areas, mini-golf and model railway.

CHINON
Musée Animé du Vin is fun, with animated figures "working" in winery.

ST-LAURENT-DE-LA-PLAINE.
Museum of old trades and crafts can be of interest to children.

Petit Trains
These little motorized trains take passengers on sight-seeing trips through the following towns, and are fun for children: Angers, Chalonnes-Sur-Loire, Chartres and Nantes.

Finally, all the quality campsites have numerous activities (*animations*) for children during the high season, usually under supervision, and all have children's play areas, with swings, slides, climbing frames and other such amusements. Most also have a special children's swimming pool.

Other Recommended Tours

At the end of the main sections of the book, each covering a different area of the Loire, are a series of car tours, walks and other tours of interest.

Fine Arts and Craftsmanship

There are several places in the Loire region where one can see craftsmen at work, and some of the many museums have some exceptionally fine works on display. The most interesting are listed here.

ANGERS
Complete collection of works by David d'Angers, sculptor and medallist, in former Eglise Toussaint.

ARGENT-SUR-SAULDRE
An exceptionally fine collection of contemporary ceramics in the Musée Vassil Ivanoff.

LA BORNE
Known as the *Village des Potiers*, there are many small studios here, specializing in grey stone pots made from the local grey clay.

BOURGES
Museum of contemporary paintings by Maurice Estève. Musée des Arts Décoratifs contains some exceptionally fine enamels and clocks.

CHARTRES
International centre for stained glass. Many small craft workshops open to view, and important International Centre in beautiful Tithe Barn. Musée des Beaux Arts has a lovely collection of faïence and 16th-century enamels, and a fine collection of glass.

GIEN
Gien china is famous for its beautiful colours and animal and bird motifs. Faïence factory can be visited.

MALICORNE-SUR-SARTHE
Pottery with a pale yellow glaze and bird decoration. Workshops may be visited.

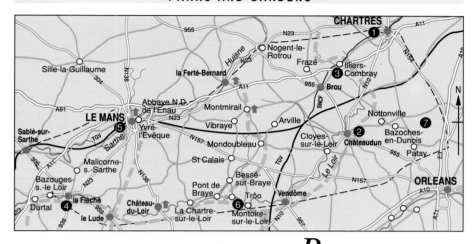

LE MANS
Fine collection of paintings in Tessé Museum.

MEHUN-SUR-YEVRE
Fine porcelain made here, and there are many small workshops where it is hand painted.

MOROGUES
Superb collection of china plates in the Château de Maupas.

ORLEANS
Particularly fine collection of 17th-century paintings from the French school in the Museum of Fine Arts.

SAUMUR
Fine collection of rare French Porcelain in the Musée des Arts Décoratifs in the château.

TOURS
Musée du Gemmail. Modern art form using particles of coloured glass bonded together and illuminated from behind. There is a reconstructed studio showing how the work is done.

*P*arks and gardens
north of Le Loir.

Parks and Gardens

The Loire Region has many beautiful parks and gardens, some formal, some informal. Garden lovers will get great pleasure devising their own routes to visit the gardens listed here.

North of Le Loir

1 CHARTRES
Very attractive riverside gardens and promenades alongside the banks of the River Eure offer good views of the cathedral. The public garden on the main road to Paris offers the best view of all. The attractive horticultural gardens are situated to the north of the city, near the stadium.

2 CHATEAUDUN
Promenade du Mail: attractive promenade and garden offering splendid views of the surrounding countryside.

3 ILLIERS-COMBRAY

Pré-Catalan gardens: made famous by Marcel Proust in his writings, which were designed and created by his uncle, Jules Amiot.

4 LA FLECHE

Public gardens with attractive view of the River Loire.

5 LE MANS

Promenade des Jacobins: terraced avenues planted with lime trees. Jardin des Plantes: botanical gardens with a rosarium, French garden and English garden.

6 MONTOIRE

Parc Botanique de la Fosse. Fine collection of trees and shrubs in château grounds.

7 VILLEPREVOST

Attractive gardens designed by a pupil of Lenôtre.

Upper Loire and Sologne

1 AUBIGNY-SUR-NERE

Parc de la Duchesse de Portsmouth: park with many mature trees surrounds the château, and which is particularly lovely in the autumn.

2 BOURGES

Beautiful gardens behind the former bishop's palace, beside the cathedral. Prés-Fichaux gardens, 20th-century gardens on the banks of the River Yèvre, on land which was once swamp!

3 CHATEAUNEUF-SUR-LOIRE

Lovely gardens in château grounds.

Exceptionally fine rhododendron walks. The park was designed by Lenôtre.

4 ORLEANS

Famous for its gardens, particularly the Parc Floral de la Source and the Roserie Municipale, where there are more than 10,000 roses on display.

5 ROMORANTIN

Square Ferdinand Buisson: gardens situated on two islands in the River Sauldre, linked by bridges.

6 ST-DENIS-DE-L'HOTEL

Attractive park beside the River Loire, and *village fleuri.*

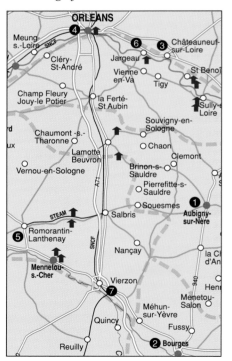

*P*arks and gardens in the Upper Loire and Sologne.

7 VIERZON

Memorial gardens beside the river, dedicated to the fallen of two world wars.

Touraine

1 BEAUREGARD

Beautiful landscaped park surrounds the château.

2 BLOIS

Terraced gardens of former Bishop's palace overlook the River Loire.

3 CHENONCEAUX

Gardens in Château de Chenonceau, especially formal gardens (Jardin de Diane de Poitiers and Jardin de Catherine de Medici).

4 ST-COSME-EN-L'ISLE

Lovely garden surrounding the ruins of the priory where Ronsard lies buried.

5 TOURS

Garden of Musée des Beaux Arts: very attractive formal gardens in shadow of cathedral. Jardin Botanique contains a collection of rare plants. Jardin des Murs Romaines contains remnants of old Roman walls. Jardin de la Préfecture offers a peaceful place of rest in the middle of the city.

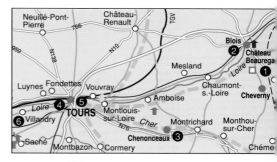

*P*arks and gardens in *Touraine.*

6 VILLANDRY

Beautiful, world-renowned formal gardens in château grounds.

Western Loire

1 ANGERS

Superb "carpet gardens" in château moats, and pretty gardens on top of the massive castle walls. Jardin du Mail: formal gardens near the town hall. Jardin des Plantes: informal gardens in the English style.

2 CHAMPTOCEAUX

Promenade du Champalaud: terraced

*P*arks and gardens in *Western Loire.*

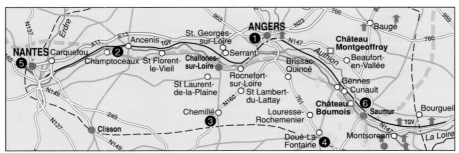

gardens with fine views of the River Loire.

3 CHEMILLE
Parc de l'Arzille: medicinal herbs and other plants attractively laid out according to colour.

4 DOUE-LA-FONTAINE
Town noted for rose-growing. Attractive public Rose Garden and annual *Journées de la Rose*, or rose show, in July.

5 NANTES
Jardin des Plantes: Botanical gardens offering a peaceful oasis.

6 SAUMUR
Jardin des Plantes: includes vine-covered terraces planted with local varieties of grape.

Old Towns and Villages

Apart from the major cities, there are many towns and villages which contain interesting old buildings, remains of city walls, etc. If you are interested in old buildings, you would enjoy making up your own routes based on this list.

North of Le Loir

ASNIERES-SUR-VEGRES
Picturesque village with 16th- and 17th-century houses and old bridge over the river.

1 BONNEVAL
Old fortified town with remains of 13th-century abbey.

2 BROU
Old town with fine market building and old chapel, once a resting place for pilgrims.

3 CHARTRES
One of the finest medieval cities in France, with many old houses and stone staircases (*tertres*) leading down to the River Eure.

4 CHATEAUDUN
Some attractive 15th-century houses can be found near the château.

5 LA FERTE-BERNARD
Renaissance houses and medieval town gate.

6 LE MANS
One of the best-preserved medieval towns in western Europe, with cobbled streets and half-timbered houses. Much of the original Gallo-Roman wall remains standing.

7 MONTIGNY-LE-GANNELON
Old walled town with Renaissance château overlooking the River Loire.

*S*ites of old towns and villages north of Le Loir.

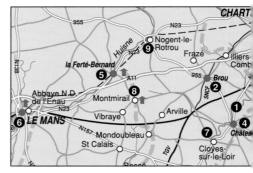

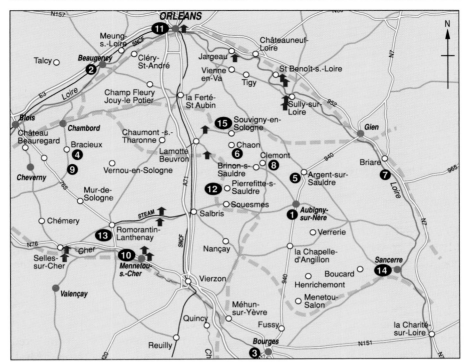

8 MONTMIRAIL
Steep narrow streets and old houses cluster round the château.

9 NOGENT-LE-ROTROU
Narrow streets and old houses dominated by ruined castle on the hill.

Upper Loire and the Sologne

1 AUBIGNY-SUR-NERE
Cité des Stuarts: remarkably fine examples of half-timbered houses in this little town.

2 BEAUGENCY
Narrow cobbled streets with Renaissance and Romanesque buildings.

3 BOURGES
Many medieval streets and old

Old towns and villages in Upper Loire and Sologne.

houses, some of which are built on the Gallo-Roman ramparts.

4 BRACIEUX
Pretty Sologne village on River Beauvron, with a picturesque bridge and half-timbered houses grouped around the market hall.

5 BRINON-SUR-SAULDRE
Pretty Sologne village with half-timbered houses and church with an interesting porch.

6 CHAON
Sologne village with typical half-timbered houses built in the local style.

7 CHATILLON-SUR-LOIRE
Very old half-timbered houses and a Romanesque church.

8 CLEMONT
Pretty village with half-timbered houses and 14th-century church with *caquetoir* or gossips' porch.

9 FONTAINES-EN-SOLOGNE
Typical half-timbered Solognot houses beside the church, which has a fine Angevin nave.

10 MENNETOU-SUR-CHER
Medieval town with cobbled streets and old gateways, and some houses dating back to the 13th century.

11 ORLEANS
Medieval houses in rue de Bourgogne and nearby streets, plus other ancient buildings scattered throughout the city of Joan of Arc.

*S*ites *of old towns and villages in Touraine.*

12 PIERREFITTE-SUR-SAULDRE
Pretty village with half-timbered houses and 15th-century church.

13 ROMORANTIN
Particularly fine half-timbered house, *le Carroir d'Orée* in the town, with carved corner posts.

14 SANCERRE
Famous for its wines, but there are also many interesting old streets and houses.

15 SOUVIGNY-EN-SOLOGNE
Beautiful Sologne village with half-timbered houses and superb *caquetoir.*

Touraine

1 BLOIS
Some streets lined with half-timbered houses, especially below the cathedral. Other old buildings scattered throughout the steep streets of the town.

2 CHINON
Fine medieval streets and half-timbered houses below the château ruins.

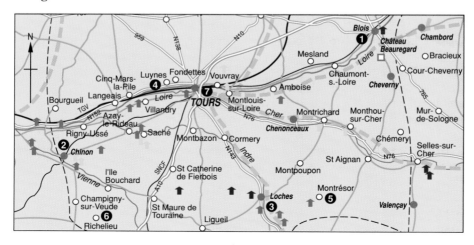

3 LOCHES

Beautiful medieval walled city surrounding the château. There are also some 15th- and 16th-century houses in the "Old Town", outside the medieval city walls.

4 LUYNES

Picturesque little town with several timber-framed houses and a fine medieval timber-framed market hall.

5 MONTRESOR

Attractive little town on river Indrois, with cobbled streets, stone cottages, and a 16th-century house with a watch tower, which is now used as a police station.

6 RICHELIEU

An early example of good town planning. Symmetrical streets with fine 17th-century classical houses, are surrounded by a wall and four identical gateways. The whole town is built around a central square.

7 TOURS

Beautiful half-timbered houses in place Plumereau and in the streets near the cathedral.

Western Loire

1 ANGERS

Some lovely 15th-century half-timbered houses, especially La Maison Adam, near the cathedral. Fine 17th-century town houses in Place du Pilori.

2 CLISSON

Town rebuilt in Italian style after the Revolution and the Vendée Wars.

3 MONTREUIL-BELLAY

Pretty town beside the River Thouet, with a good part of its medieval walls intact.

4 NANTES

Some exceptionally fine 17th- and 18th-century mansions can be found in the Place St Pierre and Ile Feydeau. Fifteenth-century half timbered houses will be found in the Quartier du Change.

5 SAUMUR

Attractive old houses in Grande Rue and Place St Pierre.

*S*ites of old towns and villages in Western Loire.

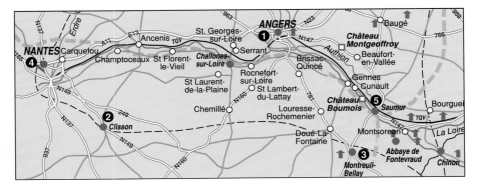

Medieval Towns, Motor Racing and one of the Prettiest Rivers in France

This chapter covers the area between Solesmes, Le Mans, La Ferté Bernard, Nogent-le-Rotrou and Chartres in the north and the River Loir in the south. Geographically, it covers about half of the *départements* of Sarthe and Eure-et-Loir and includes a small part of the *département* Loir-et-Cher. The greatest attraction of the region, apart from the two major cities, is its beautiful countryside.

Le Mans

Le Mans is the nearest major city in the Loire Region to the port of Caen, a popular entry point for many visitors to the area. Le Mans was built by the Romans (who named it *Cenomanum* after the Celtic settlement overlooking the river which it replaced), and the remnants of the walls which they erected to protect themselves from invaders can still be seen today. It is the capital of the *Département* of Sarthe, and has excellent communications by road and rail with other parts of France. Because of this it is a good place to stay when visiting the northern parts of the Loire region. There is a good selection of hotels of all kinds in and around the city.

All too often Le Mans is passed by in the haste of the visitor to reach the more well-known parts of the Loire Valley itself. Everyone has heard of the Le Mans 24-hour motor race, but there is much more to see here. It has a historic old town surrounded by Gallo-Roman walls and with a superb cathedral standing high on a rocky outcrop above the modern city. *Vieux Mans* has been perfectly restored and can stand comparison with any of

T he street market beneath the walls of the church at La Ferté Bernard is a scene which has been repeated for many hundreds of years.

89

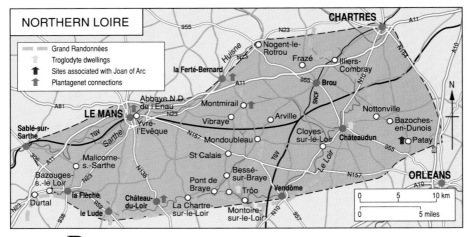

Regional map of the Le Mans and Chartres area.

*R*egional map of the Le Mans and Chartres area.

Europe's famous medieval cities. Old cobbled streets are lined with half-timbered and stone-built houses, and stone steps lead down to the river and the city walls.

Modern Le Mans owes a great deal to the insurance company *Les Mutuelles du Mans*, which began business in the city in the 19th century; but since 1977 the development of the city has progressed in leaps and bounds. It has an excellent shopping centre, with first-class shops. A very large market is held on Wednesdays, Fridays and Sundays in the place des Jacobins and the adjoining place du Jet d'Eau, below the great buttressed apse of the cathedral.

Le Mans has many connections with England, for it was in the cathedral here that Geoffrey Plantagenet married Matilda of England, the grand daughter of William the Conqueror. Their son, Henry Plantagenet, later to become King of England, was born here, and his daughter-in-law,

Berengaria of Navarre, widow of Richard Coeur de Lion, is buried in the Abbey of Epau.

Motor Racing

Much more recently, Le Mans has, of course, become famous for motor racing; this was the result of a local man, Amédée Bollée, taking an interest in motor cars. He was the first man to produce a car with the engine placed under the bonnet. It was his son's interest in racing cars which led to the building of the racing circuit, although the first 24-hour race was not held until 1923.

The American aeronaut Wilbur Wright made one of his first flights from Le Mans, and a road in the city, linking the place des Jacobins with the Quai Louis Blanc by the river, is named after him.

The Medieval Town

Around the cathedral is the medieval town, an area of cobbled streets lined with half-timbered and Renaissance houses, and elegant 18th-century mansions. Opposite the west front is **Le**

Grabatoire, built to serve as a home for aged and sick canons of the cathedral, hence its name (*Grabataire* = bedridden). It later became the palace of the Governor of Maine, and is now used as the Bishop's palace. Nearby is **La Maison du Pelerin**, (Pilgrim's House), decorated with cockleshell symbols, built in the 16th century by Jean de Courthardy on his return from a pilgrimage to Compostella. The old stone steps at the side of Le Grabatoire are known as **Les Pans de Gorron** and lead down to the riverside; there are several old houses flanking the

T*own plan* *of Le Mans.*

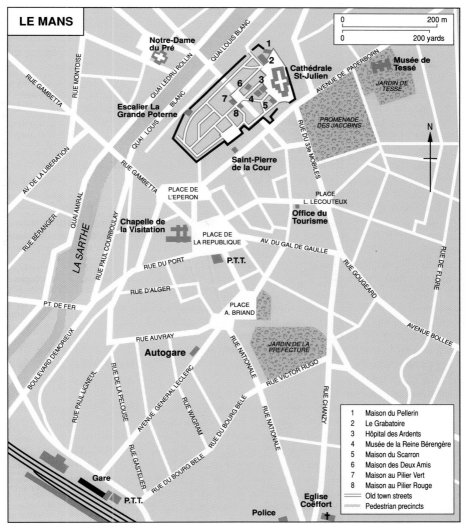

LE MANS

1	Maison du Pellerin
2	Le Grabatoire
3	Hôpital des Ardents
4	Musée de la Reine Bérengère
5	Maison du Scarron
6	Maison des Deux Amis
7	Maison au Pilier Vert
8	Maison au Pilier Rouge
═══	Old town streets
	Pedestrian precincts

The Cathedral of St Julien

St Julien's Cathedral was begun in the 11th century to replace the first cathedral built by St Aldric in AD 840, which stood to the south of the present cathedral, near the place Saint-Pierre. One of the finest views of this magnificent building is from the place des Jacobins, the market place of Le Mans. From here the beautiful flying buttresses which support the Gothic apse of the cathedral can be admired. The architect wanted to prevent shadows from being cast on to the windows of the choir, so he evolved a unique method of construction. The pillars which take the thrust of the buttresses are integral with the walls of the chapels which surround the choir. From the square below, they appear to be growing out of the roofs, rather like chimneys! There is a framework of arches connected to these pillars, some in a "V" shape, and the higher ones in a "Y" shape, which form the flying buttresses, graceful in appearance and extremely clever in their construction. To gain entrance to the cathedral it is necessary to climb the steps behind the fountain in the adjoining place du Jet d'Eau; these steps lead to the south side of the cathedral. Pause to look at the great south porch, for this is a replica of the central part of the Portail Royale of Chartres Cathedral. This porch has been given the strange name of "Pierre au Lait", or milk stone, because this was the spot where a dolmen (stone table) stood until 1770, and where the dairymaids brought their produce for sale. The west front of the cathedral is rather plain. It is Romanesque in style, and it has been altered more than once, as can be seen quite clearly if you look up at the gable. To the right of the west front of the cathedral is a strange-shaped menhir, a remnant of the days when there was a Celtic settlement on this hill. Legend says that you will forget about Le Mans if you do not put your finger into one of the holes in the stone.

Inside the cathedral, the Angevin nave gives an impression of spaciousness and light. When the fire of 1137 destroyed the roof of the building, the new nave was built on to the old Romanesque foundations. The side aisles, however, are pure Romanesque, the only complete remains of the original 11th-century cathedral. Note especially the carved capital "the lady with the lions" in the north aisle, and the beautiful 12th-century "Ascension window" in the south aisle. It is not until you reach the transept that you realize the full impact of the Gothic choir. Behind is the nave, 24m (73ft) high; in front, the choir, rising to a height of 34m (112ft), its slender columns and pointed arches soaring above, with beautiful 13th-century stained glass filling the windows of the chancel and the chapels, and the ambulatory surrounding it. This "double" ambulatory is of the same style as that found in Bourges Cathedral, the lower part being exactly half the height of the taller part. Tapestries from the 16th century relating the legend of St Julian and other saints are hung against the pillars in the choir. In the north transept, opposite the 16th-century organ, is the lovely 14th-century rose window depicting the Coronation of the Virgin.

Looking at the cathedral from the riverside, the difference in the levels of the roofs can be seen, and you might expect the interior to look rather strange. The different styles blend extraordinarily well together, however, and credit must be given to the builders of the time. When one considers that the original Romanesque chancel was demolished in order that the Gothic chancel could be built and that the intention was to demolish the Romanesque nave when the other parts of the cathedral had been finished, and replace it with a much larger one, reaching out to the edge of the bluff on which it stands, one must be thankful to those who prevented this from happening.

Rue St-Honoré in the medieval town of Vieux Mans *existed long before the invention of the motor car!*

steps, which divide half-way down. These houses, and those in the steeply sloping street of the same name, were once famous for the brothels which were there from 1796, and which were not closed until just after World War II. On the other side of the steps is **L'Hôtel Saint Paul**, sometimes known as the *Maison de la Tourelle*, a beautiful example of a Renaissance house, with a little turret on the side.

South of the cathedral is place Saint-Michel, which remains much as it was in the Middle Ages. On the corner of rue de la Reine Bérengère is the hexagonal 14th-century tower of **L'Hôpital**

Les Cénomanies–A Medieval Folk Festival

In early July, the city has its medieval folk festival, Les Cénomanies. The festival celebrates the historic origins of Le Mans, and takes place over 2 days in the old town. The city's inhabitants dress up in medieval costume, and the streets are thronging with colour. There are street entertainers and musicians appropriate to the period, dancing in the streets, plays and concerts. Craftsmen in abundance come to sell their wares, and everybody has a wonderful time–a truly medieval spectacle in a perfect setting. The festival was created only in 1986 and was an instant success, with close on 100,000 visitors attending.

des Ardents. This is all that remains of a hospital for plague victims which was founded in 1035.

The 12th-century **Maison du Scarron** stands near the top of the steps leading from the fountain, and has an exceptionally fine undercroft with rounded arches supported on a central pillar. The poet and master of burlesque, Paul Scarron, was a lay canon of the cathedral and lived in this house.

Cleric and Comic—The Poet Paul Scarron

Born in 1610, the son of a Paris lawyer, Paul Scarron became a priest, and while in Le Mans devoted himself to pleasure, indulging in the gay life of the city. After visiting Italy in 1634 he fell ill. Returning to Le Mans in 1643, he spent some time as an unordained canon attached to the cathedral, with a house to accompany the post. He consulted many specialists, but there was no cure for his illness, which eventually led to paralysis. He returned to Paris and from 1646 onwards he spent his time writing numerous sonnets, madrigals, songs, epistles and satires. Burlesque predominates throughout his work but he is best remembered for his realistic novels. *Le Roman Comique*, written between 1651 and 1657, was a reaction against the interminable affectation shown by many of the novelists of his time. In 1652 he married Françoise d'Aubigné, who, after Scarron's death in 1660 became Marquise de Maintenon before her secret marriage to Loius XIV. Many stories exist concerning Scarron's sometimes scandalous behaviour and the causes of his illness. Probably the truth is obscure but his ability as a writer and poet is not in question.

Other buildings worth looking at in the old streets that surround the cathedral include **La Maison de la Reine Bérengère**, **La Maison des Deux Amis**, **La Maison du Pilier Rouge** and **La Maison du Pilier Vert**. The old palace of the Counts of Maine is now used as the town hall, and the church next door, **Saint Pierre de la Cour** was once the palace chapel. There are many other houses, and the magnificent postern gate, **La Grande Poterne,** in the old city walls.

In addition to all these historic buildings, there are several others scattered around in the modern city outside the walls, such as the **Hôtel des Ursulines**, a former convent building which has been restored—and a hideous glass extension built onto it—for use as the *Office de Tourisme*. It is centrally situated in rue de l'Etoile at the junction with rue Mendès-France, and very busy even in early May, but unfortunately little information is available in English, not even a descriptive guide to the old town. The **Musée de Tessé** is close to the place des Jacobins, in the 19th-century former Bishop's Palace. Many of the paintings in the collection originally belonged to the Tessé family, whose house once stood on the site. Their possessions were seized during the Revolution, and the paintings, including some early Italian ecclesiastical work and French Classical paintings, form the nucleus of the collection. The most important artefact is the world-renowned 12th-century enamel of Geoffrey Plantagenet, Count of Anjou, the father of Henry II of England. This is the funeral plaque which was originally affixed to his tomb in the cathedral. The **Préfecture** is housed in the old convent buildings of the Benedictine Abbey of Saint-Pierre-de-la-Couture. The church of **Notre-Dame-de-la-Couture** has a beautiful 13th-century porch, and inside is a 16th-century white marble statue of the Virgin by the sculptor Germain Pilon. **La Maison-Dieu de Coëffort** in place George Washington, was founded by Henry II in 1180 as a refuge for the sick and poor, destitute children and pilgrims as atonement for the murder of Thomas à Becket. It has now been converted into a church, dedicated to Saint Joan of Arc. The interior is divided by two rows of elegant columns which contrast strongly with the rather severe exterior of the church.

By way of contrast, the **Chapelle de la Visitation** in the place de la République, which was built in 1730 to plans drawn by a nun, has an elaborate façade and interior with sculptures by the Le Mans sculptor Michel Chevalier.

The church of **Notre-Dame-du-Pré**, on the opposite bank of the river from the old city, was originally built in the 11th and 12th centuries on the site of St Julien's tomb to be the convent church of a Benedictine nunnery. The original layout has been maintained and the Romanesque walls are beautifully preserved.

Modern Le Mans

Le Mans has some striking modern architecture which blends well with the older buildings. Note especially **La Médiathèque Louis Aragon** in rue du Port, the "multimedia" library of Le Mans, built in 1988 and one of the most comprehensive information complexes in France.

Other modern buildings include the **Palais de Congrès et Culture** in place Stalingrad and the **Salle de Concerts** on the corner of rue de la Comédie and avenue de Rostov.

A Walk Through the City

The only way to see the old city of Le Mans is to walk! The *Office de Tourisme* arranges guided tours of the cathedral and old town in July and August, starting in the **place des Jacobins** below the cathedral at 3 p.m. However, most people will prefer to explore on their own and take plenty of time to do it. You should visit the cathedral on a separate occasion, as a walk through the old town can take quite a time. There are steep steps and alleys to negotiate, but it is worthwhile. The walk will take at least 2 hours, not allowing for stops or visiting museums and other buildings.

Begin the walk by exploring the immediate vicinity of the cathedral. The old north gate of the city stood at the end of the place du Cardinal Grente, by the rue du Château. The château which once stood here protected the most vulnerable entrance to the city. On the north wall of the cathedral can be seen traces of red and yellow markings from the fires which devastated the cathedral in the 12th century. At the far end of the north side is the entrance to the original Bishop's Palace, which was in use until the Revolution. The buildings are currently in use as the offices of **l'Agence des Bâtiments de France**, who were responsible for their restoration in 1986. The best view of this building is from the place des Jacobins.

Return to the *place* and admire the **Maison du Pelerin** and **Le Grabatoire**, then, passing the top of the Pans de Gorron and the Hotel Saint Paul, continue along the **rue des Chanoines**. On the left at no. 26 is **La Maison St Jacques**, actually two buildings, one

14th and one 15th century, linked together by a 16th-century pentagonal turret. Further along, on the right, is the **Maison Saint Martin**. Set back in a little courtyard, this house stands on the site of an old Priory. The building there today is 18th century, but it is built on an 11th-century undercroft. This large shelter, more than 20m (61ft) long and about 2m (6.5ft) high is equipped with a well and has alcoves along the walls to store provisions. Like other undercrofts of the era, the building served as a refuge in times of danger for the prominent citizens of Le Mans, and it had an "escape route" into the road behind. It now belongs to the the Duchemin family, who are particularly well known for their superb wrought-ironwork.

Continue down **rue des Chanoines** to **Square Jacques Dubois**. This pleasant little square is a monument to the man who conceived the idea of preserving the old town; it is built above the rue Wilbur Wright, and there is a good view looking down to the river.

On the far side of the square, on each corner of the Grande Rue, are two beautiful half-timbered houses. To the left, on the corner of rue du Pilier Rouge is the **Maison du Pilier Rouge**, a perfect example of a medieval timber-framed house with an elaborately carved corner post decorated with cords and rams' horns and with a death's head on the top. The red pillar does not signify anything special, apart from the decorative aspect, except as a means of locating the house. On the opposite corner, **La Maison du Pilier Vert** is somewhat larger and has a green pillar decorated with geometric designs.

Continuing down the cobbled street of the **Grande Rue** is like stepping back in time; here are houses from the 16th to 18th centuries, some with wrought-iron balconies and lamp brackets fixed to their walls, some with an air of faded elegance, and some decorated with floral hanging baskets.

Behind the Maison du Pilier Vert is the **Hôtel Rouxelin D'Arcy**. It was originally the Prior's house, and it gets its name from the Lieutenant-General of Police who lived there in the 18th century. Built in 1545, the house is one of the earliest classical buildings to be built in Le Mans but is now used by the National Conservatoire of music, dance and dramatic art. Opposite is a 16th-century house, now a restaurant, which was used as the town theatre in the 18th century. A little further along the street, on the left, is the **rue de l'Ecrevisse** where there is another fine classical mansion, **L'Hôtel de Vignolles**, known as the little Louvre because it was built at the same time as part of the Louvre in Paris, and the architect copied the window designs.

Return to the Grande Rue and turn left; no. 69 is a Renaissance house with a beautifully carved façade, known as **La Maison Adam and Eve**. Further along, on the corner of rue St-Honoré is the **Maison du Pilier aux Clefs**, so called because the corner post is decorated with three keys, the sign of a locksmith. **Rue St-Honoré** is a perfect medieval street lined with half-timbered houses leading to place St Pierre.

If you want a rest from your walk, go down the steps between the **Town Hall** and the Collegiate church of **St-Pierre-de-la-Cour** to the little garden

*S*uch *flights of steps as this,* l'Escalier de la Grande Poterne *leading up through the Gallo-Roman walls, are rather hard on the legs but well worth the effort of climbing.*

below. This 13th-century church is now used as the college of fine arts and the undercroft is used for exhibitions and concerts; access is only available at these times.

Continue past the church and turn right into the rue des Fossés St-Pierre to see the remains of the old Roman baths, discovered in 1980. The ramparts to the right contain the remains of an old wooden gallery which originally served as public conveniences—in the Middle Ages!

At the end of the street is the **rue des Boucheries**, site of the 17th-century meat market which was housed in an extension to the nearby Grenier à Sel. The **Escalier des Boucheries**, on the right, was constructed to give the city's inhabitants easy access when the meat market was moved to the site. Walk up the steps to rue Saint Flaçeau and the 18th-century **Hôtel Godard D'Assé**, and continue to the junction with the Grande Rue. Turn right and walk up the street, passing several classical houses, to the rue St Pavin de la Cité. On the corner to the left is the 16th-century **Hôtel Aubert de Clairlaunay**. In 1622 Jeanne de Beauge sold part of the house to finance the expedition which, in 1642, founded the city which was to become Montreal, Canada. Note the curious sundial affixed to the house, which only shows the hour of 12 noon! Where the street curves to the right is another stairway, **L'Escalier de la Petite Poterne**. On the corner is the **Hôtel d'Argouges**, with a rather nice 15th-century doorway in the courtyard. Continue along the street passing underneath **La Maison Suspendue**, and then turn left down rue Bouquet to rue de Vaux. Turn left again, past the Hôtel de Vaux on the right and walk as far as **L'Escalier de la Grande Poterne**. This beautiful stairway, lined with half-timbered houses, leads through the great postern gate of the city.

About halfway down to the left is a glimpse of the **Tour du Vivier** and part of the walls showing some of the beautifully decorative brickwork. At the bottom of the stairway is the **Porte Sainte-Anne** to the left and rue Saint-Hilaire to the right. Ahead is the **Quai Louis Blanc** alongside the river, with gardens either side. The best view of the Roman walls is from the gardens on Quai Louis Blanc. There are nine towers in all, most of which have been well restored. Between the towers and above the walls can be seen the backs of some of the elegant 18th-century mansions and older houses of the old city.

In the rue Saint Hilaire are several small restaurants where lunch may be obtained. The **Crêperie des Arcades**, right by the "Roman Columns" which have been erected here, serve an excellent selection of *galettes* (savoury pancakes) crêpes and ice-cream desserts at very reasonable prices.

Climb the steps to the side of rue Wilbur Wright and turn left along the rue des Chapelins. Along this road is the "emergency" exit from the undercroft of the Maison Saint-Martin. A little further along are some steps on the right; this is l'**Escalier des Pans de Gorron** which leads to the street of the same name. Continue to the top to emerge by the cathedral. Finally, turn right into rue de la Reine Bérengère. On the left is the **Maison de la Reine Bérengère**—actually built long after she died—which houses the **Regional Historical Museum**. Next to the museum is the **Maison de L'Annonciation**, with some beautiful carved statues on the front. The house is one of the last wooden houses to be built in Le Mans and the style marks the beginning of the Renaissance.

Almost opposite the museum is the **Maison des Deux Amis**, a lovely 15th-century half-timbered house with a carving of two friends on the central pillar, supporting a coat of arms. The house belonged to Nicolas Denizot, poet and painter, and friend of Ronsard, in the 16th century.

From the Maison des Deux Amis return towards the cathedral and turn right into Place Saint-Michel, and finally descend the steps to the square below.

Parks and Gardens

Le Mans has some attractive parks and gardens near the town centre. The **Promenade des Jacobins** was laid out in 1792 as a public garden when terraced avenues of lime trees were planted in the grounds of the old convents which once stood here. At the beginning of the 1980s the gardens were in a rather poor state until they were restored to the original plan. A central rectangular esplanade is surrounded by avenues on different levels linked by turfed and planted embankments. There is always something going on there—agricultural and horse shows, fairs and exhibitions.

On the south side of the gardens, adjoining place des Jacobins, is the municipal theatre. Close by is the **Jardin de Tessé**, surrounding the Museum de Tessé, and a restful spot in the centre of a busy city. The **Jardin des Plantes** in the Rue Prémartine to the east of the museum was planned by Monsieur Alphand, who was director of the Jardins de Paris under the Second Empire. The grounds comprise 8 hectares (23 acres); there is a French garden, with a rosarium, and an English garden surrounding the lake. The **Jardin de la Préfecture** is another pleasant garden adjoining the Préfecture and City administration offices fronting rue Victor Hugo.

All along the Quai Louis Blanc beside the River Sarthe are well laid-out gardens and pleasant riverside paths. On the eastern outskirts of Le Mans are the lovely woods of the **Bois de Changé**, adjoining the ancient **Abbaye de L'Epau**.

Shopping in Le Mans

Le Mans has two separate areas of pedestrian streets, one either side of the place de la République. In the place itself, part of which is set below street level, are a number of street cafés and some small shops. Below this is a very large car park. Around the square are some of the larger shops, including Monoprix. The nearby rue des Minimes contains several small arcades and precincts, including the attractive **Galerie Bérengère**. **Galeries Lafayette**, and **Nouvelles Galeries**, plus many small boutiques and jewellers are found here. Some very expensive boutiques are sited amongst others which contain quite reasonably priced goods. There are many shops in **avenue General Leclerc** which connects place Roosevelt, at the end of rue des Minimes, with the station, where there are more restaurants and several inexpensive hotels.

For those wanting big supermarkets the well-known **Le Clerc** and **Inter-marché** chains have premises situated on the outskirts of the city.

There are a few gastronomic specialities which can be found in local restaurants and *charcuteries*. *Rillettes* are one speciality which should not be missed; Le Mans *rillettes* are considered to be the best in France. Finely minced pork, often with goose flesh added, is heavily seasoned, cooked and pounded before being pressed into small pots. *Rillons* and *Rillauds* are made in much the same way, but are not pounded after cooking. *Andouillettes*, small sausages made from chitterlings, are another local delicacy.

Possibly because apples are grown in the area (the *Reinette* is the local variety and is far superior to the infamous Golden Delicious!) and because of the proximity of Sarthe to Normandy, cider is very popular.

Poultry is also a speciality, Loué capons and pullets being well known.

The nearest wine-growing areas are along the valley of the Loir, where the famous *Jasnières* wines are produced.

The Surrounding Areas of Le Mans

South of the city centre is the racing circuit. Even if visitors are not interested in motor racing, they must surely be interested in the superb collection of vintage cars, motor cycles, cycles and racing cars built from the earliest days of the motor car up to 1914 which are

T he lovely abbey of l'Epau, a short distance to the east of Le Mans, forms an ideal setting for its annual music festival.

Queen Berengaria, widow of the English king Richard Coeur de Lion, rests in her tomb in the abbey she founded in 1229 at l'Epau.

housed in the **Musée de l'Automobile**. The collection includes a steam-driven de Dion Bouton of 1885 and some of André Bollée's earliest designs.

To the east is the lovely Cistercian **Abbaye de l'Epau**, founded by the widow of Richard Coeur de Lion, Queen Berengaria, in 1229. She is buried in the abbey, and her tomb can be seen in the chapter house. Above the chapter house is the monks' dormitory, with a fine wooden vaulted roof. A music festival is held here every year in the gardens as well as inside the abbey buildings.

Further Afield

To the south and east of Le Mans are extensive areas of forest stretching as far as the valley of the Loir. In this area are some megalithic monuments, one of which, the **Dolmen de la Pierre Couvert**, is not far from Connerré on the old Chartres road. East of here is the **Forêt de Vibraye**, offering plenty of opportunities for walking, riding and cycling. In the town of Vibraye itself is an excellent restaurant in a small hotel, **Le Chapeau Rouge**, where the food is good and reasonably priced.

Further east, **La Ferté Bernard**, as its name implies, was once a fortified stronghold belonging to the Bernard family. It has a fine example of a medieval town gate, the **Porte St Julien**. Twin towers are joined by a central gatehouse and it is easy to see where the drawbridge could be lowered across the Huisne. In the gatehouse is a small regional museum, including a collection of porcelain dolls wearing regional head-dresses. In the **rue d'Huisne**, a pedestrian street leading from the gatehouse, are some interesting Renaissance houses and medieval courtyards, including a very good half-timbered house a short way along on the left, now used as a restaurant.

About halfway along the street is the **place de la République** and the huge church of **Notre-Dame-des-Marais** (Our Lady of the Marshes). The church is the second most important religious building in Sarthe, second only to Le Mans cathedral, and is a fine example of flamboyant Gothic architecture. The exterior is lavishly decorated with elaborate pinnacles and galleries. Inside are some lovely stained glass windows, in particular a 15th-century one depicting the death of the Virgin Mary. The organ is of particular interest, being suspended from a hanging keystone, known as a "birds' nest".

Outside, at the eastern end of the church, is an old fountain, and behind it, in the **place des Lices** is the old covered market, built in 1535. Although it has been restored, it has not been altered in any way since it was built. Nearby are more old houses, including one whose front is decorated with beautifully carved figures, one of whom is said to be St Stephen being stoned.

South of La Ferté is **Montmirail**, a little town with steep and narrow streets full of old houses, whose superb château dominates the countryside for miles around. The château stands on top of a huge medieval mound. Montmirail is important historically, because this was where, in 1169, Henry II of England signed a treaty with King Louis of France, in which Henry's sons acknowledged their

These turrets, part of the old Commanderie *of the Knights Templar at Arville, testify to the power of that organisation in the 12th to the 14th centuries.*

position as "Vassals to the King of France". It was also the scene of an attempt at reconciliation between Henry II and Thomas à Becket. That attempt failed, and shortly afterwards Becket was murdered in Canterbury Cathedral. The original château was destroyed, and the present one was built in the 15th century by the Count of Anjou. In the 18th century it was altered by the Princesse de Conti, who decorated the château rooms in Louis XV style.

A few miles south-east of Montmirail, in Loir et Cher Département, is **Arville**, where there is an old *Commanderie*. This was one of the bases established by the Knights Templar, where resources were gathered and recruits trained for service in the Crusades.

The church and the arch of the fortified gate at Arville date from the early 12th century, and the turrets and upper part of the gate are from the 15th century. Most of the buildings were retained in the state they were at the sale and break-up of the *commanderies,* at the time of the Revolution in 1789, and include a pigeon loft and bakery, and a barn from 1776 which has been restored. On the site of the

The Knights Templar

A religious military order of knighthood was established in 1119 and known as the Poor Knights of Christ and of the Temple of Solomon. Its founder, Hugues de Payens, and a small group of French knights vowed to devote their energy to the protection of pilgrims travelling to the holy places captured by the early Crusades. Baldwin II, King of Jerusalem, gave accommodation to the order in a wing of the royal palace which occupied an area of the former Jewish temple, hence the name of the Order.

Members of the Order were divided into four classes: knights, sergeants, chaplains and servants. Only the knight was entitled to wear the white surcoat emblazoned with a red cross. The Order was headed by the Grand Master, and each local branch or Temple was ruled by a Commander. These bases or Commanderies were used for gathering resources and training recruits for service.

All the knights took vows of poverty and chastity, and in 1139 the Order was taken under the direct command of the Pope. It grew in numbers and in power, with gifts of wealth and property, and by the mid-12th century its organization was such that the Order exerted great financial power and was used by many states as bankers, because of its ability to move goods and treasure safely and swiftly throughout Europe and the Middle East.

Bitter rivalry arose between the Templars and the military Hospitallers, and in the late 13th century proposals were made to merge the two orders.

At the beginning of the following century, Philip VI of France instigated a campaign to discredit the Templars by accusing them of heresy and irreligious practices. In 1307, members of the Order were arrested throughout France. After exerting public confessions from many of the leaders, including the Grand Master, Jacques de Molay, large numbers of the members of the Order were executed and the Order suppressed in 1312, its vast wealth and property being taken over by the state. Much of their property was transferred to the Hospitallers in exchange for large sums of money, which again went to the state.

knight's dwelling stands a 19th-century vicarage now used as a hostel for young artists and craftsmen.

South of Arville, the countryside changes to a high plateau and larger fields. At **St Agil** is an interesting moated château and, further south, is **Mondoubleau**, a small town with a large ruined castle keep leaning precariously at an angle on the hillside. The town has old narrow streets and plenty of cafés and restaurants. There is a pleasant tree-lined walk known as the **Grand Mail**, overlooking the river valley and reached from the public gardens behind the post office.

West of Mondoubleau, and back again in Sarthe, is the town of **Saint-Calais**, a market town with a very steep and dangerous hill on the main road leading down to the river Anille. The church here has an interesting Renaissance west front and a very ornate steeple. To the south, some 10km (6 miles) distant, is the little town of

This Gothic chapel is in the charming gardens of Courtanvaux château. The park with its picnic grounds is freely accessible to visitors.

Bessé-sur-Braye, on the outskirts of which is the **Château de Courtanvaux**, a Gothic building with tall pointed roofs and mullion windows; not a large château, but still very attractive. There is a pleasant park and picnic grounds which are freely accessible.

West of Saint-Calais, on the main road to Le Mans, is the **Château de Pescheray**, which has a small animal park and picnic areas in the grounds, and which provides work for the mentally handicapped adults who live there.

South of Pescheray, woodland and forests dominate the landscape. **Le Grand Lucé** is a village standing high on a hill with its own château, now used as a hospital, and with good views of the local countryside. South from here is the **Forêt de Bercé**, a beautiful area with many opportunities for walking, cycling and horse riding. At **Jupilles** is a clog and woodworking centre which aims to preserve the old crafts of the region. It is open at weekends during the afternoons, with extended hours in high season.

To the south of Le Mans on the La Flèche road, is **Spay**, with its new bird gardens containing more than 150 species of exotic birds. There is also a

*T*he massive north front of the Benedictine Abbey of Solesmes overlooks the river Sarthe. Only the abbey church is open to the public.

very beautiful church in the village. On the Sablé road, some 31km (19 miles) south-west of the city is **Malicorne**, noted for its distinctive perforated-style pottery. Malicorne pottery has a pale yellow glaze and the decoration is taken from birdlife. Nowadays other styles are made here, but much of the original ideas are still incorporated. At the **Faïencerie d'Art de Malicorne**, once the Tessier pottery, there is a museum containing some of the rarer items of local pottery. Visitors may also see today's craftsmen at work. Malicorne is also a popular centre for hiring boats to cruise along the Sarthe.

Sablé-sur-Sarthe is dominated by its château, an imposing building overlooking the town and the river. It now houses an annexe of the **National Library of France**, specializing in the microfilming of books, chemical processing, binding and restoration. There is an excellent campsite here,

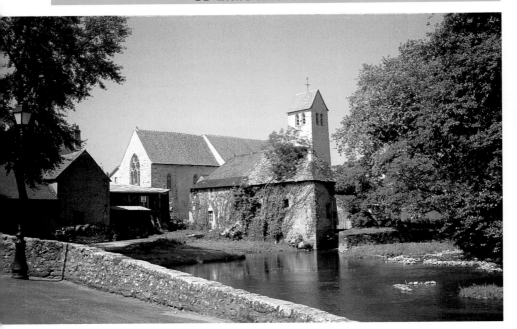

T he medieval bridge over the river Vègre offers an attractive view of the 11th-century church in the old and picturesque village of Asnières.

villages of Sarthe. There is an 11th-century church with some fine wall paintings, and an old medieval court, as well as beautifully kept 16th- and 17th-century houses. In this area it is possible to explore the lovely country lanes in horse-drawn carriages.

and an interesting cobbled square in the town centre, with some attractive shops—and small piles of cannonballs at various points!

Not far from Sablé is the magnificent **Abbey of Solesmes**, a massive structure built alongside the river. The Benedictine monks sing their Offices in Gregorian chant daily, and visitors are welcome to attend High Mass (9.45 a.m.) or Vespers (5.00 p.m.).

Just to the north of **Juigné**, the next village upstream from Solesmes, is the little village of **Asnières-sur-Vègre**, one of the oldest and most picturesque

Chartres

Chartres, the busy main town and administrative centre for the Département Eure-et-Loir is situated on the left bank of the River Eure in the plain of Beauce, the "granary of France". It is famous for its beautiful **cathedral**, a World Heritage Site, which stands on a hill above the old town, much of which remains intact and is a superb conservation area, one of the first to be created by the French Government. There are many fascinating narrow

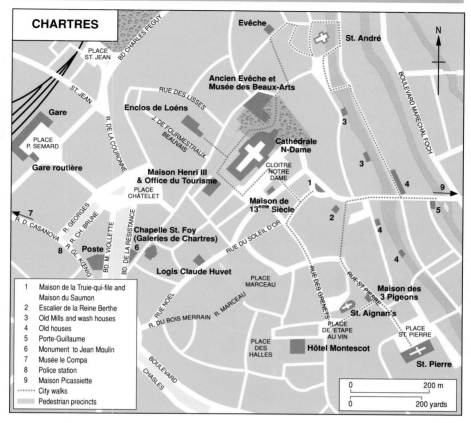

CHARTRES

Evêche
St. André
N

BD CHARLES PEGUY
PLACE ST. JEAN
RUE DES LISSES
Ancien Evêche et Musée des Beaux-Arts
Enclos de Loéns
ST. JEAN
Gare
R. DE LA COURONNE
J. DE FOURMESTRAUX BEAUVAIS
3
BOULEVARD MARECHAL FOCH
PLACE P. SEMARD
Cathédrale N-Dame
3
CLOITRE NOTRE DAME
Gare routière
Maison Henri III & Office du Tourisme
1
4
9
PLACE CHÂTELET
Maison de 13ème Siècle
2
5
R. D. CASANOVA
R. GEORGES
R. CH. BRUNE
BD. M. VIOLLETTE
BD. DE LA RESISTANCE
7
Chapelle St. Foy (Galeries de Chartres)
RUE DU SOLEIL D'OR
4
GL. KŒNIG
8
Poste
6
Logis Claude Huvet
PLACE MARCEAU
4
RUE DES GRENETS
RUE ST PIERRE
Maison des 3 Pigeons
RUE NOEL
R. DU BOIS MERRAIN
R. MARCEAU
St. Aignan's
PLACE DE L'ETAPE AU VIN
PLACE ST. PIERRE

1 Maison de la Truie-qui-file and Maison du Saumon
2 Escalier de la Reine Berthe
3 Old Mills and wash houses
4 Old houses
5 Porte-Guillaume
6 Monument to Jean Moulin
7 Musée le Compa
8 Police station
9 Maison Picassiette
······ City walks
          Pedestrian precincts

PLACE DES HALLES
BOULEVARD CHASLES
Hôtel Montescot
St. Pierre

0   200 m
0   200 yards

*T*own plan of Chartres.

streets and old half-timbered houses, steep stone staircases, known locally as *tertres*, and old stone bridges across the River Eure.

Chartres was once the settlement of a Celtic tribe, known as the *Carnutes*, from whence the city gets its name. It has been attacked many times and it was raided by the Normans on more than one occasion. It is said that, in the 14th century, when Edward III was about to attack the city with his English army, there was a violent hailstorm, making his withdrawal necessary. Chartres was attacked again in the 15th century, when the English held the city for 15 years, and in the

16th century when the Protestants tried unsuccessfully to capture the town. At the end of the 16th century, Henri IV of France conquered the town; a Protestant himself, he was later converted to Catholicism and was crowned in the cathedral in 1594.

It is recommended that the visitor obtain a guidebook from the cathedral bookshop; we recommend the English version of the Etienne Houvet guide *Chartres Cathedral*, revised by Malcolm B. Miller. This explains the

The Cathedral with the most Beautiful Windows

The original cathedral, begun in 1020, was Romanesque, and was dedicated in October 1037. Later on, the nave was extended and a new west front was built. This was done in a rather haphazard manner, by building the towers before extending the nave! Because of this, the three portals between the towers are unlike those of other cathedrals in that they are very close together, forming one great entrance known as the Portail Royal. Once richly painted and gilded, no trace of the original decoration can be seen today—indeed, much of the stonework is crumbling and some statues have had to be replaced. The west front and the towers are the only remnants, apart from the crypt, of the original cathedral which was destroyed by fire in 1194. It is said that after three days of conflagration a procession of clergy was seen emerging from the crypt bearing the cathedral's sacred relic of the Veil of the Virgin Mary, and the decision to rebuild was then made.

Apart from the west front, the present cathedral is pure Gothic; because it was built on the original foundations, and incorporated the surviving west front, the builders had to adhere to the original dimensions of the nave. However, the original cathedral had a wooden roof, and a stone-vaulted roof of this size was unheard of. To overcome the problems, the new vaulted nave rose to a record height of 37m (121ft). In addition, the whole structure was supported by solid stone buttresses to the sides of the nave aisles and elegant stone pillars towards the centre. Each arched bay is topped by a triforium, above which are double lancet windows and a rose window. Outside are the wonderful flying buttresses which keep the cathedral standing; it is these which carry the thrust from the main vault to the outer buttresses between the aisle windows. The whole cathedral is a framework for the windows, the only solid walls in the building being those of the two towers at the western end.

The windows represent the most remarkable collection of stained glass in the world, with a total area of more than $3,000m^2$ ($26,900ft^2$). The oldest windows are in the west front, and are probably the finest surviving 12th-century windows anywhere. The best of the three is the right-hand one, depicting the Tree of Jesse, which has been called "the most beautiful window ever made". The other windows were all gifts to the cathedral when it was rebuilt after the great fire. There are two modern windows, one of which is the Window of Reconciliation, given by Germany in 1971. Because the windows all contain large areas of rich, deep colours, the interior of the cathedral is very dark and sombre. Once the eyes have adjusted, however, you cannot fail to be overawed by the beauty and splendour of the place.

One interesting window commemorates St Thomas à Becket. Legend tells that when he was murdered some of his blood spilled onto a young priest, John of Salisbury, who later became Bishop of Chartres.

The cathedral contains a remarkable 13th-century labyrinth or maze, inlaid in the nave floor. Thirteen metres (42ft) in diameter, its meandering path symbolizes the Way of the Cross and has a total length of 262m (273yd). Pilgrims are said to have followed the path on their knees as an act of penance. The Treasury, in the Chapelle Saint Piat, contains the "Veil of the Virgin", donated by Charles the Bald in AD 876, and other treasures including the relics of the 13th-century rood screen, destroyed in the 18th century. The great organ was fully restored in 1971 and is now regarded as a fine, modern neoclassical instrument. Concerts are arranged on summer Sundays.

T he nave of Chartres Cathedral is supported by a system of flying buttresses, the whole forming a framework for some of the beautiful stained glass windows for which Chartres is famous.

history and architecture in a clear manner, and gives detailed descriptions of the great triple porches and the stained glass windows.

Churches

Other churches worth visiting in the city are the church of **Saint-Pierre**, close to the inner ring road through the old town to the south east of the cathedral, and the church of **St Aignan**, about halfway between the two. The old Romanesque church of St André is no longer in use and is partly in ruins, and stands below the cathedral at the bottom of the Tertre

St Nicolas. The Chapelle Sainte-Foy is another disused church, which has now been converted into the **Galerie de Chartres**. The old Romanesque doorway from the original building has survived, and can be seen from place Général de Gaulle.

Saint-Pierre church is a former abbey church of the Benedictine monks of Saint-Père en Vallée and became a parish church in the early 19th century. After the cathedral it is the finest church in the town and has some interesting architecture as well as some exceptionally fine stained glass windows. The original abbey was very vulnerable to attack because it was situated outside the ramparts of the upper town. This explains the solid keep-like bell tower, built around the year AD 1000, which still survives. The fire which destroyed much of the cathedral also destroyed most of this church, and it was rebuilt during the 12th and 13th centuries. The size and beauty of the new church show the affluence of the abbey. The earliest windows in the church, dating from the mid-13th century, are in the choir and are particularly fine. The nave windows are 14th century. One noticeable feature is that the church is much lighter inside than the cathedral; this is because the coloured glass figures are surrounded with *grisaille* or "grey" glass, which lets in much more light. Outside you can see that the windows take up an astonishing amount of wall space, separated only by slender buttresses and flying buttresses, topped by elegant pinnacles.

The church of **Saint Aignan** is built against the 9th-century ramparts of the upper town. Architecturally it is a bit of a mixture, but it contains an interesting carved coffered ceiling in one of the chapels and some beautiful 16th-century stained glass.

St André church is a Romanesque building, dating from the mid-12th century. An arch was later built over the river to carry the choir, and later still a second arch was built across the rue du Massacre. The ruins of these arches may still be seen reflected in the waters of the River Eure.

Museums

The most important museum in Chartres is the **Musée des Beaux Arts**, housed in the old Bishop's Palace behind the cathedral. It contains several important collections: medieval polychromed wood sculptures, 17th- and 18th-century Brussels and Gobelin tapestries, 16th-century enamels by Limousin, and paintings from the 17th to 19th centuries, including works by Holbein, Fragonard and Watteau. Also worth looking at are 17th and 18th century harpsichords and spinets, the Australasian collection and the Navarre collection of modern glass.

Le Compa (Conservatoire du Machinisme et des Pratiques Agricoles), is a new museum, housed in the old steam train depot by the station. As it is situated in the rich agricultural area of the Beauce, it is appropriate that this museum is the largest in France to be devoted entirely to agriculture and agricultural machinery. One of the more interesting exhibits is the tractor "Waterloo Boy", made by John Deere in the United States around 1916.

The Musée de l'Ecole, housed in the *Ecole Normale* (teacher training college) is a classroom from the days of the Third Republic, with a collection of authentic furniture and equipment.

Le Centre International du Vitrail is housed in one of Chartres' most historic buildings in **rue du Cardinal Pie**, its main aim being to promote and develop the craft of stained glass. It contains a superb collection of ancient and modern stained glass, as well as exhibits explaining how ancient glass is cleaned and restored.

Exhibitions of contemporary stained glass are staged regularly in the great tithe barn, and there is also a documentation centre which houses a specialist library of works concerning the history and techniques of stained glass art.

Curiosity

La Maison Picassiette is a strange "mosaic" house, outside the city centre near St Cheron cemetery. Inside and out the walls are covered with mosaics made from pieces of broken china and coloured glass.

Monument to Jean Moulin

Jean Moulin was the *Préfet* for the Département and was the founder of the French National Resistance movement in World War II. He was eventually captured and deported by the Germans, and was murdered by them in 1944. His monument is situated in the **Boulevard de la Résistance**, to the north of place des Epars, the largest of the city squares.

Historic Buildings

Some of the finest historic buildings are in the immediate vicinity of Chartres cathedral. Opposite the **Clocher Neuf** or new tower of the cathedral, the taller of the two towers with elaborate lace-like stonework, is the **Maison Henri III**. This house, which accommodates the tourist office, has six 13th-century windows and is considered by some people to be the most beautiful of all the historic buildings. In the **Cloître Notre-Dame** to the south, on the corner of rue des Changes, is, maybe, an even finer building from the same century, with some superb carvings above the windows. It was once the home of the cathedral canons. The **Enclos de Loëns** in rue du Cardinal Pie consists of a magnificent medieval tithe barn built over the original 13th-century cathedral wine cellars. The great undercroft has three enormous Gothic vaulted aisles. This building is the home of the stained glass centre, **Centre International du Vitrail**. In the nearby rue Chantault is the oldest house in the

city, a 12th-century Romanesque building with some amusing stone carvings. The **Maison de Saumon** and **Maison de la Truie-qui-file** (House of the spinning sow!) are 15th-century half-timbered houses in place de la Poissonnerie, and the **Escalier de la Reine Berthe** in rue des Ecuyers, is a 17th-century half-timbered house with a turreted staircase. Other interesting buildings include the **Logis de Claude Huvé**, a lovely Renaissance building which was the home of Henri II's physician, and the **Hôtel de la Caige** and **Hôtel de Champrond**. The **Hôtel Montescot** is an elegant private mansion house dating from the early 17th century in the rue de la Mairie, which has been used as the **Hôtel de Ville** (town hall) since the Revolution.

A Walk Through the City

To see some of the fine buildings in the **Vieux Quartier**, a walking tour is well worth the effort. There is a signposted route which starts from the cathedral square, although it helps to have the small map which is printed on the back of *Chartres, Ville d'art* (an information booklet published by the *Office de Tourisme*), since some signs are missing where they are most needed! A "Walkman" cassette with an excellent English commentary may be hired from the tourist office, with headsets for two persons, for an hour-long self-guided tour. The problem with these is that the leads are a bit short and it is necessary to walk at the same pace as your partner—otherwise the plug will become detached and you lose a vital bit of commentary! The tape can be stopped, if necessary, but not rewound, so you have to listen carefully to avoid missing any points of interest. A written commentary to accompany the map would enable the tour to be taken at a more leisurely pace with a stop for coffee or lunch halfway round.

Starting from the cathedral west front, immediately opposite is the **Maison Henri III** with its 13th-century windows. To the north of the Cathedral, in rue Cardinal Pie is the **Cellier des Loëns**, the beautiful half-timbered tithe barn which houses the *Centre*

The old town of Chartres has many steep flights of steps known as tertres. *One such is the Tertre Saint Nicolas, leading down towards the river from the cathedral.*

International du Vitrail. It is best to continue the walk at this point, and return to this building later to see the exhibits.

Next, walk around the north side of the cathedral to admire the north porch. Like the other cathedral porches, it has three bays with pointed arches, corresponding to the inner doors, and is richly decorated with sculptures depicting the Creation and many other biblical scenes including the coming of Christ.

From the north porch, continue round the back of the cathedral to the terrace overlooking the river Eure for a superb view of part of the old town. Here you can admire the wonderful exterior of the cathedral.

Adjoining the terrace, which was once part of the Bishop's garden, is the former Bishop's Palace which now houses the **Fine Arts Museum**. Go through a small gate in the left-hand corner of the terrace which leads to one of Chartres' interesting old, steep stairways, known as *tertres*. This is the **Tertre St Nicolas**, and about halfway down the steps is a door on the left. Go through this door and follow the small terraced path which leads out to the **rue Chantault**. Here can be found the oldest house in the city, a 12th-century Romanesque house with some amusing stone carvings. There are also several half-timbered houses to be seen.

Continue down the hill a short way, then turn into the rue du Cloître St André which curves round to emerge near the 12th-century collegiate church of **St André**, now secularized.

Turn left and walk around the church to cross the river to **rue du**

Massacre, from where it is possible to see where the choir of the church was once built out over the river; the reflection of the square tower and ruins in the river water is most attractive. Re-cross the river by the next bridge—a small footbridge—into **Place St André**, and follow the river bank to the **Pont des Minimes**. This is one of the typical humped-back stone bridges which cross the river. Turn right into the **rue de la Tannerie**. As its name suggests, this was the street of the tanners and leather workers. At the end of the bridge is one of the old fulling mills which has been converted into a very attractive bar and *salon de thé*. Not unnaturally it is called **Le Moulin**, and good meals in addition to lighter snacks may be obtained here.

The remains of other mills can be seen from this road, as well as several old *lavoirs*, riverside laundries or washhouses, some of them in a very good state of repair.

Traces may be seen of an arch over the river Eure which supported the choir of the Romanesque church of Saint-André.

Walk as far as the **Pont Bouju** and before crossing the river yet again, turn left and walk down to the remains of the ruins of the **Porte Guillaume**, a rare example of medieval military architecture, blown up by the retreating Germans in 1944.

The houses and buildings along the rue de la Tannerie were some of the first in France to be restored under a conservation order by the French Ministry of Historic Monuments. Gradually more buildings throughout the old town are being restored. Return to the Pont Bouju and cross the river again. From the bridge there is a lovely view of the cathedral spires over the roofs of the old town.

Old riverside wash-houses or laundries known as lavoirs *face onto the river Eure in old Chartres.*

Walk up rue du Bourg passing yet more half-timbered houses to **rue des Ecuyers**, where there is an exceptionally fine half-timbered house with a turreted staircase known as the **Escalier de la Reine Berthe**. If following the "self-guided walk", this will lead down a narrow lane to the rue aux Juifs and place aux Carpes, where there are more old houses, eventually emerging in the place St Pierre.

A more direct route is to follow rue des Ecuyers. Further along, the street bears to the left and becomes the rue St Pierre. To the right can be seen another Renaissance house, **la Maison des Trois Pigeons**, behind which can be seen the church of **St Aignan**, built against the 9th-century ramparts of the upper town. At the far end of rue St Pierre is the church of the same name, which contains yet more superb 13th- and 14th-century stained glass windows. These windows, and those of the cathedral, justify Chartres' reputation for medieval stained glass.

From the church, return along rue St Pierre as far as the Tertre St François and walk up to the rue des Grenets. Turn right and follow this street, which leads into the rue des Changes. After passing the covered market place on place Billard, turn right to the **place de la Poissonnerie**, where there are yet more half-timbered houses, the Maison du Saumon and Maison de la Truie-qui-file (house of the spinning sow). From this point, return to the Cloître Notre Dame on the south side of the cathedral. The south porch is another great masterpiece of carvings, featuring Christ the teacher, surrounded by the apostles, martyrs and confessors, and scenes of the Last Judgement. Chartres Cathedral is unique in that it possesses three great triple porches, which must be considered to be the finest cathedral porches in the world. In the Cloître Notre Dame, at the top of rue des Changes, is the lovely 13th-century canons' house, the ground floor of which now houses a very good bookshop.

Finally, at the end of the walk, stand in the **place de la Cathédrale** and look once more on the magnificent **Portail Royale**, depicting the life of Christ and the occupations of man.

For another aspect of the **Vieux Quartier**, a small motorized train (*Le Petit Train de Chartres*) takes the visitor along some of the old streets on a tour lasting 35 minutes, passing some of the historic buildings and the riverside. A commentary in English is available. However, to get the best from your visit, it will be necessary to go on foot.

The boulevards around the city are situated on the site of the medieval outer ramparts. There are still a few remnants to be seen, mainly to the north-west of the cathedral; from place Châtelet one can walk along the top of the ramparts to place Drouaise.

Parks and Gardens

Chartres has some beautiful parks and gardens, including some very pleasant ones beside the river. **Parc Léon Blum** provides barbecue facilities and there is boating available at **La Petite Venise** in **Parc des Bords de L'Eure**. What is considered to be the best view of the cathedral may be obtained from the public garden in the Rue d'Ablis, the main road to Paris.

Shopping in Chartres

Chartres has a bustling pedestrian shopping centre, which is particularly lively on market days. The main pedestrian shopping streets are situated between the busy **place des Epars** and the Cathedral. On the corner of place des Epars and **rue Delacroix** is an excellent *salon de thé* and *pâtisserie*. The rue Delacroix leads into the pedestrianized **rue du Bois Merain** where there are some very good *charcuteries* selling *Pâté de Chartres* and other delicacies. *Pâté de Chartres* is a rich pâté made from partridge, veal, truffles, foie-gras and cognac normally made with a raised pie crust, but it is sometimes sold in small pots without the pastry case.

In nearby **rue de la Tonnellerie** there is a *confiserie* selling superb chocolates, including *Mentchikoffs*. These are extremely expensive chocolates, made from roasted almonds, chocolate and cream, first made to celebrate the Franco-Russian alliance in 1893. They cost about 300F per kilo and each kilo contains three million calories. Definitely not for the weight-watcher!

Rue Marceau leads to place Marceau and rue du Cygne, where the flower market is held on Tuesdays, Thursdays and Saturdays. These streets make an attractive shopping centre with many small gift shops and boutiques. There are also two department stores, Monoprix and Le Printemps. The vegetable and poultry market is not in the pedestrian area, but is in the place Billard, off the rue des Changes. Market day is Saturday. The rue des Changes offers the visitor a good selection of places to eat. We found an excellent *crêperie*, **La**

Chandeleur, offering a wide variety of *galettes* or savoury pancakes which made a good lunch.

Galleries selling fine arts, stained glass, pottery, etc., are numerous. Many, particularly those specializing in stained glass, are situated near the cathedral. A particularly good one is **La Galerie du Vitrail**, in a small shop opposite the north porch of the cathedral, which exhibits works by contemporary artists, most of which are for sale. Gifts made of stained glass, including copies of typical Chartres medieval glass, and a large selection of books on the subject are available. Of special interest are audio-visual presentations on the techniques and historical aspects of stained glass which will be shown on demand, in English if required, and free of charge.

For those wanting big supermarkets, the well-known Le Clerc, Carrefour and Intermarché chains all have premises situated on the outskirts of the city.

The Surrounding Areas of Chartres

South of Chartres, in the direction of Orléans, lies the area known as **La Beauce**, a fertile region of large open fields and plains often referred to as the granary of France. Acres of wheat and corn can be seen growing here, and tall silos dominate the skyline.

To the west lies the country of **Le Perche**, an area of more rugged countryside, with sunken lanes and apple orchards between the hedgerows, small farms with the famous *Percheron* horses, and attractive forest areas, hills and dales. It is an ideal place for those who prefer more active holidays, offering plenty of walking, canoeing, riding and cycling. It is also a paradise for fishermen.

Nogent-le-Rotrou

The old town of Nogent-le-Rotrou is an ancient regional capital, with a fine château standing high above the valley of the river Huisne. There are narrow streets and old houses, and market days give that extra atmosphere. The smaller villages and towns include **Illiers-Combray**, with its association

---

A Church with a Chequered History

The Eglise Notre-Dame, opposite the tourist office, has an interesting porch, decorated in Romanesque style. Although the church was actually built in the 14th and 15th centuries, much of the decoration is in 13th-century style. In the northern side aisle there is a beautiful 16th-century set of crib figures. The church has had a chequered history. It was built originally as the chapel of the Hôtel-Dieu, which was owned by the monks of St Denis. During the Revolution it was used as a temple to the goddess of Reason, and later the floor was lifted to enable saltpetre to be extracted! In 1802 the building was reconsecrated and became the Eglise Notre-Dame.

The Duke of Sully became the owner of the château in 1624, and on his deathbed insisted that he wanted to be buried in the chapel of the Hôtel-Dieu. Since he was a Protestant this was impossible, so a tomb was constructed behind the chapel, to be integral with the building but outside the consecrated area! The tomb may be seen by entering the courtyard of the Hôtel-Dieu, behind the chapel.

with Marcel Proust, and **Bonneval**, an old fortified town, both of which lie on the upper reaches of the River Loir. **Brou** is another old town worth visiting, having an attractive château not too far away.

Nogent-le-Rotrou was once the capital of the Counts of Perche, and is dominated by the huge 11th-century keep of the Château St Jean, built on a 50m (160ft) high rocky outcrop above the river valley. The river in this case is the Huisne, which eventually flows into the Sarthe at Le Mans. Nogent-le-Rotrou has many interesting old buildings in addition to the château, and the *Office de Tourisme* at 44, rue Villette-Gâté can supply a map describing a walk through the most interesting parts of the town, although unfortunately there is no English text.

Towards the end of the 10th century the Count of Chartres installed one of his trusted supporters on the site of the château to repel the Norman invaders,

*T*he massive towers of the gatehouse protect the huge 11th-century keep of the Château St Jean which dominates Nogent-le-Rotrou.

and the construction of the keep began a few years later. The château may be visited, and there is a pleasant path encircling the old ramparts. From the château old stone steps lead down to the town below.

Old houses line the rue Bourg-le-Comte and rue Saint-Laurent, which lead to the **Abbey of Saint-Denis. The Porche Saint-Laurent** is an attractive gateway built over the street, originally the entrance to the abbey. One of the old houses in rue Bourg-le-Comte, **La Papotière**, is now a restaurant, and like several others in the town it includes local specialities on the menu. It is, however, somewhat expensive. **Hôtel**

*H*orses are a common sight on almost any farm in the region.

du Dauphin in rue Villette-Gâté is comfortable and reasonably priced, and offers a good menu. The town has a very good market, held on Saturdays.

 Illiers-Combray
This is a small town situated in the upper reaches of the Loir Valley, only a few miles from its source, and is particularly famous for its association with the novelist, Marcel Proust.

The mainly 15th-century church of **St Jacques** has an imposing nave with ribbed vaults and a panelled, painted ceiling plus some interesting windows.

Between Chartres and Illiers-Combray is the village of **Meslay-le-Grenet**. Inside the little 12th-century church is an interesting mural representing the Dance of Death. The paintings, on the south and west walls, depict 20 persons

---

Proust at La Maison de Tante Léonie
The novelist Marcel Proust is a major figure in 20th-century literature. He was born in 1871, the son of a distinguished Parisian doctor and was a semi-invalid all his life. His early years were devoted to his mother and spent in society, but after she died in 1905 he withdrew to become a recluse. It was then that he began to think deeply about life and his disillusionment with the society of the time. His thoughts gave rise to the eight-part novel which was his masterpiece, written between 1913 and 1927. *A la Recherce du Temps Perdu* appeared in 13 volumes, revealing the amazingly observant eye of the author, winning him the Prix Goncourt, awarded in 1919, and international acclaim. The novel is semi-autobiographical and makes use of material gathered during the earlier years of his life during which he spent his holidays with his Aunt Léonie in the town of Illiers-Combray. He died in 1922 and his aunt's house in rue Docteur Proust, "La Maison de Tante Léonie", has been converted into a museum containing manuscripts, photographs and other memorabilia concerning the author and his family, and the town as he knew it.

There is a pleasant riverside walk to Le Pré Catalan, the garden created by Proust's uncle, Jules Amiot, and used by the author as the setting for scenes in his books.

from different walks of life, each being led away by a grinning skeleton. A *Son et Lumière* takes place during the summer, based on the paintings, and examining the medieval preoccupation with death.

Bonneval

Situated midway between Chartres and Châteaudun, Bonneval has some fine old abbey buildings and the remains of 13th- and 15th-century fortifications including a 13th-century bridge over the river. South-east of Bonneval on the Orléans road are some small settlements along the little river Conie, a tributary of the Loir: the 11th-century abbey of **Nottonville** and the 18th-century wooden post mill at **Bazoches-en-Dunois**, as well as traditional reed-thatched houses. Approximately 15km (9 miles) east of Nottonville is the charming château of **Villeprévost**, with its gardens designed by one of Lenôtre's pupils.

Brou

This is an old town with a superb covered market building and a delightful little 12th-century chapel, now used as the local *Syndicat d'Initiative* and exhibition centre. The market here, held on Wednesdays, is noted for its poultry. North of Brou is the 15th-century château of **Frazé**, set in a valley surrounded by woodlands, with the church standing on the opposite side of the road. Like many small country towns, Brou has a hotel belonging to the *Logis de France* chain, **Le Plat d'Etain,** in the market square. It has a very reasonably priced restaurant.

Between Brou and Nogent-le-Rotrou is the little village of **Beaumont-les-Autels**, which has a

A peaceful scene behind the church in Brou, with beautifully restored old buildings.

pretty turreted château and an impressive church. At nearby **Thiron-Gardais** is a massive Abbey church, which is in need of some repairs, but is nevertheless quite impressive.

This 12th-century chapel in Brou was later used as a hospital before becoming the Tourist Office.

The Valley of Le Loir

The River Loir marks the southern boundary of the area covered in this chapter of the book.

From **Châteaudun**, the most picturesque route along the valley is signed *Route Touristique du Vallée de la Loir*, and although it could be followed in one day there would be no time to stop and enjoy the delights of the towns and villages along its banks. So take your time, and stop for at least one night *en route*, and enjoy an unhurried journey, like the river itself which flows slowly through the lovely countryside.

In the streets surrounding the château are many attractive 15th-century houses, a specially fine one at the top of rue St Lubin being the **Maison Louis Esnault** with beautifully carved timbers and decorative medallions. The rue de la Cuirasserie leads from the square at the top of rue St Lubin to the **place Cap de la Madeleine**. Cap-de-la-Madeleine is a small town in Quebec which was founded by a priest from Châteaudun. There are two buildings of special interest here, in addition to the huge Romanesque church, which was never completed because of lack of funds. One is the old **Hôtel-Dieu**, an elegant 18th-century building and the

The Dormouse River

A glance into a French dictionary tells us that *Le Loir* means the dormouse, and our English dictionary tells us that this is a hibernating rodent. So what is the connection between a dormouse and Le Loir, tributary of the much greater river of La Loire? Le Loir follows a winding course through pleasant rural scenery, and its clear waters and lakes have an abundance of fish to attract fishermen.

From just south of Chartres, the river runs to the outskirts of Angers, where it joins the river Sarthe and Mayenne before adding to the water coming down La Loire. Placid stretches of the river flow between banks lined with willows and poplars, and the adjoining meadows are backed by gentle hills. The pastoral scene is completed by grazing cattle and the hill slopes, the coteaux du Loir, are largely occupied by vineyards.

Small towns and villages with their bridges and mills, and small châteaux and manor houses, offer a pleasant and relaxing change from some of the more awe-inspiring castles and cathedrals elsewhere in the region. The landscape of **La Vallée du Loir** has been called *la Douce France* and if a lazy placid river recalls the habits of a dormouse, then so be it.

rather nice house with mullion windows, and a good view of the river.

Below the château in the lower town beside the river is the **Fouleries**, which can be reached by descending one of the many sets of stone steps from the **Promenade du Mail**, a large terrace and public garden, situated high above the river with splendid views over the surroundings.

"Fuller's Earth caves"

At one time the curing and selling of skins was an important trade in the town, and this street takes its name from the name of the clay, *foulon*, used to cure the skins. The name was later used to describe the craftsmen themselves. Hence the English words "Fulling" and "Fuller's earth".

In the rock face along the Fouleries are cavities of differing sizes from where deposits of foulon have been dug out over the years. Since 1982 it has been possible to visit some of the grottos thus formed. Guided tours are available, lasting 45min and covering a distance of about 800m (866yds). The caves are exceptionally interesting geologically, as the vaults are covered with geodes. No one knows quite how these geodes formed, or why some of them have crystallized into quartz. Silica does not usually crystallize, so this remains a mystery.

other is the **Palais de Justice**, housed in the Classical buildings of the former Augustinian Abbey.

Other interesting buildings in the town include the old porter's lodge of the abbey, which stands near the ruins of the old Roman gate. Near the château entrance is an archway leading to **Impasse du Cloître St-Roch**; go through the arch and turn right into a narrow unmade passage which twists and turns past old houses and emerges into a small square. Here there is a

Further along the Fouleries, opposite the great cliff on which the château stands, is an attractive riverside garden and old water mill.

Some 15km (9 miles) downstream is **Cloyes**, an old riverside town on the edge of the **Beauce**, and one of the stopping places for pilgrims on the ancient route of St James to Compostella. In the church is a 12th-century stone statue of St James, and a

A Most Spectacular Château

One of France's most spectacular châteaux, the château of **Châteaudun** stands high on a rocky outcrop some 60m (198ft) above the River Loir. Its foundations descend right down to the valley floor, and it is a very rare example of feudal, Gothic and Renaissance architecture. The keep is a massive 12th-century structure, some 31m (102ft) high and 17m (56ft) in diameter. The walls are some 4m (13ft) thick at the base, narrowing to 2m (6 ½ ft) thick at the top. It was one of the earliest round keeps to be built in France, and a complete military base was built around it to protect and defend the Loir valley. The present château was begun in 1450 with the chapel, at the instigation of Jean Dunois, companion to Joan of Arc. This contains some of the best examples to be found anywhere of 15th-century statues. Dunois' son François de Longueville carried on the work and built the great Gothic building and staircase at the end of the 15th century. The staircase was a revolution in construction, being wider and easier to climb. After his death, his children added the early Renaissance building which runs parallel to the valley. Here again, the staircase is particularly pleasing, being beautifully carved with elaborate decoration. The château rooms, many of which have huge fireplaces, contain some fine Brussels, Aubusson and Gobelin tapestries and a large number of Gothic and Renaissance chests and other furniture. One of the rooms was used for a revolutionary tribunal in the 18th century, and the walls, which were decorated all over with the monogram "L" and fleur-de-lys, were painted over. This room, known now as the Justice Room, has recently been restored.

*T*he castle of Châteaudun presents a spectacular mix of styles from the 12th century through to the 16th century. This elaborate Renaissance staircase is part of the later works.

Renaissance wooden carving of Christ. The chapel of **Notre Dame d'Yron** contains some beautiful 12th-century murals depicting amongst others the Flagellation of Christ, unique in France. To the north of Cloyes 3km (2 miles) away is the old walled town of **Montigny-le-Gannelon**, with its impressive Renaissance château standing on a hillside overlooking the Loir. The grounds of the château are open daily, and the château may be visited on weekend afternoons.

The route along the river follows a picturesque road through **Saint-Hilaire-la-Gravelle**, where there is an old water mill and an excellent restaurant (recommended by Les Routiers) in the shape of the **Hôtel du Loir** which offers a very good menu at prices to suit all pockets. At nearby **Courcelles** is an old ruined keep in the trees above the river and another water mill. The road follows the river for another 15km (9 miles) to enter the town of **Vendôme**.

Vendôme

Vendôme is a former Roman town (*Vindocinum*) which is directly on the pilgrims' route to Compostella. It has had a troubled history: the site of battles in the Hundred Years War and an uprising during the Revolution.

The town sustained much damage during World War II, but there are still some old buildings to be seen. The most important of these is the beautiful **Abbey Church of La Trinité**. This fine Gothic church was founded in 1033 by Count Geoffroy Martel and his wife. Only the (detached) Romanesque bell tower remains of the original church. After the Hundred Years War it was rebuilt in the Gothic style, bearing witness to the town's new prosperity. Unfortunately, many of the beautiful stained glass windows were later destroyed during the Franco-Prussian War in 1870, although some original ones, dating from the 14th century, remain in the Chancel. Also in the chancel are some beautifully carved 15th-century *misericords*. The beautiful west front of the abbey was built by Jean de Beauce, who later built the **Clocher Neuf** at Chartres cathedral.

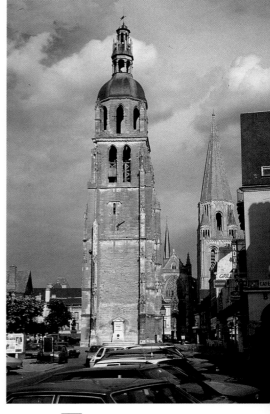

*T*his impressive bell tower is all that remains of the original abbey chuch of Vendôme.

After the Revolution, when it was sold as "National Property", the Abbey became a prison and administrative building. During the reign of Napoleon, the southern part of the abbey and the cloisters were used as a military headquarters, and they remained as such until 1940.

Today, these buildings house a local museum and a music school, as well as

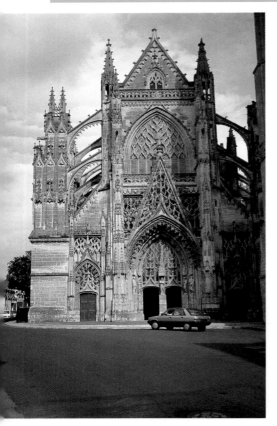

*T*he elaborate west front of Vendôme Abbey with its lace-like carvings and flying buttresses recalls features of the great Chartres cathedral.

leading to the river, and others leading to **Parc Ronsard**, around which are the buildings of the Lycée Ronsard. Balzac was a pupil here, when it was the College of Oratorians, and he hated school life. Even so, in later life, Vendôme was used as the setting for many of his novels. The local tourist office is housed in the former 15th-century **Hôtel du Bellay** in the gardens.

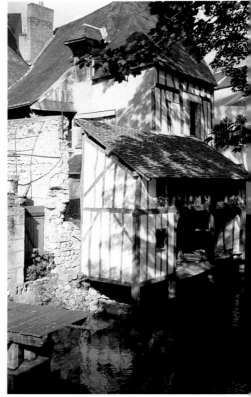

other local offices. West of the abbey is the place de la République and place St Martin. All that remains of St Martin's church is the bell tower. The pedestrian shopping street, rue du Change, leads towards the Hôtel de Ville and the **Chapelle St-Jaques**, formerly a house of rest for pilgrims and now a small museum. Off the rue du Change are little alleyways, some

*T*his Lavoir des Cordeliers *or wash-house in Vendôme dates from the 15th century.*

124

One of the alleys leading towards the river passes an old water mill, now a *brasserie*. The old water gate or **Porte d'Eau** spans the river not far from the town centre. A good view of this can be obtained from the public gardens on the other side of the river; cross the bridge at the end of rue de l'Abbaye and turn left through the gardens. Another interesting old building is the **Porte Saint-George**, spanning the river at the southern end of rue Poterie, with its twin 14th-century towers decorated with carvings of dolphins.

Above the town are the ruins of the château, reached by a steep path from the place du Château, or by road. For the road route take the Blois road after passing through the Porte Saint-George, then go left up the hill and left again into the **rue du Château**. There is plenty of parking, and a large wooded

The old entrance to the town of Vendôme from the river Loir was through the Porte Saint-George, flanked by 14th century towers and decorated in the 15th century with machiolations and carved dolphins.

area with plenty of picnic places. A 17th-century gateway leads into the courtyard, which has been landscaped into an attractive garden. There is also a *salon de thé*, open during the high season. From the château grounds there are superb views over the surrounding countryside. In addition there is a rarity here—a British-style public toilet! Vendôme is a good place to break your journey along the Loir, not least because there is plenty to see, and because accommodation is plentiful and the surroundings pleasant.

125

West of Vendôme the river Loir winds its way past *tuffeau* caves and small villages towards **Montoire**. At **Villiers** there is a wine cooperative – the *Air d'Appelation Vignobles Côte de Vendôme*. The tourist office at Vendôme will supply a list of *viticulteurs* who will sell direct to the public. Jean Brazilier, at Thoré-la-Rochette, sells some very pleasant rosé. His wife, who is Dutch, speaks excellent English. At **Les Roches-l'Evêque** are some of the best troglodyte houses to be seen along this valley.

The picturesque village of **Lavardin** and its ruined keep, once unsuccessfully besieged by Henry II and Richard Coeur de Lion, is passed on the way to **Montoire**, which also has a ruined keep standing high above the town. It was in Montoire station that Marshal Pétain met Hitler in October 1940 to discuss the fate of France for the remainder of World War II. However, the little town is more notable for its connections with Ronsard, who was titular head of the Benedictine Priory here. All that remains is the chapel of Saint Gilles, which contains some 12th- and 13th-century frescoes. There are a number of Renaissance houses in the town, many of which may be seen from the bridge over the river. The town is also the venue for an international folk festival in August, and at the nearby Château de la Fosse is the **Parc Botanique de la Fosse**. Here can be found thousands of trees and shrubs, collected from all over the world and planted by the same family since 1751. The park is only open to individual visitors about once a month, so it is best to enquire about opening times when you are in the area.

Beyond Montoire the river valley begins to open out, although there are still quite high cliffs in places. At **Troo** there are whole streets of "troglodyte" houses; it is quite a stiff climb up steps and steep alleys, but well worth the effort. At the very top is the old collegiate church of **Saint-Martin**, a massive Romanesque building. Behind is **La Butte**, an old feudal motte from which there is a superb view for miles around. The ruined keep of Lavardin dominates the skyline to the south-east.

The river Braye joins the Loir at Pont-de-Braye, and about 2km (1 mile) to the south at **Couture-sur-Loir** is the manor house of **La Possonnière**, where Ronsard was born. It is open for guided visits during the weekends in July and August.

At **Poncé** is a small Renaissance château standing alongside the main road. Not very remarkable on the outside, it contains one of the best Renaissance staircases in France. In the gardens is an interesting dovecote with revolving ladders for collecting the eggs, and an exceptionally fine maze. There is a museum of art and folklore in the outbuildings. There are many craft workshops in Poncé, including glass-blowing, pottery, weaving, and furniture making. Most of the workshops are open to the public.

Ruillé and **l'Homme** are two villages which are famous for Jasnières wines, the hamlet of Jasnières being situated between the two. Jasnières wine is a white wine, almost yellow in colour, which is always made from the Chenin Blanc grape. It is mostly rather dry, and, since so little is made, it can be rather expensive. There is a small vineyard museum in l'Homme, open during the season.

La Chartre-sur-le-Loir is a pleasant little town on a hill above the river. Although there is nothing outstanding to see here it is quite a good place to stop for a meal on a day out.

Beyond La Chartre the road follows the left bank of the river, passing tuffeau cliffs into which stores have been built. The river is crossed by a very narrow bridge at **Le-Port-Gautier** and the next village is **Vouvray-sur-Loir**. This is not the same Vouvray of sparkling wine fame, which is near Tours, although Coteaux du Loir wines are produced here, and can be tasted during weekends in July and August at the Mairie.

Château du Loir gets its name from the château which once stood here, of which only the ruined keep remains, standing in the public gardens near the town hall. At **Vaas** is a water mill museum, and at **Cherré** are some very interesting Roman remains.

Le Lude is the next town on the river. It is particularly noted for its very fine château, a former fortress built at the beginning of the 13th century with huge round towers and a deep moat. The present château is built on the foundations of the former fortress and was begun in the 15th century, with additions through the next three centuries. Despite its fortress-style, much of the decoration is Renaissance, thus softening the severity of the building. Inside is a fine collection of furniture, tapestries and paintings, including some beautiful Louis XVI furniture in the oval salon and Gobelin and Flemish tapestries in the library and dining room.

*T*he entrance to the old hospital in the town of Le Lude leads to the fascinating "La Sentinelle" collection of uniform caps and headgear.

Le Lude is famous for the *Son et Lumière* performances held there every summer. It is definitely not to be missed. In the town is another "must"; in the old hospital is the **Musée des Coiffures et Costumes** "la Sentinelle". This is a superb private collection of uniform caps and headgear from all over the world dating from 1870 to the present day. There are three hotels in the town, but for a wider choice it is better to find accommodation in **La Flèche**, which is some 20km (12 miles) downstream.

A Breath-taking Spectacle

The *Son et Lumière* at the Château Le Lude is the very best of the *son et Lumière* shows. The façades of the château are unusual, being of an Italian Renaissance decorative style on a medieval structure. Because of its superb setting, with its lovely formal gardens below the terraces by the river Loir, the château forms the perfect backdrop for the performances.

The idea originated in 1957, when, as a finale for a country fair in the park, someone suggested that volunteer saleswomen should model crinoline gowns against the backdrop of the illuminated château. The whole project then snowballed and, with the encouragement of the owner of the château, the *son et Lumière* tradition was established.

Les Féeries de l'Histoire (literally the "Fairytales of History") is an evening of magical entertainment, with wonderful costumes and slow and stately dances on a 300 m (330 yd) long grass-covered stage beside the water. The fountains and the château are floodlit, the reflections on the water adding to the atmosphere. Music and poetry complement the action on stage, and there are fireworks at the end. It doesn't matter if you do not understand the language, for the whole performance is simply breathtaking. All the 350 performers are local amateurs, their costumes made by local people. No wonder this spectacle has been awarded three stars by Michelin, and has won the French Tourism Oscar.

La Flèche is famous for the **Prytanée**, where generations of French army officers have been trained. The college was originally a Jesuit college, founded by Henri IV of Navarre in 1604. Descartes was one of the college's earliest pupils. The Château des

Now housing the Town Hall, the 17th-century buildings on the site of the Château des Carmes at La Flèche stand beside the bridge spanning le Loir.

Carmes is a 17th-century château which is now used as the Hôtel de Ville, and the gardens behind are now public with an attractive view of the river. La Flèche also has a well-known zoo to the south of the town, where the animals are kept in a woodland setting. There is a large aviary and vivarium, and a miniature farm and a natural science museum within the grounds.

At **Bazouges** is another château with two huge round towers flanking the entrance which define its origins as a fortress. It is privately owned, although it is open on Saturday afternoons during the holiday season.

Durtal, further downstream, is dominated by a château with two large 16th-century crenellated towers with pepper-pot roofs. A road runs along the remains of the medieval ramparts to the **Porte Véron**, a 15th-century gate which is part of the original curtain wall of the château. The **Forêt de Chambiers** to the south offers plenty of opportunities for walking, cycling and horse riding.

The river now flows on to enter the River Sarthe at **Noyant**, some 10km (6 miles) to the north of Angers.

Car Tours in Sarthe and Eure-et-Loir

The region between the motorway connecting Le Mans and Chartres and the River Loir lends itself well to car touring. There is a network of minor roads through very attractive countryside, passing through pretty villages and towns. In addition to the scenic route along the Loir Valley, which is well signed and described above, three further tours are suggested, two of which may be based on Le Mans, and the other on Chartres, taking in some of the interesting places described in this section.

Tour of the Châteaux and Forests to the East of Le Mans. Distance approx. 184 km (115 miles)

Leave the city via the ring road in the direction of **Chartres**, taking the road to the **Abbaye de l'Epau**, which is signed, and continuing through the woods to Changé. Then take the N23 road to **Connerré**, going into the centre of the town and taking the road on the left towards **le Luart**. After about 1km (½ mile) take the right-hand fork in the road which leads in a further kilometre to the **Dolmen de la Pierre Couverte**. This is a huge flat slab of rock balanced on a number of standing stones, resembling a large table, standing in a small enclosure beside the road. Continue along the road and then turn left at the bottom, which will bring you back to the road to le Luart. Turn right and follow the road in the direction of **Montmirail**. At the D29/D1 crossroads, a left turn will take you into the town of **La Ferté-Bernard**, about 11km (6 miles) away. Alternatively, turn right at the crossroads to **Vibraye**, and then from here follow the D302 road to Montmirail. This route will give you a good view of the château, which can best be seen from a lay-by near the bridge over the TGV railway line.

If you want to visit La Ferté-Bernard, take the road through **Cormes** and **Courgenard** (a *village* *fleuri,* and very attractive, with boxes of flowers on the pavements outside the houses) to Montmirail. Continue south to **Mondoubleau** and take the road west out of the town to **Baillou**, then follow the road south along the river Braye through **Sargé** and **Savigny** to **Bessé-sur-Braye** and the château of **Courtanvaux**. Go south again to join the valley of the Loir at **Pont-de-Braye**, and follow the *Route de la Vallée du Loir* into **La Chartre-sur-le-Loir**. Take the road out of the town in the direction of **Le Mans**, then turn left through **l'Homme** to **Chahaignes**. Turn north along the D235 and continue through the **Forêt de Bercé** along forest roads to **Jupilles**. From Jupilles, take the D13 road to **Le Grand Lucé**, then follow the D304 road back to Le Mans.

Tour to the West of Le Mans. Distance approx. 110 km (68 miles)

Leave Le Mans in the direction of **La Flèche** and after about 7km (4 ½ miles) turn off to **Spay** for the Bird Park. Continue to **La Suze-sur-Sarthe** and **Malicorne**, then take the road to **Parcé-sur-Sarthe** before turning west to **Sablé**. From here, follow the road north of the river to the abbey at **Solesmes**, then continue to **Juigné** and **Asnières-sur-Vègre**. Continue along minor roads through **Poillé-sur-Vègre** and **Chevillé** to **Loué**, and from there return to Le Mans via the N157 main road.

A Tour in the Perche. Distance approx. 162 km (101 miles)

Leave Chartres via the road to **Châteaudun** (N10), and continue as far as **Bonneval**. To the east are the wide open spaces of the **Beauce**, where you will see sunflowers, wheat and maize growing. From Bonneval, follow the D27 to **Dangeau** and **Brou**, then take the D13 road in the direction of **Unverre** and **La Bazouche-Gouët**. After about 13km (8 miles) turn right through **les Autels-Villevillon** to **Authon-du-Perche**, from where the D9 road leads to **Nogent-le-Rotrou**. The road from les Autels to Nogent-le-Rotrou passes through typical Perche country—small farms and orchards, with the Collines du Perche (Perche hills) to the north. From Nogent-le-Rotrou take the D922 road to **Thiron-Gardais**, continue to **Chassant** and turn south on the D15 to **Frazé**. Turn round in the village and take the D124 road through the **Bois du Grand Parc** to **Montigny-le-Chartif** and **Méréglise** to **Illiers-Combray**. From here, follow the D23 northwards to **Les Perruches**. About 2km (½ mile) to the west is **Saint-Eman**, the source of the river Loir. Continue in the direction of **Marchéville** and **Courville**. At the crossroads with the D302 at **le Breuil**, turn right and continue to **Magny** and **Bailleau-le-Pin**. Turn right at the T-junction and continue ahead to cross the main road, then turn left through the village to **Meslay-le-Grenet** and **Fontenay-sur-Eure**. From here drive north again to join the D921 road into Chartres.

Walks in Sarthe and Eure-et-Loir

Both **Sarthe** and **Eure-et-Loir** have some lovely countryside, and there are several *Grande Randonnées* (National

Long-distance Footpaths) in both Départements. Part of the *Grande Randonnée* 36, which runs from **Ouistreham** on the Normandy coast to the Spanish border near **Prades**, passes near Le Mans. A very pleasant stretch is that from the old stone bridge at **Yvré l'Evêque**, through the **Bois de Changé** to the *Route de Parigné* (D304). Buses from the city will take you to Yvré l'Evêque, and it is a short walk to a bus stop at the end of the walk. There are some interesting way-marked footpaths at **Coulaines** and **Sargé**, which are served by buses from Le Mans, and at **Pruillé-le-Chetif** and **Les Commerreries**, beyond **Changé**, which are within easy driving distance of the city. These walks range in length from about 3 km (2 miles) to 17 km (12 miles). Leaflets with small sketch

A bus ride from Le Mans will bring you to this peaceful scene where a medieval bridge spans the river Huisne at Yvré l'Evêque.

maps may be purchased for a small sum from the tourist office in Le Mans. Although only available in French, they are rather useful as they give details of the waymarking colour and the length of each one, with in some cases an indication of the time needed for the walk. *(Balisé* means waymark.)

The Département Eure-et-Loir produces a set of excellent leaflets describing *Petites Randonnées*, and covering the whole of the Département. Each one contains an extract of the relevant topographical map and a description of the route. These are presented in an attractive folder. Although the text is in French, the maps are easy to follow and the length of each section is marked in kilometres.

There is a particularly attractive walk along the valley of the Eure at **St-Georges-sur-Eure**. Part of this route follows the *GR de Pays de la Vallée de l'Eure*, and the rest of the route is waymarked with the support of the local authorities. It follows the line of the river, between restored gravel workings, and shady paths through the woods for 14km (8 miles) It will take about 3 ½ hours to walk the complete route, but it may be shortened if desired. It would be impossible to describe all the walks, but there are other attractive circular walks at **Bonneval**, **Cloyes** and **Brou**.

There is also a set of maps *En Marchant par le Perche* which comes in a handy-sized wallet. Each map is printed on card, with the routes superimposed in the waymarking colour, making them very easy to read. They can be linked together to make longer routes if required.

Cycle Touring in Sarthe and Eure-et-Loir

Sarthe, in particular, offers excellent cycling routes through forests and country lanes. A folder *La Sarthe à bicyclette* contains a set of 12 leaflets detailing 25 circular routes. Each route is described in fairly simple French and has an extract of the relevant topographical map. The set is published by the *Comité Départemental du Tourisme* in Le Mans, and may be purchased from *Offices de Tourisme* in the area. Particularly to be recommended are routes 5 and 6 from **La Ferté-Bernard** and **Vibraye**. These take in some lovely forest areas and offer some fine views of the Perche countryside. However, it is not essential to purchase special leaflets, because with the aid of a good map it is easy to find the minor roads which will provide the cyclist with pleasant riding. Indeed, some of the car tours described earlier could easily be undertaken by cyclists, as they are mostly on quiet roads.

Boat Trips in Sarthe and Eure-et-Loir

The River Sarthe is the only navigable river in this area, and is navigable from Le Mans to its mouth near Angers. The boat-hire centres are at **Sablé-sur-Sarthe** and **Malicorne-sur-Sarthe**. River cruisers which are fully equipped for living on board may be hired, but day cruisers also operate from these towns. Recommended are the tours in the **Sablésien**, from Sablé, which range from short trips of 75 minutes to nine-hour, all-day cruises. One of the best of these is from Sablé to Malicorne and return journey, with a superb view of the **Abbey of Solesmes** from the river. It is also possible to enjoy a candlelit dinner whilst cruising on the river.

The river Loir is no longer navigable, except for small boats used by fishermen who enjoy the abundant variety of fish in the clear water.

A Rich Historical Past in a Land of Heath, Marsh, Bulls and Valleys

This chapter covers the area bounded by the River Loire from Orléans in the north to La Charité-sur-Loire in the east, thence westwards to Bourges and along the River Cher to Selles-sur-Cher. From Selles the boundary runs north through Cheverny and Chambord to the River Loire, which it follows through Beaugency and back to Orléans. In this region is the area of wooded, marshy heathland known as the Sologne, and the lovely region of hills and steep valleys known as the Collines de Sancerre. It covers about half of each of the *départements*, Loiret, Cher, and Loire-et-Cher.

Orléans

Situated at the great bend of the River Loire, where it changes course from north-east to south-west, Orléans has always been strategically very important. In pre-Roman times it was considered to be the centre of Gaul, and was a very important trading centre.

Except for the base of the tower, the church at Gien was totally destroyed in an air raid in 1940. Reconstruction used traditional material and methods, so the town and church now look much as they did in the 15th century.

Corn from the Beauce was brought to the markets here to be sold, and was transported from Orléans by the river. A thriving port was established, and the Romans began to trade in the city. Unfortunately, they were not popular, and in 52 BC the inhabitants rose against the merchants and killed them. As a reprisal, Caesar razed the settlement to the ground. A Gallo-Roman town was built up from the ruins, which was later fortified and renamed after one of the Roman Governors of the city, **Aurelianis**, from which the present name of Orléans is derived.

Although nothing now exists in the way of building ruins from this period, there are some very fine Gallo-Roman bronzes in the **Hôtel Cabu**, now the Archaeological and Historical

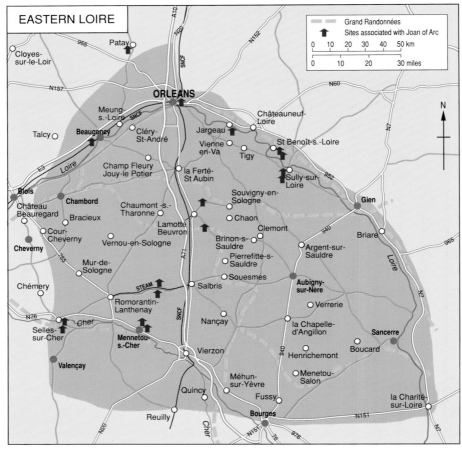

Museum. Orléans became a royal city in AD 987. In later years, monasteries and schools flourished, and eventually the schools were given university status. The siege of Orléans in 1428 caused havoc in the city, and there was great relief when in May 1429 Joan of Arc led the troops into the town which led to the lifting of the siege.

By the 15th century the town was flourishing again, and its rich inhabitants began to build some of the fine houses which can still be seen today. The University had worldwide fame, receiving many students from abroad,

*R*egional map of Orléans, the Sologne and Bourges; the eastern Loire.

including Erasmus and John Calvin. Reformist ideas began to spread, but the town suffered from Huguenot violence when civil war broke out. The cathedral and other religious buildings were badly damaged, and in retribution many Protestants were massacred. Reconstruction of the cathedral began in the early 17th century, and by the mid-18th century the town had been transformed by the building of the **rue**

Royale and the **Pont Royal**, now known as the **King George V** Bridge. The port was thriving, and the town was then one of the leading commercial centres of France. The town suffered again under the Prussian occupation of 1870–71, and during World War II. Many historic buildings were destroyed or badly damaged, and hundreds of citizens lost their lives in the air raids of 1940. An immense task of reconstruction began after the war, and many buildings were restored. In addition, the University, which had ceased to exist at the end of the 18th century, was re-established at **Orléans-la-Source** and a complete new town, which is still expanding, was built. It incorporates a scientific and industrial complex which is rapidly expanding into a large "Technoparc", and the **National Scientific Research Centre** has been established here. There are many other industrial areas around the city, but there are also many market gardens and nurseries as well as public

T own plan of Orléans.

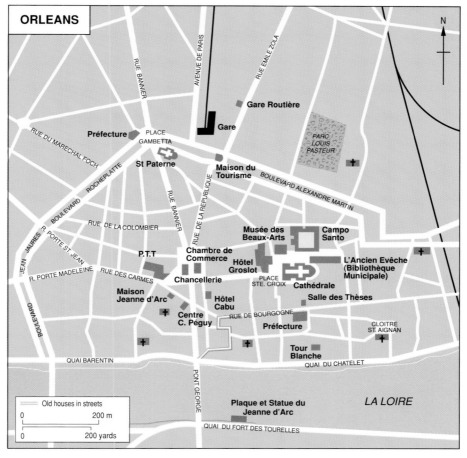

137

The river Loiret which gives its name to the département *rises as a spring in this lake in the floral park of "La Source".*

gardens, the most famous being the **Parc Floral** at **La Source**. Orléans is known as the city of roses.

Like many old French cities, the centre is surrounded by wide boulevards, which mark the site of the city

---

Orléans—History Re-enacted

The Jeanne d'Arc Festival takes place here on 29th April and 7th and 8th May each year. It was on 29th April 1429 that Joan arrived in Orléans to rescue the town, besieged by the English troops since the previous October. After only 8 days she had captured most of the English strongholds on the edge of the city, and the English soldiers finally left their positions; Orléans was liberated. Joan then went to the cathedral to give thanks, followed by a crowds of citizens. Today, on the evening of 29 April each year, these events are re-enacted. A young girl riding a white horse, dressed in armour and carrying her standard, represents Joan of Arc. She enters the city, surrounded by heralds and armed men. On 1 May is a reminder of the storming of one of the English fortresses and the crossing of the Loire, and on 7 May Joan of Arc's standard is presented to the population. In the evening it is handed to the Bishop of Orléans in front of the illuminated cathedral. On 8 May there is High Mass in the morning, followed by homage paid by all the French provinces to Joan of Arc. In the afternoon there is a long procession through the town, ending at the site of the Fortress of Tourelles, last of the English fortresses to be captured.

walls, and by the quays alongside the river Loire. Most of the older buildings are in the vicinity of the cathedral.

North of the cathedral are the remains of the old city walls, including the Gallo-Roman base. To the east are the gardens of the old **Bishop's Palace**, from where a very good view of the ornate buttresses supporting the apse may be seen. The Palace itself now houses the municipal library, and contains a 17th-century wrought-iron staircase. Opposite the library, behind the modern Ecole des Beaux Arts is **Campo-Santo**, formerly a 16th-century cemetery surrounded by open-fronted galleries, and now a public open space often used for outdoor exhibitions. Underneath is a large underground car park. Close by is the **Musée des Beaux Arts**, housed in a modern, classical-style building. It contains a fine collection of 18th-century portraits by French painters, and paintings from the 17th–18th century French School.

There are some early sculptures, including a marble virgin and child from the 14th century, plus many paintings from the Italian, Flemish and Dutch schools. There are 19th-century paintings by Courbet and Gauguin, and some 20th-century art, including sculptures by Rodin and Zadkine.

Almost opposite the west front of the cathedral, a little to the right in the **place de l'Etape**, is the **Hôtel Groslot**. Built in 1550, this red brick Renaissance mansion was the residence of the king when he stayed in Orléans. François II, husband of Mary Stuart, later Queen of Scots, died here in 1560

*T*his view from the George V Bridge looking toward the Cathedral of Sainte-Croix reveals little of the modern commercial and industrial development of the city of Orléans.

The Ugliest Church in France?

The cathedral of Sainte-Croix was begun in the 13th century, and was not finished when it was virtually blown to pieces by the Huguenots in the 16th century. Reconstruction began when the foundation stone for the new cathedral was laid by Henri IV, who undertook to rebuild it in the Gothic style, in 1601. Work progressed very slowly, however, and the towers were not added until the late 18th century. These very elaborate towers, looking rather like two wedding cakes, are 81m (263ft) high, and were severely damaged by fire in 1940. After the war, major reconstruction took place.

The cathedral is somewhat over elaborate and should be described as striking, rather than beautiful. Marcel Proust called it the ugliest church in France! None the less it is an important building, and one which dominates the skyline when approaching the city from the south. The west front has three large doorways topped by large rose windows and an elaborate gallery. Instead of the intricate carvings normally associated with the great medieval cathedral doors, here there are just four large statues of the four evangelists. Inside there is a semblance of spaciousness, with the tall nave supported by slender columns. The side aisles contain 19th-century windows illustrating the life of Joan of Arc, and her chapel is in the north transept. A monument to the Saint, placed here in 1929, shows Cardinal Touchet, Bishop of Orléans, kneeling before her. His efforts led to her beatification and eventual canonization in 1920. The choir contains some of the finest 18th-century carvings to be seen in France, in particular 32 carved medallions illustrating the life of Christ. Fortunately, these were removed during the Revolution, before they could be vandalized, and stored in the Bishop's Palace for safety. The apse of the cathedral is the oldest part, dating back to the 13th century.

In the crypt can be seen a few remains of the original churches which stood here before the 13th-century cathedral was begun. Some of the objects found in the three tombs of earlier bishops are now in the cathedral Treasury. These include a fine 12th-century *champlevé* enamel cross. Other treasures include two beautiful Byzantine enamelled glove plates, which used to be attached to the Bishop's gloves, as well as a 13th-century chalice and paten and other medieval gold and silver work.

after opening the States-General. The building was extended in the 19th century to blend in with the original, and was used as the Hôtel de Ville from 1790 to 1981. Between the two flights of steps of the beautiful external "stairway of honour" is a statue of Joan of Arc at prayer, sculpted by Princess Marie of Orléans, daughter of King Louis-Philippe. The city still uses the building for official receptions and for weddings, and the main reception rooms are open to the public. All are beautifully decorated and the Renaissance-style furniture includes some beautiful carved chests. In the main salon is another statue of Joan of Arc by Princess Marie of Orléans, depicting her on horseback, avoiding a wounded English soldier at her feet.

Behind the mansion is a pretty garden, containing the remains of the 15th-century Chapelle Saint-Jacques which once stood on the banks of the Loire.

Most of the old city of Orléans lies to the south of the cathedral. There are several medieval buildings, including the only remaining building of the original University; this is the 15th-

Set in the centre of the city, the cathedral of Orléans has suffered more than its fair share of damage from wars and fires during its existence.

century library or **Salle des Thèses** in the rue Pothier. Not far from here is the rue des Africains, where Joan of Arc's brother, Pierre du Lys, once lived. In the adjoining rue Saint-Flou is the **Tour Blanche**, or white tower, one of the old defence towers of the city which has been restored. Its Gallo-Roman foundations of alternate brick and stone have been preserved. In the rue de Bourgogne is the **Préfecture**, housed in an attractive 17th-century convent building.

In the pedestrianized section of this street, and in the old streets around the place du Châtelet there are a number of old half-timbered houses. The **Hôtel Cabu** just off the rue Sainte-Catherine the historical museum, containing the Gallo-Roman treasures from Neuvy-en-Sullias as well as many souvenirs of Joan of Arc. The 17th-century standard which is used in the Festival is kept here.

On the other side of the rue Royale are more streets with old houses, including the **Maison Jeanne d'Arc** in place Général de Gaulle, where there is an audio-visual show depicting her entry into Orléans, and the **Centre Charles Péguy** in rue du Tabour. Charles Péguy was a poet and writer who was born in Orléans. The centre is devoted to his life and work and includes a museum of manuscripts and souvenirs.

At the top of rue Royale is the place du Martrois. In the centre of the square is a fine equestrian statue of Joan of Arc. On either side of the entrance to the rue Royale are two classical buildings of note. One is the **Chancellerie**, built in the 18th century by the Duke of Orléans to house his archives, and the other is the Chamber of Commerce building, built in similar style in the 19th century. In the underground car park below the square are the preserved remains of the medieval **Porte-Bannier** (city gate).

A Walk Through the City

Orléans is, fortunately, a fairly compact city, although its medieval buildings are not neatly grouped together in one place. The walk may be started at any convenient point on the route, although the walk described starts and finishes at the **cathedral**. The walk will give visitors a good insight into the city's history, and can be followed later on by visits to the museums and other places of interest. This enables planned visits to be made, thus avoiding those lunchtime closures which can be so frustrating. Allow about 1½ hours for this walk.

Begin by exploring the immediate vicinity of the cathedral. Walk round to the north side to see the remains of the old Gallo-Roman walls, and continue to the eastern end and the gardens of the old **Bishop's Palace**, where you will have a fine view of the apse of the cathedral and the ornate central spire. Notice the lace-like stone carving on all the buttresses, which support the walls, and the high, narrow windows of the sanctuary. Cross rue Dupanloup to **Campo-Santo**, whose elegant Renaissance arcades offer a pleasantly cool spot on a hot day. From here it is only a short step to the **Hôtel Groslot**, where, behind the ornamental iron railings, can be seen the grand staircase and the statue of Joan of Arc at prayer. From here, return to the place Sainte-Croix and walk across in front of the cathedral to the south side of the square, where there are two Renaissance houses in the far corner. Walk round the square as far as rue Pothier, opposite the south door of the cathedral. Go down this street, and at the bottom left-hand corner is the old stone building of the **Salle des Thèses**.

T his bronze equestrian statue of Joan of Arc by Foyatier (1855) standing in the place du Martrois symbolizes all that Joan means to France.

Almost opposite is the **Préfecture**, in an elegant 17th-century building. If you wish to see the **Tour Blanche**, part of the original city fortifications, walk down the rue de l'Université beside the Préfecture, which leads into rue Saint-Gilles and rue de la Tour, where the tower can be seen. Return to the Préfecture and turn left into the narrow pedestrianized part of rue de Bourgogne. Along this street are many small cafés and restaurants, with plenty of choice for a meal. Many of the shops are in 18th- and 19th-century houses, but there are a few older ones to be seen, including an old wooden

house almost at the end of the street, on the left. There is a lot of atmosphere here; it may be because this was once the main thoroughfare of the city, and the road along which Joan of Arc entered Orléans in 1429.

Turn into the rue Ducerceau at the end of the rue de Bourgogne, where there is a 16th-century house with a beautiful carved doorway. Continue down to place du Châtelet, where there are several 16th- and 17th-century houses, and on to the very narrow rue de la Pierre-Percée. In this street is a lovely Renaissance house, the **Maison de la Coquille**. A few yards from the end of the street is the **Pont George V**, (formerly the Pont Royal) an elegant "flat" bridge, one of the earliest to be built in France in the 18th century. It is well worth crossing to the far side to get a good view of the city.

A little to the left of the end of the bridge, along the **Quai du Fort des Tourelles**, is the site of the fort which was taken from the English by Joan of Arc. Here is yet another statue of Joan, and, on the wall beside the river, a commemorative plaque. Return over the bridge and walk up the rue Royale as far as rue du Tabour. Turn left, and the **Centre Charles Péguy** can be found in the former mansion **Hôtel Euverte Hatte**. Gothic friezes decorate the windows, and there is a rather fine Renaissance arcade in the courtyard. The **Maison Jeanne d'Arc**, further up the street in place Général de Gaulle, is a reconstructed half-timbered house, built in the exact style of the house where Joan stayed when she came to Orléans. Next door is another Renaissance house with some beautiful colonnaded windows.

From Maison Jeanne d'Arc, cross the square and walk up rue de la Hallebarde to place du Martroi. Here is the best statue of Joan of Arc, cast in bronze in 1855. It shows her mounted on her horse with her sword drawn for battle. The pedestal on which it stands is decorated with bronze reliefs showing important scenes from her life. Walk between the two classical buildings of the Chancellerie and Chamber of Commerce down rue Royale as far as rue Jeanne d'Arc. Turn left and look down this wide 19th-century street to the cathedral. Walk along as far as the rue Sainte Catherine and turn right. A short way down the street is a small square where the **Hôtel Cabu** is situated. This elegant 16th-century mansion, much restored, houses the historical museum. There are other medieval façades to be seen nearby. Return to the rue Jeanne d'Arc and walk back to the cathedral.

Parks and Gardens

The garden behind the Hôtel Groslot is very attractive, and many of the squares are filled with flowers. Particularly attractive in the summer time are the place du Martroi and place Général de Gaulle, which are a riot of colour. Perhaps the loveliest garden of all to visit is the **Roserie Municipale**. This adjoins the **Jardin Botanique** and is situated to the south of the river Loire. To reach these gardens, cross the **Pont George V** and turn right, following the **Quai de Prague** and **Route de Saint Mesmin**. The gardens are on the right-hand side of the road, about 500m (550yds) after crossing the bridge. In the rose garden are about

La Source—Parc Floral

In 1959, in response to government demands for decentralization, the Département of Loiret bought the whole of the then neglected estate of La Source, complete with its château. The greater part of the land was to be used for the building of the new University and Science Research Centre, and a new town would be built on the remainder of the estate. About 35 hectares (86 acres) of parkland surrounding the source of the river Loiret was designated for the Parc Floral. The first section of the park, some 10 hectares (25 acres) was first opened to the public in 1964. The remainder was opened and the park achieved international fame when the International Floralies was held in Orléans in 1967. Some 5,000 bushes and conifers, 250,000 bulbs, 100,000 roses and 50,000 dahlias were planted in the château park for that occasion. Many different gardens have now been created, each with its own theme, and visitors can see many new varieties here. For example, there are now over 600 different varieties of iris, and 400 rose species. More and more are added every year when the Orléans international rose competition is held.

There are rock gardens and spring flowers in a wooded part of the park, and from Le Miroir, a semi-circular pool leading off the river, there is a superb view of the château and the "Louis XIII embroidery", a beautiful carpet garden planted on the lawn. All kinds of birds can be seen beside the river, including flamingoes and cranes.

Every visitor can enjoy the Parc Floral—gardeners, photographers, or simply lovers of beauty. Children have two play areas, and there is a small zoo. A miniature train runs through the park, and there is also a restaurant and a picnic place.

Some of the colourful displays and attractive layouts in the gardens of the floral park of La Source.

10,000 roses—trees, bushes and climbers—more than 500 varieties. If you enjoy gardens, then you must not miss this rose garden. The botanical garden contains flower borders and avenues of trees, greenhouses and an orangery. Both gardens were created in the second half of the 19th century, and are owned and managed by the city. Nearer the city centre is **Parc Louis Pasteur**, created in 1927. To reach this park, walk up the rue Fernand-Rabier, between **Campo-Santo** and the **Musée des Beaux Arts** and continue until you reach the wide

boulevard and the victory monument. Cross the boulevard and continue along rue Eugène Vignat to the entrance to the park. There is a fine collection of trees and shrubs, as well as borders and formal gardens and a small lake with sculptures. Probably the most famous of the gardens are those of the **Parc Floral** at **La Source**.

Shopping in Orléans

Orléans is probably the best shopping centre in the *Centre* region. There are good shops in the rue Jeanne d'Arc, rue de la République, rue Adolphe

The château La Source with the beautiful carpet garden known as the "Louis XIII embroidery".

Thiers and rue Charles Sanglier, but the grandest—and most expensive—shops are in the rue Royale. All the shops in this lovely street have arcaded frontages, extending from the **Pont George V** to the place du Martroi. If you like window shopping, this is the place to be. The **Chocolaterie Royale** offers a selection of mouth-watering sweets and chocolates to tempt your palate, but you will need to keep a tight grip on your purse strings! For china and glass, clocks and watches, try **Pepin**, and for tableware and silver try **Villeroy et Bosch**. High-quality ladies wear will be found at **Ann Rose**, and menswear at **New Man**. There is a lovely fabrics shop, **Soieries Lyonnaises**, in the rue Jeanne d'Arc. The fabrics on sale include silks, as the name suggests, but there are other high-quality fabrics as well, and the prices are not unreasonable.

The larger department stores, such as **Le Printemps** and **Nouvelles Galeries**, are in the rue Royale and rue Adolphe Thiers. **Monoprix** is in place de la République.

There is a large modern covered market building, **Les Nouvelles Halles** in place du Châtelet, near the bottom of the Rue Royale. Here there is fresh produce for sale, including local cheeses, pâtés and terrines. The market is open every day except Mondays, and on Sundays as well.

In the new **Centre Commercial** in place d'Arc, near the railway station, are many small shops and boutiques and a large **Carrefour** supermarket which is very good. There are a few small shops in the rue de Bourgogne, but this is an area of small cafés and bars where it is easy to get a quick snack at a reasonable price. There are plenty of good **charcuteries**, bakers and pastrycooks. For mouth-watering cakes try **Morin**, about halfway along the pedestrianized section in rue de Bourgogne.

There are plenty of large supermarkets in the surroundings of Orléans, including **Auchan** (at **St-Jean-de-la-Ruelle** and **Olivet**) and **Le Clerc** at **Olivet La Source**. There is also an **Intermarché** and **Carrefour** at **Saran**, to the west of Orléans, near the motorway interchange.

Orléans Specialities

Local gastronomic specialities include cheeses made from cows milk. *Olivet Bleu* is a small disc-shaped cheese with a slight blue mould, often wrapped in plane leaves, whilst *Olivet Cendré* is a rather stronger cheese of the same size, and is coated with wood ash. *Frinault* is a soft cheese of similar size and may also be sold as *Frinault Cendré*. Other local cheeses include *fromage de Saint-Benoît* and *fromage de Patay*. Strawberries, cherries, and asparagus, *cèpes* (wild mushrooms) and *girolles* (edible fungi) are specialities of this region. *Terrine de Gibier* (game pâté) is another speciality to look out for, as are *andouille* (smoked sausage) and *andouillettes* (small tripe sausages) from Jargeau.

Although Orléans is a wine-producing area, the wines are not very well known. However, you will find them in the local shops and they are often served in local restaurants. *Gris-Meunier de l'Orléanais*, a light red wine with a fruity flavour is very pleasant. The local white wine is *Auvernat Blanc*, which is a very fruity but dry wine.

The main wine-growing area is to the west of Orléans, between **Saint-Hilaire-Saint-Mesmin** and **Clery-Saint-André**. A simple map showing a **Route des Vins de l'Orléanais** may be obtained from the tourist office.

Around Orléans

South of Orléans lies the huge new town of **Orléans La Source**. Although it is some 10 km (6 miles) from Orléans it is still managed by the city administration, unlike **Olivet, Saint-Jean-le-Blanc** and other suburbs which have their own town halls. This leaves a narrow corridor between the two suburbs, and a large area to the south which is actually part of Orléans, and has therefore been included in the city section above.

Olivet is a charming little town spanning the river Loiret, and it is a place where many visitors choose to stay, because it is quieter than Orléans. The area is particularly well known for its nurseries and market gardens, and there are many flower beds alongside the river banks. Willow, lime and plane trees are in abundance. Olivet is also known for its cherry orchards.

There is a very pleasant riverside walk along the banks of the Loiret, some 4km (2 ½ miles) in length which passes several old water mills. The path begins at the junction of rue Albert Barbier and rue de la Reine Blanche, on the north bank of the river not far from the bridge. Rowing boats may also be hired near this point. Other independent suburbs of Orléans, namely **Saran, Fleury-les-Aubrais** and **Saint-Jean-de-la-Ruelle**, all have attractive floral decorations in the streets during the spring and summer.

Further Afield from Orléans

Up-river from Orléans lie the villages of **Chécy** and **Jargeau**. It was at Chécy that Joan of Arc and her small army crossed the Loire by boat on their way to Orléans in April 1428. Jargeau is approached by crossing the river from **St Denis de l'Hôtel**, which has won an international prize for its floral decorations. There is a beautiful floral park, at its best in June/July, and a pleasant, waymarked riverside walk. Jargeau was the scene of Joan's first victory after the relief of Orléans, in June 1429.

The church, whose large square tower can be seen from across the river, is nothing special to look at from the outside, but inside the panelled chancel is very beautiful, as well as being almost as large as the nave itself. The pulpit is 18th century and is made from wrought iron. In the town centre is a bronze statue of Joan of Arc, which depicts her rallying her troops after she had been stunned by a stone thrown from the château walls.

Châteauneuf-sur-Loire

Châteauneuf-sur-Loire is the next main town up-river from Orléans. The town hugs the river bank, and there are pleasant promenades fronting the riverside. Since the 11th century there has been a château on this site, and it was the most recent of these, the "new château", built in the 17th century, which gave the town its name. It was known as the "little Versailles", but unfortunately it was destroyed during the Revolution, and only the orangery, stables and *pavillon* remain. The old

Châteauneuf park contains shady walks among rhododendrons and an arboretum.

Reflections in the ornamental moat of the formal gardens in the park of Châteauneuf-sur-Loire, designed by Lenôtre.

stables are occupied by the public library and archive offices, and in the basement of the *pavillon*, now used as the Town Hall, is the fascinating **Musée de la Marine de Loire**. This tells the history of navigation on the Loire, illustrated with models, original shipwrights' tools, documents referring to cargoes, etc. The château park was originally designed by Lenôtre; formal gardens lead to stone terraces and steps lead down to the beautiful rhododendron walks and arboretum of rare species of trees, including giant magnolias and tulip-trees, which are at their best in early June. The local swimming pool and tennis courts are in the château park, and there are a number of waymarked walks in the surroundings. In the square behind the church is the old market hall, **Halle Saint-Pierre**, its interesting wooden roof supported on large wooden columns. Further along the Grande

---

A Carolingian Treasure at Germiny-des-Prés

The most interesting part of the church is the beautiful Byzantine-style apse at the eastern end, built during the reign of Charlemagne in AD 806 as the private oratory of Theodulph counsellor to Charlemagne and Bishop of Orléans. It was about 10m (33ft) square and 16m (52ft) high. Originally there were four large circular apses, and two smaller ones at the eastern end. The large western apse was demolished when the first nave was built in the 15th century, but its outline can be seen on the floor of the nave. The smaller ones to the east were unfortunately removed during 19th-century restorations. In the centre, supported on pillars, is a huge lantern tower, diffusing light through the whole of the oratory from windows made of alabaster. The mosaic was discovered after some plaster fell from the ceiling in 1840, and some children were found playing with small cubes of coloured glass. It was in a remarkably good state of repair, and was restored between 1841 and 1846.

The descriptive leaflet on sale in the church states that the mosaic is as old as the oratory, but many believe it is much older, and may have come from Ravenna. It depicts the Ark of the Covenant, surrounded by archangels and cherubim, with the hand of God reaching out towards it. Below the mosaic is a Latin inscription from Theodulph's writings in which he asks that the Ark should be revered, and that he should be mentioned in prayers. Below the mosaic is a gallery of 11 rounded arches, decorated with stucco and supported on carved stone pillars. Curiously, there is no decoration on the wall behind them, although one suspects that there might once have been. There are several wooden statues, the best of which is in the north apse. It is 16th century, and shows Saint Anne teaching the Virgin Mary to read. Another church treasure is a 12th-century Reliquary, made from Limoges enamel. It is kept in the sacristy and can be seen on request. In the churchyard are the remnants of an old *Lanterne des Morts* (lantern of the dead). These lanterns, built on a stone pillar in a churchyard or a prominent place near the village, used to be lit the night before a burial was to take place. There are not many of them left in the Loire Valley.

This marvellous mosaic is on the ceiling of the Byzantine-style apse of the church at Germigny-des-Prés, and is thought to be well over one thousand years old.

Rue, opposite the Post Office, is the **Nouvelle Halle**, a rare and elegant example of early 20th-century cast-iron-work.

About 5km (3 miles) up river lies the village of **Germigny-des-Prés**. This is a place which must not be missed, for it is here, in one of the oldest surviving churches in France, that a priceless mosaic can be found.

The next village upstream is **Saint-Benoît-sur-Loire**. Here can be found the beautiful Romanesque **Basilica of Saint Benedict** (Saint-Benoît). Benedictine monks settled here in the mid-7th century, and a few years after this the relics of the Saint were brought to the site from Italy. The church itself, begun in 1067, was not finally completed until the 12th century. In June 1429, after her victory at Patay, Joan of Arc and the Dauphin came to Saint-Benoît to pray before going to Sully. Most visitors will only see the beautiful **belfry porch**, decorated with carved capitals relating scenes from the bible, animals, plants and leaves. However, this is well worth seeing, and the church should not be missed just because you may not be able to see inside. Although there are guided tours arranged on summer Sundays, services take priority. Visitors are welcome to attend services, although they may not walk around the church whilst they are

The beautiful belfry porch of the 12th-century abbey church of Saint-Benôit-sur-Loire is considered to be one of the finest examples of Romanesque art.

taking place. Mass is sung in the Gregorian Chant at noon on weekdays and at 11 a.m. on Sundays and on Holy Days. The Abbey itself has no ancient buildings. It suffered badly during the Wars of Religion, when the treasures were melted down, and its precious manuscripts were sold. It was closed at the start of the Revolution, its archives transferred to the city of Orléans, and all the property was dispersed. The monastic buildings were destroyed, and the church fell into disrepair. Although the church was later restored, the monks did not return until 1944. The poet Max Jacob spent many years of his life in the village.

Max Jacob—Modern Painter and Poet

Born in 1876 in Brittany, the son of a Jewish tailor, Max Jacob played an important part in the new direction of modern poetry in the first part of this century. His work embraced a complex mixture of Jewish, Breton, Parisian and Catholic elements. He went to Paris in 1894, where he struggled against extreme poverty to achieve recognition as a poet and painter, meeting with, and sharing the life of, such friends as Picasso, Braque and Cocteau. In 1915 he was converted to Christianity and was baptized into the Catholic church, with Picasso as his godfather. In 1921 he went to Saint-Benôit-sur-Loire where he spent the years until World War II in semi-seclusion. Apart from a few breaks back to his old Bohemian life, he occupied his time painting, but was remembered in the neighbouring village for his friendly relations with the local people. When the Nazis came, he was treated in the same way as other Jews, and in early 1944 the Gestapo took him away to a prison camp at Drancy. He managed to get a message out, and a petition organized by his friends to the German Embassy pleaded for his release. This was granted, but by the time his friends arrived to take him away he had died of pneumonia in the prison hospital. At the end he asked his fellow Jewish prisoners to send for a Catholic priest. In the abbey, a plaque in his memory notes that he is buried in the village cemetery.

A further 7km (4 ½ miles) upstream is the bridge across the river from **Saint-Père-sur-Loire** to **Sully**. Here is a most imposing moated château, with a very pleasant park. A real feudal fortress, most of it was built in the mid-14th century, although there is some evidence of a previous building.

The rectangular keep is flanked by four crenellated "pepper-pot" towers at the corners, and is the oldest part of the building. It has a very fine *chemin de ronde*, or covered sentry-path, round the top, but the best part of the building is its medieval timbered boat-shaped roof. This must be one of the very finest in existence, for there are no wood beetles and no rot. It is in perfect condition, most probably because the wood was prepared over an exceptionally long period, some say more than 80 years.

The ground-floor guardroom inside the keep, and the *cour d'honneur* are the setting for many of the concerts held during the **Sully Festival** in June and July each year. Voltaire had two of his plays performed in the reception hall on the first floor, and in the **Oratory** is a copy of Sully's tomb, the original being in Nogent-le-Rotrou (*see* page 116).

Guided tours of the castle take about 50 minutes and an English translation is available. It is worth visiting if only to see the fine timbered roof and the view over the river from the sentry-path. It was at Sully that Joan of Arc persuaded the Dauphin to go to Reims to be crowned. When she

*T*he moated feudal fortress of Sully whose timber roof dating from the 14th century is in an exceptionally fine state of preservation.

returned to the castle in 1430, she discovered that the owner, the lord of La Trémoille, had influenced the king against her, and she was kept virtually imprisoned, although she later managed to escape.

The entrance to the château is on the northern side, through the esplanade and formal gardens. These were created by the famous Sully who was Chief Minister to Henri IV. He also reinforced the flood defences along the river bank. From the formal gardens a bridge leads across the moat on the eastern side to the wooded park, much of which was planted in the 19th century.

On the town side of the moat is an avenue of lime trees leading to the place Henri IV and the **Promenade des Douves**, from where there are good views of the château. There are two churches in Sully, one of which, **Saint-Ythier's**, originally stood in the château grounds. Sully had it dismantled and re-erected in the town. Inside are two good 16th-century stained glass windows, depicting the Tree of Jesse and the story of the pilgrimage to Compostella, plus a fine 18th-century organ.

The other church, almost destroyed during World War II, is dedicated to Saint-Germain. It was once the parish church of the Loire mariners, and has the highest timber spire in France. Some of the old seamen's houses can be seen nearby, and the old slipways can still be seen. In the rue du Grand Sully is an attractive Renaissance house, known as **Maison Henri IV**, although contrary to popular legend he never entered the house! The tourist office in Sully has produced a folder in English about the town, its origins and its château. A leaflet describing four local tours based on the town is available, in simple French.

Gien

The next important place up-river is **Gien**, a pleasant small town alongside the northern bank of the river. The great belfry of the church and the château, looking like one enormous building, dominate the town.

Gien was devastated in June 1940, when some 80 per cent of the town was destroyed during an air raid. The church was totally destroyed, apart from a small part of the base of the tower, and the château too was badly damaged. Reconstruction began in 1945, using traditional local building methods, designs and materials, so that much of the town retains its original appearance. This is particularly noticeable from the opposite bank of the river; the houses along the **Quai Lenoir** and **Quai Joffre** are very much in keeping with the buildings above.

The large church was rebuilt and dedicated to Saint Joan of Arc in 1954. The 15th-century base of the tower was incorporated in the new building, which blends well with the château beside it. A plaque made from Gien faïence tiles on the church wall bears witness to the fact that Joan of Arc came to Gien no less than four times during her campaigns. It is well proportioned inside, with elegant brick columns and some good, modern stained glass.

Next door, in the sensitively restored château, is the **Musée International de la Chasse**, or hunting museum. The history of hunting from the Stone Age

Florentin Brigaud. There is also a fascinating collection of jacket buttons from various hunts, including English ones, and a trophy room containing more than 500 antlers. One of the rooms is devoted to hunting horns, one of which is shown before the tube is curled up. It must be at least 4m (13ft) long, and is displayed diagonally on the ceiling! The building has well-proportioned rooms and high beamed ceilings, especially in the Great Hall, where the Desportes collection is housed.

The reconstructed town centre is pedestrianized, and it is a pleasant place for shopping. China is a speciality of the town, and although there are good shops it is best to visit the factory itself, which is near the Mammouth supermarket on the western side of the town. There is a small museum displaying some historic pieces, and there is also a shop where some of the beautiful china may be purchased. Gien china is particularly well known for its lovely animal and bird designs, and for the fine colours used.

About 7km (4½ miles) south of Gien at **Le Grand Bardelet**, it is possible to visit a working *chèvrerie* (goat farm) where cheese and cider are made. Some 12km (7 ½ miles) north of Gien, and worth the diversion if you are interested in fishing, is **La Bussière**. Standing on an island in the middle of a lake, this 16th-century château contains a museum dedicated to fishing. In addition to paintings, there are engravings and china, stuffed fish—including a large and very ugly coelacanth—and silverware, all of which are linked in some way to the sport of

T his plaque on the church wall made from local faïence tiles recalls the four visits to Gien made by Joan of Arc during her campaigns.

to the present day is shown, with weapons of all kinds including some beautifully decorated shotguns and crossbows. There are tapestries and paintings depicting hunting scenes, including a fine modern Aubusson tapestry and a large collection of paintings by Desportes (1661–1743). There are also some superb bronzes and other works by the 20th-century French sculptor and engraver,

*T*he Canal Latéral de la Loire crosses the river Loire by
this aqueduct at Briare, a monument to the genius of Gustave Eiffel,
designer of the famous tower in Paris.

fishing. There is also a large freshwater aquarium and fishing hooks, nets, etc. La Bussière is the first of the châteaux of the **Route Jacques-Coeur**.

Jacques Coeur was a wealthy merchant who put his immense fortune at the disposal of Charles VII, became his chief Minister of Finance and reorganized the tax system. It was due to his efforts that the prosperity of France was restored. He established a north–south trade route, and an interesting route has been devised which takes in the châteaux and other places of interest. The châteaux on this route show how the great private houses of the region evolved from the 13th to the 18th centuries. All are in private ownership, except for Gien and the Jacques Coeur Palace in Bourges, and many are still lived in by the descendants of those who built them.

Beyond Gien, at **Briare**, is an interesting aqueduct, built by Gustave Eiffel, who built the famous tower in Paris. This carries the Canal Latéral de la Loire across the river itself from the picturesque harbour in the town. There is a footpath along both sides of the canal across the aqueduct.

The **Musée de l'Automobile** in Briare contains an exceptional collection of more than 150 cars, dating from 1895, plus motor cycles and bicycles. There is also a collection of some 200 model vehicles. The setting is unusual; it is housed in an old lime works on the hillside above the Loire valley.

Another interesting museum is situated some 16km (10 miles) to the north-east of Briare, right on the borders of Loiret and Yonne Départements at Champoulet. Housed in the great barn of the **Château de Champoulet**, adjoining the château itself, is the **Musée de l'Outil**. Some old carpenters' tools were found by a young man in a granary on the estate in the 1960s, and this led to his researching the subject of hand tools and developing a great interest in the subject. The original tools, which have been beautifully restored and preserved, form the basis of this important and most interesting collection which is extremely well displayed. The young man who found the tools is often there, and will probably explain some of the more unusual tools to you, in English. Note that this museum is open from May to September inclusive, from 2 p.m. to 6 p.m. every day except Wednesdays in July and August and weekends only at other times.

Upstream again from Briare, on the opposite bank, is **Chatillon-sur-Loire**. Climb the **Haute Rue** of this little town to see the remains of the old château and the church, and some very old half-timbered houses. There is an interesting suspension bridge over the Loire, and between the canal and the river are the locks and canal basin, signed *Eclus de Mantelot*. Trips along the canal by boat are sometimes available from here, and the size of the old locks and the canal basin gives an idea of how busy this part of the river used to be.

Down-river from Orléans

Some 16km downstream from Orléans is **Cléry-Saint-André**, a place of pilgrimage since the 13th century, when some local peasants found an oak statue of the Virgin in a nearby bush. A church was built to house the statue, and, perhaps because many pilgrims passed this way *en route* to Compostella, the shrine became a centre of pilgrimage in its own right. The church was destroyed in the Hundred Years War, but Charles VII and Jean Dunois, the friend of Joan of Arc, soon began work on a new church. The rebuilding continued under the guidance of Louis XI, who frequently stayed at Cléry.

The building is one of the best examples of flamboyant Gothic architecture in the Loire valley, and can be seen from some distance. Both Dunois and Louis XI and his wife, Charlotte of Savoy, are buried here. The **monument to the King**, showing him kneeling on top of a marble canopy, was made by the sculptor Michel Bourdin in 1622, after the original bronze monument was melted down by the Huguenots during the Wars of Religion. They also destroyed the statue of the Virgin, but a copy was later made from memory. Louis' tomb faces the place where the statue used to be; it is now placed on the High Altar. The **choir stalls** were given to the church by Henri II, and his monogram, and that of his mistress Diane de Poitiers, are carved on some of the misericords. On the south side of the church is the **Renaissance chapel of Saint-Jacques**, with its elaborate vaulting decorated with pilgrims' staffs and girdles. There is also a 16th-century statue of the saint.

Only 5km (3 miles) to the west is **Meung-sur-Loire**, once the seat of the Bishops of Orléans. It was also the headquarters of the Earl of Salisbury during the second part of the Hundred Year's War. The original part of the château, built during the 12th and 13th centuries, contains the dungeons and *oubliettes* where the prisoners were

---

François Villon—Master of the Medieval Ballade

Although much of his life was spent in the medieval underworld of thieves and criminals, Villon was in fact a Master of Arts of the University of Paris and his mastery of the medieval ballade form was brilliant. Born François de Montcorbier in Paris around 1431, he adopted the name Villon from his foster parent. A rowdy university life was followed by a period of wandering during which he became involved in a number of suspected or actual crimes.

In 1457 he came to Blois and won the poetry prize organized by Charles d'Orléans. Two years later, Villon was implicated in another crime and imprisoned in the notorious château at Meung-sur-Loire, from where he gained his freedom on an amnesty granted by Louis XI. He was later imprisoned again before being exiled from Paris. His last years are obscure and he died around 1463.

The ballade form with its repeated refrain is typified in Villon's "*Ballade des dames du temps jadis*", composed around 1462; its refrain "*Mais où sont les neiges d'antan?*" ("But where are the snows of yesteryear?") is perhaps one of the best known lines in literature. Possibly his most outstanding example of the form is "*l'Epitaphe*", showing his capacity for sincere religious feeling. Commencing with the line "*Frères humains, qui après nous vivez*", each stanza ends with the refrain "*Mais priez Dieu que tous nous vueille absouldre!*" ("But pray God that he may absolve all of us.").

held. Because the Bishops were men of God they were not allowed to pass the death sentence; instead, their victims were lowered halfway down a cone-shaped well and left with very little food until they either died from starvation or illness. Because of the coned shape it was impossible to climb out. The poet François Villon was one such prisoner, but he was the luckiest of all, for Louis XI stopped at Meung after his coronation and gave him a free pardon.

The 18th-century wing, still lived in by the owner, contains some very fine English Chippendale furniture. The church next door is quite plain, and has a fine Romanesque doorway. In the square near the church is the **Restaurant François Villon**, which serves good food at reasonable prices, and has a pleasant atmosphere.

Beaugency

Beaugency is a lovely little town, 7km (4 ½ miles) downstream from Meung-sur-Loire, and built on the hillside above the river. It is reached by crossing the medieval bridge, parts of which date back to the 11th century. To the left of the bridge is the a tower which was once part of the original fortifications of the town. When you walk into the town it is like stepping back in time, for there are narrow cobbled streets, Romanesque and Renaissance buildings, and an enormous 11th-century square keep in the very centre.

Dunois' château, built in the 15th century, houses the **Musée Régional de l'Orléanais**, and is concerned with the everyday life of the region in times past. Each room is devoted to a particular theme, and there are mementoes of famous Beaugency citizens. The peasant's parlour shows that the inhabitants of the region lived a pretty comfortable life in the 18th century!

Other museums include an aquarium, with both local and more exotic species, and a museum of harnesses, carriage lamps and street lighting. It is well worth while spending some time in Beaugency, exploring the narrow sloping streets and little squares.

A Walk in Beaugency

Begin at the end of the bridge by the **Tour du Diable**, part of the original town defences. Walk round the back of the tower into the rue de l'Abbaye, and walk as far as the front of the 12th-century **Abbey church of Notre-Dame**. The exterior is typically Romanesque, but the interior was restored after a severe fire in the 16th century. It was re-roofed with wooden vaulting, lower than the original roof, and painted to look like stone. A great pity, as it really spoils the otherwise majestic simplicity of this lovely church. It was also badly damaged in World War II, when all the medieval windows were blown out. These have been replaced with modern stained glass, made in Orléans. It was in this church that the marriage of Louis VII and Eleanor of Aquitaine was annulled. She later married Henry II of England, and was the mother of Richard Coeur de Lion and King John.

Close to the church in place Dunois is the enormous square keep known as **César's Tower**, which is a remnant of the 11th-century fortifications built to defend the Loire crossing. Victor Hugo used it as the background for one of his plays.

Across the square, to the right of the keep is **Château Dunois**, which Jean Dunois, Joan of Arc's companion, built for himself in the 15th century. It now houses the ethnological museum for the region, and has an attractive courtyard with a graceful arcade along one wall. The **Beaugency Festival** is held each year in the square in front of the château.

Further along the Rue de l'Abbaye is place Saint-Firmin. Here is the **Tour-Saint-Firmin**, a 16th-century clock tower which is all that remains of the original parish church, destroyed in the Revolution. Close to the Tour-Saint-Firmin is one of the oldest buildings in the town, the old **Hôtel-Dieu**, which was built in the 11th century. Its Romanesque-style roof was completed in the 12th century.

North of the square is the rue de la Cordonnerie and, on the corner of the Rue du Traineau is the **Templars' House**, with some very interesting 12th-century windows. Unfortunately the façade has been ruined by the addition of a modern shop front! At the top of this street, in the rue du Change, is the **Hôtel de Ville**. In the Council Chamber of this lovely Renaissance building are eight 17th-century embroidered tapestries which originally belonged to the Abbey of

*M*edieval houses in the rue de l'Evêché in Beaugency are still used as private dwellings.

Notre-Dame. They illustrate pagan sacrifices and the four continents which were then known.

There is a very narrow alley to the left of the town hall. Go down here (there are steps to negotiate) to the rue du Pont, and then turn left. This leads you to the rue du Rû, a lovely little street with a stream running down it, with masses of flowers in boxes fixed to the rails alongside the stream. About halfway up, turn into the rue Porte-Dieu, on the left, cross the rue du Pont into rue du Martroi. On reaching the rue du Change, look left, and you will see the **Tour de l'Horloge**, or **Porte Vendômoise**, one of the gates through the 12th-century town walls. Continue to the place du Martroi, scene of the local market on Saturdays, where you will find the half-timbered building which now houses the local **Maison du Tourisme**. Walk down the square to rue de la Bretonnerie and continue down to rue Porte Tavers. Turn right, and walk through the old Tavers gate to the **Grand Mail** on the right, a pleasant tree-shaded promenade leading to the main road out of the town.

On the left of Porte-Tavers is the **Petit Mail**, offering a splendid view of the river and some pretty gardens. Walk down to the river for a good view of the bridge. The rue du Ravelin, parallel with the Quai Neuf, and the rue de l'Evêché leading off the place de la Motte at the end of the street have some very interesting medieval houses, still used as private dwellings.

There are hotels available in Beaugency, as well as a campsite and a youth hostel not far away. However, not far downstream from Beaugency is **Tavers**, where Eleanor of Aquitaine stayed during the hearing of annulment proceedings. Here is a very pleasant hotel, **Hôtel de la Tonnellerie**. Rather expensive, and listed in the Romantik hotels book and in Michelin, it is a delightful place to stay as it is so quiet. It has a very good restaurant.

Beyond Tavers can be seen the huge installations of the nuclear power station at **Saint-Laurent-des-Eaux**. Visits can be arranged by appointment for those who are interested in such things, but there is a viewing terrace and information centre which is open daily.

The Sologne

South of the river Loire between Gien and Blois lies the **Sologne**, the Royal hunting forest of France. The greater part of the Sologne lies in Loir-et-Cher Département, the most northerly part is in **Loiret**, and the rest is in **Cher**. Some 40 per cent is deeply wooded countryside and the rest is poor heathland. Small lakes and forest pools, known as *étangs* attract a lot of bird life. The marshy land and poor soil have always had an effect on this area, attracting many deer and game birds. Here is the great **Château of Chambord**, and those of **Cheverny** and **Villesavin**, as well as several smaller châteaux which are interesting.

The principal town of the area is Romorantin-Lanthenay, smaller towns including Lamotte-Beuvron, La Ferté Saint-Aubin, Argent-sur-Sauldre and Aubigny-sur-Nère. The Sologne is noted for beautiful villages, and of particular interest are Bracieux, Souvigny-en-Sologne and Selles-Saint-Denis.

The Loire Châteaux— From Fortress to Palace

The French word *château* means different things to different people at different times. One definition is "*demeure féodale fortifiée*" or fortified feudal dwelling, which could be applied to some of the older buildings. The later châteaux, however, are not and clearly never were fortified. The word derives from the same Latin source, *castellum*, as the English word "castle". In English this usually means a fortified building of medieval or older origin, including defensive earthworks. In the Loire valley the term is applied to a wide range of edifices from grim defensive keeps, through feudal castles and what in England would be termed stately homes or mansions, to the immense buildings such as Chambord, which surely merit the description of "palace".

The Earliest Traces
From the 5th century, the country under Merovingian and Carolingian rule was protected by scattered strongholds, many of which were developed from earlier Roman settlements which had been strengthened for defence. During the 9th century the depredations of Vikings led to the construction of more fortifications, added to which the conflicts between the neighbouring Counts of Anjou, Blois, Touraine and Maine gave rise to a proliferation of castles. These usually comprised a mound of earth surrounded by a wooden palisade and with a central watch-tower.

The First Keeps or *Donjons*
During the 11th century man-made mounds surmounted by square wooden towers or keeps were surrounded by earth banks, topped by a wooden fence and further protected by a ditch. Within the bank, people from the neighbourhood could take shelter with their animals. The *donjon* provided the last place of refuge should the outer defences be breached. In a number of places the keep protected living quarters built at the end of a promontory. Examples of this may be found at Blois, Langeais and Loches.

The Château Fort
The main keep began to be built of stone, and by the 12th and 13th centuries these became massive structures. The castles at Beaugency, Langeais, Loches, Montbazon and the Coudray tower at Chinon demonstrate this form. During this period, the keep, the strong point of the complex, overlooked a courtyard, known in England as the bailey, which in turn was enclosed by a curtain wall built of stone. The use of

A masterpiece of the French Renaissance, this 16th-century staircase is to be seen at Blois.

The fortified residence of Langeais has been carefully furnished and restored to its 15th-century condition.

wood for defence works was by now overtaken completely by these massive masonry structures, whose sheer size gives rise to amazement at the effort involved in the building of these strongholds or fortified castles.

The Influence of the Crusaders

Initially, these fortresses followed a compact plan in which the keep provided storage on the lower floor and a great hall was situated above, while living quarters occupied the top floor. In this way, with higher curtain walls, the stronghold was easier to defend. Through the 13th century, the experience of the Crusaders and better methods of attack led to new ideas being incorporated. Turrets and towers were added to the curtain wall, the base of which was splayed to counter attempts to scale the wall. The towers and keep followed a circular plan and a wider,

deeper moat surrounded the curtain wall. Additional outer ramparts and many practical details were included, such as battlements, machicolations through which defenders could drop missiles on attackers below, drawbridges and the portcullis to protect the entrance. At the same time more thought was devoted to the comfort of those living in the keep, with tapestries and furniture such as chests and beds making conditions somewhat more pleasant than in the past. However, the interior of the keep would be dark as the only light had to come through narrow window openings or weapon slits. Although advantage was taken of natural features such as cliffs, rocky outcrops and rivers when choosing sites for castles, these improvements in design meant that castles could also be built in more open country. A fine example of a fortress or citadel of this period is to be seen in Angers, where the deep moat surrounds a massive curtain wall reinforced with pairs of round towers splayed out at the bottom to form an almost impregnable stronghold. An impression of how these old fortresses originally appeared can also be gained from the castles of Loches and Montreuil-Bellay.

The *Demeure Féodale Fortifiée* of the 14th Century

During this time the need for strong fortresses diminished and many fortified manor houses were built. They were dwellings which were made stronger for defence but were not intended primarily for use in a war situation. At the same time their builders began taking more interest in home comforts. The larger manor houses are often described as châteaux. The massive keep evolved into a more habitable central building with larger windows, so lightening the interior. Often it would be incorporated into the surrounding walls, and higher towers with conical tiled roofs added. The overall appearance still bore resemblance to the older castles but much of this was done in order to impress rather than actually to be used in time of war. These trends may be seen at Gué-Péan and Montpoupon.

The Coming of the Renaissance

During the 15th century Charles VII and his successor Louis XI lived in various royal châteaux in the Loire region, which became the political centre of France. To be near the king, the leading merchants, financiers and religious leaders acquired or built residences appropriate to their status. Comfortable living became more important than defence. Towards the end of the 15th century the wars in Italy resulted in ideas from the Italian Renaissance being brought back to France. Charles VIII,

Azay-le-Rideau typifies the trend from castle to "mock-castle", where military features became just decoration.

who succeeded Louis XI, conceived the idea of importing a considerable number of fine objects, together with ideas and skilled craftsmen, to embellish his royal château of Amboise. This former fortress which had become a royal residence, was in the process of being renovated and enlarged with the object of making it the greatest palace on the Loire. Charles died in 1498 after an accident, and he was succeeded by Louis XII, followed by François I, both of whom had travelled in Italy and been impressed by the wealth of artistic and architectural achievement to be found there. So began the transformation of the French château from its former state of fortress or fortified manor to the magnificent and sometimes opulent structures which we see today. Most of the old buildings were either dismantled or greatly modified, and new buildings were created everywhere.

The New Look

Kings, nobles and the wealthy aristocracy and court advisors vied with each other in creating larger and more ostentatious estates, many being sited

near the river or in pleasant country surroundings which would enhance the appearance of the buildings. Moats, turrets, keeps and other aspects of the earlier military designs were retained and modified purely as decorative features. Windows became very large to allow light into the elegant rooms within, which were decorated and furnished in sumptuous fashion. The moats were incorporated into formal gardens which all added to the overall effect. Spiral stairs were replaced by elegant straight staircases, and elaborate carved chimneys and patterned brickwork appeared. The trend is well illustrated at Azay-le-Rideau, Blois, Talcy, Valençay and Villandry, while the supreme examples must surely be Chambord and Chenonçeau, the names which everyone associates with the Loire châteaux

The Final Phase

The 17th and 18th centuries saw the Renaissance style replaced by the classical style with emphasis on a symmetrical façade and restrained ornamentation, although the interior might still be richly decorated and furnished. The prime example of the classical château is Cheverny, which today has the additional attraction of magnificent furnishings which remain intact since the time of Louis XIII. Serrant is another good example.

Epilogue

So the châteaux of the Loire which we see today came into being and in the process many owners were bankrupted by the great expense involved. Many of the oldest structures are in ruins but what we see today is a mixture of fragments from all ages, the result of repeated demolition, destruction, replacement and new building. Some châteaux are empty show-pieces, others are full of the artefacts of their former glory, while some are still inhabited. Whatever they are, they are unforgettable features of the landscape of the valley of the Loire.

The supreme château of the Loire. Chenonçeau with its gardens and arched gallery mirrored in the Cher.

Romorantin-Lanthenay is the 'capital' of the Sologne, and the administrative centre for this part of Loir-et-Cher Département. In the town are two particularly fine Renaissance half-timbered houses, **La Chancellerie**, where the royal seals were housed when the King stayed in the town, and **Le Carroir d'Orée**. The latter has two fine, carved corner posts supporting the overhanging first floor of the building.

Other old houses can be seen in the **rue de la Tour**, behind the post office, and also alongside the little southern branch of the river Sauldre.

An old disused brick kiln beside the road in typical Sologne country.

165

There are lovely half-timbered water mills of interest, namely the **Moulin du Chapitre** and the old fulling mill in the public gardens. These gardens, known as **Square Ferdinand Buisson**, are situated on islands in the river, **Isles de la Motte et de la Poule**, and are linked by foot-bridges over the water. The town's public library has been built in these gardens, which are very pleasant and shady.

There is an interesting ethnological museum, housed in the nearby Town Hall, which is devoted to the life of the people of the Sologne, and, to the north of the town, a museum with a display of Matra racing cars. Plastic car bodies and mass-produced saloon cars are made in the Matra factory in **Romorantin**.

The town has its own château, where Claude de France, later to become the wife of François I, was born in 1499. It stands alongside the river Sauldre and is now used as the administrative offices for the sub-préfecture. It is not open to the public, but can be seen from the bridge over the river and from the place du Château. The bridge leads to an island on which the **church of St Etienne** stands; this 15th-century church contains some very fine Angevin vaulting.

Romorantin is noted for its **Journées Gastronomiques** held during the last weekend of October. The tourist office invites cooks, restauranteurs, bakers and caterers, wine and food growers, etc., to participate in a grand exhibition. Visitors are invited to taste and buy products and specialities of the region; a real treat for gourmets!

Another treat would be a stay at the four-star **Grand Hôtel du Lion d'Or**, probably the most famous hotel in the Sologne. It is an old coaching inn, situated in the rue Clemenceau, the old main street of the town. Michelin

---

How to Make *Tarte Tatin*

(A traditional Tarte Tatin mould is made from copper, but a 18cm (7in) or 20cm (8in) sandwich tin about 5cm (2in) deep will be quite satisfactory.)

Ingredients: 142g (5oz) caster sugar, to which ¼-tsp powdered cinnamon has been added; 142g (5oz) butter; 1.8kg (4lb) eating apples (Reinettes are best); 227g (8oz) rich short-crust pastry.

Method

Divide the sugar and butter into four equal portions before starting. Liberally butter a mould or sandwich tin with a quarter of the butter, then dust it evenly with a quarter of the sugar. Peel and core the eating apples, quarter them and cut the quarters in half again. (The slices should be quite thick.) Arrange about a third of the apples in the bottom of the tin, and sprinkle them with a further quarter of the sugar before adding a further quarter of the butter, in small pieces, on top. Repeat the process twice more, each time using a third of the apples and a quarter of the sugar and butter. Take the shortcrust pastry and roll it out to about 30mm (⅛ in) thick. Cut a circle of the pastry the diameter of the tin plus twice its depth. Centre the pastry on top of the apples and carefully tuck the edges down between the apples and the inside edge of the tin. Prick the top of the pastry with a fork to allow steam to escape. Bake in a medium-hot oven for about 45min, and then allow to stand for five minutes. Turn the tin upside down on a plate, but leave it to cool further before removing it from the tart. Do not allow the tart to become cold—it is best served warm.

classifies it as *grand confort* and gives it two stars for an excellent restaurant. Needless to say, the price charged is commensurate with the rating. Other accommodation is available, both in Romorantin and nearby **Lanthenay**, to the north. For those with more limited budgets, there is an excellent four-star municipal camping site beside the river to the east of the town.

Lamotte-Beuvron is a small town with a claim to fame, for it was here, in the 1850s, that the sisters Caroline and Stéphanie Tatin opened a hotel opposite the station, known then as **l'Hôtel Terminus**. It rapidly acquired a reputation for good food and comfort, and was a popular place to stay, both for travellers and the hunting fraternity. One day, according to legend, the younger of the two sisters, Caroline, who was also in charge of the kitchens, prepared and cooked the apples for a tart, and, without thinking, turned them into the pie plate before she had put in the pastry. Because she was very short of time, she decided to improvise, and put the pastry on top of the fruit. Once cooked, she turned the tart upside down on a serving dish; and so "Tarte Tatin" was born! At the end of the last century the hotel was renamed **Hôtel Tatin**, and it still has a reputation for good food.

La Ferté Saint-Aubin is a small town with an interesting 17th-century brick-built moated château surrounded by a park. There are eight beautifully furnished rooms on the ground floor, and a guided tour lasts about 25 minutes.

Given by Charles VII to the Stuart family of Darnley, and later owned by the Dukes of Richmond, this château at Aubigny-sur-Nère is now used as the Town Hall.

Other parts of the building, from the old kitchens in the basement, to the attics, may be visited without a guide. The outbuildings include stables, tackroom and a horse museum, and in the extensive grounds is a small children's farm and animal park.

More than 30 hectares (74 acres) of parkland include a lake and islands with picnic areas, a café and *salon de thé*—an ideal place for a family day out. Close to the château are some typical Sologne brick and timber houses.

A short distance from La Ferté is the **Domaine du Ciran**. This is an estate in typical Sologne countryside, owned by the Sologne Foundation, with forest, scrubland, meadows, streams and *étangs*. Rural crafts, agriculture, forestry and hunting are the main themes of an exhibition in the château and adjacent outbuildings which is devoted to the Sologne and its former way of life.

Argent-sur-Sauldre is a small town with a reputation for ceramics and pottery. The large 15th-century château in the middle of the town has two huge round towers, and is surrounded by pleasant gardens. It is now used by the local authority and houses two museums, the **Musée des Métiers de France** and the **Musée Vassil-Ivanoff**. The former is devoted to the tools of trades which have either disappeared or are fast disappearing, and the latter to the works of one of the masters of contemporary ceramics. Vassil Ivanoff was a Bulgarian who came to France in the 1920s to study new techniques. He made his home at **La Borne**, some 39km (24 miles) to the south-east, which is known today as the village of the potters.

The nearby parish church of **Saint-André** was once the château chapel. An interesting château near Argent-sur-Sauldre is **Autry-le-Châtel**, a plain château with a strange boat-shaped roof. This is not open to the public and can only be viewed from the nearby road. The village itself is attractive, with well-kept timber and brick houses clustered around the church.

Aubigny-sur-Nère is situated on the eastern edge of the Sologne; it is really in the Berry, but it is close enough to the Sologne to be included here. A picturesque small town which is known in France as the *Cité des Stuarts*, it was given in 1423 by the Dauphin, Charles VII, to John Stuart of Darnley, who was his constable and ally against the English.

It remained the property of the family, together with the nearby château of **La Verrerie**, until the end of the 17th century, when it reverted to the French crown. Louis XIV then gave Aubigny to Louise de Keroualle, Duchess of Portsmouth and mistress of Charles II; her descendants, the Dukes of Richmond, continued to own the town (although they were not very popular as they chose to live in England and rarely came to Aubigny) until 1812, when the château at Aubigny was seized and put up for auction. The château of La Verrerie was later sold to the Vogüé family, who still own the château.

During the time of the Stuarts, craftsmen from Scotland settled in the town and established the glass-making and weaving industries. The town was thriving, and until the 19th century it was known as Aubigny-les-Cardeux, after the carders who worked there.

Even today the rue du Pont-aux-Foulons reminds us of the once-thriving cloth industry. (The woollen cloth was "fulled" or finished by washing it in the River Nère.) The original château of the Stuarts is now the Town Hall.

Adjoining the château are **Les Grands Jardins** also known as the **Parc de la Duchesse de Portsmouth**. The gardens, laid out in the 17th century, contain beautifully clipped hedges, little arbours and mature trees. They are particularly attractive in the autumn.

The old town centre is enclosed by streets which mark the line of the ramparts. Three round towers which are part of the original ramparts, and parts of the old walls can be seen in the **Boulevard de la République** near the river.

There are some lovely 16th-century half-timbered houses to be seen in the town, all of which were built after a disastrous fire in 1512, using timber given by the Stuart family from the forests surrounding the château of La Verrerie. The most interesting of these is the **Maison du Bailly** in the rue du Bourg-Coutant, which has some beautifully carved beams. Other old houses can be seen in the same street and in the rue du Charbon. A 15th-century house, the only one to have survived the fire can be seen in the rue du Pont-aux-Foulons.

The church of **Saint-Martin** was severely damaged during the fire and was restored under Robert Stuart. The oldest parts of the church date back to the 12th century, and in spite of a number of modifications and additions its style remains transitional Gothic, which is rather rare in the Berry.

Charles VII built the original château of La Verrerie in the early part of the 15th century, but it was considerably extended at the end of the century by Béraut Stuart and completed by his nephew Robert Stuart in the early 16th century. It is in a particularly beautiful setting, beside a lake, in rather isolated countryside. In the park is **l'Auberge de la Maison Hélène**,

T ypical half-timbered house dating from the 16th century, when Aubigny was rebuilt following a disastrous fire.

a restaurant offering an excellent menu, which is open during the tourist season. One of the châteaux on the **Route Jacques Coeur**, it is possible to stay there as a paying guest.

Salbris is an important town on the route from Orléans to Vierzon, which was once an important Roman station. It has an interesting church with some attractive 17th-century furnishings, but tourists are more likely to be interested in the private railway which runs from Salbris to Romorantin, from which there is a very good view of the Sologne countryside.

*T*he church of Souvigny-en-Sologne, one of the loveliest of the Sologne villages.

The Sologne Villages

The Sologne villages are small, and many of them are picturesque. Loveliest of all is **Souvigny-en-Sologne**, with many typical Sologne half-timbered houses. Both the **Hôtel La Croix Blanche**, and the nearby restaurant, **Le Perdrix Rouge,** are in old half-timbered buildings. But the real "gem" in this village is the church. It has a fine 12th-century nave and a panelled 16th-century choir. The huge square belfry is supported from the inside by enormous oak beams and pillars. There are also some interesting 17th-century murals. The best part of all, however, is the outside. The church is partly made of black and red bricks set in patterns in a timber framework. The beautifully carved porch is a typical Sologne *caquetoir* or "cackling porch". The porch was intended to be

village women could gather for a gossip after Mass!

Other nearby villages worth visiting include **Clémont**, **Chaon**, **Brinon-sur-Sauldre** (also with an interesting *caquetoir*). **Fontaines-en-Sologne** and **Bracieux** are further west, nearer **Chambord** and **Cheverny**.

Bracieux has a beautiful 16th-century market hall, with a tithe barn above. The old houses are grouped around the market place, and there is a picturesque bridge over the river. **Selles-Saint-Denis**, in the southern Sologne, has a church dedicated to Saint-Genoulph. It is decorated inside with 14th-century murals telling the story of the saint's life. This is the only church known to be dedicated to this local saint (literally translated it means Saint Knee!) who is supposed to have miraculous powers of healing all kinds of ailments relating to the legs.

In the hamlet of **Gy-en-Sologne** is the **Locature de la Straize**, an old agricultural worker's cottage with just one living room and a few outbuildings, dating from the 16th century. Constructed from wattle and daub and small bricks, it has been furnished with typical Sologne furniture. In this former "tied cottage" one can imagine the life of the peasants of the past. In the villages of **Vienne-en-Val** and **Tigy**, in the north of the Sologne and not far from the River Loire, are small museums, one dealing with archaeological finds from the area, and the other with rural crafts.

T he epitome of the Loire château—Chambord represents the ultimate development of the château from fortress to palace.

171

The Major Châteaux of the Sologne

Perhaps the most famous château is the massive Renaissance château of Chambord (*see* below).

Cheverny is about 17 km (11 miles) from Chambord. It has a classical façade, although it was built in the late Renaissance and was completed in 1634. At one time you could only visit the château with a guide, but recently the owners have changed to non-guided visits, with a recommended route to follow. Including the private apartments, 17 rooms are open to view, and visitors are given a good leaflet in their own language on arrival. There are stewards at various locations who can answer questions. The château has been in the hands of the Hurault family since it was built, and is particularly well known for its hunting connections. The house has some interesting pieces of furniture, including a travelling trunk which belonged to Henri IV, made of Spanish leather and

---

The Magnificent Châteaux of Chambord

"The epitome of all that human artifice can create", so the Emperor Charles V called the château of Chambord.

Planned by François I as an attempt to prove that he was the greatest monarch in the western world, he wanted a large site that would give him plenty of opportunities for his favourite pastime of hunting. The estate covers some 5,000 hectares (12,350 acres), and François had a huge circular wall built around it, more than 32km (20 miles) long. This wall is still in existence today. François wanted a palace to which he would enjoy inviting his friends, and intended to live in it himself.

It is believed that Leonardo da Vinci may have had some influence on the design of the château, but he died some 5 months before work began in September 1519. There are no records of the architect. Unfortunately, François lost a great deal of money in a series of wars, and ended up as a prisoner in Spain. He returned to France in 1526, and although the foundations had only just been completed he decided to add two wings to the original plan.

By 1537, the main part of the château was finished, but François' own royal apartments were not finished until 1545. He died only two years later, and although his son, Henri II continued with the building it was still unfinished when he died in 1559. The château was eventually completed during the reign of Louis XIV in 1684.

Chambord was never lived in as François had intended, but was used mainly as a royal hunting lodge. It has more than 400 rooms and a chimney for every day of the year, and although 20 rooms and apartments are open to the public, there is usually work going on and it is rare to find them all open. Chambord is owned by the French "National Trust" (*Caisse Nationale des Monuments Historiques et des Sites*) and is one of the few châteaux where one is free to wander around the rooms at will. Only a few of them are furnished, but most visitors will be content to climb the great double staircase and go out on to the great roof terraces to admire the wonderful views. Chambord is so vast that it is difficult to take in the magnificence of the building in just one visit. The park is now a game reserve, where deer and wild boar roam free, but there are public observation hides in the park from where the animals may be observed. There are four approaches to the château along public roads through the park. The public road from Bracieux, in the south, gives the best view of the building.

This magnificent staircase at Chambord may be climbed by visitors without being escorted in a guided group.

173

Cheverny with its fine classical façade dating from 1634 contains many hunting trophies. This is another house which has adopted the idea of free circulation of visitors helped by multilingual information leaflets.

emblazoned with the arms of France and Navarre. It weighs 70kg (154lb) when empty. There are some beautifully decorated ceilings and fine 17th-century tapestries, as well as paintings and beautiful 18th-century furniture.

In the outbuildings are the kennels which house a pack of some 70 hounds, and the trophy room, containing more than 2,000 stags' antlers and a modern stained glass window depicting the departure of the hunt

from Cheverny. The grounds and park are not open to the public, but the orangery can be seen from the terrace at the rear of the château.

Cheverny gives its name to the wines which are grown on the south bank of the river Loire. Although there are many small growers, most have joined a consortium, the *Chai des Vignerons* at nearby Chitenay. They work together to produce and market their wines.

The **château of Troussay**, just 3.5km (2 miles) west of Cheverny is an attractive manor house and a typical example of a small estate in the Val de Loire. Its Renaissance style and rich decoration are reminiscent of the larger châteaux, and its **Musée de Sologne** in the outbuildings is an interesting reminder of domestic and agricultural life and customs of bygone days.

Villesavin lies between **Chambord** and **Cheverny** and is completely hidden from the road. It was built by Jean le Breton, financial secretary to François I, who was entrusted with the work of paying for the building of Chambord. The château at Villesavin was built by the same master builders and workmen who built the great royal châteaux, and it has remained virtually untouched for four centuries. The rooms are furnished with Renaissance furniture, and a collection of pewter is on display. Outside is a large dovecote with more than 1,500 holes—one for every 0.4 hectare (1 acre) of land—and a collection of horse-drawn vehicles and vintage cars.

The attractive **château du Moulin**, situated some 11km (7 miles) to the west of Romorantin, is a late 15th-century brick-built château, with two slender conical towers either side of the former drawbridge and a rather squat

The old stable buildings at Cheverny are used to accommodate a staggering collection of antlers and other trophies of the chase.

crenellated pepper-pot tower with a *chemin-de-ronde* standing at one end of the moated building. In one of the bedrooms is a 14th-century tapestry and a bedspread made from a curtain from **La Sainte-Chapelle** in Paris. In the dining room the chairs still have their original Cordova leather upholstery, and the salon contains an original painted ceiling which has never been retouched. The huge vaulted kitchens with their original roasting spit and the guardroom are also interesting.

The **château of Chemery** is more like a large medieval moated manor house, and is currently being restored. In the village is a **Cave Viticole**, open to the public. These may also be found in Contres, Mur-de-Sologne and Soings-en-Sologne.

Enjoying the Sologne Countryside

The Sologne countryside offers numerous possibilities for enjoyment; fishing in the streams and *étangs*, walking along *Grandes Randonnées* or along many of the quiet country roads and plenty of opportunities for cycling. Sailing and horse riding are also available. Many of the *étangs* belong to the communities in which they are situated, and are often reserved for wild life, although some offer fishing and water sports. The largest of the *étangs* in the Sologne which offers a wide variety of leisure activities is the **Etang du Puits** between **Argent-sur-Sauldre** and **Clémont**. The old locks on the now disused Canal de la Sauldre can be seen nearby.

Campsites are numerous and some simple *gîte* accommodation is available. Hotels are plentiful, many of them being members of the **Logis de France**. A map of the Sologne at a scale of 1:100,000, produced by IGN, is available from most local newsagents and *Syndicats d'Initiative*. This shows paths which are open to the public, and gives other useful tourist information, such as accommodation and other leisure activities.

One modern development in the Sologne is the Radio-Astronomy Observatory at **Nançay**. The site was chosen because it is level and remote from any electrical interference, an essential for such an installation. All that can be heard when standing in the car park

nearby is the quiet hum of the apparatus. Well-designed display boards and an audio tape machine beside the car park explain the purpose of the equipment and how it works. When the observatory was established in 1962 it had one of the largest radio telescopes in the world. It is not really an intrusion, for it is well screened by the trees which surround it.

Bourges

Bourges is just about the most southerly limit of the area covered by this book. Famous as the city of Jacques Coeur, it is the chief administrative town of the Cher Département. There is a beautiful **cathedral** and some fine old buildings, excellent markets and a good shopping centre. It is ideally placed for exploring the north of the Berry, including the **Collines de Sancerre**, the river Loire between **Chatillon-sur-Loire** and **La Charité-sur-Loire**, and the river Cher downstream to **Selles-sur-Cher**.

Bourges was an important town under the Romans, when it became the county town of Aquitaine, a Gallo-Roman province under its old name of *Avaricum*. It became part of the royal domain in the early 12th century, and Louis VII and his son, Philippe-Auguste, built a defensive wall around the city, parts of which can still be seen.

Work commenced on the cathedral in 1190 and for a while the city flourished. Unfortunately, in 1348 there was a severe outbreak of the plague, followed by a fire in 1353. In 1356 the old province of the Berry was given to the son of King Jean the Good, who

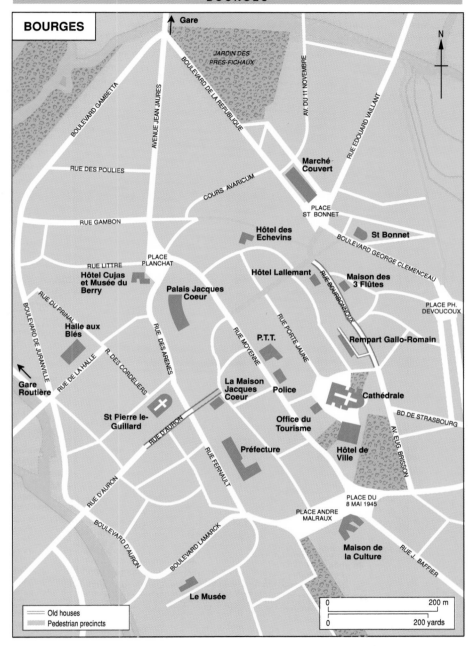

BOURGES

Gare

JARDIN DES PRES-FICHAUX

N

BOULEVARD GAMBETTA

AVENUE JEAN JAURES

BOULEVARD DE LA REPUBLIQUE

AV. DU 11 NOVEMBRE

RUE EDOUARD VAILLANT

RUE DES POULIES

COURS AVARICUM

Marché Couvert

RUE GAMBON

PLACE ST BONNET

Hôtel des Echevins

St Bonnet

BOULEVARD GEORGE CLEMENCEAU

RUE LITTRE

PLACE PLANCHAT

Hôtel Cujas et Musée du Berry

Hôtel Lallemant

Maison des 3 Flûtes

RUE BOURBONNOUX

PLACE PH. DEVOUCOUX

RUE DU PRINAL

Palais Jacques Coeur

BOULEVARD DE JURANVILLE

Halle aux Blés

RUE DE LA HALLE

R. DES CORDELIERS

RUE DES ARENES

RUE MOYENNE

RUE PORTE JAUNE

P.T.T.

Rempart Gallo-Romain

Gare Routière

La Maison Jacques Coeur

Police

Cathédrale

St Pierre le-Guillard

RUE D'AURON

Office du Tourisme

BD DE STRASBOURG

AV. EUG. BRISSON

Préfecture

Hôtel de Ville

RUE FERNAULT

RUE D'AURON

PLACE DU 8 MAI 1945

PLACE ANDRE MALRAUX

BOULEVARD LAMARCK

Maison de la Culture

RUE J. BAFFIER

Le Musée

0   200 m
0   200 yards

Old houses
Pedestrian precincts

*T*own plan of Bourges.

St Etienne Cathedral: One of the Loveliest Cathedrals in France

Comparing favourably with Chartres, Reims, Le Mans and Notre-Dame de Paris, it was begun in 1195. The main building was completed within 60 years, a record at that time, and was finally finished in 1324. It has been compared to a great ship propelled by double-banked oars. Indeed, the wonderful double flying buttresses do look like this when viewed from a distance. It has a superb western façade with five beautifully carved 13th-century doorways, the central one being surmounted by a magnificent sculptured representation of the Last Judgement. The interesting point about these doorways is that they are all of a different size. The great porches on the north and south façades are of earlier date, the south porch, through which the visitor enters the cathedral, having a carved figure of Christ in Majesty surrounded by the emblems of the four Evangelists. Inside, the visitor is immediately impressed by the enormous width of the cathedral; it is in fact the widest Gothic cathedral in France, being some 41m (134ft) wide. Unusually for a cathedral of this size there are no transepts. However, the nave has a central aisle and two side aisles on each side. The outer side aisles are lower, and they continue as an ambulatory around the back of the great choir. The windows in the cathedral are beautiful, containing some fine medieval stained glass. The oldest, and the loveliest, are those in the ambulatory and choir, which date from the beginning of the 13th century. Many of these were given to the cathedral by the various craftsmen's guilds of the time. The best time of day to visit the cathedral and get the benefit of the sun through the windows is mid-morning. In the crypt of the cathedral is the marble tomb of the Duc de Berry. The crypt is unusual in that it is built partly above ground level, and there are windows to let in the light. The north tower of the cathedral may be ascended for a fine view of the town.

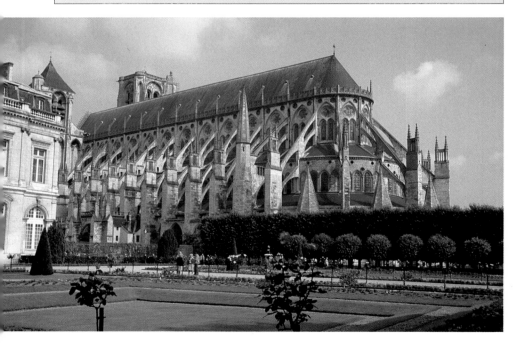

became known as Jean, Duc de Berry. He made Bourges his capital, and under his influence the city became one of the most important centres of Renaissance civilization. He was a great patron of the arts, and encouraged artists of all kinds to come to Bourges. He is particularly well known for commissioning Paul de Limbourg to create the famous illuminated manuscript *Les Très Riches Heures du Duc de Berry*. Unfortunately this is not to be seen in Bourges; it is in the Condé Museum in the château of Chantilly, some 50km (31 miles) north of Paris.

After the death of the Duc de Berry in 1416, the Duchy was handed to the Dauphin, later to become Charles VII and also known as the 'King of Bourges'. As already mentioned, Jacques Coeur was a wealthy merchant who put his immense fortune at the disposal of Charles VII, and became his chief Minister of Finance. He was a rich merchant and ship-owner. A citizen of Bourges he was probably the greatest merchant of the Middle Ages, and his mansion in Bourges, the **Palais Jacques Coeur** is a reflection of his standing.

Louis XI, son of the Dauphin, founded a university in Bourges in 1463. It attracted many students from abroad, including John Calvin, and it was here that he first heard of Martin

*T*he lovely cathedral of Bourges with its rows of double flying buttresses forms a suitable backdrop to the gardens of the former Bishop's Palace.

Luther's reformist ideas, which greatly impressed him. The Reformation in this part of France thus had its beginnings in Bourges. Today, the city is an important centre for technical studies.

Immediately outside the cathedral is the **Hôtel de Ville**, which was once the Bishop's Palace. From the beautiful gardens nearby is a wonderful view of the cathedral. Near the cathedral is the tourist office offering the visitor guided tours of the city, if required, and they have leaflets in English describing the main city sights, together with a map to help you find them. There are several pedestrianized streets, many of them containing delightful medieval houses. It is a pleasure to walk here, because although there is traffic, it is not so busy as other medieval centres like Blois and Tours.

Right next door to the cathedral is a medieval **tithe barn** with a fine enclosed half-timbered stairway above the main door, leading to the first floor. Behind this can be found the remains of the Gallo-Roman ramparts. At the end of the 12th century the inhabitants of Bourges were allowed to build their houses along these walls.

A walk along the ramparts allows the visitor to discover these old buildings, and those of a later date which were built here. The entrance to the ramparts is from the **rue Bourbonnoux**, one of Bourges' most picturesque streets, with many medieval houses. One of the finest is the **Maison des Trois Flûtes**, at the junction with rue Joyeuse.

In the same street is one of Bourges' beautiful mansions, the **Hôtel Lallement**, which is a fine Renaissance

*T*his fine octagonal staircase turret covered with Renaissance sculpture is part of the Hôtel des Echevins, built in 1487 for use by the mayor and aldermen of Bourges.

building now housing the **Museum of Decorative Arts**. This mansion was also partly built above the old walls, which explains the different levels of the courtyards. Inside the building are some beautiful fireplaces and coffered ceilings. The museum contains a fine collection of French and Dutch period furniture, including a beautiful carved ebony cabinet. There are also tapestries and *objets d'art*, paintings, clocks, enamels and glass. There is an exceptional collection of miniature furniture, including many journeymen's samples, and a good collection of antique toys.

The **Hôtel des Echevins** in rue Edouard Branly was built after the second great fire of Bourges (1487) as a meeting place for the town's mayor and aldermen (*Echevin* = alderman). It has a beautiful façade covered in relief sculptures, a fine octagonal staircase turret, and an attractive colonnaded gallery opening onto the courtyard. The building now houses the **Musée d'Estève**, a collection of modern paintings, tapestries and drawings given to the city by the contemporary Berry artist Maurice Estève and his wife.

The **Musée de Berry** occupies yet another Renaissance mansion, **Hôtel Cujas**. This building has two interesting corner turrets, one being circular and the other hexagonal. Inside are prehistoric and archaeological collections, popular and traditional art, ancient crafts and folklore of the Berry. The **Hôtel Pelvoysin** is a 15th-century half-timbered house which was built with slanting windows so that the ground floor was better lit. It is currently used as a savings bank.

Pride of place has to go to the **Palais Jacques Coeur**. This superb example of a private medieval residence built between 1443 and 1453, which, like the **Hôtel Lallement** was also partially built above the old Roman walls. Like Chambord, the palace belongs to the French National Trust (*Caisse Nationale des Monuments Historiques*). The eastern façade is especially interesting, with a richly carved stone

A typical narrow medieval street. This half-timbered house belonged to Jacques Coeur's father-in-law, and the merchant once lived there.

canopy over the main doorway. This is now empty, but it originally held a statue of Charles VII on horseback. On either side are two carved stone "windows" with figures of servants leaning out and looking down on the street. Jacques Coeur's emblems—the pilgrim's cockleshell and a heart—are much in evidence.

The interior courtyard has beautifully decorated galleries and a central octagonal tower. Inside the main building are richly carved doorways and fireplaces. There is a beautiful barrel-vaulted gallery, looking almost like an inverted ship's hull, leading to the chapel, which has a superb painted ceiling from 1488. For many years this was hidden by a false ceiling, which may explain its excellent state of preservation. Jacques Coeur's ship-owning interests are illustrated in a bas-relief and a stained glass window in one of the ante-rooms on the first floor of the building. He also installed a Turkish bath, and a pigeon loft in the attics for his homing pigeons. All this, remember, was in the 15th century.

Despite the great fire of 1487, when three-quarters of the town was destroyed, there are still plenty of medieval streets to see, most of the houses having been built during the 15th and 16th centuries. The most interesting, apart from **Rue Bourbonnoux** which has already been mentioned are **Place Gordaine**, **Rue Mirebeau**, and **Rue Coursalon**. The medieval houses in **Rue d'Auron**, include one known as "Jacques Coeur's House" which actually belonged to his father-in-law. The house where the merchant was born was situated nearby.

The **Préfecture** is an 18th-century building built on the site of the Duke of Berry's palace, where Louis XI was born. There are still some vestiges of the old building to be seen. Three churches of interest include **Notre Dame**, which has a beautiful marble font decorated with armorial bearings and a second font bearing the emblems of Jacques Coeur. **Saint-Pierre-le-Guillard** church, near the **Palais de Jacques Coeur**, has a *narthex* or vestibule inside the main door, a feature often found in early churches. According to legend, the building was paid for by a Jew, Guillard, who was converted to Christianity by Saint Antony of Padua when he visited Bourges in about 1225. Hence the unusual name of the church. **Saint-Bonnet church**, close to place Gordaine, has some rather nice 16th-century stained glass windows attributed to Jean Lescuyer. One of these depicts the Resurrection, and shows the women wearing *Berrichon* head-dress.

A modern building of interest in Bourges is the **Maison de la Culture**. This was the first centre of its kind in France and was opened in 1964 by André Malraux and General de Gaulle. It combines a cultural office which can give advice on all aspects of art and culture to those requiring it, with a music school, two theatres, exhibition rooms, café, etc. The centre organizes many artistic events and festivals in the city, when it is a hive of activity. Also of interest is the Natural History Museum, known simply as **Le Museum**, where 2,000m² (2,392yd²) under a huge structure of brick, aluminium and glass are devoted to natural science and the environment.

A Walk Through the City

Starting from the tourist office in rue Victor Hugo, close to the cathedral, where a useful map may be obtained, walk round to the cathedral itself and past the great west front to the rue des Trois Maillets. On the left is the half-timbered stairway of the medieval tithe barn. Continue ahead to rue Bourbonnoux and turn left. A short distance along, on the left, is the entrance to the **Promenade des Remparts**, a walk along the old Gallo-Roman walls.

Near the beginning of the walk is a 12th-century house which was once the home of one of the cathedral dignitaries, and at the corner of the narrow stairway, known locally as a *passage casse-cou* (break-neck alley!) but officially the Escalier Georges Sand, is a late 15th-century house. Emerging into rue Bourbonnoux again, walk as far as rue Joyeux. On the corner is the **Maison des Trois Flûtes**, now a *pâtisserie*. This lovely half-timbered house has a fine corner post, decorated with three large carved flutes.

Almost opposite is the entrance to **Hôtel Lallement**, well worth a visit at any time, but especially on Wednesdays when entry to all the museums in the city is free of charge! Continue down the street to place Gordaine, a delightful square with many half-timbered houses to be seen. There are several cafés here, and it is pleasant to sit outside and soak up the atmosphere of bygone days.

Continue the walk down rue Mirebeau, as far as the **Escalier Mirebeau**, another *"casse-cou"*. Go down the steps to rue Edouard Branly and turn right. A short way down the street, which more or less follows the line of the old city walls, is the **Hôtel des Echevins**. Continue down the street past the **Ecole des Beaux Arts** to place Cujas and then turn right down rue du Commerce. Turn right at the bottom into rue Pelvoysin and walk towards rue Mirebeau. On the corner of place de la Barre, rue Cambournac and rue Pelvoysin is the **Hôtel Pelvoysin**. Nearby is the **church of Notre Dame**, which was rebuilt after the fire of 1487 and incorporates a mixture of 15th- and 16th-century styles.

Walk back to place Planchat and cross the square to rue des Arènes where the **Musée de Berry** can be found in the **Hôtel Cujas**. Continue along the Rue des Arènes, passing the back of the **Palais Jacques Coeur**. Go up the steps between the palace and the municipal theatre into **place Jacques Coeur**. In the square is a statue of the great man, erected by the city of Bourges in the 19th century. Continue along rue Jacques Coeur past the theatre and library into rue des Armuriers. At the top of rue d'Auron, opposite the **Enclos des Jacobins** (a small modern precinct leading to the rue Moyenne) is the building known as **Jacques Coeur's house**, which is now a *pâtisserie*. From here, one can either wander down the pleasant semi-pedestrian shopping street, or walk up the stairs in the Enclos des Jacobins to emerge on the rue Moyenne, which is the main shopping street of Bourges. Turn left and walk down to the rue Coursalon, on the right. This will take you back to place Gordaine, from where you can retrace your steps to the cathedral.

Parks and Gardens

Bourges has two outstanding floral parks. The first, the **Jardin de l'Hôtel de Ville** has already been mentioned. Once the garden of the Bishop's Palace, it is believed to have been laid out by Lenôtre in the 17th century. Each year the species of flowers and their colours are changed, so the gardens take on a "new look". The outstanding gardens in Bourges, however, are the **Prés-Fichaux gardens** which were laid out on the banks of the river Yèvre between 1923 and 1930. It is difficult to believe that this was once a swamp! The designer, landscape gardener, Paul Marguerita, has created a modern garden with clipped yew arches, bold colours and shapes in the garden beds, ponds, lawns and an open-air theatre. Really beautiful gardens at any time of the year, and not to be missed.

Shopping in Bourges

The main shopping streets in Bourges are the **rue Moyenne** and **rue du Commerce**, both of which are busy streets with quite heavy traffic at times. The **rue d'Auron**, however, which is reached from the rue Moyenne via the Enclose des Jacobins, is semi-pedestrianized and a very pleasant place to shop.

The large department stores, **Nouvelles Galeries** and **Aubrun**, are both in rue Moyenne. Smaller shops and boutiques are to be found in rue d'Auron, with many of them displaying what they have to sell on the pavements outside. Shoe shops seem to be in abundance, and there are plenty of *pâtisseries* and *chocolateries* to tempt the hungry tourist in search of a snack or treat. Local specialities include *forestines*, which are little crunchy sweets filled with almond paste, nuts, chestnut purée or chocolate. *Croquets* are little biscuits rather like macaroons. *Les Sablés de Nançay* are rich, sweet shortbread biscuits.

You will have no difficulty in finding the local wines from Sancerre, Quincy and Reuilly available in Bourges. Plenty of good fruit and vegetable shops are here too, as well as small cafés and bistros, with their chairs and tables under bright umbrellas outside in the warm summer air. Prices seem more reasonable than in some of the better-known tourist cities, and the atmosphere is more agreeable. The rue d'Auron is a pleasant place to wander, even if it is only to do a bit of window shopping. A better way to pass the time perhaps is to sit at a table outside a café and watch the world go by!

Bourges is famous for its excellent markets. The best are those held on Thursdays in place des Marronniers, Saturdays in the **Halle au Blé** in the **place de la Nation**, and Sundays in the **Marché Couvert** in place Saint Bonnet. Here you will be able to buy many of the local regional specialities, such as cheeses from Sancerre and Valençay, and fresh poultry. Good potatoes are a speciality of the Berry, and are known locally as *truches*. They are often made into tasty potato cakes or pancakes, called *truffiats*. There is a good **Carrefour** supermarket at the junction of avenue Général de Gaulle and avenue du Maréchal de Lattre de Tassigny, on the road to Gien. Others can be found on the Route d'Orléans and Route de la Charité.

Sancerre and the Northern Berry

To the north-east of Bourges is quite different country to that of the north-west. Whereas the Sologne is fairly flat and marshy, the **Collines de Sancerre**, as their name implies, are hills. In places these are very steep, almost Alpine in character, with narrow winding valleys tucked between the hills. This is wine country, with vineyards stretching for miles over the steep hillsides. Many of the slopes face south, so they get full benefit of the sun and the grapes are of better quality. The river Loire lies beyond Sancerre, and forms the boundary between the **Berry** and **Burgundy**. However, there are three towns of some interest on the east bank of the river.

La Charité-sur-Loire, the upstream limit of this book, was once a busy river port. It has an attractive bridge crossing the river and a shady tree-lined quay nearby. The most interesting building in the town is the **Abbey church of Notre Dame**, which, although badly damaged in a fire in 1599, still has the original Romanesque choir, and there are some fine Romanesque sculptures in the south transept. Outside the church can be seen the original Romanesque tower and some superbly carved arcades from the original nave which was burned down in the fire. They are incorporated into the top floor of some houses. The river at this point is not very interesting, being very shallow and stony, with small flat islands in mid-stream.

Some 13km (8 miles) downstream is **Pouilly**, famous for Pouilly-Fumé wines, considered by many to be the best dry white wines in the Loire, with a higher alcohol content than many others. The **château de Nozet** has its own vineyards and produces 60 per cent of the total yield of Pouilly Fumé, although many of the grapes used are bought in from other growers. It is also of the very best quality.

The town itself is not particularly interesting, and to get a real "feel" of the countryside it is best to take the very narrow and twisting roads through the vineyards to **Les Loges**, where almost every house in this tiny rural hamlet has a board outside offering wine-tasting and direct purchase. Go into one "on spec". Maybe try some of Jean Pabiot's Pouilly-Fumé, in a small room next to the kitchen of the house. Taste it, and if you like it, buy it! That really is the only thing to do, because only you can decide what you like.

Cosne was once famous for wrought iron work, but unfortunately the trade collapsed when the river became unnavigable. There are several examples of local wrought iron to be seen along the road which runs beside the river before the bridge. Cosne also has a safe bathing beach.

Sancerre is the "jewel in the crown" of this area. Wine has been made in the region for centuries. Gregory of Tours knew of it in AD 582, but in the 11th century the Augustinian Friars began to develop the vineyards on the very stony soils of the area. Although white wines are the most famous, both rosé and red wines are produced, although not in such large quantities.

Standing perched high above the local countryside, surrounded by vineyards, the town itself is half-circled by ramparts from which there are some

*S*et upon a hill-top, the town of Sancerre is surrounded by vineyards of the Berry. A tourist route runs across the disused railway viaduct.

superb views. One of the best is the view across the river valley from the **Esplanade Porte César**, reached from the tourist office in Nouvelle Place, via rue Porte César. A château stands on the hill above the esplanade, but is not open to the public.

In Nouvelle Place, once the market square, which has quite a slope to it, and in the surrounding streets are shops selling local produce, especially *crottins de Chavignol* and various wines from Sancerre. However, it is best to buy these products from the actual cheese dairies and vignerons in the surrounding hamlets. The tourist office has a free map available which shows where they all are. What is worth buying in the town are local pastries and cakes. *Lichons de Sancerre* are almond paste cakes, *Palettes Sancerrois* are

The steep narrow streets of Sancerre look out to the distant vine-covered hill slopes.

made from almond paste, nougatine and orange peel, and *Croquets de Sancerre* are small almond biscuits, similar to macaroons. Local hams are also a speciality, and are smoked over vine roots (*sarments de vigne*).

Sancerre has several 15th-century turreted houses. Most may be found in the narrow streets and little squares below the **Tour des Fiefs:** rue des Vieilles Boucheries, place du Puits du Marché, place de la Paneterie and rue Porte-Vieille. There is an interesting story

behind the belfry next to the 18th-century church of **Notre-Dame**. Built in the early 16th century as a symbol of the town's independence, it originally had both a clock and a bell. After the siege of 1573, both were removed as a punishment to the town, and were taken to Bourges, where they still remain. (The clock can be seen in the Musée de Berry.) The original steeple blew down in a storm in 1725, and was replaced by the roof which is there today. The belfry is now used as the church tower. Nearby, in place Saint-Père, are the remains of the Romanesque church of Saint-Père-la-Nonne. These were found when foundations were being dug for the town's nursery school in 1954, and have been preserved. The **Tour des Fiefs** was once part of the original château, which was destroyed in 1621. There seems to be some doubt about when it was first built; some official leaflets say the 12th century, and the leaflet describing the old streets of the town, obtainable from the tourist office, describes it as a 14th-century tower! It is probably older than 14th-century.

Below Sancerre is **Saint-Satur**, which includes the villages of **Fontenay** and **Saint-Thibault**. The interesting Gothic **Abbey church of Saint-Satur** does not have a tower. Due to both monetary problems and the Hundred Years War, the church was never completed, and there is a huge blank wall where the west front and tower would normally be. Saint-Satur is encircled by a superb viaduct. Once it carried the railway, but now it carries a tourist route from Sancerre down to the **Canal Latéral de la Loire** at **Saint-Thibault**. This attractive little village has a small harbour, linking the canal with the river, for use by pleasure boats. There is also a bathing beach and a two-star campsite.

West of Sancerre is the little village of **Chavignol**, famous for its goat's cheese. But you will also find *caves* here, and pleasant little *auberges*.

About 10km (6 miles) to the west is **Boucard**, another of the châteaux on the Route Jacques Coeur. Built as a fortress in 1350, and still approached by a drawbridge, the château was altered in the 16th century when a Renaissance wing was added. The château may be visited, but there is not a great deal to see inside, and the guide speaks only in French. However, the outside is a good example of a feudal castle.

Further west is **Henrichemont**, a town with an unusual history. In the 17thcentury, the great Duke of Sully bought the château at **La Chapelle d'Angillon**, some 11km (7 miles) to the north of the town, on the main road between Aubigny-sur-Nère and Bourges. The land included the title of "Prince de Boisbelle", which was fortunate for him, since the Boisbelle Principality was forever exempt from paying royal taxes! With all this money saved, Sully decided to found a "free town" (Henrichemont). It has a huge market square with eight streets radiating from the centre in a star pattern. The once elegant 17th-century houses surrounding the square have now been converted into shops, and many have been spoilt by 19th- and 20th-century additions and alterations.

The **château de Béthune** at **La Chapelle-Angillon** is yet another of those on the Route Jacques Coeur.

The lovely château, with its 11th-century keep, still a stronghold, stands beside a lake. Most of the rooms in the château date from the 15th and 16th centuries. Beautifully furnished, and still lived in, it also contains a museum devoted to Alain-Fournier, the French novelist who was born in the village, and who used the château as the setting for one of his novels. He was killed in action during World War I and his name is inscribed on the local memorial.

South of Henrichemont is **La Borne**, where there are some very good potteries, and the 15th-century **château de Maupas** at **Morogues**. There is a marvellous collection of china plates lining the walls of the great staircase, and some exceptionally fine rooms with 18th-century furnishings. This château has belonged to the Agard family since 1688, although they lost it for a while during the Revolution.

To the west of Maupas is **Menetou-Salon**. This village produces some very good wines, and there are plenty of vignerons in the area where you can taste and buy. There is also a showroom run by the local wine cooperative in the village square, where there is also a map showing the location of the various vignerons. The rosé wine at Caves Jacky Rat to the south of the village is particularly good.

Menetou-Salon has a very fine château, owned since the 18th century by the Princes of Arenberg. The château once belonged to Jacques Coeur, but all his possessions were confiscated when he fell from grace and was dismissed from his post as Treasurer to Charles VII. It was after the restoration of the château to the family after the Revolution that Prince Auguste d'Arenberg decided to enlarge the château, taking as his inspiration the Palais de Jacques Coeur in Bourges. The state rooms of this beautiful château are open to the public, and are worth seeing because they have the wonderful feeling of being lived in. The outside of the château is decorated with stone carvings, particularly noteworthy being the large flat-roofed portico, decorated with elaborately carved finials. In the stables, near the entrance, is a very good collection of old family cars, and a complete collection of saddlery in the adjoining tack room. The guide speaks some English, and makes the tour very interesting.

From Bourges to Selles-sur-Cher and Valençay

The river Yèvre flows from **Bourges** to **Vierzon**, where it joins the river Cher. This in turn flows west to join the Loire beyond Tours near Villandry. The first town reached along the valley is **Mehun-sur-Yèvre**, a small town with a well-restored 12th-century town gate. Just two towers remain from the 14th-century château of Charles VII, in one of which is a small museum. It is only open on Sundays in summer.

There is a statue of Joan of Arc beside the church; it was in Mehun that she received her *lettres de noblesse* from Charles VII. The church was built between the 11th and 15th centuries, the sanctuary being the oldest part. There is a 19th-century painting depicting Saint Joan, and a fine

painting by the 17th-century Berrichon painter Jean Boucher of Christ on the Cross. This was originally in the Abbey of Saint-Sulpice in Bourges, and was given to the parish of Mehun by the cathedral authorities in 1824.

To the west is **Quincy**, which, with the village of **Reuilly** to the south, is another well-known wine area.

Vierzon is a fairly large town, which has a few old half-timbered houses in rue Galilée, rue Maréchal Joffre and place des Bancs. Le Beffroi, the 14th-century old town gate was also once the town's prison. In the 19th century, a clock tower and lantern were added to the old gate, thus ruining what would have been a fine monument. Behind the *Office de Tourisme* in Place Thorez is the **Auditorium**, a large open-air concert platform beside the river.

Not far from here are the old locks and basin of the **Canal de Berry**, which linked the Cher with Bourges. Beside the canal are the beautiful **Memorial Gardens** dedicated to those who died in two World Wars. There are many opportunities for water sports here—fishing, sailing, canoeing—and being on the very edge of the Sologne there is also plenty of riding and walking. There are several hotels, a campsite and a Youth Hostel here.

The next important place down-river is **Mennetou-sur-Cher**. This fascinating little medieval town allows the visitor to step right back into history. As you walk through the narrow cobbled streets you almost expect people in medieval dress to meet you as you turn the corners. It is still partly surrounded by the 11th-century ramparts. On the remains of the keep beside the **Hôtel le Lion d'Or** is a plaque which,

*T*his old drawbridge leads to one of the town gates giving access to the cobbled streets of the medieval town of Mennetou-sur-Cher. It is probable that Joan of Arc passed through this very gate.

translated, reads "Joan of Arc passed through Mennetou-sur-Cher on March 3rd 1429 on her way from Gien to Sainte Catherine de Fierbois. (Commemorating the) 500th anniversary". This was on the journey to Chinon, where she recognized the Dauphin.

At both ends of the **Grande Rue** are remnants of the old town gateways, and there are some lovely medieval houses, some dating back to the 13th century, in the street. The **Grange aux Dimes**, the remains of two medieval barns, is now in use by the local Finance Office.

Selles-sur-Cher has two châteaux which are linked together by a long wall. The old château was built in the 13th century and is a typical moated fortress. It was bought by the Duke of Sully's brother in 1604, and he built the 17th-century brick building. The dining room of the château is the former guardroom, and has a huge fireplace which is one of the largest in France. Both Charles VII and Joan of Arc stayed here, as did, much later, the Count of Chambord, pretender to the French throne in the 19th century.

South of Selles is **Valençay**, one of the loveliest of the French Renaissance châteaux. There is a superb view from the approach to Valençay from the north, and parking is easy under the trees alongside the wide road. Valençay was originally built in 1540 by Jacques d'Estampes, who had married the daughter of a wealthy financier. She brought with her a large dowry, so d'Estampes demolished the existing château and began to build a new one more in keeping with his new position as a man of wealth.

Because of various factors, including financial constraints, the château was never finished, and it has only two wings instead of the four which were planned. Talleyrand, the famous Minister under Napoleon, bought Valençay in the early 19th century, as a prestigious place for the emperor to

Cranes strut proudly where Talleyrand, Napoleon's Minister, once walked in the grounds of the château of Valençay.

entertain important foreign guests. Lovely though it is, with beautiful furniture and art treasures in the salons, with wax figures of Talleyrand and other courtiers dressed in period costume, the tour of the building is not very good. With everything roped off in the rooms, it would be far better if the system used at Cheverny and Chenonçeau was implemented here. The English "translation" is completely inadequate and the *grande salle-à-manger* and kitchens cannot be seen as part of the tour. An extra fee must be paid, and they are only open at certain times, normally by booking in advance which is very disappointing. There is, however, a very interesting automobile museum in the park—a superb collection of more than 60 cars of all kinds, all of which are in working order. There are some early models with right-hand drive; so that the driver could see the curb! One model had the steering wheel in the centre! Also in the park are deer, llamas, black swans and flamingoes, as well as other animals and birds.

Car Tours, Walks and Cycling in Orléans, the Sologne and Bourges

The whole region of the Sologne and the Northern Berry has a network of small country roads which are ideal for leisurely touring. With the aid of a good map, it is possible to find the way along the very small country roads, seeking out the many private châteaux in the area, which are marked on the map, and which may often be seen from the road. In addition, the river Loire can be followed from **Orléans** to **La Charité-sur-Loire**, much of the way being close to the banks of the river. Between **Briare** and **la Charité** a very pleasant road follows the banks of the **Canal Latéral de la Loire**.

A Tour of Some Sologne Villages. Distance approx. 194km (122 miles)

Leave Orléans by way of **Pont George V** in the direction of **Olivet**. Go straight ahead, under the N20 road bridge and about 500 m (550 yards) after crossing the bridge over the Loiret turn left in the direction of **La Source** and the **Parc Floral** to **Saint-Cyr-en-Val**. In the village, turn right along the D108 road to **Marcilly-en-Villette**, go left along the major D921 road for a few metres then turn right opposite the cemetery on the D64 which leads to **Sennely** and **Souvigny-en-Sologne**. The road numbers change twice on the way, becoming first the D17 and then the D126. Take some time to wander round the little village of Souvigny and admire the old houses and the lovely church.

Go south to **Chaon**, then turn left and follow the D126a, which becomes the D77 when you cross the boundary into Cher *département*, and leads to **Brinon-sur-Sauldre**, another picturesque village. Go east from here along the D923 towards **Clémont**, then north through the village, turning right to take the minor road (D176) which passes the **château de Lauroy**. After about 5 km (3 miles) turn left along a

narrow road leading to the **Etang du Puits**. Approaching the lake you pass the sluices on the now defunct **Canal de la Sauldre**. The Etang is a very pleasant place to have a picnic, and there are also opportunities for swimming. Continue ahead to the main road (D948) and follow this into the little town of **Argent-sur-Sauldre**. If you are interested in châteaux, it is worth the 8km (5 mile) diversion to see **Blancafort**, to the east along the D8 road. From Argent, go south along the D940 to **Aubigny-sur-Nère**.

It is well worth stopping for a walk round this lovely little town and its beautiful park. Leave the town by the D89 road which leads to **Château de la Verrerie**. If you arrive at a time when the château is closed, or if you do not have time to go in, do park to one side of the road and get out to admire the reflection of the château in the lake. Turn round and follow the D39 through the **Forêt d'Ivoy** to reach the D926 in the middle of the forest at **Le Grand Rond**, a junction of some ten roads and tracks which converge at this point. Turn right here and follow the main road to **La Chapelle d'Angillon**.

From here, take the D12 north-east to **Presly**, then continue in a westerly direction across the heaths and woods of the Sologne along road D29E. At the junction with the D79 turn left in the direction of **Neuvy-sur-Barangeon**, and in 500 m (550yd) turn right in the direction of Nançay. After about 5km (3 miles) take the right-hand fork, which brings you to the major D29 road.

Turn right again to the radio telescope, where there is a large car park and information boards. From here, continue north to **Souesmes** and **Pierrefitte-sur-Sauldre**, another attractive village with an interesting church. From here, take the D55 and D923 to **Lamotte Beuvron**, passing several châteaux, most of which can be seen from the road. From Lamotte Beuvron take the main road north to Orléans through **La Ferté-Saint-Aubin**.

A Tour Up-river from Orléans. Distance approx. 188km (118 miles)

Leave Orléans on the road which follows the northern bank of the Loire (the D460) to **Chécy** and **Saint-Denis de l'Hôtel**. If you have the time, stop here to admire the lovely gardens beside the river. Continue along this road to **Châteauneuf-sur-Loire**, another place where there are some lovely gardens. Continue through the town, then take the road off to the right, the D60, to **Germigny-des-Prés** and **Saint-Benoît-sur-Loire**. Continue to **Saint-Père-sur-Loire**. The road lies on top of the embankment for part of the way, and continues almost as far as **Ouzouer-sur-Loire**. From the road there are excellent views across the river to the **château of Sully**.

Keeping to the northern bank, there is a choice of route at Ouzouer. Either turn south and follow the river bank, passing the huge nuclear power station at **Dampierre**, or, if you prefer to avoid this, take the main road (D952). Either way, the route will bring you into **Gien**. Stop here for a look at the château (hunting museum), a visit to the faïence factory, or simply for some shopping or a meal. Continue, again

on the northern bank, to **Briare**. Go right into the town centre and park the car on the quay near the end of the **Pont-Canal**.

Walk along the tow-path across the bridge, and return on the opposite side. This is a superb example of 19th-century engineering. With luck you will see some canal traffic using the aqueduct, although these days it is only used by pleasure craft. Walk back into the little town to the harbour basin. The boats have to make quite a complicated journey through several locks to reach the basin from the canal. Continue to **Bonny-sur-Loire**, and if you are there during the weekend make a diversion along the D48 north to **Champoulet** and the interesting **Musée des Outils**. This will add about 30km (19 miles) to your journey. Still continuing on the north bank, and into Burgundy, drive as far as **Neuvy-sur-Loire** and cross the river to **Belleville-sur-Loire**. In about 2km (1 mile) turn right along the D951 road which follows the Canal Latéral de la Loire to **Beaulieu** and **Chatillon-sur-Loire**.

A short stop here is worthwhile to see the old locks, **éclus de Mantelot**. To reach them, turn right in the centre of the town and right again just before the suspension bridge. Follow the signs to **les Mantelots**. Go back into the town and turn right again, following the road beside the canal to the end of the Pont-Canal on the south bank of the river at **Saint-Firmin-sur-Loire**. Notice the huge flood doors on either side of the road under the aqueduct.

The road now continues alongside the river Loire itself, passing the **château of Saint-Brisson** high above on the left. Continue for another 5 ½ km

(3 miles) passing under the high new bridge at Gien. There is an excellent view of the town and the château from this side of the river. Continue through **Poilly-lez-Gien** and **Lion-en-Sullais** to **Sully-sur-Loire**.

A stop here to wander through the château park and admire the great fortress is worthwhile. It is also a useful stopping place for refreshments. From Sully the road goes to **Tigy** and **Viennes-en-Val**, each with their own small museums, thence via **Saint-Cyr** and **Olivet** back to Orléans. It is possible to drive with care along the bank of the river through Guilly and Sigloy to Jargeau, then cross the river to return to Orléans To do this, fork right to leave the D951 some 7km (4 miles) after leaving Sully.

The Châteaux of the Sologne. Distance approx. 180 km (113 miles)

This route passes through some more lovely Sologne villages, and by many of the private châteaux to be found in the Sologne. These, though they cannot be visited, may often be seen from the road. Travel across typical Sologne heathland and woodland to reach the greatest château of them all, **Chambord**. However, a visit to this great château should be planned for a separate occasion, preferably going out from Blois. It will not be possible to visit the château on the same day as this tour if you wish to see the inside.

Leave Orléans by crossing the river and taking the D951 along the south bank to **Cléry-Saint-André**. Turn left here and take the D18 to **Jouy-le-Potier**. Just after passing the road to **La Ferté-Saint-Aubin** on the left, there is another turning; go down this road, passing the **Château du Lude** (not the one of *Son et Lumière* fame), and after a sharp bend in the road go left again to pass another private château. Turn right on reaching the major road and continue towards **Ligny-le-Ribault**. After 5km (3 miles) at the next major road junction, take the D19 road to **Yvoy-le-Marron** and **Chaumont-sur-Tharonne**. Here, take the minor road leading westwards towards **la Marolle-en-Sologne** and after about 7km (4 ½ miles), after passing the château of **Villebourgeon**, go left to **Neung-sur-Beuvron**. Turn right at the main road, then left to follow the D923 along the valley of the Beuvron. At the next main road turn left to **Vernou-en-Sologne**. Turn right and follow the D63 through **Courmemin** towards **Mur-de-Sologne**. This road passes a very attractive brick château beside an *étang* just beyond Vernou, and there are several other peaceful *étangs* along the way.

From Mur-de-Sologne take the minor D20 road north through the **Domaine de la Morinière** towards **Fontaines-en-Sologne**. Turn right on reaching the major D119 road, then go left again on the D78 to **Cour-Cheverny**.

In the village, to the west of the main road, is the château of **Cheverny**. This graceful, classical mansion cannot be seen from the road but is worth visiting. From here, take the D102 towards **Bracieux**. The **château de Villesavin** is just outside the village, but is behind large wooden gates so cannot be seen from the road. From Bracieux, take the D112 through the forest to **Chambord**. Note that it is not

*H*orse ploughs are still used in some country districts in the Loire.

permitted to stop in the forest, neither are there any facilities for turning round. On reaching Chambord, follow the road to the left around the château, then turn right towards the car park. It is sometimes possible, on a quiet day, and if you want a brief stop, to park under the trees at the edge of the road near the junction with the road to the car park. From Chambord drive along the **Route François 1er** to **Muides** and cross the river to Mer. At the main road, N152,

turn right to **Beaugency**. Here is a good stop for refreshment and a wander through the town before going back to Orléans through **Meung-sur-Loire**.

A Tour through the Hills of Sancerre. Distance approx. 118 km (74 miles)

Leave Bourges by the D940 road north towards **La Chapelle d'Angillon** and **Gien**, and at **Fussy** fork right to **Menetou-Salon**. Stop here to admire the lovely château, and perhaps try some of the local wine from a nearby *vigneron*. Take the road leading from the top right-hand corner of the square to **Parrassy** and **Morogues** (D59)

passing the **Château de Maupas**. If you wish to visit the potteries at **la Borne**, follow the very winding road north from Morogues. Otherwise, continue along the D59 to join the main D955 road to **Sancerre**.

Along this road there are many breathtaking views of the vineyards and hills of Sancerre as you approach the town, some 18km (11 miles) distant. On a clear day the town stands

One of the old mills on the river at Romorantin.

out on top of its own hill, high above the surrounding hills and valleys, a silhouette of the **Tour de Fiefs** and the buildings of the upper town against the clear skies. Park the car at one of the car parks on the old ramparts, and walk into the town. Enjoy the magnificent views over the Loire Valley and into Burgundy from the esplanade **Porte César**, and wander through the old medieval **rue des Vieilles Boucheries**.

Leave the town via the **Rempart des Augustines**, below the esplanade which leads down a winding road to join the tourist road across the viaduct to **Saint-Satur**, and continue into the little village of **Saint-Thibault**, between the canal and the river Loire. Stop on the beach for a swim or a picnic, or simply watch the pleasure boats. Look back up at the wonderful sight of **Sancerre**, high above on the hill, with the viaduct in the foreground.

Take the main road (D955) back towards Sancerre, turning right after 3 ½ km (2 miles) to **Chavignol**. Down the hill is a turning to the left leading to the **Caves de la Mignonne** where a good selection of wines may be tasted. Continue to the village of Chavignol, famous for its goat's cheeses, which can be soft or firm, according to the process of making and maturing. Sometimes they are sold *cendré*, or coated with ashes from burned vines. They are delicious when served hot.

From Chavignol continue up the steep hill through the vineyards to emerge on a small hilltop road beyond a hairpin bend. Turn left here, admiring the view as you turn, continue to a T-junction and turn right to **Menetou-Râtel**. Turn left along the D85 to **Boucard**, stopping a while to admire the outside of this feudal château.

Continue along the D85 to a T-junction in the **Bois de Boucard**, then turn left towards **la Chapelotte**. Take the winding D11 road to **Henrichemont**,

and then the D20 to join the main **Gien** to **Bourges** road. Turn left, and follow this road, which runs through some attractive fruit-growing areas, back to Bourges.

A Tour through The Southern Sologne and Valençay.
Distance approx. 212km (132 miles)

This tour takes in historic **Mennetou-sur-Cher** and **Romorantin**, and the **château of Valençay**, together with the wine-growing area between Valençay and Bourges. Leave Bourges via the main road (N76) to **Mehun-sur-Yèvre**, **Vierzon**, and **Mennetou-sur-Cher**. From here take the D123 north 9km (5 ½ miles), then turn left along the D75 to **Romorantin**. Follow the minor D159 road out of the town, rather than using the main road, to **Pruniers-en-Sologne**. Turn north here and continue to **Château-du-Moulin** near the little hamlet of **Lassay-sur-Croisne**. After visiting the château, return to the main road at Lassay and take the minor road on the right, after the bend in the road, which leads south and then west to **Gy-en-Sologne**. Turn right and go along the narrow country road which leads across the heath to the **Locature de la Straize**, an interesting country museum. Continue to **Soings-en-Sologne**, then turn left along a minor road, passing the **Lac de Soings**, which leads towards Sassay. At the main road, turn left and go south to **Chemery** and **Selles-sur-Cher**.

Still following the main road, continue south to **Valençay**. Visit the château if you wish, and hope it is not too crowded! The grounds and motor museum are, however, well worth

198

visiting. From the château, go south to cross the river Nahon, then turn left along the D960 to **Poulaines**. Go left here, and follow the D16 to **Graçay**, then the D68 through **Nohant-en-Graçay** to **Reuilly**. This, together with Quincy, is another of the smaller wine-growing areas of the Berry, and the furthest south of the "Loire" wine region.

From Reuilly, take the main road towards **Vierzon**, then, where the road turns sharp left, continue ahead to **Quincy**. This is a typical wine-growing village, which has been producing wine for centuries. In fact, it was only the second district in France to receive an *appellation d'origine contrôlée*. From here, continue to **Mehun-sur-Yèvre** and return to **Bourges** along the minor D60 road along the river valley through **Berry-Bouy** and the suburb of **Saint-Doulchard**.

A useful booklet, *Circuits touristiques en Cher-Berry* is published by the *Comité Départemental de Tourisme de Cher* and may be obtained from the main tourist offices. Although the directions are in French, each route is accompanied by a good map marked with road numbers and distances, and is easy to follow. Of the ten routes described, four come within the boundaries of this book, and two more cover a part of the area.

Cycling

With many quiet country roads, this region is ideal for cycling, especially in the **Sologne**. Although it can be hilly in places, notably around **Sancerre**, many of the minor roads are quiet and relatively traffic free, and offer some really enjoyable cycling. With the aid of a good map, sections of the routes described for motorists can be linked by other minor roads to make a good tour. Some of the routes in the booklet described above are also suitable for cyclists.

Walking

There are so many opportunities for walking in this region that one could fill the whole book with good walks. Folders full of leaflets outlining walks in Loiret and Cher are obtainable for a modest fee from local tourist offices, and sometimes from book shops in the area. These are produced by the Comité Départemental de Randonnée Pédestre for the *département* concerned. Local authorities may also produce their own simple maps of local routes. For example, the town of Châteauneuf-sur-Loire has an excellent leaflet with a map showing some eight waymarked circular walks in the area. These may be combined to provide a longer walk if you so wish. The town of Romorantin, in Loir-et-Cher has produced a duplicated leaflet and map describing a circular walk to the west of the town. If you do not want to buy any of these folders—although the leaflets are normally free of charge—then you will find that many local authorities have signed routes in the region, with waymarked trails for both pedestrians and cyclists. An indication is given of the time needed to complete the walk, and whether or not it is circular, returning to the same spot.

You are allowed to walk in the Forêt d'Allogny, Forêt de Boulogne, Forêt de Lamotte-Beuvron, Forêt de Vierzon and Forêt de Vouzeron, provided that you keep to the marked paths and do not enter with vehicles. Always respect the rule of the countryside, being especially careful not to start fires. In the autumn, keep away from areas where hunting may be in progress, and do not stray from the marked trails. Remember that the sign *Chasse Gardée* means private land. In the **Parc de Chambord**, certain areas, which are clearly marked, are open to pedestrians only. Several *Grandes Randonnées* pass through the region, and are marked with the familiar red and white stripes on trees and posts. These are shown on the IGN 1:100,000 maps by an interrupted orange line.

By combining the major walks detailed on the map from **Châteauneuf-sur-Loire**, a walk of some 19km (12 miles) may be taken which links the bridges across the river at Châteauneuf and **Saint-Denis-de-l'Hôtel**. It follows the opposite bank of the river from Châteauneuf to **Jargeau**, where it crosses the river to Saint-Denis. It then runs through the attractive **Parc Henri-Coullaud** and then turns inland to the **Château de Chenailles** before turning east again through the woodlands and back to Châteauneuf. The route is marked with brown markings as far as the end of Parc Henri-Coullaud, when it changes to blue.

Another lovely walk, this time in the Sologne, is centred on the village of **Ménestreau-en-Villette**, not far from **La Ferté-Saint-Aubin**. There are in fact two walks, each 12km (7 ½ miles) long, and each lasting about three hours, although they may be combined to make a day-long trip. The **circuit de l'étang du donjon** is signed by brown wooden finger posts, and follows part of the *Grande Randonnée* from Gien to Chambord. The walk starts in the centre of the village; go to the right of the village store, past the church towards the *mairie* and keep straight ahead on the road towards **Moinard**. In about 500 metres leave the road and take a track on the left leading to the woods ahead. At the cross-tracks, take the junction on the right, following the *Grande Randonnée* until you reach the tarmac road again. Go straight ahead on a forest road for approx. 1km (½ mile) and you will come to the *étang*, which you cross. On the left is a path which you follow as far as the D17 road to **La Ferté-Saint-Aubin**. Turn left, and a short distance after passing the power lines take the road on the right, following it round under the power lines. Just beyond them is a path on the right which you take, then keep straight on in the same direction until the path meets another track.

Go to the right descending to cross an open area where you can see, on the left, the **château du Mazuray**. Follow the track through the woods to the **Etang du Ménil**, and the *étang communal*, from where it is a short walk back to the village.

From Sancerre, there is a lovely walk around the hillside which offers some superb panoramas, and it continues to the nearby hill, l'**Orme au Loup**, from where there are views of Sancerre itself. Although it is only 5km (3 miles) long, allow plenty of time, not only to admire the views but to allow for the steep ascents on this walk.

Park in **rue Honoré de Balzac**, one of the roads leading off the big road junction at the edge of the town, and which is now part of a *Route Touristique*. Walk along this road which runs round the hillside. From it there is a fine panoramic view of the nearby vineyards, the hilltop villages of **Amigny** and **Bué** to your left and the **Bois de Charnes** ahead of you to the north. At one point you can see the church tower of Chavignol.

On the other side of the hill you come to a steep road which descends to **Saint-Satur**. The viaduct at **Fontenay** seems very close, and **Cosne-sur-Loire** can be seen in the distance across the valley beyond. Turn right to climb the steep, winding road leading to the road junction below the **Esplanade de la Porte César**. Take the steep road ahead to the bottom of the hill and at the "stop" sign continue downhill for a few metres, then turn right onto a track which runs through the vineyards. This leads to the source of a little stream which feeds the **étang du Manoir**, and then reaches the **croix de Pignol**.

At this point the route meets the GR31; turn left and follow the red and white waymarks for about 500 m (550 yds). Leave the GR to climb to the right by the stony track between the vines. **Sancerre** begins to appear, its old houses grouped together on the summit, and, on the slopes, more modern houses which rather spoil the view.

Soon you reach the access road to the old flint quarries which have cut deeply into the side of the hill, the **Colline de l'Orme au Loup**. Turning around, you can see the whole of Sancerre, covering the peak and the western slopes of the hill. Follow the track which contours around to the left, and when you reach the road climb to the top of the rise.

As you come out of the woods, a new panorama unfolds over the vineyards of **Amigny** and **Bué**. In the far distance you can see the extent of the **Champagne Berrichonne**, and to the left are the wooded hills of **Humbligny** and **la Borne**. The route now descends to join the road from **Vinon** to **Sancerre**, now not too far away.

There are several other possibilities in this area. By walking a short section of the waymarked *Grande Randonnée* from **Sancerre** to **Chavignol** and returning by road, a good walk through the vineyards can be made, some 8km (5 miles) long. Going the other way, you can walk from Sancerre down to **Ménétréol**, by the river, and along to **Saint-Thibault** and **Saint-Satur**, returning along the viaduct and up the steep hill into Sancerre. This makes a walk of about the same distance.

A Land of Contrasts—from Châteaux to Cave Dwellings

This chapter covers the old administrative area of Touraine, together with a small part of the present *département* of Loir-et-Cher lying mainly to the south of Blois. Part of the area lies between the Loire and its tributary to the south, the Cher, and this is the part called the garden of France. Along the Loire valley and throughout Touraine there are a great number of interesting châteaux, some famous and others not so well known but worth seeing.

Blois

Blois, the first major town when travelling downstream along the Loire from Orléans, should be approached from the south if possible. The old town is situated on rising ground on the north bank of the river, which was originally crossed by a medieval bridge lined with houses. This bridge was

The magnificent west front of the cathedral of Saint-Gatien, whose 16th-century towers overlook the city of Tours. The soft limestone used for the intricate carvings is in constant need of repair and restoration.

destroyed by a flood in 1716 and replaced in 1726 by the present elegant structure, named **Pont Jacques Gabriel** after its designer.

The **château** stands on a rocky promontory overlooking the river and, together with the high tower of Blois Cathedral, is most impressive. The first reference to a château on the site was in the 9th century, and successive Counts of Blois rebuilt the fortress several times before the end of the 13th century. It is one of the most important of the Loire châteaux and is easily reached from the river bridge by following **rue Denis Papin** to **place Victor Hugo**, thence to **place du Château**. The main entrance to the château is surmounted by a carved equestrian statue of Louis XII, very strongly

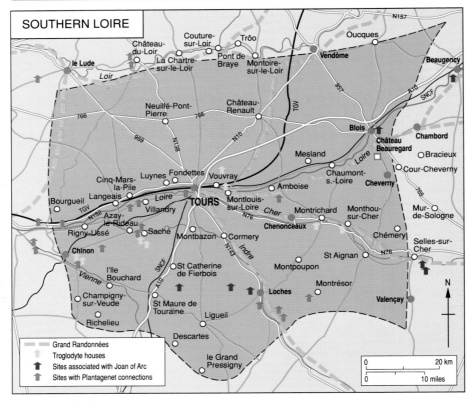

SOUTHERN LOIRE

Map of the Blois, Tours and Southern Touraine region; southern Loire valley.

Gothic in style, erected in 1857 to replace the original statue destroyed during the Revolution. If you stand in the central courtyard you can see buildings from the 13th to the 17th century, reflecting the architecture and the history of the period. In the same way history has stamped its mark upon the city, leaving a rich inheritance of old buildings in the steep and narrow streets overlooking the river.

At the end of the 14th century the county of Blois was sold to Prince Louis of Orléans, son of Charles V. In 1498 his grandson became Louis XII, King of France, and Blois became the capital of the kingdom until part way through the 16th century, after which time the kings of France only paid short visits to the town.

After a period of neglect and following the Revolution, the château was saved from demolition by becoming a military barracks. In 1810 it was presented to the city and subsequently restored. Finally, after further damage in 1944, it has again been restored. The largest remaining parts of the medieval 13th-century château comprise a corner tower, the **Tour du Foix**, parts of the ramparts, and in the north corner the **Salle des Etats**

Généraux (the council chamber of the Counts of Blois), which has survived almost unchanged since it was built in the early 13th century. On the walls are two 17th-century tapestries. Adjoining this hall, along the eastern side of the central courtyard, is the so-called **Louis XII wing**, part of the Renaissance château from the end of the 15th and early 16th centuries.

Between 1498 and 1501 Louis XII had the early fortress transformed into a royal residence, built of brick and stone in contrast to the medieval

*T*own plan of Blois.

fortress. The façade fronting on to the central courtyard has galleries, balconies and windows enhanced by carvings including the porcupine and ermine emblems of the king and his consort, Anne of Brittany. At each end of the arcaded gallery facing the courtyard, spiral staircases give access to the upper floors. The grand staircase adjacent to the old Council Chamber leads to a **Museum of Fine Arts**, beautifully furnished and decorated and exhibiting some fine 16th- and 17th-century paintings and portraits, together with musical instruments, ceramics, costumes and examples of the former clock-making industry of Blois. The remaining portion of the Louis XII wing

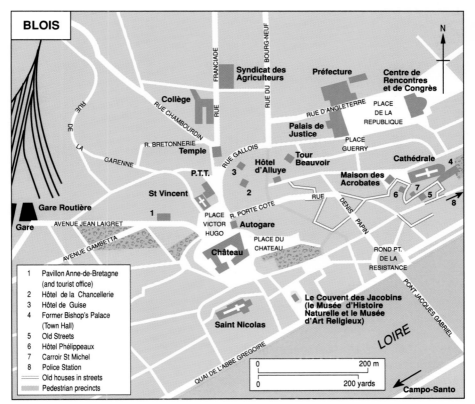

1 Pavillon Anne-de-Bretagne (and tourist office)
2 Hôtel de la Chancellerie
3 Hôtel de Guise
4 Former Bishop's Palace (Town Hall)
5 Old Streets
6 Hôtel Phélippeaux
7 Carroir St Michel
8 Police Station
══ Old houses in streets
░░ Pedestrian precincts

The main entrance to the château of Blois is surmounted by an equestrian statue of Louis XII which although Gothic in style only dates from 1857—the original was destroyed at the time of the Revolution.

consists of the **Chapel of St Calais**, built in 1508, of which only the chancel remains. It was originally the private chapel of the royal couple, and again follows strong Gothic traditions. War damage from 1944 has been repaired and the stained glass windows by Max Ingrand date from 1957.

The north-west side of the courtyard is occupied by the **François I wing**, built between 1515 and 1524 and largely an adaptation of parts of the original 13th-century fortress. It is one of the very earliest examples of French Renaissance work, and although still exhibiting Gothic influence it became, with its decorative schemes and moulded ornamentation, the pattern for many of the Loire châteaux.

The outstanding feature of the courtyard façade of the François I wing is the octagonal spiral staircase with its three open balconies looking on to the court. The openwork of the side walls and the delicate carvings are a masterpiece. The wing contains a number of splendid state apartments, largely restored and furnished with period objects relating to the history and time of François I and Henri III. The chamber once occupied by Catherine de Medici is situated on the first floor.

On the second floor is the Council Chamber, scene of the murder, in 1588, of the Duke of Guise, at the

During its various periods of alteration and enlargement, the château of Blois gained a whole wing built under the orders of François I. An outstanding example of early French Renaissance work, it includes this masterpiece, a carved octagonal spiral staircase.

instigation of King Henri III whose chamber adjoins this room. It is still possible to see traces of the older fortress buildings where these have been incorporated into the later reconstruction.

The ground floor houses an **Archaeological Museum** with exhibits from Blois and Loir-et-Cher regions dating from prehistoric and Gallo-Roman times. The **Robert-Houdin Museum** is in a small circular room, part of the older building, and illustrates the work of a famous 19th-century illusionist, scientist and inventor, and former citizen of Blois.

The largest part of the present-day château is the **Gaston d'Orléans** wing, facing the Louis XII wing across the central courtyard. Originally, Gaston d'Orléans, exiled brother of Louis XIII, intended to demolish all the older buildings and replace them with a palace comprising four wings built in the classical style. Work on this impressive structure continued from 1635 to 1638, but it was never completed owing to financial restrictions. This wing houses the Municipal library and large conference and concert halls.

Visitors to the château may see an audio-visual presentation before going around the various rooms, and a leaflet and excellent guidebook in English are available. Each year, the château provides the setting for *Son et Lumière* performances from April to September, some performances being in English.

An excellent view of the fine **Façade des Loges** of the François I wing may be obtained from the **Pavillon Anne de Bretagne**, which now houses the tourist information office. The Pavillon once stood in the vast gardens of the château, of which only the small **Jardin du Roi** remains, overlooking place Victor Hugo. From the terrace on the place du Château there are magnificent views over the city and towards the river. Below is the **Jacobin Convent**, dating from the 15th and 16th centuries and now home to a **Museum of Religious Art** and a **Natural History Museum**. Nearby is the church of **St Nicolas**, built as an abbey church between 1136 and the 14th century. There is a particularly fine view of this building from across the river. Nearer the château, on the north side of place Victor Hugo, is the church of **St Vincent** built in the mid-17th century. Some streets in the centre of the city have been pedestrianized and there is a good choice of shops.

Scattered through the steep streets are some interesting buildings, many having been built for court officials, or for the wealthy merchants and others who were attracted to the royal town to serve those who served the king. One of the finest is the **Hôtel d'Alluye** in rue St Honoré. Built in 1508 as a private mansion for the Treasurer to three successive kings, the façade with Gothic Renaissance sculptures conceals a courtyard surrounded by Italian Renaissance galleries. The building is now occupied by an insurance company, and the courtyard may be viewed during office hours on request.

In contrast, the nearby **rue Beauvoir**, with half-timbered houses and a 15th-century stone house, gives access to the **Tour Beauvoir**, a 10th-century square keep which was later incorporated into the town's fortifications.

Dominating the eastern side of the city is the cathedral of **St Louis**. The present building is rather strange looking from the outside, as the tower appears not to match the remainder of the structure. A church existed on the site in the 9th century, the crypt of which still remains. A larger cathedral with a high Renaissance tower was built in the 16th century but was almost completely destroyed by a hurricane in 1678, only the west front and the tower remaining. Rebuilding and enlargement resulted in the present cathedral, with a graceful, light and imposing interior and the odd-looking tower from the earlier building. The organ was presented by Louis XIV, the Sun King, in 1704.

Behind the cathedral the old **Bishop's Palace**, built about 1700, has been used as the Town Hall since 1940. From the ornamental gardens there is a wonderful view over the lower city and river.

Beyond the cathedral towards the eastern outskirts is the modern **Basilica of Notre-Dame de la Trinité**, built between 1937 and 1949, and containing some fine stained glass. The 61m (200ft) high campanile offers outstanding views and houses one of the finest carillons in Europe, comprising 48 bells. Beyond the basilica a modern bridge, **Pont Charles de Gaulle**, carries the N252 road across the river to join the Autoroute 10 to the north of the city. On the far side of the city, by way of contrast, is the **Poulain chocolate factory**, opened in 1848 and still very much in business. Visits to the factory may be arranged by telephoning 54-78-39-21 (Extension or *poste* 339) in advance. Finally, across the river on the south bank is the cloister of **St Saturnin**. Formerly a cemetery with timber-roofed galleries built around 1515, it is now a museum housing a collection of fragments of sculpture from old houses, churches and other historical buildings which no longer exist. Concerts are also held here and in the adjacent church of **St Saturnin**.

A Walk Through the City

With its network of steep narrow streets and flights of steps, the only practical way to see the many interesting buildings and scenes in the old town is to walk. A convenient starting point is place Victor Hugo with its attractive flower beds and fountain. The walk can follow a visit to the château, and a call at the tourist information office in the **Pavillon Anne de Bretagne** off avenue Jean Laigret may be worthwhile. After looking around the church of **St Vincent** and glancing back at the château, leave place Victor Hugo on the north side along rue Porte Côté. After a few metres turn left along rue Chémonton, a very steep street. At the corner of rue du Lion Ferré on the right is the **Hôtel de la Chancellerie** (late 16th century) with a rare framework and wooden archway over the main entrance. Further up rue Chémonton on the left (no. 18) is the Renaissance **Hôtel de Guise** with a frieze of medallions along the front. Return and turn along rue du Lion Ferré, most of the buildings along which date from the time of Louis XII. They have not all been well preserved but no. 7 has a beautiful medieval turret.

Turn left at the end of the street, then first right into rue St Honoré to see the fine **Hôtel d'Alluye** a mansion from 1508, to which reference has already been made. At the end of the street, a turn to the right reveals the top of **l'Escalier Denis Papin**, a flight of steps down which one can look right across the **Jacques Gabriel bridge** far below. Halfway down the steps is a statue of Denis Papin.

Go right down the graceful flight of steps and turn left down rue Haute, lined with beautiful façades from many periods, then left into rue Pierre de Blois. This leads into an area of narrow, winding medieval streets and alleys, linked by steep flights of steps, and offering fascinating glimpses of old houses and courtyards, many of which

> **Denis Papin—An Inventive Genius**
> Denis Papin was born in 1647 of an old Huguenot family in Blois. He was an engineer and medical doctor who worked in England and Germany during the Huguenot persecution in France, and never returned to his native land. He worked with Boyle in England and became a member of the Royal Society. A century before Watt perfected his steam engine, Papin had developed a steam-operated piston machine, and his invention of the "marmite de Papin" was the forerunner of the pressure cooker. In Germany he built and tested the world's first steamboat on the River Weser in 1707. Papin returned to London but his resources ran out and he died in poverty in 1714.

have been restored with care. You are sure to find some fresh detail or unexpected view here. The first house in rue Pierre de Blois dates from the late 16th century and has a beautifully sculptured door bearing the enigmatic motto *"Usu Vetera Nova"*. The street contains several houses ranging in date from the 14th to the 18th centuries, often with exquisitely sculptured doors. One 15th-century half-timbered house completely bridges over the street, and at the top is the **Maison des Acrobates**, dating from the end of the 15th century, with a half-timbered

T *ypical of old Blois are the numerous flights of steep steps. This, l'Escalier Denis Papin, gives a view right down to the Jacques Gabriel bridge far below, past the statue of Denis Papin.*

façade carved with beautiful figures of acrobats and jugglers.

From the top of rue Pierre de Blois enter place St Louis, overlooked by splendid 17th-century façades. Ahead is the cathedral and former Bishop's Palace, now used as the Town Hall. From the south side of the cathedral, two flights of steps descend. From the top of the larger flight, the **Grands Degrés St Louis**, you will gain a fine impression of the medieval town below. Go down the steps and turn left into the steep and narrow rue des Papegaults, one of the principal streets of Blois in the Middle Ages. The name of this street comes from the parrots which used to be used as practice targets for crossbowmen. Now the street displays several fine buildings as targets for modern cameras. The 16th-century **Hôtel Phélippeaux** has a beautiful carved oak doorway, and at no. 10 the **Hôtel Belot** has a lovely courtyard beyond an iron gate.

At the top of the street turn right in front of the entrance to the ornamental gardens and descend the steps of the **Petits Degrés St Louis** into rue du Puits-Châtel, originally occupied as military lodgings and prisons but then upgraded during the time of Louis XII. Some houses still have bars over the lower windows, but the results of the raising of the status of the dwellings may be seen in the façades, balconies and carving.

Turn right at the bottom of the steps, along the street, and at no. 15 there is an alley called **Cour des Miracles** which leads to a group of medieval houses. Further down the street turn left into rue du Grenier à Sel and go down here to place Vauvert and

right into rue Vauvert, where there is a delightful little botanical garden. Go along rue Vauvert to the corner, where on the left is the **Fontaine des Elus**, next to a bakery. Turning right along rue Fontaine des Elus leads to rue des Juifs, but note the lovely half-timbered gabled house **Carroir St Michel** at the junction of rue du Puits-Châtel and rue des Papegaults on the right.

Continue up rue des Juifs past more fine 16th-, 17th- and 18th-century façades, then turn left down yet more steps into rue des Trois Clefs which leads into the main shopping area of the city. In this street there are three enormous keys as a reminder that this is where the locksmiths and ironworkers used to carry on their trade. The street crosses the wide rue Denis Papin, the main shopping street which leads directly to the **Jacques Gabriel bridge**.

Even in the centre of the modern shopping district there are half-timbered façades dating from the 16th century above many of the shop fronts. At the corner of rue des Trois Clefs turn right into rue du Commerce, noting the particularly fine half-timbered façades. Take the second turning on the right into rue Pardessus with more interesting houses, then left at the end into place du Marché Neuf with the 15th-century Puits Quartier or **St Jacques Fountain**.

From here, it is not a very long distance along rue Porte Côté, back to the starting point of the walk in place Victor Hugo. This is a good point for some well-deserved refreshment to be taken. The **Auberge de la Duchesse Anne** on the east side of the square is recommended.

Parks and Gardens

As Blois is set on a hilly slope, there is little scope for extensive parks or gardens within the city. One oasis on a hot day is the place Victor Hugo, lying between the château on one side and the church of St Vincent on the other. Surrounded by a busy road, a garden with fountains, a large cedar tree and benches to sit on provides a welcome resting place after walking up and down the interminable flights of steps linking the steep narrow streets of the old town.

Le Jardin du Roi which is on a high terrace overlooking the Place Victor Hugo is one of the only remaining parts of the once extensive gardens of the château, which originally stretched from there as far as the railway station. The avenue Jean Laigret cuts through where the gardens used to be, separating Le Jardin du Roi from the small gardens surrounding the **Pavillon Anne de Bretagne**, now the tourist information office but built in the time of Louis XII.

Gardens and grass areas on the outer ramparts of the château allow fine views over the river, and so do the pleasant gardens of **la terrasse de l'Evêché,** the terrace and gardens adjoining the former Bishop's Palace behind the cathedral, now the Town Hall.

In the shopping centre of Blois narrow streets such as the rue Porte-Chartraine still have 16th-century façades above modern shop fronts.

Shopping in Blois

The main shopping area of the city lies between rue Denis Papin and the château. The central area, comprising part of rue Commerce and rue Porte Chartraine, with rue St Martin, rue des Trois Clefs and the small streets between rue Commerce and the southern section of rue Denis Papin, is pedestrianized so that the whole area forms a very pleasant shopping precinct. At 29, rue Denis Papin is the department store **Le Printemps**. With the local chocolate factory it is not surprising that there are a number of very good *patisseries* to tempt the eye and the appetite. A good variety of boutiques, jewellers, gift shops, antique dealers, book shops and others, covering all price ranges, can be found within this central area. Restaurants, cafeterias, *crêperies* and pizzerias are to be found to suit all requirements. There are a number of shops selling Loire wines, particularly those of Touraine.

Hypermarkets are situated on the north of the city off avenue de Châteaudun (E. Leclerc) and south off D956 at **Vineuil** (Euromarché). A number of shops and other establishments display a sign saying "No Francs? No Problem!" in English. These shops will accept payment in any European currency, as well as in dollars and yen! This is in addition to the usual acceptance of credit cards or Eurocheques.

The Surrounding Area

About 4km (2½ miles) north-east of the city along the D951 road towards Orléans, on the south bank of the river, is the **Lac de Loire** , where a barrage has been built across the river to form a lake with facilities for water sports, other leisure facilities and a campsite.

Further Afield

About 20km (12 miles) to the northeast of Blois in an area of open farming country dotted with small villages lies **Talcy**, which would be unremarked but for the gables and turrets of the château. The two-storied keep is joined to only one wing, the other having been destroyed by fire.

Talcy is rather off the normal tourist track, so retains its quiet rural charm, and the château, although rather severe on the outside, has been kept in its original state inside. Furniture, hangings, *objets d'art* and kitchen equipment remain as they were in the early 16th century, and include Flemish and Aubusson tapestries. The 13th-century fortified manor was enlarged and altered in the late 15th and early 16th centuries, and has a covered well in the courtyard. The garden has been restored to its original appearance and a large dovecote and 400-year-old wine press add to the interest.

Historically, Talcy was the place where, in 1562, Catherine de Medici arranged a fruitless meeting between Catholic and Protestant leaders to try and resolve their differences. The original owner was a rich businessman who was the French king's banker. He was also father of Cassandre, the young girl who inspired the poet Ronsard to write his *"Amours de Cassandre"*. There is a well-restored wooden post mill outside the village. Both the mill and the château may be visited.

About 8km (5 miles) up-river from Blois on the north bank of the river Loire is a complete contrast in the form of the château of **Ménars**, begun in 1637 then coming into the possession of Madame de Pompadour in 1760. It has been described as unequalled as an example of graceful domestic architecture of the age of elegance. The original central part of the building was extended by the addition of two wings and other outbuildings. The château is surrounded by terraces and gardens which extend to the river bank, but unfortunately neither château nor the grounds are open to the public. However, a good view may

T he portrait gallery in the elegant little château of Beauregard is notable for its unusual collection of over 300 historical portraits of royalty and contemporaries from the reign of Phillipe VI to Louis XIII.

be obtained from the road on the opposite side of the river.

 South from Blois in the Forest of Russy, overlooking the green valley of the river Beuvron is the small elegant Renaissance **Château of Beauregard**, said to have been built around 1520 as a hunting lodge for François I, and subsequently owned by various Ministers of State. It is not one of the major châteaux listed on the tourist trails,

but it is wonderful inside. Of particular interest are the panelled and painted study, and the long gallery whose walls carry no less than 363 portraits of 15 sovereigns of France and other notables of the times. The ceiling is also painted, and even more remarkable is the floor covering of Delft tiles bearing pictures of soldiers of the time of Louis XIII. With a rare 16th-century kitchen, the whole building is well worth a visit.

Down the hill from Beauregard is the little village of **Cellettes**. There are vineyards in this area and the growers have formed a consortium based in

B eauregard also has a particularly fine painted ceiling in the small Cabinet des Grelots.

214

Chitenay to produce white wines under the Cheverny VDQS appellation.

Some 8km (5 miles) south of Chitenay, just to the west of Fresnes, lies the château of **Roujoux**. The estate has been turned into a leisure park and the château and grounds with various amusements, model railway, small zoo and animated puppets is called "*Le Château Enchanté*". The admission charges seemed excessive for what was provided. Along the river valley to the west is the little village of **Fougères-sur-Bièvre** standing among nursery gardens, and dominated by its château. The Renaissance building was built close to the original 11th-century square keep in 1470 and has fine wooden doors and beams. All the furniture was removed when the castle was used as a spinning mill during the last century, but it is now open to visitors.

About 10km (6 miles) south-west in an agricultural area, the town of **Pontlevoy** has been the setting for a Benedictine abbey since 1034 and became a notable centre of learning under the tutelage of such prominent figures as Cardinal Richelieu.

The scope of the educational establishment, opened here in 1644, was widened in 1776 to include an *Ecole Royale Militaire* which gave military training to scholars selected by the king from among the gentry.

Today, the former abbey provides technical training related to road transport, and in the old riding school is the **Musée du Poids Lourds**, a collection of some 20 trucks built between 1910 and 1960 illustrating the technical development of road transport. In the west wing of the main building, up a splendid staircase, are two floors devoted to outstanding collections of photographic prints and plates, models and other material relating to local village life and early ventures into publicity, the latter being the work of the founder of the Poulain chocolate factory in Blois.

The abbey church was damaged during the Hundred Years War with England, and was only partly rebuilt in the late 15th century. In the abbey refectory can be seen a large Delftware stove, one of four commissioned by Maréchal de Saxe for the château of Chambord.

Two other museums in Pontlevoy are the archaeological museum in the **Maison du Carroir Doré**, covering prehistoric, Gallo-Roman and medieval history, and the **Musée de la Course Automobile** which has cars and information relating to Formula 1, 2 and 3 international motor racing.

About 8km (5 miles) south-east of Pontlevoy, near the village of Monthou-sur-Cher and approached along a long winding road, is the picturesque Renaissance **Château of Gué-Péan**, square in plan with three pointed towers and one with an unusual bell-shaped top. Built as a country house in the 16th and 17th centuries on the site of a feudal castle, it stands in a wooded valley surrounded by parkland.

The château has, in its time, hosted among others Louis XII, François I, Henri II and Henri III, and is now in private ownership and inhabited, but is open to the public. It was in the private chapel of this château that Mary of York, sister to Henry VIII of England secretly married Charles Brandon,

Duke of Suffolk, following the death of her first husband Louis XII. Mary was the grandmother of the ill-fated Lady Jane Grey, so again we see how the history of England and of this part of France are so closely interwoven. Apart from the furnishings of the various rooms, reflecting their past and present use as a family home, the library contains a valuable collection of souvenirs, while of special interest is a small exhibition devoted to the wartime Resistance movement, in which the present owner, the Marquis de Keguelin, played a leading part. It is possible to stay at this château as a paying guest.

The southern edge of Loir-et-Cher lies more or less parallel with the valley of the attractive river Cher, across which lies the town of **Saint-Aignan**. A good view of the château and church can be obtained from the island in the river or from the bridge.

Standing in parkland in a wooded valley, the château of Gué-Péan saw the secret marriage of Mary of York, sister of England's notorious Henry VIII, to Charles Brandon, Duke of Suffolk, following the death of her first husband, Louis XII of France.

Old streets with 15th-century stone and half-timbered houses lead to **St Aignan's** church, dating from the 11th and 12th centuries, with a crypt decorated with frescoes from the same and later periods and surmounted by an impressive tower. From the porch of the church a great flight of steps leads up to the château courtyard from which there is a fine view over the town. The earliest parts date from the 14th century with later additions, but only the courtyard is open to the public. The long distance walking route GR 41 passes through St Aignan and two local *Sentiers de Petite Randonnée* of 16km (10 miles) and 10km (6 miles) respectively are described in a leaflet (no. 198) published as part of a set under the title *Circuits pédestres en Loir-et-Cher*. A short distance south of the town on the road D675 is the **Parc Ornithologique de Beauval** with an exceptional collection of exotic birds. The park is devoted to the breeding of threatened species and is open daily.

The country to the south lies just within the eastern boundary of the *département* of Indre-et-Loire, and the long straight road south from Beauval leads to **Nouans-les-Fontaines**. In the 13th-century church is a very fine painting of the Descent from the Cross, attributed to Jean Fouquet (1420–1480). The quality of the painting is unusually good for a provincial church. Across the road is **Le Lion d'Or**, a small restaurant offering good simple food cooked in the traditional way at a reasonable price.

About 8km (5 miles) to the west, in attractive countryside, lies the little town of **Montrésor** on the banks of the river Indrois, a tributary of the Indre. The 16th-century Gothic church houses the tomb of the Bastarnay family who built the present château. The curtain wall and ruined towers were built by Foulques Nerra in the 11th century, and the present residence was added within the original walls, from which attractive views over the town and river can be obtained.

The half-wild gardens are very attractive, and the interior of the château, restored by the Polish Count Branicki in 1849, remains just as he left it. The château contains a **Museum of Polish art** which may be visited, and is owned by descendants of the count. The town with its cobbled streets, stone cottages and medieval timber market is well worth a visit.

North towards the river Cher is the imposing-looking château of **Montpoupon** overlooking a wooded valley. Only the towers of the original 13th-century fortress remain, the main buildings having been added in the 15th century. The château has been inhabited almost continuously ever since by a family with a great interest in hunting. In the stables is a fine display of hunting costumes and souvenirs together with carriages, harness and trophies of the chase.

Another fascinating aspect of this establishment is the ancient kitchen which was in use until 1978 and all the copper and other utensils and implements have been preserved, together with beautiful linen and lace garments in the laundry. This is another château which takes paying guests.

Returning to the Cher at St Aignan, the northern bank runs west past more vineyards to **Thésée-la-Romaine**, with a museum in the *Mairie* exhibiting finds from local Gallo-Roman sites. The local wine production is mainly handled by a collective based in Oisly, to the north of the forest of Choussy, most of it being white, but with some reds and rosés.

The cliffs along the north bank of the river from east of Thésée downstream past Bourré are riddled with caves, many of them "troglodyte" dwellings. The stone was quarried extensively in the past and the resulting openings often turned into surprisingly comfortable homes, a number of which are still in use. Other caves are used as wine cellars or for growing mushrooms.

In Bourré itself there are very extensive underground galleries from which limestone has been quarried since Roman times and which has been used for building many of the châteaux and houses in Touraine.

The conditions of temperature and humidity which exist in these caves are ideal for the large-scale cultivation of mushrooms, the *champignons de Paris*. This has been going on since the end of the last century, and many tonnes of mushrooms are produced every year. The mushroom caves are located on the road D62 leading north out of the village and guided tours are available.

Between Bourré and the town of Montrichard, just before the railway bridge, are the **Caves Monmousseau**, cellars under the chalk cliffs belonging to the firm of that name which is owned by the Taittinger champagne house. They are noted for their sparkling Touraine wines made by the *méthode champenoise* and aged in the caves which maintain a constant temperature of 12°C. The cellars are open to visitors during working hours.

Montrichard itself is long and narrow, squeezed between the river and the cliff on which stands the great square keep of the castle, built around 1010 by Foulques Nerra and reinforced by further outer walls in 1109 and 1250. During the struggles between the Plantagenets and the kings of France, Richard Coeur-de-Lion was besieged here by Philippe-Auguste in 1188, and was imprisoned in a cell in the base of the keep for a short time. Much later, in 1940, German artillery virtually destroyed a round tower south of the keep. Although in ruins, it is well worth the admission fee and effort to climb to the top of the keep for the magnificent view over the town and surrounding country. There is a small museum in a room near the entrance.

Below the keep is a flight of steps, the **Grands Degrés Ste-Croix**, leading down into the town. At the top of the steps is the church of **Ste-Croix**, dating partly from the 11th and 12th centuries. It was originally the castle chapel and is now the parish church. Here in 1476 Louis d'Orléans, aged 14, later to become Louis XII, and the 12-year-old Jeanne de France, his cousin, were married.

The town has a number of very interesting old houses dating back to the 11th century.

On the opposite side of the river is a pleasant beach, rather crowded in summer but giving a wonderful view of the keep overlooking the town and church. A short distance further along the valley at **Chissay-en-Touraine** is the **Distillerie Fraise d'Or** where visitors may see and buy the liqueur distilled from locally grown strawberries.

Almost due north from Chissay is **Chaumont-sur-Loire**, on the south bank of the river Loire. The village itself consists of one single street along the bank of the river, while the château is above among tall trees, dominating the landscape. A wooden stronghold occupied the site in AD 980, but the later stone fortress was destroyed and rebuilt several times. Bought in 1560 by Catherine de Medici after the death of Henri II, and later given by her to Diane de Poitiers, favourite of Henri, the decoration and furnishings of some of the rooms mark these events. Subsequently the castle passed through various hands.

During the 18th century an Italian named Nini produced fine ceramics in a factory established in the stable block here, using clay from the nearby river,

and a kiln constructed specially in the corner of the stables. Nini produced medallions of famous people such as Benjamin Franklin, who stayed here often.

For a while in 1810 Madame de Staël lived here after being sent away from Paris by Napoleon. In 1875 the château was bought by a very rich sugar-refiner named Say for his daughter, who later married a prince De Broglie. Enormous sums were spent on

refurbishing, altering and modernizing not only the château but most of the village, until the sugar-refining business collapsed.

In 1938, the state bought the château, restored and furnished it and opened it to the public. Guided tours of the interior are very strictly controlled and may not be considered worthwhile by everyone, as not all the rooms are furnished, not having been lived in. However, the exterior with its

views from the 18th-century terrace, the extensive and lavishly fitted stables dating from 1877 and the park and grounds, extended by the De Broglies and containing fine old cedar trees, make it worth paying the entrance fee at the bottom and walking up the long approach through the trees.

A fine view of Chaumont village and château is gained from the bridge over the river and from the north bank, where the village of **Onzain** lies across the main road and railway, against the rising cliffs, separated from the main river by the tributary river Cisse.

At this point along the Loire in June 1856 there was a great flood and the *levée* gave way along a 400m (438yd) length, sweeping away the hamlet of Ecures together with 20 houses, although no lives were lost. A castle existed in Onzain in the time of Louis XI but it was pulled down in the 19th century and only a few stones remain.

In the village a wine co-operative supported by many local growers produces wines under the *appellation* Touraine-Mesland, and wine may be sampled and purchased here. There is an interesting little wine museum in the local tourist office (*Syndicat d'Initiative*).

The river Cisse flows virtually parallel with the Loire eastwards for about 5km (3 miles) to **Chouzy-sur-**

*T*his old wine press mounted on a plinth stands at the entrance to the vineyard of Domaine de Lusqueneau at Mesland.

Cisse, then turns north through a delightful valley, passing a number of villages with churches dating back to the 11th century and interesting manors and old mills, mostly ruined now. Their names make interesting reading —Coulanges, Chambon-sur-Cisse, Molineuf, Orchaise, St-Lubin-en-Vergonnois. The valley curves around the western edge of what remains of the ancient oak forest of Blois, of which an area of about 5km by 8km (3 miles by 5 miles) is criss-crossed by long straight rides which provide good walking. A series of leaflets detailing walks in this area and along the valley of the Cisse are available from local tourist information offices or *Syndicats d'Initiative* in the neighbourhood.

Heading west from the Cisse valley a minor road runs from St-Lubin to **Herbault** where the **Auberge des Trois Marchands** provides good food at very reasonable prices, shown by the fact that it is well patronized by the locals.

South from Herbault through Santenay, this countryside lies at the centre of the production of the Touraine-Mesland wines whose quality is due, in part, to the particular stony soil on which the grapes grow.

In general, the red wines from **Mesland** are most notable although some rosés are produced. The whites, which may only be made from the Chenin Blanc grape, are not always so successful.

The village of Mesland is notable not only for its wines but for its church, which dates back to 1060. Like so many other early Christian churches, it stands on the site of a pagan temple, and incorporates fragments of this earlier structure. In particular the porch, known as the **Porche des Barbus**, bears 26 carved heads with beards.

The local wines may be tasted and purchased at a number of vineyards, one notable *vigneron* being Philippe Brossillon of Domaine de Lusqueneau. Most of their production is red, with small quantities of rosé and white, also some sparkling rosé and white.

By going from Mesland down to the valley of the Loire again, the town of **Amboise** may easily be reached.

Amboise

Amboise is yet another town owing its existence to a natural feature on the river which was fortified in former turbulent times. An island in the middle of the river Loire, **Ile Saint-Jean**, also known as **Ile d'Or**, is now largely occupied by a well-equipped campsite, but it also forms a convenient place for bridging the river. A bridge existed here from very early times, thus making this a strategic position.

A flat-topped hill spur overlooking the river on the south side was the site of a Stone Age settlement, later fortified by a ditch and rampart in the Iron Age. Not surprisingly, in the early 12th century Foulques Nerra built a fortress on the same site, and successive owners altered, strengthened and enlarged the castle until it passed into royal hands. Through the reigns of Charles VII, Louis XI, Charles VIII and Louis XII many changes took place, culminating in a wing finished in the time of François I. Through successive periods of new building and extensions to the

original fortress, alterations and the destruction of older buildings have left the present-day complex much smaller, and a large part of the area within the ramparts is now occupied by the terrace gardens, approached by way of a

*F*ramed *by bunches of mistletoe, the castle and royal residence of Amboise stands above the far river bank.*

The Château of Amboise—Birthplace of the French Renaissance

The entry to the château via the covered ramp leads under the walls and emerges near the entrance to the Chapelle St-Hubert. Built around 1491 it has fine Gothic doors and a carved lintel, with some later additions. Set astride the walls, the chapel is all that remains of the buildings which formerly bordered the ramparts. The largest buildings comprise the two remaining wings of the Logis du Roi, the royal residence built during the reigns of Charles VIII, Louis XII and François I. One wing overlooking the river is Gothic and the other Renaissance. Although visitors may wander freely around the gardens and terrace, to see the interior of the royal apartments, it is necessary to wait and join a party taken round by a guide. Unless there are sufficient numbers of English-speaking visitors to make up a group you will have to follow a French-speaking guide. The tour is very rapid and the English language translations on loan do not match the spoken explanations. Through the Gothic wing and the Salle des Gardes is an arcaded terrace giving a fine view over the Loire valley. The first floor of the Gothic wing includes the Salle de Justice or Court Room which saw, in 1560, the trial of many Calvinist protestors who were subsequently executed on the terrace above the river. Two massive round towers, the Tour des Minimes and Tour Hurtault, are interesting for the spiral ramps inside, large enough to allow horses and riders to enter the castle. During the summer months, *Son et Lumière* performances take place in the château.

*T*he Tour de l'Horloge
in Amboise.

The Genius at le Clos-Lucé

Leonardo da Vinci was granted a pension and offered le Clos-Lucé as his home. Already aged 64, he spent his remaining years peacefully here until his death in 1519 at the age of 67. The house has been restored and furnished in the state it would have been in Leonardo's time, a number of the rooms containing rare and delightful items including paintings, drawings and tapestries. Although none of Leonardo's own pictures is here, there is a museum devoted to his life and works. A video presentation depicting aspects of his work as scientist, engineer, inventor and artist can be followed by a tour around rooms filled with drawings and models built from his original notebooks and sketches. The amazing thing about many of these devices is that they were never actually made during da Vinci's lifetime, as technology was at least three centuries behind his ideas. They only existed in his extremely detailed descriptions and drawings. All the models on display are modern, and prove that his ideas, although far ahead of their time, actually work.

vaulted ramp which was formerly protected by drawbridges. The views over the town and the Loire and its valley and the surrounding countryside from the terrace are magnificent and well worth the admission fees to the castle if the weather is clear. The massive retaining walls overlook the town on the north side.

A pedestrianized shopping street runs from the castle entrance to the 12th-century church of **St-Denis**. The street is dominated by a clock tower built by Charles VIII on the site of one

The bridge linking the main buildings of the château of Chenonceau to the opposite bank of the river Cher was added during the time the property was owned by Diane de Poitiers, and further enlarged by Catherine de Medici.

of the gates in the ramparts. The old **Hôtel de Ville** (Town Hall) now houses a local museum, while on the Loire embankment is a surrealist fountain by

Max Ernst. In the town is an early 16th-century mansion, the **Hôtel Joyeuse**, which now accommodates an interesting **Musée de la Poste** depicting all aspects of postal services through the ages.

Perhaps the most interesting feature of Amboise must be **le Clos-Lucé**, a red brick and stone manor house, originally dating from the 13th century and acquired by Charles VIII in 1490 for his queen, Anne de Bretagne. There is said to be an underground tunnel connecting the house with the château of Amboise. François I spent some time here, and it was he who in-vited that amazing genius Leonardo da Vinci to Amboise in 1516.

Further Afield

The road south from Amboise towards **Bléré** runs through some lovely coun-try, rising some 61m (200ft) above the river and leading into the **Forêt d'Amboise**, mixed woodland with a number of oaks and scattered lakes, formerly the hunting ground for the Valois kings. About 2½ km (1½ miles) out of the town is the **Pagode de Chanteloup**, a strange-looking tower which was copied from the Chinese pagoda in Kew Gardens in England. It

---

Chenonceau—A Pleasant Place to Visit

An estate belonging to the Marques family was sold in 1460 to Thomas Bohier, a tax collector under three kings. Around 1513 he commenced construction of a new château, having demolished all except the keep and moats of the Marques structure, which in turn had replaced an even earlier manor. This third Chenonceau in the form of a square villa with watch towers at each corner was built in the middle of the river and pro-vides a link between the earlier fortress-type buildings and the newer Renaissance coun-try mansions. Much of the work was supervised by Bohier's wife, Catherine Briçonnet, but after his death his son had to relinquish ownership to the crown in 1535 to set-tle the debts incurred in the building. The château was given by Henri II to his mis-tress, Diane de Poitiers, and during her occupation she had extensive gardens created and a bridge with a gallery on top built as an extension to the main building, linking it with the opposite bank of the Cher. On Henri's death his widow Catherine de Medici took over the château, giving Diane the château of Chaumont. Catherine continued the enlargement and embellishment of Chenonceau, including the addition of a three-storey extension on top of the bridge in classical style.

Following her death the château passed through a succession of owners, becoming a Capuchin convent in the 17th century and seeing a number of distinguished guests from the fields of art and literature during the 18th and 19th centuries. It became a military hospital in World War I, and in World War II provided an escape route be-tween occupied France on the north side of the river and the "Vichy" territory to the south. The buildings are set in extensive gardens and the stable block houses a wax-works museum with tableaux depicting the history of the château. There is also an ex-cellent tearoom and restaurant, and it is possible to buy the excellent white, red and rosé wines produced on the estate under the *Appellation Contrôlée Touraine*. The gen-eral charm and attractiveness of Chenonceau may perhaps be attributed to the influ-ence of so many talented ladies over the years of its development, and today the es-tate is owned and managed by the Menier family in a way which could well be copied at other famous tourist attractions in the region.

T hese beautiful formal gardens were created at Chenonceau by Diane de Poitiers during the 16th century.

is a folly built in 1778, and is all that remains of the Château de Chanteloup, built by Louis XV's Chief Minister who offended Mme du Barry, resulting in his banishment to this estate. The house was demolished in 1823, having become disused and neglected.

A picturesque road through the forest leads directly to the village of **Chenonceaux**. The same name spelt without the final "x" is the name almost universally associated with the

great Loire châteaux, yet the **Château of Chenonceau** lies on the river Cher. Not only is it one of the most delightful of all the châteaux, it is also one of the best administered. No groups of tourists herded around by rapidly speaking guides here. On entry you are given an explanatory brochure, well written in the language of your choice (including Japanese!) and invited to walk around. Smartly dressed custodians are to be found in most of the rooms, ready to answer questions should you wish, but otherwise it is a pleasant change to be able to follow a leisurely tour of the rooms, which have explanatory plaques and are also fully furnished, including the kitchens set in the supporting piers in the river bed.

Tours

Tours is the capital of the *département* of Indre-et-Loire, a university town and the see of an Archbishop. Situated in a rich and fertile countryside at an important crossing point of the river Loire, it has a long and varied history. Before Roman times it was the capital of the **Turones**, a tribe of ancient Gaul, and under the Roman occupation it grew in importance. During the 4th and 5th centuries AD Tours became one of the capitals of Christianity, due largely to St Martin, Bishop of Tours. He was followed in the 6th century by Gregoire de Tours (538–594) who wrote the celebrated *History of the Franks*. It became a centre of learning under the influence of Alcuin of York, until the Normans destroyed the abbey. Prosperity was reflected in the fine buildings and trade in luxury silks and gold cloth, but the religious troubles took their toll, as did the Revolution.

The river and bridges maintained the town's importance as a communications centre, boosted by the arrival of the railway in 1846. The city has been involved in several wars in modern times. It was heavily bombarded

Town plan of Tours.

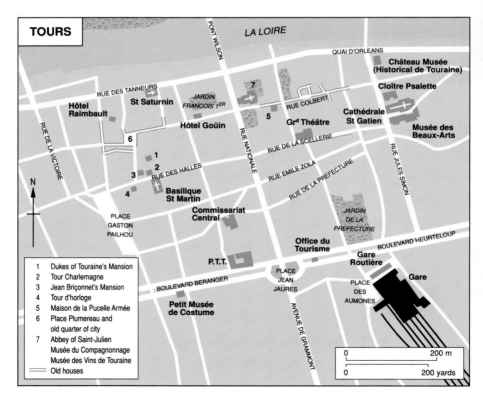

TOURS

LA LOIRE

PONT WILSON

QUAI D'ORLEANS

Château Musée
(Historical de Touraine)

Cloître Psalette

RUE DES TANNEURS

Hôtel
Raimbault

St Saturnin

JARDIN
FRANÇOIS 1ER

RUE COLBERT

Cathédrale
St Gatien

Hôtel Goüin

RUE NATIONALE

Grd Théâtre

Musée des
Beaux-Arts

RUE DE LA SCELLERIE

RUE DE LA VICTOIRE

6

1

2

3

RUE DES HALLES

RUE EMILE ZOLA

RUE DE LA PREFECTURE

RUE JULES SIMON

N

4

Basilique
St Martin

PLACE
GASTON
PAILHOU

Commissariat
Central

JARDIN
DE LA
PREFECTURE

Office du
Tourisme

BOULEVARD HEURTELOUP

Gare
Routière

P.T.T.

PLACE
JEAN
JAURES

PLACE
DES
AUMONES

Gare

BOULEVARD BERANGER

Petit Musée
de Costume

AVENUE DE GRAMMONT

1 Dukes of Touraine's Mansion
2 Tour Charlemagne
3 Jean Briçonnet's Mansion
4 Tour d'horloge
5 Maison de la Pucelle Armée
6 Place Plumereau and
    old quarter of city
7 Abbey of Saint-Julien
    Musée du Compagnonnage
    Musée des Vins de Touraine
═══ Old houses

0   200 m
0   200 yards

and occupied during the Franco-Prussian War of 1870, and was the headquarters of the American administrative centre in World War I. During World War II there was heavy German bombing in 1940 and further damage by Allied bombers in 1944. Since then, much of the damage has been repaired and the city today is a thriving modern industrial and commercial centre stretching over the flat ground between the Loire and the Cher.

The **Pont Wilson**, a stone bridge over the Loire built in the 18th century has had more than its share of trouble. It was blown up by the French in 1940 and by the Germans in 1944, and damaged by floods in 1978. After that it was rebuilt in its original style. The

The interesting gargoyles and lovely Renaissance carving of the Psalette or choir school of Tours date from about 1440 to the early 16th century.

main thoroughfare, the **rue Nationale**, leads south from this bridge and, together with the streets leading from it forms an outstanding shopping centre. Many of the modern buildings have been built to replace large areas of the city destroyed by fire during World War II. Separated by this modern town centre are two areas which survive from the past.

A Serene and Harmonious Design

This description aptly fits the cathedral of Tours with its soaring west front built of tufa limestone which unfortunately has suffered and is still suffering from the ravages of time. Much of the delicate carving is crumbling and is constantly having to be repaired. The whole building took many years to complete and it shows every stage of development from early 13th-century Gothic through to the Renaissance.

The present cathedral stands on a site occupied by three former churches, the first of which was the burial place of St Martin of Tours who died in AD 397. This was replaced by a Frankish church which stood for 400 years. A Romanesque cathedral, traces of which still exist, was destroyed by war and fire after about a century. Construction of the present choir began in 1236 and the pure Gothic carvings show examples of Touraine flora and fauna. Outside, the apse is supported by two tiers of elegant curved flying buttresses. The tall stained glass windows date from about 1260 and more 13th-century windows are to be found in the chapels opening from the choir. In one of the chapels is the tomb of Charles VIII's children, moved here from the Basilique de St Martin. More very fine stained glass including two magnificent rose windows which date from the 14th century are in the transept. The vaults of the nave were raised around 1460 and the great rose window above the west door dates from the same period. Finally the towers, which are not exactly similar, were completed in the 16th century, the same period which saw the installation of the organ. Although not large compared with other cathedrals, so lacking in spaciousness, St Gatien has some exceptional stained glass. Much of this is over 700 years old and by great good fortune survived the bombing of World War II. Leading from the north aisle is the beautiful Cloître de la Psalette (choir school). Part of it dates from about 1440 while the remainder was completed in the early 16th century. The north-east tower contains a fine Renaissance staircase. Converted into an apartment house after the Revolution, the Psalette has now been restored to its original form.

To the east beyond the **Cathédrale St-Gatien** lies the district once occupied by the Gallo-Roman arena, traces of which can still be seen.

The former Archbishop's Palace from the 17th and 18th centuries is overlooked by the cathedral, and faces a very pleasant garden. The building now houses the **Musée des Beaux Arts** with fine collections of furniture and French and foreign paintings from the Middle Ages to the present day.

Between the cathedral and the river Loire is the **Château Royal de Tours**, a royal residence from the 13th to 15th centuries. It was abandoned in the 17th century and partly destroyed in the 18th, the materials being used to strengthen the river dyke. The site was occupied as a military barracks until after World War II; now after years of neglect the château has been renovated and rebuilt by the municipality. A conspicuous round tower, the **Tour de Guise**, survives from the 12th century. Today, the château provides the setting for the **Historiale de Touraine**, a particularly well-planned waxworks exhibition telling the history of Touraine from Roman times to the present century in a series of life-size tableaux. There is also a tropical aquarium within the château complex.

Between the château and rue Nationale are some interesting 15th- and 16th-century houses. To the east of rue Nationale, between rue Colbert and the river, lies the 13th-century abbey church of **St Julien** which, together with other buildings from the former abbey, lies below the level of the present road. Well worth a visit are the **Musée des Vins de Touraine** and the **Musée du Compagnonnage** which occupy the cloisters and cellars of the church. The wine museum is set in the 13th-century wine cellars of the abbey, and a series of displays explains the relationship between wine and mythology, religion, family and social rituals and health, together with well-illustrated explanations of the whole art and science of vine culture and harvesting, wine making and associated trades. The Musée du Compagnonnage may best be explained as a museum devoted to craft guilds. Probably founded by the craftsmen who built the early cathedrals in the 15th century, they were later to become active in the fight to improve workers' conditions. Members of the *compagnonnage* had first to prove their skill and the museum contains many examples of the masterpieces made by various craftsmen in order to demonstrate their ability. The whole museum

*T*wo *interesting museums, dealing with wine and craft guilds, are located in the 13th century cellars and cloisters of the abbey church of Saint-Julien in Tours.*

presents a fascinating picture of social history and sheer excellence of manual skills.

To the west of the modern shops and offices on rue Nationale is the old quarter, much of which was destroyed in World War II. However, the narrow streets lined with half-timbered houses have been very skilfully restored, giving the area a strong feel of the Middle Ages. One survivor of the bombing was the elegant façade of the **Hôtel Goüin** which has been described as the finest Renaissance house in Touraine. A medieval dwelling built on Roman foundations, it was decorated around 1510 by a wealthy Tours merchant. A Breton banking family, the Goüins, owned it from 1738 to 1940, and after restoration following wartime fire damage it is now the **Archaeological Museum of Tours**. Very well-arranged displays cover the prehistoric, Gallic and Gallo-Roman periods and subsequent history of the area.

The **Basilique Saint-Martin** was built in the 19th century to replace an older building from the 13th century which was sacked by the Huguenots in 1562. It fell into disrepair during the Revolution and collapsed. Originally a sanctuary had existed from the 5th century covering the tomb of St Martin but this was destroyed by the Normans. The **Tour Charlemagne**, rebuilt after collapsing in 1928, and the **Tour de l'Horloge** are the two towers of the earlier basilica, and the shrine of St Martin is in the crypt of the modern building, in its original position.

The **Hôtel Raimbault** is an elegant 19th-century mansion which now houses the **Musée du Gemmail**. Here, examples of this modern art form are displayed, using particles of coloured glass illuminated from behind. The stables contain a studio and an underground 12th-century chapel has been decorated using the technique. The **Petit Musée du Costume** contains the R and G Pesché collection of dolls and old mechanical toys. The dolls are beautifully and authentically dressed to illustrate the history of costume through the ages.

A Walk Through the City

The City of Tours has produced a series of leaflets describing walks around the city based on various themes. These are available, in English, from the *Office de Tourisme* near **l'Hôtel de Ville** in boulevard Heurteloup. Guided tours are also arranged by the tourist office if required.

A walk taking in the main places of interest in the old city can start from the tourist office. This walk will take about 2½ hours, not allowing for stops or visiting museums and other buildings.

Walk along boulevard Heurteloup towards the railway station and turn left along rue de Buffon, passing the gardens of the **Parc de la Préfecture**. On the right at the junction with rue de la Préfecture is the 17th-century former Convent of the Visitation which is now the **Préfecture**. Continue ahead to the end of rue de Buffon where the **Grand Théâtre** (Municipal Theatre) was built at the end of the last century over the remains of the Couvent des Cordeliers (Greyfriars' Convent). A door from that church is still visible on the side of the theatre facing rue Voltaire. To the right, rue de la Scellerie has a number of half-timbered house fronts, many of which are occupied by antique dealers. The name of the street recalls its Roman origins, the wall of the old Chancellerie being still visible at no. 93. The street leads to place François Sicard with large plane trees and a statue of Michel Colombe the sculptor. Turn left along rue de la Barre then right into the narrow rue de la Cloche. Right again and an unobstructed view of the west front of the cathedral of **St Gatien** may be had from place de la Cathédrale.

Walk to the east end of the cathedral and place Grégoire de Tours. On the right is the balcony of the **Salle des Etats**, formerly part of the Archbishop's Palace which is now the **Museum of Fine Arts**. From the balcony, judgements of the ecclesiastical court were pronounced. Passing along rue du Général Meusnier which follows the line of the old Gallo-Roman arena, a turning on the right leads into rue des Ursulines. Follow this to the left and a passage leads into a public garden bordered by a section of the Roman city wall built around AD 275. Return along rue des Ursulines to the lawns and shrubberies of the Archbishop's Palace gardens from which the whole front of the palace may be seen. The oldest part is a 17th century mansion. The cedar of Lebanon tree in the courtyard was planted in 1804, and on summer evenings the gardens are lit and classical music is played.

Across place de la Cathédrale, rue Lavoisier leads to the **Château Royale** where the **Historial de Touraine** and the **Tropical Aquarium** are situated. Return along rue Lavoisier and turn right along rue Colbert, a street with many excellent small shops, and a number of interesting old houses along this and the adjoining streets. On the right is place Foire le Roi where François I authorized free fairs to be held in 1545. Medieval market stalls once stood where today there are garden beds. On the right of the square is the **Passage des Jacobins**, at the far end of which, on the right, is the mansion where the poet Ronsard is supposed to have lived. On the left a narrow arch leads into the **Passage du Coeur Navré** (Passage of the Broken Heart) which in turn leads back into rue Colbert.

Turn right and continue, noting numerous half-timbered houses. No. 39 is the **Maison de la Pucelle Armée** (House of the Armed Maiden) standing on the site of the armourer's shop where Joan of Arc's suit of armour was made in 1429. Beyond here on the left rue Jules Favre leads to the **Jardin de Beaune-Semblançay**. This attractive garden lies between rue Jules Favre and rue Nationale and contains the **Fontaine de Beaune** erected in 1511. Here also are the ruins of the 16th- century mansion of Jacques de Beaune, Lord of Semblançay. From the garden go through one of the gates into rue Nationale and turn right. Go down into the cloister of the former abbey of **Saint-Julian** for the **Musée du Compagnonnage** and the **Musée des Vins de Touraine**.

Cross rue Nationale and follow rue du Commerce which leads towards the old city, much of which has been restored following the devastation caused during World War II. Past the **Ecole des Beaux Arts** on the right is the Renaissance front of the **Hôtel Goüin** where the **Archaeological Museum** is located.

This fine Renaissance façade is on the Hôtel Goüin which houses the Tours Archaeological Museum.

Beyond this point is the medieval quarter, beautifully restored with a network of old streets lined with houses of all ages. Turn right down rue Constantine, beside the François I garden, left along rue des Tanneurs then second left into rue Littré. This leads to a small pleasant square facing the church of **Saint Saturnin**, given by Louis XI to the Carmelites in the 15th century. The rue des Carmes passes along the south side of the church. Turn right into rue Paul-Louis Courier, a street with considerable character. At the end, turn right again along rue du Commerce, and enter the pedestrianized zone near **place Plumereau** at the heart of the city's conservation area. The busy square is lined with finely restored half-timbered houses dating from the 15th and 16th centuries. This makes a convenient and pleasant stop for refreshment at one of the many open-air cafés, and a number of the houses on the square will repay closer inspection.

To the north of the square a high arched passage leads to a pleasant garden in place St-Pierre-le-Puellier, where the foundations of an old church and a Gallo-Roman and medieval cemetery have been discovered. Follow rue Briçonnet north then turn left into rue du Murier, where the **Hôtel Raimbault** is situated. Turning left again, rue Bretonneau leads past several more fine mansions. Cross rue du Grand Marché then turn left along rue de la Rôtisserie, still within the pedestrianized zone of the old quarter. At the end, turn right into rue du Change. At the corner with rue de Châteauneuf is a tall 15th-century mansion built for Jean Briçonnet, the first elected Mayor

*M*uch of the old city of Tours was devastated during World War II but it has been carefully restored. These medieval houses may be seen in the old quarter.

of Tours in 1461. Going left to **place de Châteauneuf**, the 14th-century mansion of the Dukes of Touraine may be seen on the left.

Across the square is the dome and apse of the **Basilique St-Martin**. At the foot of the **Tour Charlemagne** on rue des Halles there is a plan of the former basilica which shows where remains may still be found and just how extensive the old building was. To the west along rue des Halles the **Tour de l'Horloge** stands on the left, with remains of the arches of the ancient nave on its north side. Turn left into the narrow rue Julien Leroy which leads into rue Rapin. Turn left again, passing the **Saint-Martin Museum** located in the 14th-century chapel of Saint-Jean.

Turn right into rue Descartes, across rue Néricault and along rue de la Grandière to the boulevard Béranger where a flower market is held on Wednesdays and Saturdays. On the far side of the boulevard, at no. 54, is the **Petit Musée du Costume**. Along the Boulevard to the left is the place Jean Jaurès, the city centre, Hôtel de Ville and the starting point of this walk.

Parks and Gardens

There are a number of squares in the city which have small but pleasant gardens. Larger gardens near the city centre include the **Jardin du Musée des Beaux Arts**, the garden of the former Archbishop's Palace in place François Sicard (near St-Gatien Cathedral). Nearby is the **Jardin des Murs Romains** in which are substantial remains of the old Roman wall, as its name suggests. It is reached from rue des Ursulines, on the opposite side of which the rue François Cluet leads to the **Parc Mirabeau**. Alongside rue Nationale near the former **Abbatiale St Julien** is the **Jardin de Beaune-Semblançay** and to the west, surrounding the **Ecole des Beaux Arts** in rue du Commerce is the **Jardin François I**. The extensive **Jardin de la Préfecture** lies north of boulevard Heurteloup, opposite the railway station.

Still within the city, in a residential area west of avenue Grammont, the **Jardin des Prébendes d'Oë** replaces water meadows formerly liable to flooding. On the western edge of the city, reached via the long rue d'Entraigues, the **Jardin Botanique**, established in the last century, has rare plants, animals and greenhouses. Around the city, to the north near the Autoroute bridge over the Loire, the **Parc de Sainte Radegonde** occupies part of an old island in the river Loire known as **Grande Ile Aucard**, reached from **Pont Mirabeau**. Downstream is another island with a park, **l'Ile Simon**.

To the south of the city, an island in the river Cher provides the location for the Parc **Honoré de Balzac** while south of the Cher is **Parc de Grandmont** in the suburb of **St Avertin**. In the same area the **Lac de Cher** nautical and swimming centre is surrounded by extensive parkland.

Shopping in Tours

The city is one of the best shopping centres in the region with branches of many international chains. The principal shopping streets are rue Nationale, avenue de Grammont, rue des Halles and rue de Bordeaux, a pedestrian precinct near the railway station. Large department stores include *Monoprix*, *Nouvelles Galeries* and *C&A*, all in rue Nationale, and *Le Printemps* in rue de Bordeaux. *La Maison de la Touraine* on boulevard Heurteloup near the *Office de Tourisme* displays a wide selection of quality products of Touraine, including wines, cheeses, confectionery, pottery, silks, works of art and many other items suitable for souvenirs.

*F*resh vegetables on a French market stall—a delight for the hungry tourist.

Throughout the central area will be found numerous smaller shops catering for all requirements, and prices may be lower than in some of the prestige establishments. A good place to shop for fresh food of all kinds is the covered market, *Des Halles*, at the west end of rue des Halles. The major banks are situated along boulevard Heurteloup, boulevard Béranger and around place Jean Jaurès. There are many cafés and restaurants, both along the main shopping streets and in the many smaller squares, particularly in the pedestrianized areas of the historic old town. Here you can enjoy some of the local specialities. Some examples are *rillons*, small chunks of breast of pork eaten cold or hot as a starter, *rillettes*, potted shredded pork or goose meat, or *andouillettes* which are grilled, seasoned sausages made from tripe.

237

These may also be purchased in local *charcuteries*. Many of the dishes will be prepared using local Touraine wines and local fruit appears in such dishes as *porc aux pruneaux* (pork with prunes). Locally grown plums and melons appear frequently on menus. Cakes, pastries and confectionery from Tours are very tempting. One establishment not to be missed is *La Livre Tournois* at 6, rue Nationale, adjacent to the Cloître Saint-Julien. Described as a *Confiserie Tourangelle*, it sells very expensive confectionery including the local *Pruneaux Farcis*, which are prunes stuffed with very rich almond paste. In this shop you can taste these and other local specialities and watch them being made. It is quite an experience. Major hypermarkets include **Mammouth** at Chambray-lès-Tours, a suburb south of the river Cher, and in the Centre Commerciale **"La Petite Arche"** north of the Loire in the suburb of St-Symphorien. **Centre Leclerc** is in rue de la Bondonnière in the suburb of Joué-les-Tours south of the Cher, and **Euromarché** in the Centre Commerciale north of the Loire in the suburb of St-Cyr-sur-Loire.

The Surrounding Area

About 3km (2 miles) to the west of the city centre in the suburb of La Riche between the rivers Loire and Cher is the ruined priory of **Saint-Cosme-en-l'Isle** set in an attractive and well-cared for garden. Its history goes back to the 10th century when a chapel existed on an island in the Loire. In 1092 a priory was founded, and it was enlarged during the 15th century. Remains of the church still exist. Of more interest are the 12th-century refectory and the prior's lodging dating from the 15th century. It was in the latter building that Pierre de Ronsard, "prince of poets" lived, worked and died.

Pierre de Ronsard and the Pléiade

Born in 1524 in the manor house of La Possonnière near Vendôme, Pierre de Ronsard became a royal page. Later he studied in Paris, where he met other student poets including Joachim du Bellay. The group of seven became known as the *Pléiade*, and they promoted the use of the French language instead of Latin in poetry, raising its standard to a new richness of expression. Although du Bellay published what was, in effect, the manifesto of the group, Ronsard was its acknowledged leader. He is known today as the creator of some of the greatest love lyrics, and his sonnets to Cassandre (Amours, 1552), Marie (1555), Hélène and other ladies have led to the belief in some quarters that Ronsard's relationships with these women were far from compatible with his position as a royal chaplain and lay prior of the priory of Saint-Cosme in Touraine. However, it seems most likely that his interest was platonic. Nevertheless, he wrote some of the most beautiful verses, with a recurrent theme of the short-lived beauty of a rose:

"Je vous envoye un bouquet, que ma main
Vient de trier de ces fleurs épanies"

Ronsard's work extends far beyond his love lyrics. Up to the time of his death at Saint-Cosme in 1585 he had written some 50,000 lines of verse including odes and works on philosophic and religious problems. Ronsard has been described with some justification as the "prince of poets". A small museum portraying his life and work is located in the prior's lodging.

Also in **la Riche**, about 1km (½ mile) south-east of the Priory, is all that remains of the **Château of Plessis-lès-Tours**. In this context the word "*lès*" means "near" to Tours.

The manor, which was originally named Montils-lès-Tours, was purchased in 1463 by Louis XI who had a new residence built on the site. He died there in 1483 and during the reigns of Charles VIII and Louis XII the château was enlarged and altered. Following years of neglect all that remains of the original three wings is a small brick and stone building which was the south part of the royal apartments. On the first floor is an attempted restoration of Louis XI's bedroom, also a room devoted to St François de Paule, the founder of the Order of the Minimes.

Along the north bank of the Loire, to the east of the Autoroute bridge, an inconspicuous entrance leads to the **Abbaye de Marmoutier**. Little now remains of this ancient foundation, once one of the most powerful abbeys in Christendom. Founded by St Martin in AD 372 on becoming Bishop of Tours, the caves in the neighbourhood had been used by St Gatien, first Bishop of Tours, to say Mass a century earlier. A great monastic school was established here in the time of Charlemagne, and after plundering by the Normans in AD 853 it rose again under the Benedictines of Cluny. Today, a bell tower from 1096 still stands, virtually all that is left after destruction by Huguenots in the 16th century and the suppression during the Revolution. Now the site is occupied by nuns of the Congregation of the Sacred Heart.

A further 3km (2 miles) along the river the village of **Rochecorbon** lies below a high cliff on top of which is a 15th-century watch-tower known as **La Lanterne de Rochecorbon**. The cliff is full of tunnels, not only wine cellars or *caves*, but actual "troglodyte dwellings", some three storeys high and still inhabited.

Overlooking the river and partly within caves in the cliffside is a four-star hotel and restaurant, **Domaine des Hautes Roches**. The village lies within the area which produces wines under the *appellation* Vouvray which applies to the white *pétillant* and *mousseux* wines produced from locally grown *Pineau de la Loire* or *Chenin Blanc* grapes. Some red wine is also made.

Beyond Rochecorbon is the village of **Vouvray**, where the river Cisse joins the river Loire. Here again there are many cellars dug into the limestone cliffs, interesting old houses and a 12th-century church. A number of vineyards are open to visitors. A small local museum deals with vine culture and wine making, the attractive local embroidered bonnets and caps, and local history.

Across the river from Vouvray, but not connected directly by a road bridge, is **Montlouis**, another charming village on the bank of the river and backed by cliffs. It too has its *appellation contrôlée* Montlouis. Its wines are very similar to those of Vouvray and again there are a number of vineyards open for visiting and tasting.

Some 5km (3 miles) to the north of Vouvray lies the village of **Parçay-Meslay** and just beyond the junction between the Autoroute A10 and the main N10 road is the fortified farm

of **Grange de Meslay,** which was built in 1220 for the Abbey of Marmoutier. An arched gateway in a tower leads into a large courtyard where the most striking building is a superb 13th-century tithe barn.

*T*his *arched gatehouse dates from 1220 and leads into the courtyard of the fortified farm of Grange de Meslay, in the great tithe barn of which the annual Touraine Music Festival is held.*

Life Underground— The Strange World of Troglodytes, Mushrooms and Wine

With cliffs formed of soft limestone *tufa* overlooking the river valleys it is not surprising to find caves dug for shelter and for storage. When one sees smoking house chimneys sticking up out of the ground, then that is a cause for surprise. "What on earth is a chimney doing here?", you may ask. The answer must be that in the earth below there is a dwelling, dug into the rock. The idea of digging out a shelter is so simple that it is not confined to any particular country or period of history, neither is it confined to the less-favoured classes of society. Throughout France, wherever man has been able to quarry stone, troglodytes or cave dwellers may be found, and the region of Anjou, Poitou and Touraine is the most important centre for such dwellings, many of which are still inhabited.

In the south-east of Maine-et-Loire are located a wide range of isolated dwellings, hamlets and villages embracing all types of habitation: mansions, rural and urban dwellings and religious sites representing a mode of life which has endured through several centuries, giving rise to a special tradition, a language, culture and legends peculiar to the environment. The origin of these dwellings is ancient, with some confirmed datings going back to the 12th century and many from around the 15th century.

This entrance door leads into a surprisingly comfortable underground dwelling in a troglodyte village near Saumur.

These ancient troglodyte villages and farm buildings are important sites when studying the history of this way of life, and in studying the history, geography and ethnology of the region in general. Because of alterations, damage, and changes in their use over the centuries, it is difficult to assign exact dates to the first troglodyte dwellings; nevertheless, they present a living record of a completely organized society with homes for all classes, underground streets and lanes, chapels, dovecots and mansions, bakers' ovens and provision stores, quarries and sailors' homes.

Around a century ago many of these villages possessed perhaps two or three houses above ground, and many had none. The troglodyte dwellings underground were secure, insulated against cold, cheap to build and cheap to maintain. They could be enlarged and

improved as circumstances required. They were usually constructed in caves left after stone had been quarried and sold, thus paying for building and furnishing the home. Often, however, they were dug with the sole intention of being inhabited.

The two types of soft limestone are tufa and falun. The first has been used since earliest times for building houses, manors, châteaux, churches and monuments throughout the valley of the Loire, while falun or "shell stone" was used extensively as lime on the fields. They have been quarried extensively and over 40 quarries or mines were in use at the end of the 19th century in the Anjou region alone. Two remain in production today, but many have been abandoned. Often these old quarries, with networks of galleries and chambers, are now utilized for mushroom growing or wine storage, and there are around 1,000km (60 miles) of such caves in the Saumer region.

Two methods of quarrying were employed. The tufa was extracted through underground tunnels two or three metres (6–9ft) high serving underground galleries extending over several kilometres. This type of excavation is very common in the cliffs bordering the Loire, the most important examples being found in the villages of Souzay, Turquant and Montsoreau. A different method was used to dig falun. A hole was made through the top soil into caverns which opened out below ground level and were linked together. This method is no longer used. The most impressive example exists at Doué-la-Fontaine. Rock faces 12–15 m (13–16 yd) high enclose rows of five to ten adjoining chambers.

The cliff villages along the Loire between Saumur and Montsoreau were created over a period of several centuries, and the old quarry tunnels and troglodyte dwellings were served by alleyways or paths in the cliff face. Collapse and change have often destroyed the continuity of these ways. At Turquant a path along the cliff face serves a number of dwellings, among which several are still occupied. It passes a site now used for mushroom cultivation and leads to a group of inhabited caves with chimneys, ovens, wine presses and so on. In several places such as Turquant, Coutures and Souzay it is possible to find traces of façades, chimneys and other architectural features remaining from former manor houses and their ancillary structures. They have often been altered or destroyed during the past two centuries but are, nevertheless, very interesting from the point of view of preserving the scarce remaining evidence of the past.

There are a number of underground dovecots which recall the ancient *droit de fuie* or right of the nobility to keep doves and pigeons, the total number being restricted to one nesting hole per *arpent*, an old land measure of about one acre. This is part of the historical heritage of rural Anjou. The only visible part above ground of these structures is the exit tower through which the birds left and returned.

Underground chapels were excavated as places of worship or as refuges, their creation often dating back to the 12th, 13th or 14th century. One of the most interesting is *La Cave de la Frairie* in Doué-la-Fontaine.

In the village of Rochemenier not far from Doué is an excellent example of a complete farm complex below ground level. The central farmyard is dug out from the level ground, and it is surrounded by a series of separate or interconnecting chambers which provide living rooms and other accommodation such as stables, barns and cow sheds, all underground. The whole complex includes exhibition rooms and forms a museum of troglodyte life as it was. The two farms in this complex are furnished as they would have been when abandoned at the beginning of the present century, and they were started in the 17th and 18th centuries. The village of Rochemenier has a total of about 250 caves, in all about 40 similar farms, the oldest of which dates from the Middle Ages. The village church of Sainte-Emérance, on the surface near the caves, has an underground chapel beneath it, probably established in the

Many dwellings are dug into the walls of stone quarries, and extend beneath other buildings on the surface.

16th century when the church was burnt down during the religious wars.

A further reason for excavating underground caves was to provide safe refuges in times of war or strife. Such an example is to be found at Dénezé-sous-Doué. During the same religious wars of the 16th century the Protestants were forbidden to practise their religion and were liable to the death sentence if found in groups of three or more. A number of Protestant stone-masons held secret meetings in a group of caves at Dénezé, and as a result there remains a most extraordinary collection of over 400 sculptured figures on the walls, ceilings and even the floors of the chambers. Many of these are of an extremely satirical nature, expressing the feelings of the oppressed. Much effort has been devoted to restoring this unique record, which is now open to the public.

Reference has been made to the cliff dwelling at Coutures, on the River Loir, and other similar troglodyte dwellings are to be found in a cliff face formed in a loop of the river at Ansières, between Montoire-sur-le-Loir and Vendôme.

So, in this part of the Loire region, all is not always what it seems. An unobtrusive doorway beside the road may lead to a *cave* lined with racks containing hundreds, or even thousands of bottles or casks of wine, maturing in a steady temperature. On the other hand, the door may open to reveal a vast and well-organized operation devoted to the growing of fine mushrooms, again in the special temperature conditions which exist in these underground caverns. It is just possible, however, that you may find behind that door a very cosy comfortable house, complete with its small terraced garden overlooking the valley below, and "all mod. cons." inside!

Touraine Music Festival, Grange de Meslay

This beautiful medieval tithe barn is used as the setting for the Touraine Music Festival. The 13th-century building was built on the instructions of the Abbot of Marmoutier in 1220. Some 55m (180ft) long and 21m (70ft) wide, it is divided into five naves by four rows of 18m (60ft) high oak pillars. It is a truly remarkable building, with a high timber roof supported by many beams presenting a fine example of 15th-century architecture. Up to 1,200 people can be seated in the building, whose accoustic properties are outstanding. The only disadvantage might be the noise from nearby Tours-St Symphorien airfield. The festival was founded by Sviatoslav Richter in 1964, and he has given recitals at many of the festivals since then. In 1990, artists appearing included Richter himself, Stephen Hough, Shura Cherkassky, Budapest Philharmonic Orchestra and Barbara Hendricks, as well as other international musicians.

Further Afield

Tours is an ideal centre for visiting the many interesting places downstream along the Loire, in the valley of the Indre and in the country to the south.

About 4km (2½ miles) north-west of Tours near the village of **Mettray** is a large dolmen, one of the biggest in the area. About the same distance along the Loire valley west of Tours, past numerous "troglodyte" dwellings and caves in the cliffs, is the small but attractive town of **Luynes**, overlooked by a 13th-century château, which is *not* open to the public. In the square is an interesting 15th-century covered market with intricate timber construction.

To the north of the town is a row of stone and brick columns, some linked by arches, the remains of a Roman aqueduct built about 1,800 years ago to bring water to the Roman town of what is now Tours.

Another reputed Roman relic is **La Pile**, a solid stone pillar about 20m (70 feet) high, whose purpose is a mystery. It gives its name to the village of **Cinq-Mars-la-Pile**, which stands at the confluence of the Loire and Cher.

In the square in the little town of Luynes stands this 15th-century covered market hall with an interesting timber structure supporting the roof.

The village itself is dominated by a medieval fortress dating from the 11th century, of which two round towers remain.

A suspension bridge crosses the Loire at **Langeais** but the main point of interest is the château. Remains of the original keep built in AD 994 by Foulques Nerra still stand. Externally, the present 15th-century château appears as a fortress, entered over a drawbridge. This was where Charles VIII married Anne de Bretagne in 1491. In 1886 it was bought by Jacques Siegfried who devoted much time and money to having the interior restored to what it must have been at the time it was built. The furniture and decoration are outstanding, especially a collection of over 30 valuable Flemish and Aubusson tapestries. In 1904 Siegfried gave the château and gardens to the *Institut de France* who, with the Historic Monuments Fund, maintain it for the nation.

These arches are 1,800 years old and carried the water supply to the Roman settlement now known as Tours. The aqueduct is just to the north of Luynes.

Away from the river to the north, **Bourgueil** is the site of an imposing abbey. It is also the centre of a district producing excellent red wine, with some rosé. Both Bourgueil and the neighbouring village of **Saint-Nicholas-de-Bourgueil** have their own *appellation contrôlée* .

South of Bourgueil, the view across the river is dominated by the silver sphere of the nuclear power station between Avoine and the river bank near the confluence of the Indre and Loire. A museum and exhibition explains the processes involved in the generation of nuclear power.

Upstream from here is the château of Ussé, on the edge of the **Forêt de Chinon**, overlooking the Indre. In appearance it is the typical romantic castle of fairy tales, gleaming white from the tufa stone. Most of the present château dates from the 15th and 16th centuries, but it was built on the foundations of a medieval fortress. Terraces and formal gardens surround the buildings which are furnished with many items of artistic and historic interest. It is alleged to have formed the inspiration for the legend of the *Sleeping Beauty* and the story is represented by waxwork figures in rooms in the towers, access to which is rather cramped.

Near where the river Cher joins the Loire stands the château of **Villandry**, the last great Renaissance château to be built on the banks of the Loire. As is so often the case, it was built around 1530 on the site of a former feudal fortress, the one remaining tower of which existed in 1189. Dr Joachim Carvallo bought the estate in 1906 and his family still lives there. He devoted himself to restoring the exterior of the château and gardens to its original Renaissance state. The interior was remodelled in 18th-century style, and the owner's fine collection of Spanish paintings was housed there.

The most outstanding and interesting feature of Villandry must undoubtedly be the gardens which enjoy an international reputation. A full description of these is beyond the scope of this work but well-written and well-produced books are available at the château which describe the gardens in detail and explain the techniques involved. The formal ideas of the 16th century have been re-created. Briefly, the gardens are terraced on three levels, the lowest is the kitchen garden, next the ornamental gardens and herb gardens, and at the highest level the water gardens. The overall visual impact at any time of year is astounding, but behind the scenes all the hard manual work and the skilled raising of plants in the greenhouses and planning and organization of the year's work on such a scale can only be a source of admiration and wonder.

The little town of **Savonnières** on the Cher gets its name from the pink *saponaria* or soapwort flowers which were used as soap in Roman times and are still abundant. There are many small caves in the tufa cliffs in the neighbourhood used for commercial purposes. Just to the west are two very large caverns, the so-called "**Grottes Petrifiantes** ". Dripping water carrying lime in solution has formed stalactites and cascades of solid limestone. Objects placed under the dripping water become coated with layers of solid stone.

Straddling the river Indre and the main N10 road south of Tours, the town of **Montbazon** is dominated by a square keep, remains of a fortress built in AD 994 by Foulques Nerra. In 1866 a massive figure of the Virgin in copper was placed on the top. Of no great artistic merit, the statue has become black with age. A three-star campsite, Camping Municipal "**La Grange Rouge**" is sited by the river.

To the west in pleasant country with orchards and water mills overlooking the Indre is the village of **Saché** with its pleasant 16th-century manor house, in which the writer Honoré de

Balzac and the Human Comedy

Although Honoré de Balzac was born in Tours in 1799 and lived mainly in Paris from 1819 to 1830, most of his creative work was done in the manor house at Saché, to which he often retreated to find the peace and quiet he needed for his writing. After an unhappy period in college at Vendôme, he studied law at the Sorbonne because his father wanted him to become a notary. However, he wanted to be an author but he never made much money and was in fact frequently hounded by creditors and publishers. The Margonne family, friends of Balzac's mother, provided him with a welcome refuge and work-place whenever he needed it, and he described the house as melancholy but "dear to the aching souls of poets". Many of his novels were set in the area, including "*Le Lys dans la Vallée*" which is largely autobiographical. Balzac is best known for the monumental series of novels making up "*La Comédie Humaine*", which explores all aspects of French life and society. He showed phenomenal industry, working for 15 to 18 hours a day and writing over 85 novels during 20 years, often correcting his own proofs.

He had corresponded with a rich Polish lady, Eveline Hanska, for a number of years, and when his health broke in 1849 he went to Poland to convalesce. The couple were married in 1850 but Balzac died 3 months later. The room he used in the manor house in Saché has been restored to exactly the same condition as when he worked there, and a fine collection of manuscripts and other material relating to the man and his work is maintained as a museum.

Balzac (1799–1850) stayed with close friends, and where he created some of his best works.

Osiers grow extensively along the river in this area and have given rise to a craft industry centred on the village of **Villaines-les-Rochers** about 6km (4 miles) to the south-west. The willow stems are cut in December, sorted, bundled and stacked on end in the water until May. They are then peeled and made into basket or wickerwork (*vannerie*) of all kinds. After the

*A*lmost the entire population of Villaines-les-Rochers is occupied in some way in the business of basket-making. Baskets and wickerwork items of all sizes are made, as shown here.

original craft had almost died out, a cooperative was formed in 1849 and the business is now thriving.

Back to the river Indre, where the village of **Azay** dates back to Roman times. In the Middle Ages a small fortress guarded a ford over the river. Ridel d'Azay and his descendants owned it from the 12th century, and later it passed to the Duke of Burgundy who in 1418 fell foul of the Dauphin Charles. As a result, the castle and its garrison were destroyed. An important financier, Gilles Berthelot, owned the estate at the beginning of the 16th century and began reconstructing the château in 1518. It is set on piles over the water and the design owes much to the influence of Berthelot's wife Philippa. A combination of Gothic and Renaissance styles enclose what was to be a pleasant residence. Subsequent owners continued to add to, and improve, the château and it was finally sold to the State in 1905.

The buildings and park have been restored and the rooms turned into a Renaissance museum with furniture, paintings, tapestries and objects of everyday use. One striking feature of the interior design is the four-storey Grand Staircase, unusual for its time. The whole building when seen reflected in the surrounding water makes a memorable scene and lends itself to the *Son et Lumière* performances which are held during the summer.

The best approach to **Chinon** is from the south, when the view across the river Vienne shows the old town backed by the castle ruins along the high ground on the opposite bank.

A position of strategic importance, the first stone fortress on the site was built in AD 954 to replace an earlier wooden structure. Originally there were two forts, Coudray and Milieu. These were joined and more towers added in 1044. In 1154 Henry Plantagenet became king of England. He

The present château of Azay-le-Rideau reflects the result of restoration and improvements carried out by a succession of owners since the early 16th century.

created a new Fort St George and he and his descendants continued to strengthen the château until 1205. Chinon was Henry's favourite château, and he had a stone bridge built across the river and marshes. Both he and his son, Richard Coeur de Lion, died at Chinon and his second son, King John was married to Isabelle d'Angoulême in the château in 1200. Five years later it was captured by Philippe Auguste, King of France, and major reconstruction took place from then on up to the 15th century.

It was at Chinon that Joan of Arc first met and recognized the Dauphin Charles in 1429, and she stayed in the château until she left for Orléans at the head of Charles' army. Chinon continued to enjoy prosperity until the château eventually passed into the hands of Cardinal Richelieu in 1634.

A castle has overlooked the river Vienne at Chinon since the 11th century, and the vast structure stands high above the old fortified medieval town.

This marked the beginning of its decline, and not until the 19th century, after years of neglect, was an attempt made to restore it to some of its former grandeur. Much has already been achieved and the lower floors of the Royal Apartments have been restored and furnished. In the **Clock Tower** is a museum devoted to the life of Joan of Arc. There is also some material relating to the château, with objects discovered during archaeological digs within the ruins. There are outstanding

Traditional Markets in the Old Town of Chinon

During the first weekend of August each year, the old streets of Chinon, and the château grounds, come alive when a medieval market is held. The townspeople dress up in period costume, and more than 150 craftsmen are there, demonstrating medieval crafts. Music and dancing in the streets, strolling players, jugglers, tumblers and fire-eaters are much in evidence. Local taverns have plenty of local wine and cold drinks to refresh the traveller, and old recipes can be tasted. Later the same month, the *Marché Ancienne* takes place in the place de la Mairie. This is a revival of the markets of the last century. At dawn, the country people of the area set out for Chinon. They arrive at about 10 a.m. to the sound of music, their carts and horse-drawn wagons full of sheep, pigs, geese and other animals, plus barrels of Chinon wine. Their baskets and panniers are overflowing with vegetables and cheeses. You can taste and buy the wine and the farm produce, admire the local costumes and head-dresses and collection of old carts. You are also likely to hear some of the traditional old songs of Touraine.

views overlooking the river Vienne and the town from the gardens and ramparts.

The river bank below the château has a pleasant landscaped "English Garden". Between the river and the high ground supporting the ramparts lies the old town of Chinon, with many houses from the 14th to 16th centuries in the narrow steep streets.

Within the old town are two museums of interest. The **Musée du Vieux Chinon et de la Batellerie** in the restored 15th-century **Maison des Etats-Généraux** is concerned with folk art, local history and in particular it has a collection of models of the old boats which used to trade on the river. The **Musée Animé du Vin et de la Tonnellerie** contains an outstanding collection of tools and implements used in the 19th century for the cultivation and harvesting of grapes, wine making and barrel making. Animated models demonstrate some of the work and free sampling of wine is available. A recorded commentary is available in English.

Wherever you go in Chinon it is difficult to escape references to Rabelais and St Jeanne. An additional attraction for many will be the steam train which runs to and from the town of **Richelieu**, taking one hour in each direction. Finally mention must be made of the wines of the district, mainly red, but with some rosé, made famous by Rabelais and having a well-deserved reputation. The Chinon reds tend to mature quickly but with care can last for years. There are plenty of opportunities for tasting and buying wines in the town and locally. In the town itself the shop of **Couly-Dutheil**, owners of the Clos de l'Echo vineyard near the north side of the château, is a good place to purchase matured red Chinon wine of good quality.

*B*etween the castle ramparts and the river, the old town of Chinon has many half-timbered houses dating from medieval times, many of which are occupied as shops or offices.

Rabelais—Master of Satire

The town of Chinon is famous for the humanist and satirical writer François Rabelais (1494–1553), who spent much of his time here.

François Rabelais was yet another of those French men of letters who combined a number of talents. Known as one of the most popular and widely read satirical writers, he was in turn a Franciscan monk, a Benedictine priest and a well-qualified doctor of medicine. The son of a Chinon lawyer, he was born in the manor house of La Devinière in 1483—although there is some doubt as to the exact year of his birth, this date seems to be the most likely as it allows time for the young François to become familiar with the countryside in the way revealed in his subsequent writings. After being educated at the Benedictine abbey of Seuilly, followed by a period in the Franciscan house of La Baumette near Angers, he became a novice in the monastery of Fontenay-le-Comte. He studied Greek, Latin, Hebrew and the works of early French authors, later transferring to a Benedictine house near Orléans.

It was not until 1532 that he published his famous work *Pantagruel*, followed two years later by *Gargantua*. These books, based on folk tales about two benevolent giants, were used to comment on a wide range of subjects including law, education and religion. Rabelais mocked contemporary learning in quite an outrageous way and his use of extravagant and frank language gave rise to the word "rabelaisian", used to describe such satirical humour. In these and other books, Rabelais used such language and burlesque farce to mock lawyers, theologians, philosophers, and all who thought in abstract terms, although he himself displayed great erudition. He died around 1553 but during his life his wisdom made him many friends although the riotous licence of his mirth made as many enemies. His work displays an amazing fund of humour, common sense, wisdom and satire.

Approximately 4km (2½ miles) west of Chinon near the village of **Seuilly** stands the country house of La Devinière, birthplace of Rabelais. It is now a museum devoted to his life and work and contains exhaustive documentation of Rabelais, his writings and of Rabelaisian folklore.

On the main road south from Chinon to Richelieu, which lies 21 km (13 miles) distant, is **Champigny-sur-Veude**. Here there is a beautiful 16th-century Renaissance chapel, **La Sainte-Chapelle**, which has elaborate stonework on the exterior and some beautiful stained glass windows. A large château once stood here, which Cardinal Richelieu purchased, only to pull it down! The stables and other outbuildings remained, and were later converted into a home for *"La Grande Mademoiselle"*, niece of Louis XIII. The chapel was only spared from destruction by the intervention of the Pope. The story goes that Richelieu wanted to use the stones from the Château at Champigny to build his new town, 6km (4 miles) to the south.

The town of Richelieu must be one of the earliest examples of town planning. In 1624, Cardinal Richelieu, Prime Minister under Louis XIII and one of the most powerful French statesmen, decided to transform the family mansion into a palace. He also decided to have a town built nearby for his "court". Planned as a large square surrounded by a high wall and moat, to which three high gates give

*T*he statue of Cardinal Richelieu stands looking over the town he planned in 1624 to accommodate the households of his "court".

*T*his beautiful 16th-century Renaissance chapel at Champigny-sur-Veude contains some very fine stained glass windows. The Sainte-Chapelle is the only remaining portion of the old castle, which was demolished on the orders of Cardinal Richelieu.

access, building commenced in 1631. Along the **Grande Rue** are 28 identical town houses with carriage gates opening onto courtyards. In the south square, place du Marché, is a baroque church, the **Market Hall** with a splendid timber roof and the **Town Hall**, now a museum. The buildings in the north square used to be a convent and college, and are fine examples of classical architecture.

The Cardinal died in 1624 and his palace was demolished in the 19th century. The magnificent park now belongs to the University of Paris and only a domed pavilion, the cellar and orangery remain.

The Romanesque church of **Saint Nicholas** at **Tavant** on the river Vienne is remarkable for its rare 11th-century frescoes and carved capitals. **Sainte-**

The town of Richelieu had four identical gates, one of which gave entrance to the park surrounding the Cardinal's palace.

Maure de Touraine has a fine medieval covered market erected in 1672 and the remains of a 15th-century château built on the site of one of Foulques Nerra's keeps. Restored rooms accommodate a museum of local history, geology and rural arts and crafts.

The town is noted for Sainte-Maure cheese made from goat's milk, usually sold in a cylindrical shape. Farm-produced cheese bears a green label, and that from a dairy has a red label.

254

Some 6km (4 miles) south of Sainte-Maure the river Vienne is joined by the Creuse, another of the attractive rivers of this region. About the same distance up the Creuse is the town of **Descartes**, birthplace of René Descartes who has been described as the greatest French thinker. The small house where he was born is now a museum containing documents, manuscripts and other material relating to his life and work.

There is a Romanesque church on the Tours road leading out of the town. On Sundays, people come from miles around to shop at the **market**; the streets in the town centre are packed with stalls selling all kinds of produce and other goods. Traffic is excluded whilst the market is in progress.

The country between the river Creuse and its tributary, the Claise in southern Touraine, provided an abundant supply of natural flint which, in prehistoric times, formed the raw material for the production of flint tools and weapons which were traded all over Europe. Traces of this activity are to be found at various sites in the area, but in the château of **Le Grand-Pressigny** an outstanding collection of

*F*rom in front of the Town Hall, the statue of René Descartes looks down on the Sunday street market which fills the town centre of Descartes.

Descartes—Father of Modern Philosophy

René Descartes, philosopher and mathematician, was born in 1596 in the small town of La-Haye, near Tours, now called La-Haye-Descartes. He was educated during the years 1604 to 1614 at the Jesuit College of La Flèche and remained a Catholic all his life. After studying law at Poitiers he enlisted at his own expense for private military service with the Prince of Orange and later in the Bavarian army, to enable him to travel and to think. He settled in Holland from 1628 to 1649 during which time he produced his major works. His ideas had a wide impact as he was the first philosopher to write in his native language and not in Latin.

His philosophical system was based on doubt —to accept nothing as true until it could be proved. In the field of mathematics, Descartes in his study of algebra and geometry laid the foundations of analytical geometry and calculus, based on Cartesian coordinates. His fundamental thoughts on logic were set out in his *"Discours de la Méthode"* published in 1637. He also made important contributions to the study of astronomy. In 1649, Descartes was invited to Stockholm by Queen Kristina, but caught pneumonia and died in 1650. He was buried in Stockholm but his body was subsequently moved to Paris and then to Germigny-des-Prés.

*T*he ruined castle of Le Grand-Pressigny occupies an almost impregnable position on a hilltop.

*T*he ramparts and fortifications of the medieval walled town
of Loches run down to the banks of the river Indre.

flint objects has been assembled, together with a large collection of fossilized shells from the region.

Perched on a steep hill above the small quiet village, the remains of this once large château built between the 12th and 16th centuries are being restored. It has a drawbridge and gatehouse flanked by round towers, an impressive keep and an unusual tower with internal spiral staircase. Apparently the castle resisted attack by English and Burgundian forces for 50 years before being captured.

On the river Indre some 40km (25 miles) south-east of Tours, is the town of **Loches**, one of the best-preserved small towns in France. It stands on a bluff above the river where a fortress is known to have existed in the 6th century AD. Foulques Nerra had a square keep built during the 11th century to which ramparts were added, and further works during the 13th century made it almost impregnable. Then royal apartments were added at a later date. The whole complex, including the keep, royal lodgings, the church of St Ours and other medieval buildings are enclosed within 2km (1¼ miles) of ramparts.

The fortress was held by Henry II of England, and later by Philippe August, from whom it was captured by Richard Coeur de Lion in 1194. After its recapture in 1205 it remained the property of the French crown until the Revolution. In 1429 after her victory at Orléans, Joan of Arc came to Loches to persuade Charles VII to go to Reims to be crowned. It was here that he first met Agnès Sorel, later to become his mistress, and who is buried here. After her death in 1450,

the king spent much of his time in Loches, and he and his son, Louis XI, both added to the château and its defences. Many famous personages were either guests or prisoners in the château of Loches until after the Revolution. Its importance declined at the end of the 18th century and during the 19th century steps were taken to save the remainder from deterioration. The **royal apartments** contain a number of tapestries and paintings, and the tomb of Agnès Sorel, which was removed from the nearby church and restored after being desecrated during the Revolution. The fine **church of St-Ours** was founded as a collegiate church in the 10th century, but was rebuilt during the 12th century. It has some fine Romanesque vaulting and decorated columns, plus two very unusual pyramidal domes, known as *dubes*. The remnants of some fine Renaissance carvings, badly damaged during the Revolution, can be seen in the great west porch.

The **11th-century keep, round tower** and **Martelet** form an impressive group of fortifications, below which are dungeons and a torture chamber, which can still be seen today. Notable is the cell of Ludovic Svorza, the walls of which he decorated with his paintings during the 8 years he was a prisoner here.

T he belfry known as the Tour de Saint-Antoine stands up from the lower town of Loches and can easily be seen from the castle ramparts.

The **Porte Royale**, which is still the only way into the château and the church, now houses a museum which contains a reconstruction of a typical 19th-century Touraine room. A nearby studio houses a collection of paintings by E. Lansyer (1835–1893) and other notable artists.

In the lower town, there are two interesting gates. The 14th-century Porte Picois, a tall watch-tower with a *chemin-de-rond* and crenellated openings under the roof, adjoins the fine Renaissance building of the Hôtel-de-Ville which was built from 1535–43.

Opposite the *jardin publique* beside the river is the turreted Porte des Cordeliers. Both lead to picturesque streets with some attractive shops. Between the two gates is the Tour de Saint-Antoine, a 16th-century tower which was built as a belfry and was never part of a church building. In the rue du Château, which leads to the Porte Royale, is the Maison de la Chancellerie, a 15th-century house decorated with fluted columns and wrought-iron balconies. There are other medieval houses in the Grande Rue. Excellent views of the walled town may be had from the public gardens and nearby car park, close to the tourist office.

In 1007, at nearby **Beaulieu-lès-Loches**, on the other side of the river Indre, an abbey was founded by Foulques Nerra, where, it is said, he wished to be buried. This was partly destroyed during the Hundred Years War, but the beautiful Romanesque belfry still stands among the ruins. Part of the abbey church is also Romanesque, but the nave and chancel were rebuilt in the 15th century. Here too are some old houses in the narrow streets, including a Knights Templars' house from the 12th century.

On the road north from Loches at the village of **Cormery** a Benedictine abbey was founded in AD 791. It has since been demolished but a huge 11th-century bell tower and remains of the prior's lodging, refectory arches and other fragments give an idea of its size. The 12th-century church of **Notre-Dame-de-Fougeray** overlooks the valley and in the cemetery is a 12th-century *Lanterne des Morts*, unusual in this part of the country. It is a tower in which bodies awaiting burial were placed while a lamp would be lit in a window higher up the tower.

Car Tours and Walks in Blois, Tours and Southern Touraine

Car Tour from Blois. The Valleys of the Cisse, Cher and Indrois. Distance approx. 170km (105 miles)

Blois is a good centre for touring the attractive country in the valleys of the rivers Cisse and Cher, both of which run into the Loire downstream from Blois.

From the centre near the château follow avenue Gambetta across the railway and at the first roundabout take road D766 through the **Forêt de Blois**. At **Molineuf** turn left onto D135 with the forest on one side and the river Cisse on the other. Continue through **Chambon-sur-Cisse**, following D135 and signs towards **Coulanges**. Take the first turn right across the river into the village, then left. A sharp bend to the right across the river is soon followed by another turning to the right, still following D135 back across the river to a T-junction. Turn left to **Chouzy-sur-Cisse**. Take the turn to the right just beyond the river, then right again onto road D58. The route from Molineuf has been within the area producing wines under the AC Touraine-Mesland, and there are opportunities for *"dégustation"* and a look at some of the attractive old buildings in most of these villages along the valley of the Cisse.

The road D58 from Chouzy runs between the Cisse and the sloping hillsides dotted with vineyards. Follow the road D58 through **Onzain**, **Monteaux**, **Cangey** and **Limeray**. Beyond Limeray, cross the main D31 road. The road number changes from D58 to D1 but continue ahead following signs to **Pocé-sur-Cisse**. At the T-junction turn right then keep left towards **Amboise**. Continue until the road crosses over the railway then bear right to join road N152 **rue de Blois**. Turn right then left and cross the Loire by **Les Vieux Ponts** with the château of Amboise ahead. A separate day would be required to explore Amboise itself. Follow signs for **Le Clos-Lucé** and continue past the house, keeping to the right at the road junction to cross the little river. At the next crossroads (avenue Léonard-de-Vinci) turn left and continue to the new bypass road. From here, follow the D61 road towards **Montrichard**.

If you do not wish to find your way through the town on this trip, turn left along the D31 bypass before reaching Pocé-sur-Cisse and continue until the D61 is reached, then turn left and continue on this road through the **Forêt d'Amboise** where there are numerous long straight drives. The forest was once used by the Valois kings for boar hunting. Stopping places off the road are convenient for picnics. At the far side of the forest, the road number changes to D115. Continue into Montrichard, which makes a good stop for refreshment. After looking around the town, cross the bridge over the river Cher on road D764.

This road passes **Faverolles-sur-Cher** and climbs up from the valley. There are few villages along the road but after about 6km (3½ miles) the road runs through woods and the château of **Montpoupon** appears on the right. After going down across a stream the road rises to where there is a pleasant *"aire de pique-nique"* on the right. Parking is free and it provides the best view of the château across the valley.

Continue along D764 through pleasant country, through **le Liège** and down into **Genillé**, a quiet village in the valley of the Indrois.

Beyond Genillé the D764 rises to enter the **Forêt de Loches**, a former hunting forest of the English Plantagenets. The forest contains many tall oak trees and there are places along the road where vehicles may pull off. In about 4½ km (3 miles) the road is crossed by a long straight drive 8km (5 miles) long, marked at intervals by four pyramids erected in 1770 as rendezvous for hunters. This drive, known as the **Route de St Georges d'Amboise**, is a public road. Turn left along it, through the forest, and at the **Pyramid de Chartreux** turn left onto road D760, still within the forest. In a short distance the ruins of the monastery of

Chartreuse du Liget appear on the right of the road. One of many founded in 1178 by Henry II of England in atonement for the murder of Thomas-à-Becket, a walk around will give some idea of how large and impressive the buildings must have been before demolition in the 18th century. Nearby in the forest is the round chapel of **St-Jean-du-Liget** with fine 12th-century frescoes.

Continue along the D760 into the old village of **Montrésor** with its château and Renaissance church. After looking around and perhaps visiting the château, leave the village still following road D760 along the Indrois valley, where the river is lined with willows, alders and poplars and runs through lush meadows with orchards on the slopes. On the right beyond the river are the remains of a former Benedictine abbey. At **Nouans-les-Fontaines** go through the village onto road D675. The road runs north for about 8km (5 miles) in a straight line, passing through the **Forêt de Brouard** before following a winding course down into the Cher valley, past the turning to the ornithological park of **Beauval** on the left and into **St-Aignan**. The town and château may be visited, then continue across the bridges over the Cher.

The road continues as the D675 through undulating country with market gardening and fruit growing, including some vineyards. After **St-Romain-sur-Cher** the road becomes straight again most of the way to **Contres**.

At the road junction at the entrance to the village keep straight ahead onto road D956 and continue through **Cormeray**, where more vineyards will be seen on both sides. Beyond is **Cellettes** and the **Château de Beauregard**, from where the road passes through the **Forêt de Russy** and back to **Blois**.

Car Tour in the Valley of the Indre in Southern Touraine. Distance approx. 115km (72 miles)

Tours makes an excellent centre for journeys along the valleys of the Cher and Indre rivers and through the surrounding country.

Leave the city by going south, across the river Cher and through the suburb of **Chambray-lès-Tours**. Follow *Route de Bordeaux*, the straight N10, until it goes down and crosses the river Indre into **Montbazon** with the statue of the black Virgin on the castle keep on the left. Continue through the town and along the N10 through **Sorigny** to **Sainte-Catherine-de-Fierbois** with its interesting church where, following instructions given by Joan of Arc, a sword was found for her. A number of 15th-century houses may be sufficient reason for a short stop here.

Continue along the N10 to **Ste-Maure-de-Touraine**, through the village and at the junction beyond, turn left onto D760. At the left bend go straight ahead on D59 through **Sepmes** and **Bournon** to **Ligueil**. Bear right then cross the D50 and follow D31 for Loches. Note the restored decorated wooden wash-place on the edge of the town on the Loches road. About 1½ km (1 mile) along the D31 take the second turning on the left and follow road D95 through **Vou**. Still on the D95, in about 5km (3 miles) cross D760 and after another 5km (3 miles) turn right into **Dolus-le-Sec**. Continue through the village and follow D94 signed to **Chambourg-sur-Indre**.

Cross the main N143, go under the railway into the centre of Chambourg then turn left by the church and take the road D17 to **Azay-sur-Indre**. The road follows the river Indre and continues through **Reignac-sur-Indre** and the pretty village of **Courçay**, and passes a number of small mansions. At **Cormery** turn right along the main N143 road across the river Indre. In about 1 ½ km (1 mile) turn left onto

*T*he 16th-century formal gardens around the Renaissance château of Villandry have been re-created to delight visitors the year round.

D17 to **Esvres**. The route is signed "*Vallée de l'Indre*".

In Esvres there is a picnic area by the river. Continue along the valley to **Veigné**, turning left to cross the river then right along D250 into Montbazon. Return to Tours along the N10 main road.

Car Tour in the Loire, the Vienne and the Manse. Distance approx. 125 km (78 miles

Leave Tours through the suburb of **Joué-lès-Tours** along road D7 south of the river Cher. Go through **Savonnières** to **Villandry**. Just opposite the château entrance, turn right through an avenue of trees then left, to follow the road along the river embankment, which becomes the D16 after it crosses the road

to **Langeais**. The road continues along the river for about 20km (12 miles) with fine views across to the opposite bank. The river Indre converges from the left. Take a left turn to **Château d'Ussé**, then right along D7. At **Huismes**, a sharp turn to the left on to the D16 road leads to the village, from which point the road leads over the hill to **Chinon**.

Through the town, turn left along the riverside on road D8 and follow the north bank of the river Vienne to **l'Ile-Bouchard**. Turn left here and follow D757 north for about 2km (1¼ miles), then fork right on to road D21 along the river valley of la Manse. A left turn (D138) leads to the village of **Avon-les-Roches**. Turn right in the village, passing the interesting 12th-century church and continue to **Crissay-sur-Manse** with a ruined castle on the left. Continue on road D21 to **St-Epain**.

Turn right in the village along D57 and almost immediately turn left and follow the road straight ahead with the river Manse on the right. After passing under the railway bear left to **Courtineau**. The road runs up the valley between the Manse and the cliff with scattered troglodyte dwellings. After passing under the autoroute and through the village of Courtineau note the 15th-century chapel of **Notre-Dame-de-Lorette** carved into the cliff face on the left of the road. On reaching the main N10 road turn left to Montbazon and return to Tours.

Walks in Touraine

The area is well provided for by leaflets published by the various local tourist offices, and by the fact that a number of *Grandes Randonnées* pass through. The GR3 runs from east to west through Blois to Chinon and beyond, and many minor routes link with it. The *Comité Départmental de la Randonnée Pédestre*, 11 place du Château, 41000 Blois has produced a set of leaflets describing walking routes in Loir-et-Cher.

A Walk from Monthou-sur-Cher

This walk runs beside vineyards and follows the River Cher for a while before returning to **Monthou-sur-Cher**. From the village, another way-marked walk leads to the château of **Gué-Péan**. It should be noted that both walks are guided by yellow waymarks, so be sure you start this walk in the right direction.

Start from the *Mairie* and follow the red and white waymarks of GR41 for 100m (110 yards) to **Villa Ariane** then for a further 1,500m (1 mile) to a large stone. Turn right and follow the path to cross the Thésée road and down through the vineyard – note the view. In 1,500m (about 1 mile) turn left by the Roman ruins, go along the road for 50m (60yd) then under the railway to reach the bank of the Cher. At this point leave the GR41 and follow the yellow waymarks to the right, along the river, until you come to a bridge under the railway. Don't go through this bridge, but continue along the river bank to cross the railway and the D176 road to **Le Bois de Vineuil**. Continue following the yellow waymarks to the **Bois de Vigneau**, then follow the GR41 to the right as far as **La Jarellerie**.

Continue in the same direction (leaving GR41) past the houses of **les Bois**

Berniers and cross the D85. In 200m (220yd) leave the road and take a dirt track on the left. Follow this path to **Le Rolland Gué**, (gué = ford) where there is a footbridge and a water mill on the left. Cross the bridge and follow the path to the right to **Assenay**. Cross the little bridge over **Les Anguilleuses** and in 100m (110yd) take the middle path at the junction. This leads towards a large cedar tree at **La Mardelle**, then bears left. At **Peu** go down to the left beside the last house to return to the village. Distance: 15km (10 miles).

A Walk in the Forêt de Chinon
This walk follows part of the GR3 and returns along forest drives. The starting point is **La Chapelle-Saint-Blaise**, across the river Indre from **Azay-le-Rideau**. Suitable car parking should be possible in either place.

Pick up the red and white waymarks of the GR3 in the middle of La Chapelle and walk along the D17 in a westerly direction for about 1km (½ mile). Turn left to **Bourg-Cocu** then right through **Baigneux** and **Beaulieu**, past the **château de la Cour** to **Cheillé**. The route leads past the 13th-century

church to a crossroads. Take the road to the left to **La Belle Croix** on the edge of the **Forêt de Chinon**. Continue along the edge of the forest to the road D119 near **Le Bois Boureau**, cross the road and follow the path south into the forest. On reaching the forest drive **Allée de Marie-d'Anjou**, leave the GR3 and turn left. Follow this drive through the forest, across the road D119 at the junction (**Carrefour de Charles VII**) and continue to **Carrefour d'Agnès Sorel** . At this point take the forest road **Route d'Agnès Sorel** , leading half right, as far as the **Carrefour de François I** . Turn left to follow the forest road **Route de Françoise de Foix** , cross over the road D757 at **Carrefour de Bayard** and continue ahead, crossing a minor road in about 2km (1 ¼ miles). Continue along the edge of the forest past **La Fosse Laslin** to meet the red and white waymarks of the GR3 at the crossroads. Follow these along the path to the left, to reach the edge of the forest again. After a winding route along the edge of the trees in a generally northerly direction, past **La Cave**, turn left onto the D17 and back to La Chapelle-Saint-Blaise. Distance 24km (15 miles).

The Old and the New,
Accompanied by Good Wines

This chapter covers the area from the boundary of the *Centre* region with the Pays de la Loire, through Saumur and Angers to Nantes, the end of our journey downstream. Again we have an overwhelming variety of interests from ancient fortresses to the most modern armoured vehicles, from underground dwellings to the busy port of Nantes, and from outstanding châteaux to what may be considered as some of the finest wines of the Loire. This is also the area where market gardens and nurseries may be found, including the rose nurseries at Doué and bulb fields at Beaufort-en-Vallée.

Saumur

Saumur is famous for two things in particular: its sparkling wines, and its famous *Cadre Noir*, the display team of the internationally renowned *Ecole nationale d'equitation* (National Riding School). It has a fine château, several interesting museums, and a good shopping centre. There are some very fine Romanesque churches and abbeys in the area, including the wonderful abbey of **Fontevraud** where two English kings are buried. Mushrooms, megalithic monuments and Roman remains, troglodyte villages and underground caves, plus some interesting towns and châteaux can all be seen around Saumur or further afield. Since it is also the meeting place of several *Grandes Randonnées*, it makes a good base for those who enjoy walking.

The best way to approach Saumur is from the north side of the river Loire. This is where the best view of the château, standing high above the town, a real fortress overlooking the river, is obtained. Like Amboise, it was an obvious place to build a fortress, and, because of the island in the river, an ideal place for a bridge, but in the

A few of the 5,000 roses grown in the extensive nursery gardens at Doué-la-Fontaine, the town of roses.

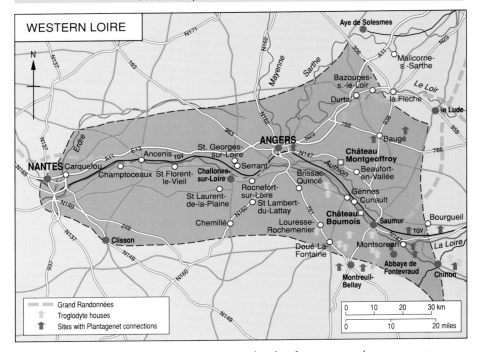

WESTERN LOIRE

Grand Randonnées
Troglodyte houses
Sites with Plantagenet connections

M ap of the region containing Saumur, Angers and Nantes.

case of Saumur, the island is larger. **Ile d'Offard** has its own local community, with shops, houses and hotels, schools, sports centres and a campsite. (It also has a site for "travellers" at the opposite end of the island!) The roads from Tours, Rouen and Angers meet at the northern end of the **Pont des Cadets**, which leads to Ile d'Offard. A wide boulevard links this bridge with the **Pont-Cessart**, leading into Saumur itself. Because of its strategic position, it has always been an important place, even though it is not a large town.

In the 9th century, Charles the Bald built a fortified monastery here, but despite these precautions many successful attacks on the town ensued. There has been a succession of fortified buildings built on top of the hill, the present château being a mixture of 13th- and 14th-century buildings. Although it is a fortress, it has elaborate decorations, with battlements decorated with *fleurs-de-lys*, pepper-pot towers with turreted roofs, and beautiful mullioned windows. The star-shaped ramparts were added in 1590 when Saumur became a Protestant stronghold. "Good King René", Duke of Anjou, and incidentally the father-in-law of Henry VI of England, who lived from 1409 to 1480, was also a poet and playwright of the time. He called Saumur his *"Château d'Amour"*, and it was also illustrated in the famous *Très Riches Heures du Duc de Berry*. During the time of Napoleon it was used as a state prison, but was restored early this century, and now houses three museums.

The château is floodlit at night during the summer, and looks superb, its white tufa stone shining under the powerful arc-lights.

The royal apartments are the home of the **Musée des Arts Décoratifs**, which has a fine collection of rare French porcelain, ceramics and enamel work, plus wood, stone and alabaster carvings, church ornaments, furniture and tapestries from the 14th to 18th centuries. On the upper floors of the building is the **Musée de Cheval**, a unique museum which shows the his-

tory of horse riding from the earliest times to the present day. It includes the skeletons of some famous French horses as well as other items connected with equitation.

After visiting the museums, the watch-tower may be climbed for a fine panoramic view over the town. You would perhaps expect to be able to walk through the rooms of a museum

T own plan of Saumur.

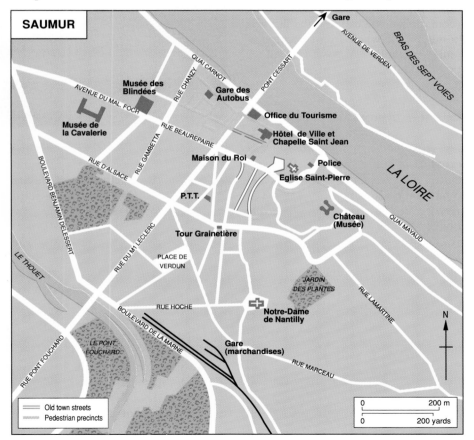

Gleaming in the afternoon sun, the château of Saumur commands the river and the town at its feet, and looks down on to the spire of the church of Saint-Pierre.

at will, even though you might be asked to follow a one-way route. Not so in Saumur. All visits are guided, and although there is an English-speaking guide, you have to see the horse museum first, and listen to a lecture about some of the objects in each room, before you can visit the fine arts museum. The whole tour of both museums takes 1½ hours and is not all that enjoyable. The tourism officer in Saumur says that the system will be changed in the future. It is to be hoped so, but in the meanwhile, before you part with your cash, check whether it is a *visite guidée* or *visite libre*. In the grounds of the château, in the casemates, is a museum of toy soldiers and other figurines, and there are good views over the river valley from the ramparts.

The streets of the *vieux quartiers* lie between the château and the bridge, those in the **Grande Rue** being particularly attractive. Many new buildings have been built in medieval style to try and maintain the atmosphere, although there are some more modern buildings to be seen. In rue Dacier is the **Maison du Rois**, built by Louis II, Duke of Anjou, the brother of "Good King René", and often used as a *pied-à-terre* by the kings of France on their journeys. At the top of rue des Paiens,

in the place de l'Arche-Dorée is the **Tour Grainetière**, once the town's granary, and the 16th-century house where Duplessis-Mornay, the so-called Huguenot Pope lived.

The town hall has a beautiful Renaissance façade with some very fine carvings. Its foundations were once part of the town walls. In the rue Saint-Jean, the bustling pedestrianized street behind the town hall, and in the nearby place Saint-Pierre, there is a real mixture of medieval and classical buildings.

One historic building which is not in the town centre but on Ile d'Offard is the **Maison de la Reine de Sicile**, built by King René for his mother in the 15th century.

Of the four churches in Saumur the oldest, **Notre-Dame de Nantilly**, is a Romanesque building containing some beautiful tapestries, dating from the 15th century. They include eight 17th-century Aubusson tapestries depicting the life of Christ and the Virgin Mary. There is an epitaph to King Rene's nurse close to the baptistry which was once the private oratory of Louis XI.

The church of **Saint-Pierre**, which was built between the 12th and 17th centuries, has some 16th-century choir stalls and a beautiful baroque organ loft. Tapestries from the 17th century depict the story of Saint Pierre and Saint Florent. The **Chapelle-Saint-Jean** is a little 13th-century building with fine Angevin vaulting.

Along the river bank, to the east of the town, is **Notre-Dame-des-Ardilliers**, a graceful domed building and a place of pilgrimage since the 15th century.

Saumur is famous for its military connections. The French Cavalry School was founded in Saumur by Louis XV, and it occupies an imposing 18th-century building opposite the huge **place du Chardonnet**. In this square, every July, there is a cavalry display, including the more modern mechanized elements.

Whilst on the subject of military operations, during World War II, the cadets of the Military Academy, under the command of their instructors, made a valiant stand against the advancing German forces, and held out

271

The Cavalry School and its Museums

Officially the cavalry school is the *Ecole d'application de l'armée blindée et de la Cavalerie*, the name adopted during World War II. The school trains the élite of the French cavalry, including officers for the armoured regiments. Inside the barracks is a museum of souvenirs of the school, including swords and weapons, uniforms, helmets, medals and photographs. The story of the cavalry during two world wars is told, together with that of the campaigns in Indo-China and Algeria. Entrance to this museum is free, and you may wander around at will. However, to get in you will have to go to the guardroom, hand over your passport to the guard commander, for which he will give you a receipt, and be escorted through the building to the museum! It is, however, well worth the effort, but it is not open on Mondays or Saturday mornings, and is closed for the whole of August.

Nearby is the Musée des Blindés, or tank museum, illustrating the history of 20th-century warfare through the development of armoured vehicles. The museum has a collection of more than 700 tanks, vehicles and guns from 12 different countries and is said to be the largest of its kind in the world. Many of the vehicles on show have been restored and are in working order, and some take part in the cavalry display each year. It should be pointed out that not all 700 tanks are on display in the museum!

for 3 days with only the most basic weapons. They blew up the bridges which were being crossed by the Germans at Saumur, Montsoreau and Gennes, where there is a monument to their heroism.

Parks and Gardens

The grounds of the château have been well laid out and are very pleasant. Between the château and the church of Notre-Dame de Nantilly is the **jardin des plantes**, which includes a **station viticole** and several vine-covered terraces. Although not a garden, there are some lovely views to be had from the rue des Moulins, above the cliffs, offering fine views over the Loire. At **Bagneux**, to the south of the town, there are pleasant woods with many paths for pedestrians and cyclists only.

Shopping in Saumur

Saumur wines are world renowned. The **Maison du Vin** in rue Beaurepaire has all the wines of local producers on display, and you can also taste and buy. You can also buy wine at the *caves* of most of the famous wine houses nearby.

The town is well known for the production of rosaries and other religious objects, and a good choice may be found here. There are plenty of antique shops, most of which are to the west of the rue Franklin Roosevelt and rue d'Orléans, the wide shopping streets which lead from the bridge into the town. **Monoprix** and **Printemps** department stores are in rue Franklin Roosevelt, and there are some good boutiques (perhaps not so surprizing since Coco Chanel was born in the town). The pedestrianized rue Saint-Jean has small shops of all descriptions in the attractive old houses lining the street.

The main market is on Saturdays in the modern covered market in place Saint-Pierre, and there are also markets on Tuesday and Wednesday mornings. These markets are the best

*A*mong *the tufa caves at Saint-Hilaire, many are used for mushroom cultivation, the quality of the product being apparent from the contents of the baskets illustrated here.*

273

place to buy fresh fruit and vegetables, including, of course, mushrooms. There is a large **Leclerc** hypermarket, with a very good restaurant, on boulevard de Lessert, west of the town near the end of the new bridge, and an **Escale** supermarket on the route de Rouen, on the north bank of the river.

The Surrounding Area

At **Saint-Hilaire-Saint-Florent**, a suburb to the west of Saumur, is the **Musée du Champignon**. In the underground galleries of this area, from where the tufa stone used for many of the châteaux and other famous buildings in this part of France was hewn, are a number of mushroom "farms". The galleries are used because mushrooms require a constant temperature during their cultivation, and such conditions can easily be obtained in these caves.

The mushrooms grown here are the famous *champignons de Paris*, and the area produces about three-quarters of all the national output. The visit starts with an interesting video, in English, about mushrooms, and on a walk through the galleries, visitors can see, step by step, how the mushrooms are cultivated.

Also in this suburb are the *caves* of some of the famous wine houses which produce the sparkling wines for which Saumur is famous. Bouvet-Ladubay, Ackerman-Laurance and Veuve Amiot are all here. Some of them offer tours of their premises, as well as wine tasting. Tours can be arranged with an English guide, but it is best to make enquiries in advance. The tourist office may be able to help arrange a tour. Bouvet-Ladubay take their visitors

*T*he public displays of riding given by members of the famous "Cadre Noir" from the National Riding School at Terrefort are superb examples of horsemanship.

through the underground caves where their wine is stored and bottled. It is fascinating to see how a large, fat straight cork becomes a mushroom-shaped champagne cork! They do not own any vineyards themselves, but buy in their grapes from other growers.

The **National Riding School** is situated at **Terrefort**, above Saint-Hilaire-Saint-Florent. Guided visits, sometimes including displays of horsemanship by the famous Cadre Noir, are available. Times vary, and if you want to see the Cadre Noir in action it is best to check with the tourist office.

At the little village of **Bagneux**, some 2km (1 mile) south of Saumur, is one of France's best megalithic monuments, called **le Dolmen de Bagneux**. Eight upright slabs, in two parallel rows, together with an end slab, form a rectangle which is covered by three huge horizontal slabs and one smaller one. It is amazingly regular in shape, and the total area covered is 90m^2 (970ft^2) with a volume of 200m^3 (7,000ft^3) and a total weight of more than 500 tonnes.

Further Afield

North of Saumur, along the northern bank of the Loire towards Angers, are the châteaux of **Boumois** and **Montgeoffroy**, and the towns of **Beaufort-en-Vallée** and **Baugé**. Boumois was built in the 15th and 16th centuries and shows the transition from Gothic to Renaissance architecture. It has a particularly interesting dovecote, with a revolving ladder and space for more than 1,500 pigeons. Montgeoffroy is a very elegant 18th-century mansion, standing at the top of a long drive behind beautiful wrought-iron gates. It has remained in the same family since it was built, and has been preserved in its original state. There are many original furnishings still in use in the château, and each piece of furniture is placed in the exact spot for which it was designed, 200 years ago.

Beaufort-en-Vallée contains the ruins of a 14th-century château, from where there is a fine view of the valley below.

Between Beaufort and the river is a large stretch of reclaimed land, or polder, and the story of how it was made is told in the museum at **Saint-Mathurin-sur-Loire**, 10km (6 miles) to the south. About 4km (2½ miles) upstream is the little town of **la Menitré**, noted for its folklore traditions.

La Menitré

This little town offers an interesting spectacle on the last Sunday in July. There is a head-dress parade, which brings together many local folklore groups, and a great variety of traditional costumes and head-dresses can be seen, some of them very old. Although it is common to see such costumes in Brittany and parts of Normandy, they are less common in this region, and this parade offers the visitor a chance to see some of the beautiful head-dresses which were once worn as a matter of course on high days and holidays.

Baugé, another old town with a château and some old houses, possesses a priceless relic, the 13th-century Cross of Anjou, believed to have been made from part of the true cross. It is most unusual, with two arms and a crucifix on both sides. It is richly decorated with pearls, turquoises and amethysts. Above the crucifix on one side is the dove of peace, and on the other the paschal lamb. The cross was venerated by King René and his descendants, and one of these was René, Duke of Lorraine. After he had beaten Charles the Bold in battle, his troops, in order to recognize each other, adopted this cross as their symbol and it

On the last Sunday in July the market square of La Menitré comes alive with the colourful parade of traditional folk costumes and head dresses.

has since been known as the Cross of Lorraine. In the hospital is an interesting old pharmacy, still in its original condition after more than two centuries. In the château, which is now the town hall, is an interesting local museum. At **Brain-sur-Allonnes** are the ruins of a 14th-century fortified house, and a museum containing thousands of decorated floor tiles which were discovered there.

On the south side of the river, about 11km (6 miles) upstream from Saumur, is the château of **Montsoreau**, built high above the river in the middle of the 15th century and later altered to include a very fine Renaissance staircase.

In the village are some "troglodyte" houses, preserved in their original state. Behind them are extensive galleries dug out during the 15th century to provide stone for building, and which are used today for mushroom cultivation.

In the area are some typical Anjou windmills, postmills which are set on a conical base. These may be reached on foot up steep hills from Montsoreau. From the **Moulin de la Herpinière**, which lies about 2km (1 mile) uphill from the town there is a fine view across to the mill at **Montsoreau**, with the steam from the cooling towers at Chinon as a background.

Some 1½ km (1 mile) from Montsoreau is the beautiful church of **Candes-Saint-Martin**, a monument to the Saint who died here in AD 397. The church has a wonderful porch, with a single central pillar supporting the beautiful Angevin vaulting. Behind the pillar, surrounding the church door, are many carved statues, but these are unfortunately in a bad state of repair. Inside the church, the chapel of Saint Martin is built on the spot where he is said to have died. Legend tells that the monks who were left guarding his body fell asleep, and the monks from Tours came and stole the body, taking it upstream to Tours where he is

At the end of a long drive beyond wrought iron gates stands the 18th-century mansion of Montgeoffroy.

The Great Abbey of Fontevraud—Resting Place of Kings of England

The superb Abbaye Royale de Fontevraud where two Plantagenet kings of England are buried, was built in the 12th century to house not just monks, but also nuns. In addition, it had a leper house, a hospital, and a house for "fallen women". These five separate establishments were ruled over by an abbess; the first of these was chosen by the founder of the abbey, and subsequent abbesses were often chosen from the nobility and a few were of royal blood. The abbey was richly endowed by the Plantagenets, and later by the French kings, and its buildings are a testament to their generosity.

Although many of the buildings are still in process of restoration, the visitor can see for himself how impressive they are. The great church was consecrated in 1119, and is a superb example of Romanesque architecture. There is just one great nave, divided into bays with domed roofs. Beautiful rounded columns and arches decorate the side walls. The chancel is a masterpiece of tall columns topped by an arcaded triforium. In the abbey are the four beautifully decorated tombs of Henry II, Eleanor of Aquitaine (his wife), Richard I, Coeur-de-Lion and Isabella of Angoulême, his sister-in-law, the wife of King John. The tombs are normally in the south transept, but the church was being restored in 1990, and they were temporarily placed on a platform in the chancel, where they could be seen from a temporary viewing platform. These monuments are some of the finest polychrome monuments to be found, dating from the early 13th century and made from tufa limestone. Except, that is, for Isabella's tomb, which was made from wood. Despite being severely damaged during the Revolution, they are in a remarkable state of repair. The adjoining cloister is a haven of peace and quiet, with its lovely garden in the centre and beautiful carvings on the vaults of the cloisters around it.

On the opposite side is the refectory, with the strange, circular Romanesque kitchen leading from it. It has a central conical roof surrounded by smaller conical roofs with extraordinary chimney pots. Between the two, on the eastern side of the cloister, is the beautiful chapter house with its carved Renaissance doorway and murals depicting the Passion of Christ. The community room, once the only heated room in the abbey, adjoins the chapter house.

Other buildings have been restored and may be seen from the outside. The religious orders were driven from the abbey during the Revolution, and it fell into disrepair until 1804 when Napoleon converted it into a prison. Even the church was used to house prisoners. At the turn of the century the abbey church was handed to the Ministry of Culture, who began to restore it.

It was not until 1963 that the rest of the buildings ceased to be used as a prison, and the Historic Monuments Commission began restoring the abbey. It is now known as *Centre Culturel de l'Ouest*, and every year there are concerts and plays, seminars and courses held in these fine buildings.

buried. As they journeyed, the flowers in the nearby fields are supposed to have burst into flower, giving rise to the saying "Saint Martin's summer".

The cobbled street to the right of the church leads to the meadows above the village, where there is a lovely view over the confluence of the rivers Vienne and Loire. **Fontevraud** with its famous abbey is only 6km (4 miles) from Candes.

South of Saumur, 18km (11 miles) away, is the town of **Montreuil-Bellay**, yet another place with a superb feudal

From the air some idea may be gained of the vast extent of the Abbey of Fontevraud, much of which dates from the 12th century.

château standing high above the river valley. The barbican, moats and fortified ramparts date from the time it was built, in 1025. The underground passages and kitchens date from the Middle Ages, the kitchens being in very good condition.

The other buildings, including the church, were built during the 15th and 16th centuries. There is a lovely turreted staircase with mullioned windows and carved balustrades – which are, in fact, an illusion, for there are no balconies behind them. The rooms in the château contain some fine furniture, and the oratory has some lovely frescoes on the walls, depicting angel musicians with their instruments.

Much of the original town wall still stands, including the massive remains of the 15th-century **Porte-Saint-Jean**. From the gardens by the river there is an impressive view of the castle.

There are many narrow streets and steep alleyways in the town, which also has an aquarium devoted to the fish and other aquatic creatures which are found in the local rivers, and a museum of crafts and traditions, with tools, everyday objects and costumes related to the local area.

The forest of Brossay separates Montreuil-Bellay from the ruins of the 13th-century abbey of **Asnières**. The building was built in Angevin Gothic style and the choir, transept and belfry are in a very good state of preservation.

Doué-la-Fontaine is known as the town of roses. Every year, a rose festival is held in the town's amphitheatre, **Les Arènes** which attracts many visitors to the area. The rose gardens themselves contain some 5,000 roses, with 500 varieties representing the production of the growers of the area.

The amphitheatre is believed to have been converted from an old quarry in the 15th century, when all the terraces were carved from solid rock. In addition to the rose shows, it is used for plays and concerts. Doué has made good use of its old quarries, for the zoo is also located in some. The deep pits with their natural vegetation have

This is the central farmyard of the troglodyte village of Louresse-Rochemenier. It is below the level of the surrounding land and dwellings are excavated into the sides.

been changed into open-air compounds for lions and other large animals. There is a vulture pit, and several islands for colonies of a rare breed of monkeys.

On the southern outskirts of the town is the **Maison Carolingienne**, built in the 9th century and subsequently transformed into a keep during the 10th and 11th centuries.

Troglodyte dwellings are a great feature of this whole area. In Doué there are some large quarries, known as **Les Perrières**, which have been

converted into troglodyte homes that have been occupied continually since the 19th century.

At nearby **Louresse-Rochemenier** is a complete troglodyte village, with cave dwellings surrounding a central square. It is now an interesting museum, showing the way of life in the caves in the last century.

At nearby **La Fosse** is another troglodyte hamlet, still in use as a family home. Both these places are different from the troglodyte dwellings along the banks of the Loire, in that they have been dug out from the plains. At **Dénizé-sous-Doué** is an extraordinary underground cavern filled with carved figures cut into the rock. It is believed these may have been created by 16th-century stonemasons who met in secret at the time of the persecution of the Huguenots.

The surprisingly comfortable interior of an underground dwelling at Louresse-Rochemenier.

Gennes is the site of an impressive Roman amphitheatre, one of the best preserved in existence. Many of the artefacts found on the site are housed in a nearby archaeological museum. In the neighbourhood are a number of megalithic monuments, including an impressive dolmen, and about 3km (2 miles) to the south-west is an interesting 16th-century water mill which is still in working order. Standing high above the river Loire, overlooking the bridge, is the ruined 12th-century church of Saint Eusèbe, where, in 1940, some of the cadets from Saumur stood firm against the German army. It is a fitting site for the memorial to

The 15th-century crenellated tower beside the church is all that remains of the castle at Trêves.

all those cadets who lost their lives defending the Loire from Gennes to Montsoreau.

Between Gennes and Saumur there are some lovely old churches. The priory church at **Cunault** is the finest of them, a beautiful tall Romanesque church, with beautiful carvings over the west door, and on top of the very tall pillars inside. A pair of binoculars might be useful here. There is also a beautifully carved and painted reliquary of Saint Max, who was a disciple of Saint Martin of Tours.

There is a rather nice public park in the former abbey grounds. Another Romanesque church and a ruined keep can be found at **Trêves**. **Chênehutte-Trèves-Cunault**, a different village, has an 11th-century priory church, **Notre Dame des Tuffeaux**.

*T*own plan of Angers.

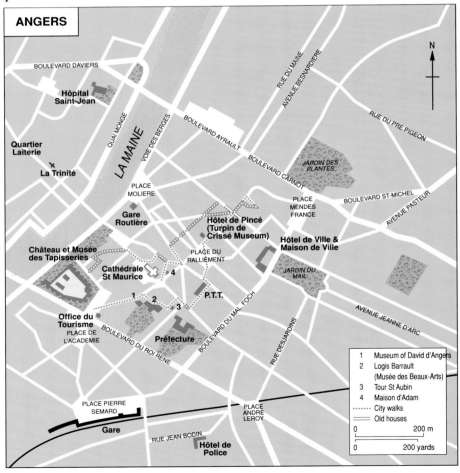

Angers

Angers, the old capital of Anjou, and principal town of Maine et Loire *département*, stands on a slope above the river Maine. It is known that there were prehistoric settlements in the area around Angers, and the Romans built a settlement where the city now stands in the 2nd century. Later, Foulques the Red, first count of Anjou, established the Angevin dynasty, and one of his descendants, Foulques Nerra, built a château at Angers. The dynasty reached its peak in 1154, when Henry Plantagenet, who had already acquired much of the land to the south by his marriage to Eleanor of Aquitaine,

T he only entrance to the fortress of Angers lies over the drawbridge, but today a herd of deer grazes in the dry moat.

succeeded to the throne of England. The French kings tried for more than 50 years to capture Anjou from the English, and finally succeeded in doing so in 1205, when King John had to relinquish his lands to King Philippe-Auguste. About 30 years after this, Louis IX began to rebuild Foulques Nerra's château. A university was founded in Angers in 1364, and soon achieved an international reputation. But it was "Good King René", a great scholar and patron of the arts, who developed the city's reputation as a centre of culture and learning.

The Revolution and the Vendée Wars left their mark on the city, when many of the old churches and other buildings were destroyed. At the beginning of the 19th century Napoleon ordered the ramparts to be pulled down, but in the same century the city began to rise again, with the construction of wide boulevards, beautiful gardens, and the rebuilding of the quays and docks.

Today, Angers is a busy university city, having two universities and a number of other institutes of higher education, many of them specializing in technological subjects. A new science park has been developed on the University campus at **Belle-Beille**, called **Technopole**. The main industries include garment manufacture and textiles, including tapestries, and of course the production of Cointreau. In addition, it is an important commercial centre, the head offices of many national organizations being situated in the city.

Angers is also a stopping place for travellers, both from home and abroad, on their holiday journeys to and from the south, which makes it an important tourist centre.

The first thing the visitor sees on entering the city from the main autoroutes is the **château**. It is doubtful if there is such a fine example of a massive feudal fortress existing elsewhere. The huge walls, complete with no less

---

The Tapestries of the Apocalypse

The largest known set of tapestries in the world, they are housed in a purpose-built gallery reached via the little turreted lodge by the Logis Royal. Louis died not long after the tapestries were finished, and his grandson, "Good King René" gave them to the Church in Angers. They were maintained by the cathedral and considered one of its greatest treasures, but in the mid-18th century they were removed on the instructions of the canons. Apparently, they deadened the sound, so it was difficult to hear the services! The tapestries rapidly deteriorated, mainly because they were stored in the wrong conditions, and many were severely damaged or lost completely during the Revolution. It was not until the mid-19th century that some were rediscovered in the Bishop's Palace, and an attempt at restoration began. Other remnants were sought out, purchased and restored, and after many years of work, they were returned to the castle for which they were designed. Of the original 90 tapestries, 75 still remain. Sadly, the cartoons from which they were made disappeared long ago, so it is not known what the missing ones looked like. The original length of the tapestries was 130m (142yd) in total, and each had a height of more than 5m (16 ½ ft). It is a superb work of art, and should not be missed.

T his illustration shows a small detail of the great Tapestry of the Apocalypse in the château at Angers, but it cannot do justice to the real thing—it has to be seen in its entirety to appreciate fully the magnificent work of art.

than 17 towers, occupy a distance of more than 1km (¾ mile), and are some 40m (130ft) tall. Originally there were pepper-pot roofs and *chemins-de-rondes* at the top of each tower, but these were removed in the 16th century. The great moats are now filled with beautiful gardens, and in one section a small herd of deer grazes peacefully, only a few yards from busy traffic. The entrance is via the **Porte de la Ville**, on the north side of the outer walls. Inside, across the drawbridge, is a very large courtyard, planted with trees and flower beds, and containing several buildings. The largest of these is the beautiful 15th-century chapel and **Logis Royal**. The chapel has some fine vaulting, and on one of the keystones there is a carving of the Cross of Anjou. In the Logis Royal are some lovely 15th-century tapestries, decorated with flowers of all descriptions, and known as *Milles-Fleurs* tapestries. In the **Governor's Lodging**, on the far side of the courtyard, are more tapestries, this time from the 16th century.

The most famous of all, however, are the tapestries of the Apocalypse, made in Paris for Louis I, Duke of Anjou in the 14th century.

Outside, in the courtyard between the two wings of the building, are the remains of the original Romanesque château chapel.

Before leaving the grounds, take a walk along the top of the château walls, where some beautiful gardens have been created, including a medieval garden. Some vines have also been planted here. There are fine views from the **Tour du Moulin**, the tallest of the remaining towers, both across the city and over the river to **La Doutre**.

The cathedral of **Saint-Maurice** was built mostly during the 12th and 13th centuries. It is a fine example of early Gothic, or Angevin architecture, and has a beautifully carved entrance portal on the west front showing Christ in Majesty, surrounded by the symbols of the four Evangelists. Unfortunately this was badly damaged during the Revolution, but the skilled carving is still clearly visible. The tall steeples were added in the 15th century, and the octagonal bell tower during the Renaissance. Inside, the main nave is supported on the original pillars of an earlier church, and the vaults were built on top of these. The stresses involved in building the high roof were reduced by having diagonal arches built above the transverse and longitudinal arches. This is probably the earliest example of Angevin vaulting, which originated in Anjou and gives a more domed-shaped roof. The transept and chancel are of later date, and have taller, more pointed arches and eight ribs to the vaults instead of four. The cathedral contains some fine stained glass and a beautiful baroque altar. There is also a statue of Saint Cecilia by David d'Angers, and a number of fine tapestries. The interesting one of *The Last Supper* mysteriously depicts 14 figures, instead of 13! The cathedral treasury contains, amongst other valuable relics, a green marble font used for the baptisms of the Dukes of Anjou, and an urn given by Good King René.

In the old **Abbaye Toussaint** (All Saints Abbey), is the **Museum David d'Angers**. The old abbey church, in ruins until only a few years ago, was covered with a glass roof to make a fine setting for the collection of the sculptor's works. A lovely arcaded cloister adjoins the building.

A colourful scene typical of the Loire countryside. As well as wine and market garden produce, there is also much arable farming in the area around Anger.

David d'Angers— Artist and Sculptor

Pierre-Jean David was born on 12 March 1788 in a cramped and humble dwelling in the old rue de l'Hôpital, the street which now bears his name in Angers. The son of Pierre-Louis David, also a sculptor, he was the youngest of four children. He was a rather sickly lad, and had an extraordinary childhood. He was barely five years old when his father enlisted as a volunteer in the Republican army and took the young lad with him into the Vendée.

The Vendéen War
The French Revolution had taken place in 1791, and had offered little of advantage to the peasants in the countryside—townspeople, on the other hand, saw more benefits, and the peasants resented this favouritism. The final straw came when mass conscription was imposed by the convention in March 1793, and the peasants of the Vendée and Les Mauges, in the south of Anjou, decided to fight against it. These people were basically royalists and rose in revolt. The revolt began in Saint-Florent-Le-Vieil on 12 March 1793.

By 15 March the Royalists had captured Cholet, but the Republicans counter-attacked. The Vendéens were forced to retreat to the River Sèvre, beyond Cholet. They soon regrouped, however, and were able to fight back, so that by the end of June the Royalists had gained control over the whole of Anjou. The following autumn the Republicans retaliated again, attacking the royalists from the south. On 18 October the Vendéens were defeated at Cholet and retreated, taking with them their prisoners and their wounded, among them General Bonchamps, to Saint-Florent-le Vieil.

The model of Jean Bart by David d'Angers, from which a bronze statue was made for the town of Dunkirk in 1845.

A Lasting Effect
The Vendée War was a particularly bloody civil war, and it was an unhappy time for the boy; what he saw there would remain etched in his memory for ever. His father was captured, and was one of the 5,000 Republican prisoners who were held captive in the church of Saint-Florent in October 1793. Such were the atrocities committed by the Republican armies during the war that the Vendéens were planning to massacre all the prisoners they held. The dying Bonchamps heard about the plan, and begged that his men should spare them. His cousin ran to the church, crying *Grâce aux Prisonniers* and the

287

prisoners were spared. On the following day, some 80,000 Vendéens crossed the River Loire. They were massacred by Republican troops, shot down in their thousands, and many drowned in the fast flowing waters of the river.

The Return Home

After the war ended in 1796 Pierre-Jean David returned home with his father. Times were very hard, and the family was reduced to living in very poor circumstances in the rue St-Aubin, as very little money had been paid to them during the war. His father was commissioned to sculpt *L'autel de la Patrie*, and the young David watched him with admiration. He himself wanted to be a sculptor, but his father, strangely enough, was greatly opposed to this.

Early Studies

Pierre-Jean David became a pupil at the Central College in Angers, where he became a friend of his drawing master, Delusse, who gave him much encouragement. During this time he worked with his father, putting the theory he was learning at the college into practice, and helping to support his family. His father was still strongly opposed to his vocation, however, and when the course at the school finished David had a new struggle on his hands.

Paris

In despair because of his father's opposition, the young David, with just 15 francs in his pocket, ran away to Paris, but he was brought back, and for a while was quite desperate. Eventually his father gave way, Delusse giving the boy his modest savings to supplement David's meagre purse. So, in 1807, at the age of 19, David came to Paris for the second time, with plenty of courage and determination but with barely enough money to survive. He spent all his free time studying hard, both day and night, in an attempt to gain a place at the Ecole des Beaux-Arts. He became a pupil of the sculptor Philippe Laurent Roland, but he also had to earn his living, and managed to obtain employment as a craftsman, working on the decoration of the Louvre. He also attended anatomy classes at the Hôtel-Dieu, which gave him valuable experience. The painter Louis David also accepted him as a pupil. Encouraged by his teachers, David spent long hours modelling a bas-relief of one of Poussin's etchings.

Success Begins

David was admitted to the Ecole des Beaux-Arts at the end of his second year in Paris, and was given a medal of encouragement. In 1810 he won the second *Prix de Rome*, and then received something which was, to him, of far greater value. This was a bursary from the town of Angers, to the tune of 600 *livres* per year, which seemed to him a fortune.

This enabled him to study full time. The following year he won the first *Prix de Rome* for a bas-relief *The Death of Epaminondas*. The prize enabled him to go to Rome to further his studies, but he was most anxious that his home town should have some tangible proof of his gratitude. He asked them if they would accept the models for his prize-winning works for the museum in Angers. The first of these were dispatched to Angers as early as 1811 and formed the basis for the collection of his works.

Rome

In Rome, David worked at the studio of Antonis Canova, and made the first of his many medallions. The model he used was a young girl, Cecilia Odescalchi, of whom he became very fond. It is her image which inspired his statue of St Cecilia which is in St Maurice Cathedral, Angers. David remained in Italy for five years, visiting Florence, Venice, Bologna, and Naples. He visited Herculanum and Pompeii, and produced many classical-inspired designs.

Return to France

In 1816, David returned to France. That same year his former teacher, Roland, had died, and left unfinished his statue commemorating *Le Grand Condé*. David was asked to complete the statue, which stands today in the Cour d'Honneur in Versailles. In 1817 he obtained his first commission, which was the Pont de la Concorde in Paris. The statue of Condé attracted much favourable comment when it was completed in 1820, and as a result further commissions poured in. In 1825, he completed the monuments to Bonchamps and King René, and was recognized as a master of his art. The following year he was elected to the Académie and became a professor at the Ecole des Beaux-Arts.

Bonchamps Monument

In 1824 when the monarchy was restored, the king authorized the erection of an official tomb for Bonchamps. It is interesting that David, a staunch Republican, should have received the commission. One wonders what he was thinking whilst he was working on it, knowing that Bonchamps was responsible for saving his father's life, and probably his own too, since he would have been held captive with his father. David attended the inauguration of the monument in the church at St Florent,

and was deeply moved by the occasion. Some of the survivors from Bonchamps' army were there, standing in the church, "worn down by the passing of the years, yet still carrying their old weapons". He recorded all that he saw, and his notebooks contain 58 individual drawings of these men, each one a fine character portrait and a wonderful historical record.

In Search of Great Men

David had now begun to embark on a new career as "the sculptor of history". He travelled throughout Europe in search of great men, and made busts of

The most famous of David's works is this statue of Gutenberg, inventor of the printing press, erected in Strasbourg in 1839.

289

Goethe, Paganini, Victor Hugo, La Fayette and many more. At some time he must have gone to America, because he is known to have made busts of Washington and Jefferson, and also a statue of the latter. He was commissioned to make the pediment to the Panthéon, which took him nearly seven years to complete as work was suspended for four years. The design was to illustrate the inscription "To great men, from a grateful country". David combined allegorical figures with certain historical ones, representing the Nation distributing crowns to Genius.

Family Life

David married, in 1831, the daughter of a Republican family from Anjou, and they had two children, Robert and Hélène. Both children were used as models in some of his works, one of the best being *Child with Grapes*, modelled by the four year old Robert in 1837. The family lived in Paris, and after his marriage David refused to travel further afield. David had always signed his work simply "David", but in 1840 he began to sign his work *David d'Angers*. It seems strange that he did very little work for his home town. Apart from the statue of St Cecilia and a Crucifixion in the Cathedral, the only piece of work to be seen on the streets is a statue of "Good King René" which stands near the château.

Politics

David wanted to go into politics, but his early attempts resulted in defeat. In 1848 he accepted the post of Mayor in the district of Paris where he had his studio, and was elected a member of the Constituent Assembly, representing Maine-et-Loire. The Revolution which deposed Louis-Philippe had taken place, but David voted against the return of Louis-Napoleon. He refused the post of Director of the Académie, and never set foot in his studio again. He considered it was more important to be a citizen than an artist. In 1849 he lost his seat in the Assembly and in 1851, when Napoleon returned, he went into exile. He stayed away from France until 1854 when, thanks to his friend, the poet Béranger, he was able to obtain a passport and return to France. He went back just once to Anjou before returning to Paris, where he died in January, 1856.

A Complete Record

Because of his generosity in giving his home town the original plaster casts of most of his work, there is now an almost complete record of it housed in the Galérie David d'Angers. The works were originally housed in the Fine Arts museum, in a gallery which was opened during the artist's lifetime. In the 1970s, the town Council had been looking for a permanent, separate building in which to house the artist's work, and in September 1980 it was decided to restore the ruined buildings of the abbey church of All Saints (église Toussaint). The walls were reinforced and the gables rebuilt to support a new timber-framed roof which would be covered with tinted glass. The effect is of a ruined building, open to the elements, but it also gives a wonderful clarity of light to the interior. This provides a fine setting for the works of Angers' famous son, the only French artist to have given a record of his complete works to his home town. It is right that there is a museum devoted exclusively to his works. He only created statues to great men who had died, made busts of the living whom he considered worthy and superior to others, and made medallions of otherwise talented people. It is interesting to note that Bonaparte was only considered worthy of the latter.

The **Logis Barrault**, now occupied by the **Musée des Beaux Arts**, is a Gothic Renaissance mansion with an elaborate turreted staircase tower, built at the end of the 15th century by Olivier Barrault, Treasurer of Brittany and several times Mayor of Angers. On the north side of the building is a little vaulted gallery. Many famous people were entertained here, including Cesar Borgia, Mary Stuart and Marie de Medici. Later it was sold to the Bishop of Angers and used as a seminary, new buildings being added in the 17th century. After the Revolution, in 1797, a museum, library and school were opened in the buildings. The collections in the museum include medieval and Renaissance furniture, carvings and enamels, and a fine collection of paintings from the 12th to 19th centuries, including works by Ingres, Watteau, Fragonard, Corot and local painters.

Hôtel Pincé is another fine Renaissance building with an elaborate staircase tower and some fine mullioned windows. It was given to the city in the 19th century and now houses the **Turpin de Crissé Museum**. This local painter was also chamberlain to the Empress Josephine, and his fine personal collection forms the basis of that in the museum. There are Greek, Roman, Etruscan and Egyptian *objets d'art* and antiquities, plus a fine collection of Chinese and Japanese art.

The **Hôtel de Ville** is a graceful 19th-century building facing the **jardins du Mail**. Beside it is the 16th-century **Maison de Ville**, with its round tower built onto the bare rock. This was once the College of Anjou and was later used as the town hall.

The **Tour Saint-Aubin** is a 12th-century combined keep and belfry tower which was part of a Benedictine Monastery which stood nearby. This was rebuilt in the 17th century and the buildings now house the **Préfecture**. Some of the remains of the original abbey can be seen inside the building by arrangement during working hours.

*T*he fine half-timbered 15th-century house known as Maison Adam in place Sainte-Croix is very near the cathedral and should not be missed when visiting Angers.

There is one exceptionally fine house in Angers which should not be missed. This is the fine 15th-century half-timbered **Maison Adam** in place Sainte-Croix. If you do not have the time to explore the rest of the old town, which is rather scattered about, then at least try to see this one. It should present no difficulty, because it stands very close to the cathedral.

Apart from the cathedral and the museums, there are several other houses, ranging from half-timbered merchants houses to elegant 18th-century mansions within the old city. The best way to see them is to walk. It will take about 1½ hours, not allowing for stops to visit museums and other buildings *en route*. There is a *petit train* which tours the city, but it cannot use some of the streets, because they have built-in steps and are too steep.

A Walk through the City

Start the walk by the main entrance to the château, cross over the promenade du Bout du Monde and walk up rue Saint-Aignan. About halfway up the street is a lovely old house, part half-timbered, part stone-built, with a little corner turret. There are other half-timbered houses nearby, but turn left here, along the little rue des Filles-Dieu, and at the end turn right again to climb rue Donadieu de Puycharic. This is a fascinating street, with some interesting old doorways, which follows a series of wide, shallow cobbled steps to reach the **Montée Saint-Maurice**. This is a true flight of steps, leading from the river straight up to the cathedral, from which there is a fine view in both directions. Turn right and climb to the cathedral square. To the left of the cathedral is the former Bishop's Palace, a 12th-century Romanesque building which was restored during the last century. Go past the palace and turn into rue d'Oisellerie. In this street are two attractive 16th-century half-timbered houses. Go past these and turn right along rue Montault to place Sainte-Croix. As you emerge, on your left is the half-timbered house known as the **Maison Adam,** already mentioned. Believed to be 15th-century, it has a number of richly carved vertical

A fascinating glimpse of old Angers seen in rue Saint-Aignan.

292

The Montée Saint-Maurice is a flight of steps leading from the river straight up to the very fine Gothic cathedral of Saint-Maurice.

beams on the façades, and unusual curved beams which stand proud of the gables to support the roof framework. All four storeys overhang each other, and the little corner turret is supported by a corner post in the shape of an apple tree. Unfortunately, during the Revolution, Adam and Eve disappeared! Walk round to the other side of the building and go down rue Chaperonnière, then go left again

along rue Plantagenet. Turn right into the pedestrianized rue Saint-Laud.

From this point on your walk, you will find plenty of opportunities for refreshment at the numerous little cafés to be found in these pedestrianized streets. rue Saint-Laud is a pleasant little shopping street with several old houses. Notice particularly no. 21, a 15th-century house with some fine carvings. On the right is the little **Impasse Fourmi**, a reminder of what Angers used to be like in days gone by.

Continue to rue des Poëliers and walk down towards the rue du Mail, passing more half-timbered houses on the way. In rue du Mail are some 19th-century houses. Turn into place du Pilori, and you enter the town's old legal quarter. As well as old half-timbered merchants, houses, in this district are some fine town houses from the 16th and 17th centuries. Go down rue Pocquet de Livonnière and you come to place Louis Imbach, which was once the city's market square. Go to the left and turn left again to place du Pilori. In the rue du Canal, to the right, are some of the town houses mentioned above.

From place du Pilori walk up rue Lenepveu, another attractive pedestrianized street, which leads to place du Ralliement. Just before reaching the square, on the right, is rue de l'Espine where the **Hôtel de Pincé** is situated. place du Ralliement has a large underground parking area beneath the square. Above, it is dominated by the 19th-century theatre, and is a hive of activity. Walk across the square and along rue Saint-Denis towards the main post office. Take the street to the right of the building, which leads to rue Saint-Aubin, the main pedestrianized shopping street. Turn right along here, then left along rue du Musée, passing the keep of the **Tour Saint-Aubin** and continuing past the **Logis Barrault** to reach rue Toussaint. Turn left and walk down past the **David d'Angers museum** to the château at the bottom of the hill.

Parks and Gardens

Angers has some beautiful parks and gardens, which is not surprising, since it is one of the leading horticultural areas in France. There are beautiful "carpet gardens" in the château moats and less formal gardens on top of the walls. Public buildings such as the **Hôtel de Ville**, **Préfecture** and the **Musée des Beaux Arts** each have their own gardens, those of the Hôtel-de-Ville being particularly attractive. The **Promenade du Port Ligny** beside the river Maine is a pleasant green spot beside a very busy road, and even the roundabouts are planted with flowers and shrubs, and the bus station with trees. The **Jardin du Mail** is a formal garden near the town hall, and the **Jardin des Plantes** contains more informal gardens of the "English" style. These were planted in the 18th-century, and have pretty tree-lined walks, more informal flower beds, several statues and swans on the lake. Among the trees is a cedar planted in 1789.

In the south of the city is an arboretum with a unique collection of every species of oak tree, as well as other trees.

Across the river, the **Museum Saint-Jean** has a beautiful garden, and beyond **La Doutre** is the **Parc de la Garenne**, a wooded area beside the long *étang* **Saint-Nicolas**. This extends to the **Parc de la Haye**, another large wooded area, where there are opportunities for boating and walking, and children's activities.

To the west of Angers is **Le Lac de Maine**, a huge leisure area with a large lake offering all kinds of leisure activities, including sailing, sailboarding and canoeing. There is also a bathing beach with pedaloes and a restaurant and cafeteria, tennis courts and 'swin-golf'. There is a campsite in the park.

Shopping in Angers

Angers is particularly well known for its small shops, and there are many to be found in the various pedestrianized streets. Some larger shops can be found in place du Ralliement, including the department store **Nouvelles Galeries** and the menswear shop **New Man**. In the square are several small shops selling children's wear, which is made locally, and some good boutiques. This is also where you will find one of the best restaurants in the town, **La Rose d'Anjou**. Because it is a university town there are many small *créperies* and cafés to be found, and you can be sure of finding something to suit your pocket. There are good restaurants offering local dishes such as *Saumon de Loire Beurre Blanc Angevin*. In addition to the usual ingredients of shallots, butter and wine vinegar, the Angevin sauce includes dry white wine plus a very small quantity of the *lie de vin*, the sediment left in the vats when the wine has been drawn off. *Matelote d'anguilles de Loire à l'angevine* is an eel stew made with mushrooms, small onions, *julienne* vegetables and red wine. Also in the city are a variety of

Indian, Italian, and oriental restaurants. For chocolates and pastries, try **D. Saussereau** in rue Chaussée Saint-Pierre. There is also a good *salon de thé* here. Other *pâtisseries* and *chocolateries* can be found in rue Lenepveu, rue Saint-Aubin, and rue des Lices. The orange liqueur Cointreau is, of course, a local speciality, and is used in some of the more expensive chocolates.

You will find wine shops in Angers, including the **Maison du Vin** opposite the château, but it is more enjoyable to find a local *vigneron* in one of the villages in the area and taste before you buy. The area is noted for its wines under the general AC of Anjou. Most of the vineyards are south of Angers itself. Over half of the total production is rosé, with whites and a small production of reds. The Rosé d'Anjou, a medium sweet wine, is made all over the general Anjou region, with a much smaller production of Rosé d'Anjou *Pétillant*, a semi-sparkling Rosé d'Anjou.

There is a vast new covered market, **Les Halles** in place de la République, which is open daily except Mondays and Saturday afternoons. The open-air market is held on Saturdays in the boulevard de la Résistance, selling flowers, fruit and vegetables and clothing. Soft fruit is a speciality of the area, and the markets are the place to go to buy.

Like all the other major towns, Angers has a good selection of hypermarkets. Most of these are situated on the outskirts of the town in *Centres Commerciaux* where you will also find other shops. There is a large **Espace** (Leclerc) hypermarket in rue du Grand Montrejeau, on the road from the city centre to Saumur, and a **Carrefour** on the south side of the river near the new Jean Moulin bridge and the motorway. In the city itself, but to the south of the railway station is a **Supermonoprix**, in rue Létenduère, and to the west, reached by the exit to Lac de Maine, is a large **Euromarché**, in rue du Grand Launay.

The Surrounding Area

Across the river from the town is the suburb of **La Doutre**. *D'Outre Maine* means across the Maine, and it was once the area where the poor of the city lived. There has been a monastery on the north bank since the Middle Ages, and there is one there still. Tradesmen set up their businesses in La Doutre, and greatly contributed to the prosperity of the city. Today, the centre of La Doutre has been restored, and it is well worth a trip across the river, either by car or in the local bus, to see this interesting area. Pride of place must be given to the **Hôpital Saint-Jean**. Founded in 1175 by Henry II, possibly as part of his penance for the murder of Thomas à Becket, it served the purpose of hospital for the sick and also as a resting place for pilgrims, as did the Maison-Dieu de Coëffort in Le Mans.

The building was in continuous use as a hospital until the 19th century. The ground on which it stands was given by the Abbess of Ronçeray, whose abbey was nearby. Throughout its history, it was open to all patients regardless of their religious beliefs, and this continued, even through the Wars of Religion, right up to the Revolution. Historical records show that at

This cloister lies behind the great hall of the Hôpital Saint-Jean, founded in 1175 by Henry II and in almost continuous use ever since. It is now used to display contemporary tapestry work.

one time the building could house up to 500 patients! At the front entrance is a little colonnaded walkway, in front of which is a pretty garden. Inside this lovely building is the great hall or patients' room, with a double row of slender columns down the centre supporting typical Angevin vaulting. The very colourful tapestries which brighten the walls were designed by Jean Lurçat, and are known as *Le chant du Monde*. These are considered to be the modern equivalent of the tapestries of the Apocalypse in the château. They have a total length of 103m (338 ft), and there are 74 tableaux. Other contemporary tapestries are on display in an upstairs gallery. Just inside the great hall, to the right, is the old dispensary of the hospital, containing pots and jars and other equipment, mainly from the 18th century. Behind the great hall is the hospital chapel and the cloister, although these are not in a very good state of repair. The building to the rear is the original granary of the hospital, with its lovely rounded windows above a massive double entrance.

To the west of the hospital is the old centre of La Doutre, with some of the best-preserved half-timbered houses in the city. This part of the town is known as the **quartier Laiterie**. The 12th-century church of **La Trinité** was once the abbey church of Ronçeray, and is a lovely Romanesque building. The old abbey buildings are now used as the college of arts and technology.

Les **Ponts-de-Cé** lies about 7km (4 miles) to the south of Angers, at the confluence of the little river Authion with the Loire. It was here, in 1562 that the Huguenots who had been defending the château were overcome and thrown without mercy into the river. The town was also a scene of massacres during the Vendée Wars after the Revolution, and again in 1944 when many civilians were taken hostage and shot. The remains of the château, which was once King René's country house, are now used as the local town hall. An interesting museum of head-dresses from the region is housed in the keep.

Reflected in its moat the Château de Plesses-Bourré is an almost perfect 15th-century castle.

Some 5km (3 miles) upstream is **Trelazé**, famous as a quarrying centre for the black slate of Anjou. A museum has been established here where you can see how slate used to be quarried and watch demonstrations of slate-splitting. It is open every afternoon except Mondays, and a visit lasts about 2 hours.

A little further north, at **Saint-Barthelmy**, is the Cointreau distillery. Regular public tours of the distillery are arranged, including a visit to the museum, which tells the story behind Cointreau. Enquiries should be made at the tourist office in Angers as the times vary.

Further Afield

To the north of Angers are two châteaux with very similar names, which, although just out of the area covered by this book, are worth visiting. The **Château du Plessis Bourré**, about 18km (11 miles) north of the

The rather grim appearance of the exterior of the château of le Plessis-Bourré gives little clue to the beautifully decorated and furnished interior, of which this richly painted ceiling is an example.

city, is a lovely moated château flanked by four massive pepper-pot towers on the corners. It was built between 1468 and 1472 by Jean Bourré, secretary to the Treasury of Louis XI. It is a massive fortress, but is not at all grim inside, as there is a very large courtyard. To get to this you have to cross a 43-m (47-yd) long bridge over the moat, and a drawbridge. The château is unusual in that it has a narrow terrace around the base of the walls, designed to trap any heavy artillery and prevent damage to the walls. The rooms inside are beautifully furnished, and there is a fine painted ceiling in the guardroom. In the library is an interesting collection of fans from the 17th century to the present day.

Le Plessis-Macé stands 14 km (8 miles) north of Angers and when first seen looks as though it is partly in ruins. However, once inside there is an ornate 15th-century country house with a very fine carved stone balcony over the doorway, and an interesting square staircase turret which is stepped about halfway. The gables of the left-hand wing are elaborately decorated, as is the chapel roof. Inside, the rooms are hung with tapestries, and the chapel still contains its original Gothic panelling. The word *plessis* will be found at a number of places in Anjou, and is an old French word meaning an enclosure.

South of the river Loire is another château, **Brissac**, which is a mixture of different styles but very impressive because of its height. It was built originally in the 15th century, and the two round towers standing at each end of the building are clearly from this date. It was almost destroyed during the Wars of Religion, and the owner then decided to rebuild the château completely. However, having completed the first stage, he died before the remnants of the old chateau could be pulled down and rebuilt. The result is the strange appearance of an elaborate 17th-century building supported by two medieval pepper-pot towers. Since the early 16th century the château has been in the hands of the same family, the Dukes of Brissac. Inside are elaborately decorated rooms with some fine painted ceilings. In the dining room is an interesting gallery which looks just like marble, but is, in fact, painted wood. The furniture includes a beautiful 16th-century four-poster bed and some fine 18th-century Gobelin tapestries. There is also a rather nice theatre, built at the end of the 19th century. It is possible to stay at the château as a paying guest, but you would need to be fairly affluent to do so!

South of Brissac are the **Coteaux du Layon**, where the vineyards stretch for miles. At **Saint-Lambert du Lattay** is a very interesting museum, **La Musée de la vigne et du vin d'Anjou**. This tells the story of wine making from the first planting of the vines through to the finished product. It includes examples of what happened when a parasite

T o the north of the château of Brissac, on the road to Angers, stands this handsome restored windmill, one of a number to be found in the region.

The whole story of the growing of grapes and the production of wine is explained in this museum at Saint-Lambert du Lattay, outside of which is an old wine press.

(*Phylloxera*), destroyed nearly all the European vineyards at the beginning of the century, and explains how disease is now combated. There is a display of all kinds of equipment related to wine making and cask making, and an interesting collection of wine presses. The visit concludes with a video about the harvesting of grapes, and of course a taste of the local wine. Nearby is a waymarked path through the vineyards.

Chemillé is a small town 26 km (16 miles) south of Angers which is known for its medicinal herb garden, containing some 350 species of wild plants from all over the world. It is situated in the attractive **parc de l'Arzille** adjoining the town hall. The tourist office is in a little stone building in the centre of the park. You will find camomile, peppermint, hyssop, lemon balm and many other scented herbs and flowers. Most of the flowers are planted according to colour, and a very pleasant hour can be spent here. In the nearby documentation centre are books and brochures on the subject, and you can try a *tisane* free of charge.

The town has two churches called Nôtre-Dame. The old church is situated in the main street and, according to local legend, was consecrated by the Pope in 1096. The Romanesque belfry is considered to be one of the finest in Anjou. Sadly, the interior is much in need of repair, but there is an old baptismal font and some wall paintings to be seen. It is believed there are many more waiting to be uncovered.

The modern church of Nôtre-Dame stands on the hill above the town and was built towards the end of the 19th century. The ruins of the old gateway to the château can still be seen in the town, with a sculpture of a rather large man preparing to throw a huge stone on to the heads of his enemies as they pass through. Other remnants of the château, destroyed in the Wars of Religion, are scattered throughout the little town.

Saint-Laurent-de-la-Plaine, about 17km (10½ miles) north-west of Chemillé has a very interesting museum, **La Musée des Vieux Métiers.** Of all the museums of this kind, this is one of the largest and, when all the alteration works have been finished, will be one of the best. In 1968, the local blacksmith was clearing out some old tools from the forge to make more working space, and intended to throw them away. However, the local carpenter realized their potential, and suggested that they should be kept so that future generations would learn how men worked in the past. As a result, a small exhibition was arranged in the village which was such a success that many more old tools were offered to the collection. The museum now houses exhibits devoted to crafts of all kinds, from lace making to weaving, from carpentry to printing. Most of the exhibits have been collected from all over France by a team of local volunteers. Currently the old village cinema, where the first exhibition was held, is being incorporated into the museum. Rooms are being constructed to show old furniture, and many other exhibits are being expanded. The buildings themselves are fine examples of the carpenter's craftsmanship, for the carpenter, whose idea it was, has built some of these buildings according to the old methods. It is a fascinating museum, and well worth the visit.

Chalonnes-sur-Loire, 5km (3 miles) from Saint-Laurent, is an important centre for the wine industry of Anjou. At one time it was also a centre for growing hemp, used for making ropes for ships and other purposes.

The local church, **Saint-Maurille,** is built right beside the river, and there are beautiful gardens beside the river Layon, which flows into the Loire at Chalonnes. The local *Caveau* is the centre of activity here, with its opportunities for tasting the local wines.

The *vignerons* have also acquired a *petit train* which takes visitors through the village along part of the **Corniche Angevin** and through the vineyards. The valley of the river Layon has some interesting villages and picturesque sites, particularly **Chaudefonds-sur-Layon** with its old lime kiln and 17th-century *lavoir*.

Rowing boats may be hired at **Saint-Aubin-de-Ligny** for a peaceful trip along the river.

Between Chalonnes-sur-Loire and Rochefort-sur-Loire is the **Corniche Angevin,** a twisting road with superb views over the valley of the Loire. On the opposite bank are the villages of **Savennières** and **la Possonnière,** and the island of **Béhuard**. It was to this island, which still retains its 15th-century chapel and some old houses, that Louis XI came to pray before taking Anjou from King René. **La Roche-aux-Moines,** almost opposite Béhuard village on the north bank of the Loire, is the site of the château, long since

The attractive moated château of Serrant with its library and magnificent interior is near Saint-Georges-sur-Loire. It came into the ownership of an Irish family who supported the Stuart cause in 1749 and is still owned by a direct descendant.

disappeared, where King John had been defeated by Philippe-Auguste 250 years earlier. Savennières has a lovely Romanesque church and the most northerly vineyard in Anjou. There are only 100 hectares (250 acres), and its wines were much favoured by the kings of France.

The château of **Serrant** lies about 8km (5 miles) back from the river, near **Saint-Georges-sur-Loire**. It has changed hands several times since it was built, but in 1749 it was sold to Antoine Walsh, an Irishman, living in Nantes, who wanted it for his brother Francis, Earl Walsh. The family were known for their support of the Stuart cause. Louis XV rewarded the family for their support by creating Francis the Count of Serrant. A direct descendant of Francis Walsh, the Prince de Ligne still lives in the château. It is an imposing moated building, built during the 16th and 17th centuries and symmetrical in appearance with two large domed towers at either end. The courtyard is used for the performance of plays, often Shakespeare, during the Festival of Anjou. Inside is a magnificent stone staircase with a beautifully decorated curved ceiling. The library contains more than 20,000 books, and above the fireplace is a picture of Bonnie Prince Charlie giving a message for the French court to Francis Walsh. One of the bedrooms was prepared for Napoleon, who was due to stay at the château in 1808. He actually arrived, rather late in the evening, but only stayed for 2 hours before leaving for Angers, so he never slept in the room, which has an interesting domed ceiling and beautiful Empire-style furniture.

Down the river from Chalonnes is **Montjean-sur-Loire**, a little town offering a fine view from its church across the river valley to **Champtocé**. This is where the story of Bluebeard, made famous by the French storyteller, Charles Perrault, is believed to have originated, in the old ruins of the castle. Downstream a further 5 km (3 miles) is **Ingrandes**, once quite a large port when the river was fully navigable, but its main interest is that it once stood on the borders of Brittany and Anjou. In former times, when salt was taxed, Brittany was for some reason exempt from the charge, and a profitable smuggling operation used to take place here.

Nantes

The city of Nantes is not usually included in what is popularly called the Valley of the Loire. However, it seems to be too important to ignore, and in

T*own plan of Nantes.*

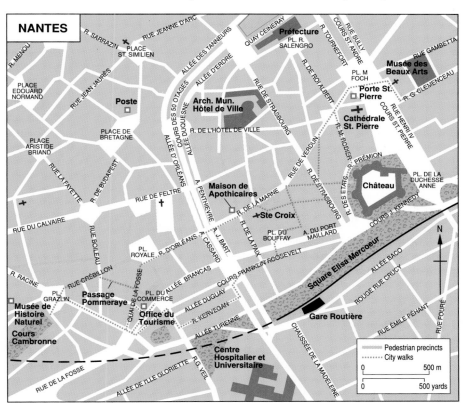

A Castle with Three Museums

The Château des Ducs de Bretagne is at the east of the old town, beside the Cours John Kennedy, one of the new wide boulevards which carry heavy traffic through the city. At the end of its occupation as a barracks during the 17th and 18th centuries a large explosion damaged many of the buildings within the château complex. After this the city bought the site and has carried out much restoration, including the establishment of three museums within the château.

Entrance is from rue des Etats across a wide paved bridge over the dry moat, now laid out as a park. The bridge leads between two massive round towers into the building known as the Grand Gouvernement. Here is the Museum of Regional Folk Art containing notable collections of Breton head-dresses and costumes from the 16th century to the early 20th century, together with furniture, wrought-ironwork, ceramics and implements. Across the courtyard in the building known as the Harnachement is the Salorges Museum which traces the maritime, commercial and industrial history of Nantes since the 18th century, with many model ships and boats. A third museum, in the Horseshoe Tower, is the Museum of Decorative Arts, an important collection of contemporary textile art including modern tapestry. Admission to the museums includes viewing the ramparts and the rest of the château complex.

fact it could be thought of as the gateway to the Loire. Today, it is the chief town of the *département* of Loire-Atlantique, a university city and one of the leading cities in France, a centre for commerce and technology and still expanding. Its origins, however, lie in Celtic and Gallo-Roman times. It was captured by the Bretons in AD 850 and later became the home and capital city of the Dukes of Brittany.

A wall was built to protect the town from Norman invaders during the 9th

*T*he Château des Ducs de Bretagne in Nantes saw the birth of Anne de Bretagne in 1477, and some of the earlier buildings remain intact. The central courtyard of the castle is reached by crossing the bridge over the dry moat and passing between two massive round towers.

and 10th centuries and the castle was rebuilt in 1466. Anne de Bretagne was born here in 1477 and in 1532 Brittany was united under the French crown. The treaty of union was signed in Nantes by François I, and in 1598 Henri IV signed the Edict of Nantes by which the Protestants were given freedom to follow their beliefs.

Its position on the river Loire led to the development of Nantes as an important commercial centre and port during the 16th and 17th centuries. In the 19th century ocean-going ships found the lower Loire too shallow so much of the trade moved to St-Nazaire.

However, Nantes has remained an important harbour and shipbuilding centre. In addition to the older parts dating from the 15th century, much of the city reflects the affluent period during the 18th and 19th centuries. Much of the damage caused by bombing during World War II has been restored and many modern buildings and wide boulevards testify to the active growth of the city.

The **cathedral of Saint-Pierre and Saint-Paul**, started in 1434 on a site occupied by earlier churches, lies to the north of the Château des Ducs de Bretagne, facing Place St-Pierre. The crypt dates from these earlier times. Construction of the cathedral continued until the 17th century. Much damage was caused during the Revolution (1793) and by the gunpowder explosion in the château (1800), the resulting restoration and some further building being completed in 1891. The nave is particularly impressive and in the south transept the tomb of François II sculpted by Michel Colombe (1502–

1507) is considered to be one of the finest examples of Renaissance sculpture. A tablet on the wall commemorates British soldiers who fell during World War I. The cathedral suffered a terrible fire in January 1972 which nearly destroyed the whole building, but complete restoration of the interior was undertaken, being completed in 1985.

The **Musée des Beaux Arts**, one of the finest in France, is housed in a large 19th-century building, completely restored. It contains collections of works by major artists from the 13th century to the present day, both French and foreign, well displayed in chronological order.

An Anglo-Norman family of ship owners named Dobrée who settled in Nantes in the 18th century bequeathed a collection to the *département* of Loire-Atlantique. It comprises an outstanding library of rare books, manuscripts, and engravings, together with enamels, oriental porcelain and other objects, and the museum bearing their name was established in 1894. The **Musée Thomas Dobrée** and the **Musée Archéologique** share space in the **Manoir de la Touche** (early 15th century), the **Palais Dobrée** (late 19th century) and a new building erected in 1974. The archaeological collections illustrate the prehistory and history of the Pays de la Loire from its origins to the Renaissance.

The **Natural History Museum** in Nantes, established in 1799, has been entirely modernized and is classed as one of the best in France. Other museums in the city include the **Jules Verne Museum**, established in 1978 by the Municipal Library, which is a

Nantes Festival d'Eté (Summer Festival)
This major festival takes place every year in early July. It is probably the most important event in France dedicated to worldwide music and dance, and is staged in the château in the centre of the city. The main stage is built in the central courtyard of the château, and, in addition, there are three secondary stages constructed in the old château moats (*douves*). There is a wonderful atmosphere in the town during the festival, for every day there are parades in the streets, street entertainers, spontaneous entertainment – the whole town is *en fête*. The festival village, in the place de la Duchesse Anne, is accessible to everyone from noon to midnight, and here you can find craftsmen from all over the world, try out traditional dishes and meet artistes from the festival. There is always a service in the cathedral and a procession through the city of all the artistes who are taking part on the Sunday afternoon. Performers come from Africa, Eastern Europe, India, South America, and Hawaii, as well as from France and other countries of western Europe. In 1990 there were gipsy musicians and dancers from Spain, France, Hungary, Poland, Romania, Yugoslavia and Albania performing together for the first time in France.

*E*very year in early July Nantes holds a festival of music and dance. Performances by groups such as these bagpipers from central France take place on temporary stages in the castle moat.

permanent exhibition dealing with the works of the famous author who was born in Nantes. A **Postal Museum** in the stores depot of the Regional Postal Administration, a **Museum of Dolls and Old Toys**, a **Printing Museum** and a **Planetarium** offer something of interest to everyone.

A Walk Through the City

A walk around the central part of the city will show the old town together with some of the elegant architecture from later years. A good starting place is the **Maison du Tourisme** in the former Bourse du Commerce, an elegant building facing on to the place du Commerce, part of a pedestrianized area. Walk around the building to the right into place de la Bourse and turn right, along rue de la Fosse. Walk past the 18th-century façades to place Royale, completed in 1794. The elaborate fountain symbolizes the city of Nantes surrounded by the Loire and its tributaries. To the right, rue d'Orléans leads to the busy and strangely named cours des 50 Otages, commemorating one of the atrocities committed against the citizens of Nantes during World War II. On the opposite side of this boulevard, continue ahead along rue de la Barillerie to place du Change in the old **Quartier du Change**, one of the oldest quarters of the city, where the 15th-century half-timbered **Maison des Apothicaires** still stands. Nearby is the church of Sainte-Croix, built in the 17th century. Go along the side of the church, rue Ste-Croix, and along the pedestrianized streets of rue de la Juiverie and rue de l'Emery. Here are more half-timbered houses and some former stables known as **Maison des Palefrois**. Take a look down some of the side turnings.

At the end, cross over rue de Strasbourg and go left. Fork right along rue des Carmelites and ahead into place St-Pierre to the cathedral. From here, the rue de l'Evêché leads to place Maréchal Foch where there is a tall column commemorating Louis XVI.

Elegant 18th-century mansions surround the square, with views along the boulevards cours Saint-Pierre and cours Saint-André. Turn round and look back towards the cathedral to see the **Porte Saint-Pierre,** built in the 15th century over the remains of the original 3rd-century city walls. Across the boulevard is the 17th-century **Eglise de l'Oratoire**, and to the right of it rue Georges Clémenceau leads to the **Musée des Beaux Arts**.

Return across the front of the cathedral and along rue Mathelin-Rodier to place Marc-Elder and the entrance to the **Château des Ducs de Bretagne**. Access to the park within the moat is further along in rue des Etats.

From Place Marc-Elder go along rue du Château, cross rue Strasbourg and continue ahead to place du Pilori. Turn left along rue des Chapeliers and rue des Petites-Ecuries then right, along rue des Echevins into place du Bouffay, the oldest square in Nantes. Formerly the residence of the Counts of Brittany stood here, followed by a law court and prison. All this was demolished and replaced in 1843, but a market place has been here since the 15th century.

South of the place du Bouffay another of the boulevards, cours Franklin Roosevelt runs along the line of a former arm of the river Loire. Cross over and go right to cross cours Olivier de Clisson. On the other side the *quartier* of the former Ile Feydeau contains perfect examples of 18th-century architecture in the mansions of wealthy merchants and ship owners. The wrought-iron balconies and carved stone masks along rue Kervégan, place de la Petite Hollande and

The fantastic and ornate Passage Pommeraye, a glass-roofed shopping gallery in Nantes which brings back memories of a bygone age.

along quai de la Fosse are certainly worth seeing.

Turn back and follow rue de la Fosse past place de la Bourse, and on the left is the somewhat unbelievable **Passage Pommeraye**. Built in 1843, it looks today exactly as it might have done 150 years ago. Three ornate flights of steps lead up between statues and through archways, with galleries on each side lined with shops which seem from another age, the whole arcade being covered by its original glass roof. At the top is rue Crébillon, a pedestrian street lined with elegant shop windows. To the left the street leads to place Graslin, passing **La Cigale**, a famous restaurant with décor straight out of a nineteenth century fantasy. In place Graslin is the classical façade of the theatre, and almost opposite is the cours Cambronne, lined with façades from the same period facing on to wide lawns and garden beds. Leading back from the square to the left is rue Jean-Jacques-Rousseau, where Jules Verne lived. At the end of the street, turn left along rue de la Fosse and so back to the starting point of the walk.

Away from the Centre of Nantes

The walk described above only covers the area around the city centre. A number of interesting places are situated further out, although still within the city. If they are too far to reach on foot there is a good bus network and a tramway runs from the north-east of the city past the main railway station and château, past the bus station near the place du Commerce (Maison du Tourisme), then west to the district of Bellevue beyond the Port Maritime. Details may be obtained from the Maison du Tourisme or from the SNCF railway station.

The Quai de la Fosse runs along the waterfront and continues as **Quai Ernest-Renaud**, overlooking the Loire. It passes the berth used by the sail training ship *Belem* when she is not on a cruise. On the right the rue de l'Hermitage diverges and runs uphill to the **Belvédère Sainte-Anne** from which a very fine view over the river and harbour can be obtained. Steps run down to the road along the riverside, and on rue de l'Hermitage overlooking the river is the **Jules Verne Museum**. Nearby is the **Planetarium** in square Moysan.

Not far away the long straight line of the Boulevard Saint-Aignan leads to place Général Mellinet, a perfect example of 19th-century town planning. Its octagonal shape is surrounded by eight elegant private mansions, each at the start of a long tree-lined avenue.

Beyond **place Maréchal Foch** near the cathedral the river Erdre is channelled beneath the city. There is a pleasant walk along the **Quai de Versailles**, which passes the embarkation point for the modernistic-looking craft known as River Palaces. These operate sightseeing cruises on the river Erdre at a leisurely pace as far as Sucé-sur-Erdre, during which the passengers may, if they wish, wine and dine in luxury. The best way to see the river.

Parks and Gardens

Many of the squares and wide boulevards (*cours*) in the city are lined with trees and have gardens. The drained moat of the château is laid out as a park, and it is here that many of the performances of the annual Nantes summer festival are staged. On the other side of the cours John Kennedy the **square Elisa Mercoeur** extends alongside the coach station. Opposite the main railway station the **Jardin des Plantes** (Botanical Garden) provides a restful oasis near the city centre. To the north-west along the banks of the river Chézine the **Parc de Procé** has extensive lawns and flower beds with walks along the river. North of here is **Le Parc de la Gaudinière**, a wooded valley stretching along both sides of the river Cens, a stream which runs into the Erdre.

On the Erdre, not far from the river cruiser berth, the **Ile de Versailles** has been laid out as a Japanese garden. A wooded park surrounds the 18th-century château known as **Le Grand Blottereau** to the east of the city.

Shopping in Nantes

As a major city Nantes is, of course, a good shopping centre. The main shops are to be found in the partly pedestrianized area bounded by place Graslin, place du Commerce, place Royale and place de Bretagne, including rue Crébillon, Rue Scribe, Rue Rubens and rue Contrescarpe, not forgetting the Passage Pommeraye. The area in the old town around **Sainte-Croix** has a network of streets with smaller shops, while rue d'Orléans and rue de la Marne running north-east from place Royale also have major shops and boutiques. Galeries Lafayette is located in rue du Calvaire and so is Monoprix. Nouvelles Galeries are in rue de la Marne. Places to eat range from the most expensive restaurants to small but good restaurants in the old town offering dishes from practically every part of the world. One such recommended establishment is the Restaurant Le Carrousel in rue du Bouffay. The many pavement cafés such as those in the place du Commerce provide welcome rest from sightseeing. Nantes is a centre of the biscuit trade and the region is an important fruit and vegetable producer. It is also the centre of the Pays Nantais region, producing Muscadet and Gros Plant white wines. Special dishes from the Nantes area include *brochet beurre blanc* (pike in butter sauce), *alose grillée* (grilled shad), *sandre de Loire* (freshwater fish similar to perch), *civelles* (baby eels) and *canards nantais* (duck).

Hypermarkets are either on the edge of Nantes or in the suburbs. E. Leclerc and Carrefour are both off route de Paris to the north-east of the city, in the *Centre Commercial "Paradis"*. To the north-west, Hyperloire is off route de Vannes and Euromarché is off boulevard du Massacre. Carrefour is also in the *Centre Commercial* on Beaulieu island between the two branches of the river Loire south of the city. Branches of E. Leclerc are at Atout Sud, rue Ordronneau in the southern suburb of **Rézé**, in *Centre Commercial "Atlantis"*, Route de St-Etienne de Montluc, in the suburb of **St-Herblain** and in the *Centre Commercial "Conraie"* in the suburb of **Orvault**, both the latter being to the north-west.

A lovely stretch of the river Erdre at Sucé-sur-Erdre, a popular stop for motor cruisers from Nantes.

Further Afield

The river Erdre has been described as the most beautiful river in France. This will, no doubt, be disputed elsewhere but it certainly is a beautiful river. Flowing north from Nantes through pleasant scenery, between wooded banks with châteaux and country mansions, once the river clears the suburbs of Nantes there are few roads running close to it along the valley.

The best way to appreciate the scenery is by boat and the river cruisers which run from the **Quai de Versailles** provide such an opportunity. The river is popular with owners of private motor cruisers and sailing boats, particularly to the north of **Sucé-sur-Erdre**. At this town the road D37 crosses the river, and beyond it widens to form the **Plaine de Maze-rolles**, where the river cruisers turn around. The canal from Nantes to Brest begins here and a few kilometres further north the town of **Nort-sur-Erdre** marks the limit of navigation.

About 11km (7 miles) east of Nantes is the **Château de Goulaine** which has been occupied by the family of Goulaine for over 1,000 years. The present building was erected in the 15th century over the remains of an earlier castle. It is the last château of the Loire, although its position is on the edge of Bretagne. The beautifully furnished apartments on the first floor may be visited, and a large greenhouse contains hundreds of tropical butterflies which fly freely around visitors. The Marquis de Goulaine, present owner of the estate, is a leading grower and producer of Muscadet wine.

T he red-tiled roofs and houses show the Italian style of the town of Clisson.

The vineyards of the area are concentrated to the east and south of Goulaine and are noted for their Muscadet (white) and Gamay (rosé) wines. It might seem surprising to find that a few miles to the south-east, around **St-Créspin-sur-Moine** and **Clisson**, there are extensive uranium mines.

Clisson is an attractive town on the borders of Anjou, Poitou and Brittany. Its impressive medieval castle overlooks a deep valley at the confluence of the rivers Sèvre and Maine. Built on a rocky spur overlooking the river in the 13th century, it was enlarged and improved during succeeding years culminating in the construction in 1590 of further outer defences. In the 17th century the château was modified as a residence, but during the Revolution, in 1793 and 1794, the town was subjected to acts of terrorism and completely

The only building to survive the fires which destroyed Clisson during the Revolution was the covered Market Hall, whose fine and intricate timber construction may be seen here.

destroyed by fire, only the market hall surviving.

A diplomat named Cacault had been an ambassador in 1790, and on his return found Clisson in ruins. He planned to establish a museum and school at Clisson and invited the sculptor Frédéric Lemot to come there. Lemot found that the scenery reminded him of Italy so he set to work to rebuild the town. Many of the houses and the church are in Italian style. Lemot bought the ruins of the castle and saved them from further destruction. Finally, he created a neoclassical villa and park in the Italian style across the river, known as the **Domaine de la Garenne-Lemot**. The estate is now the property of the Département de Loire-Atlantique and the villa and other buildings are used for art exhibitions and musical events.

Above Nantes, the Loire is wide and is divided by islands. About 25km (15 miles) upstream hills close in again and on the south bank a rocky hillside is crowned by the ruined castle of **Champtoceaux**. Celtic and Roman occupation were followed by stronger fortifications including defences on the river bridge. After two sieges in 1230 and 1234 the castle was ordered to be destroyed in 1430 by the Duke of Brittany. Two round 15th-century towers linked by an arch are the main visible remains of the castle, surrounded by trees. A terrace behind the church, the **Promenade du Champalud**, offers a spectacular view over the river and islands, and the bridge at the foot of a steep winding road down through the trees.

Near the bridge some ruined walls and arches are the remains of the old 13th-century ferry and toll house which collected dues from passing river traffic.

The town is pleasant with several good hotels and restaurants and a small museum in the *Syndicat d'Initiative* building on Le Champalud. Across the bridge on the other side of the river, **Oudon** has an old keep dating from about 1400 which also provides fine views across the river.

Above Champtoceaux the river valley widens again with more islands. Another 8km (5 miles) and a long suspension bridge crosses to **Ancenis**. The bridge supports carry the arms of Anjou at one end and of Brittany at the other, as the river formed the boundary. In fact, the castle whose ruins lie to the right just across the bridge has been called the key to Brittany. The **Château d'Ancenis** was first established around AD 980 and the medieval town and port grew up around it.

Virtually no trace of the medieval town remains and the castle was destroyed during the 17th century on the orders of Louis XIII. There remain two massive towers, the main part of a Renaissance dwelling and some 17th-century houses around the church. A magnificent view over the river is obtainable from the terraced gardens of the château.

The next crossing point over the river upstream from Ancenis is at **Saint-Florent-le-Vieil**. The town itself is on rising ground overlooking the river which, at this point, is divided by an island, **l'Ile Batailleuse**.

The settlement developed around a Benedictine monastery which was established here on the hill known as Mont-Glonne. Around AD 852 Viking ships appeared on the river so the monks fled. The island became a base for these Norman raiders until about AD 936, when Breton forces drove them away. The monastery was in ruins but was re-established, being later rebuilt in 1720. The tower and nave of the abbey church of that date are still in being, and the crypt and choir were further rebuilt in the last century.

GRÂCE AUX PRISONNIERS!

T his very fine sculpture by David d'Angers forms the monument over the tomb of the Vendéen leader Bonchamps in the church at Saint-Florent-le-Vieil.

Along the hilltop a tree-lined avenue extends from the church to a column which commemorates the Duchess of Angoulême. The abbey farm (**Ferme Abbatiale des Coteaux**) has been restored and the buildings house a tourist information centre and exhibitions and displays showing products of the Mauges region and fishery on the Loire, together with historical and religious exhibits from the area.

There is an aquarium with all kinds of fish found in the river. In the town is another museum dealing with local history. Saint-Florent saw the uprising which started the Vendée war in 1793. After the defeat of the Vendéens at Cholet a large body of them converged on Saint-Florent in order to cross the river. They had about 4,000 Republican prisoners held in the church and planned to massacre them. The Vendéen leader Bonchamps, mortally wounded in the battle, persuaded his men to spare the prisoners before he died. In recognition of this act of mercy, the sculptor David d'Angers, who was 5 years old at the time and whose father was one of the reprieved prisoners, created in 1825 the very fine monument over the tomb of Bonchamps in the church at **Saint-Florent**. The inscription on the statue reads simply "*Grâce aux Prisonniers!*"

Car Tours and Boat Trips from Saumur, Angers and Nantes

Although parts of the routes are suitable for cyclists, some areas are rather hilly, and it could be hard work getting up those hills! However, the tough climbs can be rewarded with some fine views, so may be considered worth the effort.

Car Tour from Saumur. Distance approx. 100km (63 miles)

The first part of this tour can be done as a separate short route to enable you to have more time to visit the abbey at **Fontevraud**. The whole tour will allow time for visiting some, but not all, of the interesting places on the way.

Leave Saumur by the bridge over the Loire and turn right in the direction of Tours, following the main road to **Varennes-sur-Loire**. From this road there are some excellent views of the hillside across the river, including the mill of **La Herpinière** and the château at **Montsoreau**. Cross the bridge at Varennes and take the road through Montsoreau to **Candes-Saint-Martin**. Stop here to look at the lovely old church or climb the hill above for a fine view over the river.

Take the road through the village in the direction of Fontevraud, which leads up to a main road which you will have to follow if you wish to visit the abbey. Return along the main road towards Candes, but fork left at the D947/D751 junction and in about 500m (550 yards) take the small road on the left. This leads past the mill of **La Herpinière**, from where you can examine the mill more closely, although unfortunately it is no longer open to the public. Continue along this road through the vineyards and back to the outskirts of Saumur. Go past the water towers, then turn right along **rue des Moulins** which leads to the large car park behind the château. There is a superb view over the river just before you reach the car park.

Continue down into the town and turn left into rue Maréchal Leclerc to continue ahead on the N147 towards **Montreuil-Bellay**. The dolmen at **Bagneux** is signed from this road and is worth the short diversion to the left to see it. Continue on the Montreuil-Bellay road through **Distré** and past the large electricity substation. After passing under the power lines, take the second turning on the left into the village of **le Coudray-Macouard**, then turn right to follow the road along the river valley through **Bron** to **Montreuil-Bellay.**

The road passes through vineyards, and there is a fine view of the château as you approach the town. Follow the road up to the town centre and park the car in the square before visiting the château or taking a walk round the town.

Leave Montreuil-Bellay by returning downhill and then take the road on the left alongside the river. Go under the bypass and continue for another 4km (2½ miles) before turning right uphill towards **le Puy-Notre-Dame**.

The road goes through vineyards to le Puy, where you join the D87 road to **Doué-la-Fontaine**. This is a good stopping place for refreshment, or to buy food for a picnic, or you can spend some time in the rose gardens or the zoo.

Take the D69 road north out of the town towards **Dénezé-sous-Doué** and Gennes. After passing the **Château du Pont-de-Varenne** on your right, turn left to **Rochemenier** to visit the troglodyte village, or go straight on to

Dénezé. The **Caverne-Sculptée** is in a small road going off to the left, and is signed. Continue to **Gennes**, and stop near the ruins of the old church up the hill on the left to admire the view over the river Loire. Go back down into the town and take the D751 along the river bank, which goes back to Saumur, stopping at **Cunault** to see the old abbey church, or to visit the **Mushroom Museum** at **Saint-Hilaire**.

**Car Tour From Angers.
Distance approx. 133km (83 miles)**

This route goes through the vineyards of the **Coteaux du Layon**, allows time for a visit to the wine museum or Crafts museum, and returns to Angers along the **Corniche Angevine**. There are some superb views to be had *en route*.

T his ancient dolmen stands beside the road on vine-covered slopes near Beaulieu-sur-Layon and is a fine example of many such relics of the past history of Anjou.

Leave the town in the direction of **Les Ponts-de-Cé** and cross the river to **Erigné**. Take the main road towards Doué-la-Fontaine as far as **Brissac**, leave the main road and go through the town to the château. From here, continue as far as the main road again, then turn right, taking the D748 in the direction of Martigné-Briand. After about 5km (3 miles) you pass through the village of **Notre-Dame d'Allençon** and go right on the D24 road to **Thouarcé**, a village on the river Layon.

Turn right on entering the village to follow the D120 road along the river for about 3km (2 miles) before going to the right again to **Faye d'Anjou**. Turn left in the village to follow the picturesque route through the vineyards to **Beaulieu-sur-Layon** and the main road. On the way you will pass a large dolmen among the vines on the left of the road. Follow the main road as far as **Saint-Lambert-du-Lattay**, where you can visit the wine museum. In the village, take the road to the right, and, keeping to the right of the cemetery, continue down to the river valley and up through the vineyards on the other side to **le Breuil**, to reach the D54 road leading to **Rochefort-sur-Loire**. Turn left, and in about 1km (½ mile) take the left fork which leads past the radio mast at Bellevue. Here, there is indeed a beautiful view, right across the valley to Angers.

Turn left along the D106 to **Saint-Aubin-de-Luigné**, then turn right to follow the river valley to **Chaudefonds-sur-Layon**. Here it is worth stopping to look at the lovely old wash-houses. The village gets its name from a warm-water spring, which is where the old

lavoirs are situated. There is also a very interesting old lime kiln here, standing beside the road. Continue for another 3km (2 miles) to the main road, cross over, and in a further 1½ km (1 mile) turn right to **Saint-Laurent-de-la-Plaine**.

After visiting the museum of old crafts, take the road back to **Chalonnes-sur-Loire**. Here, turn left and follow the road through more vineyards to **Montjean-sur-Loire**. Cross the river to **Champtocé**, then turn right to follow the main road to **Saint-Georges-sur-Loire**. This will allow you to visit the **Château de Serrant**. Go back to Saint-Georges, and cross the river again to Chalonnes-sur-Loire. Turn left and follow the steep and twisting picturesque **Corniche Angevine**, as far as **Rochefort-sur-Loire**. There are some superb views along this road.

At Rochefort, cross the Loire again to **Savennières**, then follow the north bank of the river to **Bouchemaine**, which stands at the confluence of the Maine and Loire. Take the road from here to **Pruniers** and Lac de Maine, and then return to the city by the main road.

Car Tour from Nantes. Distance: approx. 210km (130 miles)

It is possible to shorten this tour at several points by crossing over the Loire and returning to Nantes along the north bank. Alternatively, it could be split into separate sections. It goes through the valley of the Sèvre and through the vineyards to Clisson, before returning to the Loire to follow the river upstream. After crossing to the north bank, a more direct cross-

*T*he view over the valley from the Cirque de Courossé, a little-known natural amphitheatre near the village of la Chapelle-St-Florent.

country route is followed to Nort-sur-Erdre before returning to Nantes.

Leave Nantes to the south over Pont Pirmil and road N149 signed to Clisson. Immediately past the hospital on the right take the left fork D59 to Vertou. On reaching **Vertou**, after passing the château on the right, go

right at a crossroads onto road D115. This winding road leads across the river Sèvre. Strictly speaking it is the Sèvre-Nantaise to distinguish it from other rivers of the same name. Immediately across the bridge turn left and follow the road D58 through **Portillon** towards Châteauthébaud. About 4km (2½ miles) after leaving Portillon, go left along D63, cross the little river Maine and continue up the winding road to **St-Fiacre-sur-Maine**, which lies almost exactly halfway between the two rivers, the Sèvre and its tributary, the Maine. At St-Fiacre turn right onto D59 towards Clisson but then take a left fork on D76 to **Monnières** and **Gorges**, with fine views over the vineyards on both sides of the valley. About 2km (1 mile) beyond Monnières the road turns sharp left under the railway then turns right into Gorges. From here, turn left along D59 into **Clisson**.

From Clisson take the N149 main road, signed to Nantes, then after 2½km (1½ miles) continue ahead on road D763 to **Vallet**. In the town, pick up road D37 to the left to **le Landreau**. Keep to the left of the church and follow the picturesque road D307 through vineyards to **le Loroux-Bottereau**. At the beginning of the town rejoin road D37 and follow it to **St-Julien-de-Concelles** and continue to the bank of the river Loire.

Turn right along D751 which follows the river, then after about 9km (6 miles), the road begins to climb through vineyards to **La Varenne** and **Champtoceaux**, where it drops to the river again before climbing up to the town. There are fine views across the river to the cliffs on the opposite bank.

Continue along road D751 through **Liré** to **Bouzillé**. Just beyond the village fork right along road D201 to **la Chapelle-St-Florent**. Go straight ahead through the village and take the first turn to the left, signed **Cirque de Courossé** and **Château de la Baronnière**. Continue ahead, ignoring the next sign to the château, until you reach some large wrought-iron gates with a car park on the right. Paths and steps through the woods lead to a "hidden valley" among rocks, forming a natural amphitheatre with a river below. A notice in English warns that children must be held by the hand! The 100-year-old "promenade" belongs to the château. A small shrine in a grotto was set up in thanksgiving for the return of deportees and prisoners in 1946. Access to the area is only on foot but there are some pleasant walks to be made around the *cirque*.

Return to the car and retrace the route, taking the left fork back onto road D201, turn left and follow the winding road with superb views until it reaches road D752. Turn left and follow it to **St-Florent-le-Vieil**. Continue ahead across the bridge to **Varades** then follow the main road, N23, to **Ancenis**. Beyond the town, at **St-Géréon**, turn right onto road D164 and follow this to **Nort-sur-Erdre**.

Cross the bridge over the river Erdre and in the town take a turn on the left on D16 signed to Héric. Almost immediately go left again on the D26 road to **Casson**. Bear left beyond Casson and follow road D37 to **Sucé-sur-Erdre**. Beyond the railway bridge, go right onto D69 and continue along the Erdre valley, through la Chapelle-sur-Erdre and so back to Nantes.

Boat Trips

Below Angers the Loire becomes navigable by motor cruisers. Angers Croisières operate the cruisers *Le Roi René* from Quai de la Savatte. A variety of cruises with or without full restaurant facilities covers the river down as far as **St-Florent-le-Vieil**.

From Nantes the Erdre is navigable as far as **Nort-sur-Erdre** and the Sèvre as far as **Monnières**. Luxury cruisers with restaurant facilities are operated by River Palace of Nantes. Erdre cruises and cruises up the Loire start from **Quai de Versailles**, and cruises on the Sèvre start from **Parc de la Sèvre** in **Vertou**.

Walks in Maine-et-Loire

The *département* Maine-et-Loire publishes a series of 1:50,000 maps, based on the IGN maps, showing both short walks and long-distance paths in the area. The maps also show horse riding trails and cycle routes, but there are no accompanying descriptions of the routes. Since these maps are printed in black and white, with only the routes, forests and rivers in colour, better maps will be needed. The maps do, however, give the locations and addresses of suitable accommodation for ramblers, plus the location of the tourist offices and places of interest.

A Walk from Saumur—The Dolmen, Cave Dwellings and Woods

This walk follows the GR3 from Saumur westwards before returning near the National Riding School.

Local footpath routes are very well signed showing destinations, directions and distances, often with an estimated time for completion of the journey. This example is in the Sologne.

Start in Saumur at the south end of **Pont Cessart**. Walk through **place de la Bilange** and continue up the straight main avenue to **Pont Fouchard** at the far end of rue du Maréchal Leclerc. Note that this is the GR3 but it is not signed through the town. The red and white waymarks will be seen outside the town. Cross the bridge and turn left onto the footpath beside the rue des Peupleraies. After about 300m (325 yd) turn left onto a tarmac path between walls leading up to rue Desmarets. Follow this to place de l'Avenue, turn right along rue du Vieux Bagneux to **place du Dolmen**.

From the Café Grand Dolmen take rue de l'Arche almost opposite, continue across road N147 and along rue de la Bergère. Turn left at the cemetery, cross a road and continue ahead along the road opposite for 2km (1¼ miles). The road then becomes a path skirting Pocé wood before crossing a road to go down into **Riou.** Turn right and follow a winding road lined with cave dwellings, to bear right along road D305 into **Marson.** Turn left at the church, continue on D305 for 500m (550yd) and at the end of the wall of the château grounds turn right on a path along the edge of Marson pond and up into the woods.

About 1km (⅔ mile) from the pond the forest trail comes to a fire break and 100m (110yd) further the GR3 turns left onto a path leading downhill out of the woods. Follow wide paths between plots of land to reach road D161, cross over and enter **Villemolle.** Go through the hamlet and turn left at the crossroads to head north-west along a path leading towards some woods. Just after entering the wood turn left along a path leading to a wide avenue. Turn right and follow the avenue to the hamlet of **La Croix.**

At La Croix, leave the GR3, which goes to the left. Turn right and follow the road, which is a recommended cycle route, to the hamlet of **la Poitrineau.** Take the turning on the right after the hamlet and go straight ahead at a crossroads to **la Tour de Ménives.** Turn left and bear to the right on a road leading to a T-junction with road D161. This is on a *Petite Randonnée* and will be waymarked, but not with the red and white signs of a GR.

Turn left along D161 for about 500m (550yd) then right through woods along a forest road. Where it meets another road near the **Ecole Nationale d'Equitation** turn left and follow the road in an easterly direction. In about 1¼ km (¾ mile) there is a pond on the right. Immediately past the pond take a path to the right, cross

the road ahead, then follow the road along the airfield boundary. Turn left along rue François Bédouet to cross the main road D751. Continue ahead until you reach road D161, avenue du Maréchal Foch. Turn right and follow this back to the town centre and the starting point of the walk. Distance: 21km (13 miles).

A Walk from Rochefort-sur-Loire—Vineyards and River Bank

Rochefort is a small riverside town on the south bank of the Loire about 12km (8 miles) downstream from Angers. This walk follows parts of the GR3 and the GR3D through vineyards and along the Loire bank. It also drops into the valley of the **Layon.**

Start from the square behind the church in Rochefort. Follow the red and white waymarks of the GR3. Cross the square and turn left up a street which becomes narrow, then turns right, leading to a road. Immediately turn left onto a path leading downhill through vineyards to cross the Saint-Lézin stream and back uphill. In about 1km (¾ mile) it comes to a road. Turn right and immediately left along another path on the edge of a small wood. The GR3 then follows a track around the estate of l'Eperonnière.

At the next bend do not follow the GR signs to the right but keep straight ahead to join the road D125. Turn left to a crossroads then right down road D106 through le Grand Beauvais to **St-Aubin-de-Luigné** which lies in the pleasant valley of the river Layon. At the road junction, before crossing the bridge, the GR3D comes in from the left. Follow this route to the right between houses. The path heads north through vineyards and in about 600m (650yd) it bears left up the hillside, following a winding course. After about 1½km (1 mile) north-west, turn left along a road for a short distance then right onto a path leading uphill. Turn left again after about 250m (270yd) and walk into **la Haie-Longue**.

At la Haie-Longue, cross over the D751 road, turn right and pick up the route of GR3 going west. This passes a road leading to the beach and a refreshment room, then runs down to a tarmac path alongside an arm of the river Louet. Near **le Pressoir Girault** turn left onto road D751, follow it for a short distance then turn off right and go uphill on a track through vineyards. The path bears left past la Piécière and another *Petite Randonnée* leads off left, down to **Pic Martin**. Before reaching road D751 look for waymarks to the right, past Pic Martin then left into **Rochefort-sur-Loire** and the starting point. Distance: 14km (9 miles).

Walking in the Nantes Area

The Department of Tourism for Loire-Atlantique produces an excellent booklet containing walks, complete with maps and notes on the areas concerned. The GR3 runs through the area from east to west, with many branch routes.

A Walk from Le Cellier—The Tow-path along the Loire

Le Cellier is a village on the north bank of the Loire about 20km (12 miles) upstream from Nantes. This walk starts on the tow-path along the river and returns along the GR3 route.

Start from Rue Notre-Dame in le Cellier. Go down the road towards the Loire and under the railway line. Go left onto the tow-path and follow this along the river, following red and white waymarks of GR3. The path passes in front of a restaurant "Beau-Rivage" and around the railway tunnel at **Château de Clermont**. Continue along the towpath, with fine views ahead across the river. Beyond the next railway tunnel go left under the railway and take a small footpath which leads into the woods and the ruins of **les Folies-Siffait**, a rather mysterious place the origins of which are not too certain. The ruins are on a promontory with more magnificent views over the Loire. Return to the tow-path and continue left until level with **Saint Méen**, then leave the towpath and go up on the left towards the village.

At the crossroads take the road to the left and when level with **Château Guy** take a path to the right, which is waymarked in yellow, across the vineyard in the direction of **la Rousselière**. Bear left past **la Rocherie** with its old chapel and follow the path which turns to the left. Continue ahead as far as the D84 road, cross over and continue ahead towards **la Savariais**. Go through the hamlet and cross the D68. Continue straight on and on reaching **les Noues** go to the right as far as the bend in the road. Go left towards **la Vinalière**. Take the road to the right and in 50m (55yd) go left on a path which descends a wooded valley. After passing through **le Cul Froid** keep left and return to le Cellier and the starting point of the walk. Distance: 12½km (8 miles).

Things to Do, Places to See and a Few French Tips

The area we cover in this book has very good possibilities for many sports, from walking to riding, canoeing to golf, and not forgetting angling. Many of these activities have local committees who produce local information, but these often involve voluntary effort. For published information on local possibilities enquiries should be made to the major tourist offices or to local *Syndicats d'Initiative.*

Sports and Leisure Activities

Walking

There are many footpaths which cater both for those wanting short strolls or the more energetic who prefer long-distance walking, either carrying camping gear or using hostels or other indoor accommodation. The type of equipment and clothing required in more rugged regions is not necessary here, although good wet-weather clothing and lightweight walking boots or shoes are to be recommended. Note that the going can be wet in places.

In France there is a good system for establishing and maintaining walking routes. *Sentiers de Grandes Randonnées* (National Long-distance Footpaths) are marked in orange on the IGN 1:100,000 and larger scale maps, and are given a number prefixed by the letters "GR". All are waymarked (*balisé*) on the ground with horizontal white and red stripes on posts, using a standardized method of indicating changes of direction and junctions with other routes.

*W*hatever your interest, you'll find something to do in the Loire valley.

Regional long-distance paths cover particular areas, usually in the form of a circular route. They are called *Sentiers Grande Randonnée de Pays*, and are waymarked yellow and red. In addition, the network of *Petites Randonnées* provides shorter local walks, usually circular and which may be completed within a day. These are generally waymarked in yellow. All these paths are kept in order by volunteer members of the *Fédération Française de la Randonnée Pédestre* (the French Ramblers Association). Other local walking routes also abound, marked with different colours but almost always clearly signed. There is always the possibility of taking sections of a GR or other route and linking them to form your own circular walk. The choice is yours.

Full information on the GR network may be obtained from the *Fédération Française de Randonnée Pédestre*, 8, Avenue Marceau, 75008 Paris, who publish a series of *Topoguides*, in French, covering each GR route, with maps and other information. The English guide *Walks in the Loire Valley* is one of a regional footpath series, Footpaths of Europe, based on these Topoguides. It covers the GR3 within the boundaries covered by our book. The title is rather misleading as it does not cover any other possibilities in the Loire area apart from the main GR3.

Maps, leaflets or booklets giving information on *Petites Randonnées* and other footpaths may be obtained from the departmental tourist offices or from local *Syndicats d'Initiative*. Some are free but a small charge is made for most of them.

A map showing all the paths in France, with an explanation in English, is available from McCarta Ltd in London and from other good map shops. Both *départements* produce leaflets which are available from local *Syndicats d'Initiative*.

The region is traversed from Orléans to Nantes by the *Grande Randonnée* GR3 (*Le sentier de la Loire*), and a number of other GR routes cross the area from north to south or run through parts of it.

Cycling

Cycling is a very popular way of seeing the country, either cycle touring with or without a tent or simply by cycling around local routes. Many regions and *départements* publish descriptions of cycle routes which enable the visitor to see areas of special interest or beauty. These route descriptions usually include details of accommodation along the way. General information on cycle touring may be obtained from the *Fédération Française de Cyclo-Tourisme*, 8, rue Jean-Marie Jego, 75013 Paris. Tel: (1) 45-80-30-21. Information on local routes may be obtained from the departmental tourist offices. Information on hiring cycles may be obtained from the same sources or from local *Offices de Tourisme* or *Syndicats d'Initiative*.

Horseriding and Pony Trekking

There are many riding stables in the region, also centres organizing pony trekking with overnight accommodation. Many areas have waymarked routes for horse riders. Of particular interest are tours on horseback in Sologne, details of which may be obtained from *Loisirs-Acceueil du Cher*, 10, rue de la Chappe, 18000 Bourges. Tel: 48-70-74-75.

Similar trips can be made in the Perche and Sologne of which details are available from *Tourisme en Loir-et-Cher*, 11, place du Château, 41000 Blois. Tel: 54-78-55-50. Information on other possibilities may be obtained from the departmental Tourist Offices or local *Syndicats d'Initiative*.

In a number of areas touring by horse-drawn van is available. For example, information on week-long tours in Sarthe or Cher will be provided by the Tourist Offices, and details of many other local arrangements can also be obtained.

Angling

With so many large and small rivers and lakes, fishing is a popular sport. Perch, pike, striped mullet, carp and tench are to be found in the Loire lower reaches, the Indre and the Loir, also in pools in the Sologne. Trout are in the streams of Anjou and tributaries of the Loir. Salmon fishing is normally not allowed, being reserved for professionals. Permits are required and full information on these and on close seasons and other restrictions are available from local tourist offices or *Syndicats d'Initiative*.

Canoeing and Sailing

In some places, particularly on the river Loire itself, there are deceptively strong currents and eddies, and local advice should be sought. Canoe-kayak trips or camping tours are possible on many of the rivers and canals in the region, and cater for most levels of expertise. Tours may be organized in groups or craft can be hired by individuals. The firms catering for this activity are well organized and insist on minimum requirements as regards swimming ability and supervision of children. Visitors bringing their own canoes have plenty of opportunities for exploring the region's waterways.

Many of the larger lakes (*plans d'eau* or *étangs*), and some of the rivers offer the possibility of sailing in dinghies or small boats, either hired on the spot or brought with you. Here again, if sailing on the rivers take local advice regarding possible hazards. Sailboarding is getting very popular in many of these places, so visitors bringing their own boards are well catered for. Once again, enquire from the tourist offices or *Syndicats d'Initiative*.

River Cruising

Cruises on the Sarthe, Mayenne and Loire in the *Roi René* cruisers with catering facilities run from Angers. For full details and booking apply to Anjou Croisières, quai de la Savatte, 49100 Angers. Tel: 41-88-37-47.

Cruises on the rivers Erdre, Loire and Sèvre from Nantes are made by the River Palace fleet of luxury cruisers with restaurants. Full details and booking information are obtainable from Armement Lebert-Buisson, 24, quai de Versailles, BP 249, 44008 Nantes. Tel: 40-20-24-50.

River cruises on the Sarthe are operated by Le Sablésien, Quai National, BP 33, 72301 Sablé-sur-Sarthe. Tel: 43-95-93-13. Day and shorter cruises on boats with catering facilities operate on the canal from **Briare**. For details and booking, apply to Les Bateaux Touristiques, Maison Eclusière, Port de

Plaisance, BP 58, 45250 Briare. Tel: 38-37-12-75. Details and booking information on day cruises from **Gien** and from **Orléans** are available from Loisiers-Accueil Loiret, 3, rue de la Bretonnerie, 45000 Orléans. Tel: 38-62-04-88.

Cruises with a difference include day trips on the Mayenne in a horse-drawn boat operated by Féérives, BP 28, 49220 Le Lion-d'Angers. Tel: 41-88-88-78. Longer cruises on the barge "La Belle Marinière" depart from Le Mans harbour. For details apply to Captainerie du Port, quai A. Lalande, 72000 Le Mans. Tel: 43-28-82-00.

"Self-drive" hire cruisers are available from Chatillon-sur-Loire and Briare, bookings for which are handled by Loisirs-Accueil Loiret, 3, rue de la Bretonnerie, 45000 Orléans. Tel: 38-62-04-88. Information and bookings for firms providing cruisers on the Erdre and the Nantes-Brest canal are dealt with by Loisirs-Accueil de Loire-Atlantique, Maison du Tourisme, place du Commerce, 44000 Nantes. Tel: 40-89-50-77. Similar arrangements for cruisers on the Mayenne and Sarthe are handled by Maine Réservations, Place Kennedy, BP 2207, 49022 Angers. Tel: 41-88-99-38.

Golf

There are numerous possibilities for keen golfers, both beginners and experts. A selection of courses includes: Golf d'Avrillé, 5½ km (3½ miles) north of Angers at Château de la Perrière, 49240 Avrillé. Tel: 41-69-22-50. Anjou Golf and Country Club, north of Angers at Route de Cheffes, 49330 Champigné. Tel: 41-42-01-01. Le Golf d'Ardrée, 12km (7½ miles)

north of Tours at Château d'Ardrée, 37360 St-Antoine du Rocher. Tel: 47-56-77-38.

A group of four golf courses, two in Sologne, one in the forest of Orléans and one in the Gâtinais, have joined forces to operate what they call the "Golf Pass". This covers the green fees for 1 day on each of the four courses. An optional, more expensive pass includes hotel accommodation. The courses are at Sully-sur-Loire, Marcilly-en-Villette south of Orléans, Donnery at Château de la Touche in the forest of Orléans, and Vaugouard near Montargis. Full details are obtainable from Loisirs-Accueil Loiret, 3, rue de la Bretonnerie, 45000 Orléans. Tel: 38-62-04-88. Information on other golf courses can be obtained from the tourist offices or local *Syndicats d'Initiative.*

Aerial Trips

Trips by helicopter over the châteaux and countryside around are possible from, among other places:

Amboise-Dierre: Touraine Hélicoptère, BP 13, 37370 Neuvy-le-Roi. Tel: 47-24-81-44.

Blois: Apply to Office de Tourisme de Blois, 3, avenue Jean Laigret, 41000 Blois. Tel: 54-74-06-49.

Bourges: Apply to Loisirs-Accueil du Cher, 10, rue de la Chappe, 18000 Bourges. Tel: 48-70-74-75.

Tours: Tours Aéro Services, 4, rue des Augustins, 37540 St-Cyr-sur-Loire. Tel: 47-51-25-65.

Trips by light aircraft are also possible.

An unusual way of seeing the country is by hot-air balloon, known in France as a *montgolfière*. One example is in Indre-et-Loire starting near Amboise. For details apply to Loisirs-Accueil d'Indre-et-Loire, 38, rue Augustin-Frésnel, BP 139, 37171 Chambray-les-Tours. Tel: 47-48-37-27.

Other Sports

Most towns have sports and recreation parks or centres which may include tennis courts, swimming pools, both indoor and outdoor, indoor bowling rinks and other facilities. Local enquiry will show whether or not these are available to visitors.

The Loire for Children

Beaches

Although this area has no seaside, there are many beaches and sandy areas which are safe for children. These are mainly in recreation areas which also provide other facilities. Examples include the **Lac de Loire** near Blois, the **Lac de Maine** near Angers and **l'Etang du Puits**, all of which have bathing beaches, play equipment, walks and canoeing.

Animal Parks

There are several animal parks and children's zoos, such as the Parc Animalier at Château de Pescheray near Le Mans, the Parc Floral La Source at Orléans which has a small zoo and a miniature train, the zoo at Doué-la-Fontaine (Maine-et-Loire) and La Flêche (Sarthe). There is an animal park and children's farm in the château grounds at La Ferté-St-Aubin. Bird gardens are at Spay near Le Mans and at Beauval near St-Aignan.

Museums

Museums which may be of particular interest to boys are Le Compa Museum in Chartres with tractors and agricultural machines, and the car museums at Le Mans, Briare, Valençay and Romorantin. In Saumur is a museum of Toy Soldiers, and the museum of Tanks may interest the older boys. Leonardo da Vinci's models and machines in le Clos-Lucé at Amboise usually create much interest, and steam trains are always a good attraction. The lines from Chinon to Richelieu and from Salbris to Romorantin are worth enquiring about.

The girls are not forgotten. Tours has a good Doll Museum, and Nantes has its museum of dolls and old toys to amuse children of all ages.

Leisure Parks

The leisure park in the grounds of **Château Roujoux** has play areas, mini-golf and a miniature railway, and the **Château of Ussé** contains the waxwork tableaux illustrating the story of *Sleeping Beauty*. The **Museum des Vieux Métiers** at St-Laurant de la Plaine can be of interest and at Chinon the **Musée Animé du Vin** has some amusing animated displays.

Several towns have *Petits Trains* which take passengers on tours around the sights, examples being at Nantes, Angers, Chartres and Chalonnes-sur-Loire.

Finally, all the quality campsites have numerous activities (*animations*) for children during the high season. These are usually under supervision, and all have children's play areas with swings, slides, climbing frames and other such amusements.

Nature and Wildlife

Plants

Much of the chalk and limestone areas of the Loire valley have similar flora to the chalk Downs in England, with short turf and flowers such as field scabious, cowslip, harebell, gentian and various orchids. Roadside verges are often masses of colour with laburnum, lilac, and wild rose. Fields red with poppies or yellow with sunflowers make a striking picture, while meadows seem carpeted with cowslip, daisy, vetch, clover, cornflower and other species. One common sight is dark clumps of mistletoe in the trees, mostly poplar, looking from a distance almost like rooks' nests. Many of the extensive forests have oak and chestnut in abundance. Apart from the open plains of the Beauce fields are bordered by hedges with scattered copses which provide shelter.

Birds

Along the river banks, ducks and king-fishers are to be found. In the Sologne with its marshy ponds, heath and deciduous woods, herons, ducks, harriers and other species of water bird are common and the bittern may also be heard. In most areas with deciduous woodland, and where there are ponds with uncultivated land, hoopoes, woodpeckers, pheasant, partridge can all be encountered.

Other Animals

Both red and roe deer, some wild boar, and rabbit and hares are quite commonly seen. Red squirrels, hedgehogs, moles and various varieties of shrew, also badger, otter and red fox all occur fairly commonly.

Toads include the midwife toad and occur almost anywhere in damp places. Frogs add to the night sounds near ponds and marshes. Slow-worms and grass snakes, which are harmless, and poisonous vipers may all be seen. The latter do not attack people unless disturbed, and even then they usually slide quickly away.

Crickets fill the air with their song in spring, and many species of butterfly are attracted by the great variety of wild flowers. Many species of moth occur and dragonflies may often be seen flitting over streams in the sunshine.

Many species which were once common are becoming rare due to intensive agriculture and the activities of collectors and hunters. Collecting insects and birds' eggs is not to be encouraged. In fact, hunting with a camera is a far more friendly activity. Unfortunately, the French seem very much addicted to hunting birds and animals with shot guns, which can be hazardous at times. Signs reading *Réserve de Chasse* or *Chasse Privé* indicate that the shooting is reserved for the landowner, so treat such warnings with respect.

Useful Expressions and Vocabulary

This list contains words and phrases to help the traveller when shopping, eating out, and getting around. Some useful "courtesy" words are also included which may be helpful. French is quite a complicated language. A good language course should be followed, and this will greatly increase your enjoyment of the country. Always try to speak slowly, and ask others to speak slowly to you. Do try *some* words of French; it will be much appreciated, and you will very likely get more co-operation if you have to resort to your native tongue! No one will worry if you get your masculine and feminine words mixed up!

Shopping

I would like to buy	Je voudrais acheter
How much? (is it)	C'est combien?
Do you accept credit/charge cards?	Cartes de crédit?
VISA card	Carte-Bleu
I need	J'ai besoin de
Do you have some, a—?	Avez-vous des, un—?
That's too expensive	C'est trop cher
That's not expensive	Ce n'est pas cher
I am looking for a —	Je cherche un—
Where is the—	Où est le, la—?
Where do I pay?	Où est la caisse?
Where is the shopping centre?	Où est le centre commercial?
What time do the shops open/close?	A quelle heure ouvrent/ferment les magasins?
I need some money	J'ai besoin d'argent
Have you any change?	Avez-vous de la petite monnaie?
Annual holidays	fermeture annuelle
weekly closing	fermeture hebdomadaire
Sale	Solde
a discount	un rabais
shops	les magasins

baker	la boulangerie
bank	la banque
butcher	la boucherie
cake shop	la pâtisserie
chemist	la pharmacie
fishmonger	la poissonnerie
delicatessen	le charcuterie
grocer	l'épicerie
hairdresser	le coiffeur
health-food shop	la boutique des produits diététique
paper shop	la maison de la presse
stationer	la papeterie
bookshop	la librairie
sweet shop	la confiserie
watchmaker	l'horloger
wine-shop, cellar	la cave

Things to Buy—Food

bread (wholemeal)	du pain (complet)
butter	du beurre
jam	de la confiture
ham	du jambon
rolls	des petits pains
cheese	du fromage
fish	du poisson
eggs	des oeufs
yoghurt	le yaourt
sausages	les saucissons
meat	des viandes

Things to Buy—Non-food

a film	une pelicule
slides	des diapositifs
shoes	des chaussures
clothes	des vêtements

presents	des cadeaux
tights	un collant
trousers	un pantalon
stamps (postage)	des timbres (de poste)
telephone card	une télécarte
suntan cream	de la crème solaire
soap	du savon
toilet paper	du papier hygiénique

Eating Out

I'd like something to eat	Je voudrais manger
Do you have an area for non-smokers?	Avez-vous un endroit pour non-fumeurs?
Do you have a set menu?	Avez-vous un menu?
May I have the menu?	Puis j'avoir la carte?
Do you have any local dishes?	Avez-vous des spécialités locales?
What do you recommend?	Que me recommandez?
May I have a glass of water?	Puis-je avoir une verre d'eau potable?
soups	les potages
cold meat selection	une assiette anglaise
poultry	des volailles
chicken	du poulet
turkey	de la dinde
beef	du boeuf
lamb	d'agneau
game	les gibiers
well-cooked	bien-cuit
rare	saignant
very rare	bleu
underdone	pas assez cuite

Getting Around On the Road

left	à gauche
right	à droite
straight on	tout droit
bends	les virages
slow down	ralentir
one-way	sens-unique
no entry	entrée interdit
give way (to traffic from right)	priorité à droite
give way	vous n'avez pas priorité
give way (at junction)	cédez le passage
No parking	Interdit de stationner
No through road, road blocked	Toute barrée
Road works	Travaux
Poor surface	Chaussée déformée
Speed limit	Limite de vitesse
Toll	Péage
Watch out, take care	Prenez garde
I need some help	J'ai besoin d'assistance
Help! (emergency)	Au secours!
Someone's injured	Personne est blessé
I'm lost!	Je me suis perdu!
I've lost my keys	J'ai perdu mes cléfs
Alternative route	Bison Futé (bis)
Traffic lights	Les feux
Height limit (bridge, etc.)	Hauteur limité
Motorway rest area	Aire de repos
Diversions	Déviations
Parking disc	Disque de stationnement
Self-service	Libre service
Petrol (gasoline)	Essence
Lead-free	Sans plomb
traffic police	garde mobile

332

Car Problems

breakdown service	dépannage
My car's broken down	Ma voiture est en panne
I'm out of petrol	Je suis en panne d'essence
Something's wrong with	J'ai une problème avec
the brakes	les freins
the exhaust	le pot d'échappement
the radiator	le radiateur
one of the wheels	une roue
My car won't start	Je n'arrive pas à démarrer
It's overheating	Le moteur chauffe
I've got a flat tyre	J'ai un pneu à plat
The battery is flat	La batterie est à plat
How long will it take?	Combien de temps faut-il?
The windscreen is broken	Le pare-brise est cassé
Would you please repair it?	Pourriez-vous le réparer s'il-vous-plaît?
pedestrians	les piétons
cycles	vélos
for hire	à louer

Some Other Useful Phrases and Words

guided visit	visite guidée
visit at your own leisure	visite libre
free entry	entrée gratuite
thank-you	merci
please	s'il vous plaît
good morning	bonjour madame, monsieur
(always add 'madame, monsieur', and always said on entering and leaving a shop)	
Would you please speak a little slower	Vous parlez un peu plus lentement, s'il vous plait
tomorrow morning	demain matin
this afternoon	cette après-midi
tonight, this evening	ce soir
reception (in hotel, campsite)	reception, accueil
no entry	défense d'entrer
private land	chasse gardée

333

Information to Help You Have a Good Trip

French Government Tourist Offices Abroad

Canada
French Government Tourist Office
1981 Avenue Mc Gill College
Tour Esso
Suite 490
Montréal QUE H3 A2 W9
Tel: 514-288-42-64

French Government Tourist Office
1 Dundas Street West
Suite 2405
Box 8
Toronto ONT M5 G1 Z3
Tel: 416-593-47-23

Great Britain
French Government Tourist Office
178 Piccadilly
London W1V 0AL
Tel: 071-491-7622

United States
French Government Tourist Office
610, Fifth Avenue
Suite 222
New York NY 10020-2452
Tel: 212-757-11-25

French Government Tourist Office
645 North Michigan Avenue
Chicago, ILL. 60611 2836
Tel: 312-337-63-01

French Government Tourist Office
9454, Wilshire Boulevard
Beverly Hills
California 90212-2967
Tel: 213-272-26-61

French Government Tourist Office
2305 Cedar Springs Road
Stc 205 Dallas
Texas 75201
Tel: (214) 720-4010

Diplomatic Addresses

Australian Embassy
4, rue Jean Rey
75015 Paris
Tel: (1) 45-75-62-00

British Embassy
35, rue du Faubourg St Honoré
75383 Paris
Tel: (1) 42-66-91-42

British Consulate
5, rue des Cadeniers
44000 Nantes
Tel: 40-63-16-02

Canadian Embassy
35, avenue Montaigne
75008 Paris
Tel: (1) 47-23-01-01

Irish Embassy
4, rue Rude
75016 Paris
Tel: (1) 45-00-20-87

New Zealand Embassy
7ter, rue Léonard-de-Vinci
75016 Paris
Tel: (1) 45-00-24-11

United States Embassy
2, avenue Gabriel
75382 Paris
Tel: (1) 42-96-12-02

Tourist Information Offices

Principal Offices in the Loire
Cher
Office de Tourisme
21, rue Victor-Hugo
BP 145
18003 Bourges
Tel: 48-24-75-33

Eure-et-Loire
Office de Tourisme
place de la Cathédrale
28005 Chartres
Tel: 37-21-54-03

Indre
Office de Tourisme
place de la Gare
36000 Châteauroux
Tel: 54-34-10-74

Indre-et-Loire
Office de Tourisme
boulevard Heurteloup
37042 Tours
Tel: 47-05-58-08

Loire-Atlantique
Maison du Tourisme
place du Commerce
44000 Nantes
Tel: 40-89-50-77

Loiret
Maison du Tourisme
place Albert I
45000 Orléans
Tel: 38-53-05-95

Loir-et-Cher
Office de Tourisme
Pavilion Anne de Bretagne
3, avenue Jena-Laigret
41000 Blois
Tel: 54-74-06-49

Maine-et-Loire
Maison du Tourisme
place Kennedy
BP 2148
49021 Angers
Tel: 41-88-23-85

Sarthe
Office de Tourisme
Hôtel des Ursulines
rue d'Etoile
72000 Le Mans
Tel: 43-28-17-22

Tourist Offices in the Main Centres
Office de Tourisme
quai du Général de Gaulle
BP 233
37402 Amboise Cedex
Tel: 47-57-09-28

Maison du Tourisme
place Kennedy
BP 2397
49023 Angers Cedex
Tel: 41-88-69-93

Office de Tourisme
28, place du Martroi
45190 Beaugency
Tel: 38-44-54-42

Office de Tourisme de Blois-
Accueil de France
Pavillon Anne de Bretagne
3, avenue Jean-Laigret
41000 Blois
Tel: 54-74-06-49

Office de Tourisme
21, rue Victor Hugo
BP 145, 18003 Bourges
Tel: 48-24-75-33

Office de Tourisme
Parvis de la Cathédrale
BP 289, 28005 Chartres Cedex
Tel: 37-21-54-03

Office de Tourisme
1, rue de Luynes
28200 Châteaudun
Tel: 37-45-22-46

Office de Tourisme de
Châteauneuf
1, place Aristide Briand
45110, Châteauneuf-sur-Loire
Tel: 38-58-44-79

Office de Tourisme
12, rue Voltaire
BP 141
37501 Chinon Cedex
Tel: 47-93-17-85
and 47-93-36-91

Office de Tourisme
Hôtel-de-Ville
72205 cédex La Flèche
Tel: 43-94-02-53

Office de Tourisme—Syndicat
d'Initiative
rue Anne de Beaujeu
45500 Gien
Tel: 38-67-25-28

Office de Tourisme
Place de Wermelskirchen
37600 Loches
Tel: 47-59-07-98

Office de Tourisme—Syndicat
d'Initiative
Hôtel des Ursulines
rue de l'Etoile
720000 Le Mans
Tel: 43-28-17-22

Maison du Tourisme
place du Commerce
44000 Nantes
Tel: 40-89-50-77

Maison du Tourisme
place Albert 1er
45000 Orléans
Tel: 38-53-05-95

Office de Tourisme
place Raphael-Elizé
72300 Sable-sur-Sarthe
Tel: 43-95-00-60

Office de Tourisme
place de la Bilange
BP241
49415 Saumur Cedex
Tel: 41-51-03-06

Office de Tourisme de Sully-sur-
Loire
place de Gaulle
45600 Sully-sur-Loire
Tel: 38-36-23-70
and 38-36-32-21

Office de Tourisme de Tours
boulevard Heurteloup
37042 Tours Cedex
Tel: 47-05-58-08

Office de Tourisme
avenue de la Résistance
36600 Valençay
Tel:54-00-04-42

Office de Tourisme—Syndicat
d'Initiative
Hôtel du Bellay
41100 Vendôme
Tel: 54-77-05-07

Office de Tourisme
Hôtel de Ville
place Maurice-Thorez
18100 Vierzon
Tel: 48-75-20-03

Emergency Telephone Numbers

General
Police: dial 17
Fire brigade: dial 18
Ambulance: phone police

Angers
Doctor on call (SAMU): dial 15
Anti-poison centre:
Tel: 41-48-21-21

Chartres
Doctor on call: 37-36-20-20
Anti-poison centre: 47-66-85-11
Ambulance: contact police

Le Mans
Ambulance: 43-24-64-18 or
  contact police

Nantes
Accident: 40-08-38-95
Doctor on call (SAMU): 40-08-
37-77

Orléans
Doctor on call: 38-54-44-44
Anti-poison centre: 47-66-15-15 or
47-66-85-11 (TOURS)
Emergency medical help (Service
d'assistance médicale d'urgence
(SAMU): 38-63-33-33

Saumur
Doctor on call (SAMU)
Tel: 41-48-44-22 (Angers), or con-
tact police
Anti-poison centre: Tel: 41-48-21-
21 (Angers)

Tours
Urgent medical help: 47-28-15-15
Anti-poison centre: 47-66-85-11
Ambulance: 47-53-13-53
Doctor on call: contact police

General Useful Information

Angers
Office de Tourisme
place de la Gare
Angers (for personal enquirers)

Railway station:
Gare Saint-Laud
place de la Gare
Tel: 41-88-50-50
(travel enquiries and information)

Bus station:
Gare-Routière
place de la République
Tel: 41-88-59-25

Post office:
rue Franklin Roosevelt
Tel: 41-88-45-47 (also in place de
  la Gare)

Police:
Commissariat Central
15, rue Dupetit-Thouars

Hospital:
1, avenue de l'Hôtel-Dieu (in la
Doutre)

Blois
Railway station:
SNCF
Gare de Blois
avenue Jean-Laigret
Tel: (information) 54-78-50-50;
      (reservations) 54-78-83-49

Bus station:
Autogare
4 place Victor Hugo
Tel: 54-78-15-66

Main post office:
rue Gallois
(off place Victor Hugo)

Police station:
rue Jehan de Saveuse
Tel: 54-74-00-89

Hospital:
Centre Hospitalier
Mail Pierre Charlot
Tel: 54-78-00-82

Bourges
Railway station:
place du Général Leclerc

Bus station:
rue du Champ de Foire

Post office:
rue Moyenne

Police station:
rue Moyenne

Hospital:
Centre Hospitalier
34, rue Gambon
Tel: 48-68-40-00

Chartres
Railway station:
place Pierre-Sémard
Tel: 37-28-50-50

Bus station:
place Pierre Sémard
(next to railway station)
Tel: 37-21-30-35

Post office:
Boulevard Maurice-Viollette

Police station:
57 rue du Docteur Maunoury

Hospitals:
Hôpital Fontenoy
rue des Chaises
Le Coudray
Tel: 37-30-30-30
(approx 3km—2 miles—south of
the city centre)

Le Mans
Railway station:
place du 8-Mai
(boulevard de la Gare)

Bus station:
Autogare STAO
avenue du Général Leclerc

Post office:
place du 8-Mai
(next to railway station).
Also at place de la République

Police station:
rue Coëffort
Tel: 43-84-50-00

Hospital:
Centre Hospitalier
avenue Rubillard (direction
Laval)

Nantes
Railway station:
SNCF Gare de Nantes
boulevard de Stalingrad
Tel: 40-08-50-50

City transport information:
Tel: 40-29-39-39

Coach station:
Gare Routière
allée de la Maison Rouge

Airport:
Aeroport International de Nantes
Château Bougon
44340 Bouguenais
Tel: 40-84-82-17

Post office:
PTT, place de Bretagne

Police station:
Centre Cambronne
place Waldeck-Rousseau
Tel: 40-74-21-21

Hospital:
Hôtel-Dieu
place Alexis-Ricordeau
Tel: 40-08-33-33

Museums

Orléans
Railway station:
avenue de Paris, near place d'Arc

Bus station:
rue Emile Zola, near Natural
Science museum

Post office
place Général de Gaulle

Police station:
place Gambetta

Hospital:
Centre Hospitalier Regional
1, rue Porte Madeleine
Orléans
Tel: 38-51-44-44

Saumur
Railway station:
avenue David d'Angers
(On the north bank of the Loire)
Tel: 41-50-50-50

Bus station:
place Saint-Nicolas
Tel: 41-51-27-29

Post office:
place du Petit-Thouars and
avenue David d'Angers

Police station:
rue Montesquieu
Tel: 41-51-04-32

Hospital:
Centre Hospitalier
rue Seigneur
Tel: 41-53-25-00

Tours
Railway station:
Gare SNCF de Tours
place Maréchal Leclerc
Tel: (information) 47-20-50-50
(reservations) 47-32-18-48

Bus station:
Gare Routière
place Maréchal Leclerc
Tel: 47-05-30-49

Main post office:
1, boulevard Béranger
Tel: 47-21-50-15

Police:
Commissariat Central
14, Rue de Clocheville
Tel: 47-05-66-60

Angers
Musée des Beaux Arts
10, rue du Musée
Angers
Tel: 41-88-64-65

Galerie David d'Angers
33 bis, rue Toussaint
Angers
Tel: 41-87-21-03

Musée Pincé
32 bis, rue Lenepveu
Angers
Tel: 41-88-94-27

Musée des Coiffes
les Ponts-de-Cé
Tel: 41-44-60-44

Musée de l'Ardoise
32, rue de la Maraîchère
Trelazé
Tel: 41-69-04-71

Blois
Musée d'art religieux
Aux Jacobins
rue Anne de Bretagne
Tel: 54-78-17-14

Musée d'archéologie; Musée des
beaux arts; Musée de la magie
Château de Blois
Tel: 54-78-06-62 and 54-74-16-06

Musée d'histoire naturelle
Les Jacobins
rue Anne de Bretagne
Tel: 54-74-13-89

Musée Lapidaire, Au cloître
Saint-Saturnin
rue Munier
Tel: 54-78-06-62

Bourges
Musée des Arts Décoratifs
Hôtel Lallement
6, rue Bourbonnoux
Tel: 48-57-81-17

Musée du Berry
Hôtel Cujas
4–6 rue des Arènes
Tel: 48-57-81-15

Musée Estève
Hôtel des Echevins
13 rue Edouard de Branly
Tel: 48-24-75-38

Le Museum
rue Messire-Jacques
Tel: 48-57-82-44

Palais Jacques Coeur
rue Jacques-Coeur
Tel: 48-24-06-87

Chartres
Musée des Beaux Arts
Palais épiscopal
29, Cloître Notre-Dame
Tel: 37-36-41-39

Musée de l'école
1 rue du 14-Juillet
Tel: 37-28-57-90 and 37-35-46-85

Conservatoire du machinisme
agricole (Le Compa)
rue Danièle-Casanova
Tel: 37-36-11-30

Centre International du vitrail
Enclos de Loëns
5 rue du Cardinal Pie
Tel: 37-21-65-72

La Maison Picassiette
22 rue du Repos
Tel: 37-34-10-78

Le Mans
Musée de Tessé
2, avenue Paderborn
Tel: 43-47-47-47

Musée de la Reine Bérengère
7, rue de la Reine Bérengère
Tel: 43-47-47-47

Musée de l'Automobile
rue du Panorama
Tel: 43-72-50-66 (inside 24-hour
racing circuit)

Nantes
Musée des Beaux Arts
10, rue Georges-Clémenceau
Tel: 40-41-65-65

Museée des Arts Décoratif
Château des Ducs de Bretagne
Tel: 40-47-18-15

Musée d'Art Populaire Régional
Château des Ducs de Bretagne
Tel: 40-47-18-15

Musée des Salorges
Château des Ducs de Bretagne
Tel: 40-47-18-15

Musée Thomas Dobrée
place Jean V
Tel: 40-69-76-08

Musée Archéologique
place Jean V
Tel: 40-69-76-08

Musée d'Histoire Naturelle
12 rue Voltaire
Tel: 40-73-30-03

Musée Jules Verne
3, rue de l'Hermitage
Tel: 40-69-72-52

Le Planetarium
Square Moysan
8, rue des Acadiens
Tel: 40-73-99-23

Musée de la Poupée et des Jouets
Anciens
39, boulevard Saint-Aignan
Tel: 40-69-14-41

Musée de l'Imprimedrie
24, quai de la Fosse
Tel: 40-73-26-55

Musée de la Poste Pays de la
Loire
10, boulevard Auguste-Pageot
Tel: 40-29-93-07

**Orléans and
Surrounding Areas**
Musée des Beaux Arts
rue Paul-Belmondo
Orléans
Tel: 38-53-39-22

Musée Charles-Péguy
11, rue du Tabour
Orléans
Tel: 38-53-20-23

Hôtel-Musée Groslot
place de l'Etape
Orléans
Tel: 38-42-22-30

Musée Historique et
Archéologique de l'Orléanais
(Hôtel Cabu)
place Abbé-Desnoyers
Orléans
Tel: 38-53-39-22

Musée Jeanne d'Arc
3, place de Gaulle
Orléans
Tel: 38-42-25-45

Musée des Sciences Naturelles
2, rue Marcel-Proust
Orléans
Tel: 38-42-25-58

Musée de la Marine de Loire
Le Château
Châteauneuf-sur-Loire
Tel: 38-58-41-18

Musée International de la Chasse
Château de Gien
Tel: 38-67-69-69

Musée de la Faiencerie de Gien
place de la Victoire
Gien
Tel: 38-67-00-05

Musée de l'Automobile
avenue de Lattre de Tassigny
Briare
Tel: 38-31-20-34

Musée de l'Outil
Ferme du Château
Champoulet
Tel: 38-31-94-44

Musée Régional de l'Orléanais
Château de Dunois
2, place Dunois
Beaugency
Tel: 38-44-92-73

Musée-Aquarium
2, promenade de Barchelin
Beaugency
Tel: 38-45-92-73

Musée de l'Attelage et de
l'Eclairage des rues
6, route Nationale
Beaugency
Tel: 38-44-51-42

Saumur
Musée des Arts Décoratifs and
Musée du Cheval
Château de Saumur
Tel: 41-51-30-46

Musée de la Figurine-Jouet
Château de Saumur
Tel: 41-67-39-23

Musée des Blindés
place Charles de Foucauld
Tel: 41-67-20-96

Musée de l'Ecole de Cavalerie
avenue du Maréchal Foch
Tel: 41-51-05-43 ext. (poste) 306

Musée du Champignon
La Houssaye
St-Hilaire-St-Florent
Tel: 41-50-31-55

Tours
Aquarium Tropical
Château de Tours
quai d'Orléans
Tel: 47-64-29-52

Musée des Beaux Arts de Tours
18, place François Sicard
Tel: 47-05-68-73

Musée du Compagnonnage
Cloître St Julien
8, rue Nationale
Tel: 47-61-07-93

Musée du Gemmail
Hôtel Raimbault
7, rue du Mûrier
Tel: 47-61-01-19

Musée de la Société
Archéologique de Touraine
Hôtel Goüin
25, rue du Commerce
Tel: 47-66-22-32

Historial de Touraine
Musée Grévin
Château de Tours
quai d'Orléans
Tel: 47-61-02-95

Musée des Vins de Touraine
Celliers St Julien
16, rue Nationale
Tel: 47-61-07-93

Petit Musée du Costume
54, boulevard Béranger
Tel: 47-61-59-17

Campsites

Amboise
Camping Municipal "Ile d'Or"
Entrepot
Amboise
Tel: 47-57-23-37

Angers
Camping Caravaning du Lac de
Maine (3 star)
Route de Pruniers
Tel: 41-73-05-03

Blois
Camping Municipal de la Boire,
off Levée de Saint Dyé (D951)
on south bank, (3 star)
Tel: 54-74-22-78

Camping-Caravaning du Lac de
Loire, off D951 Vineuil (4 star)
Tel: 54-78-82-05

Bourges
Camping Municipal (3 star)
26, boulevard de l'Industrie
Bourges
Tel: 48-20-16-85

Camping Municipal de Bellon
(2 star)
Route de Bellon
Vierzon
Tel: 48-75-49-10 and 48-75-20-03

Camping Municipal Les Chênes
(3 star)
Valençay
Tel: 54-00-03-92 (on road D960
on edge of town)

Chartres
Municipal Campsite (3 star)
Les Bords de l'Eure
rue de Launay
Tel: 37-28-79-43
(open from April to September)

Le Mans
Camping du Vieux Moulin
(3 star)
Neuville-sur-Sarthe
(Direction Alençon, 10 min from
Le Mans)
Tel: 43-25-31-82

Camping de l'Hippodrome
La Prairie du Château
Allée du Québec
72300 Sable-sur-Sarthe
Tel: 43-95-42-61 (recommended)

Nantes
The following are all within 20km
(12 miles) of the city centre:
Camp de St Simon (2 star)
Road N751
La Chapelle-Basse-Mer
Tel: 40-54-01-40

Camp Municipal du Val du Cens
(4 star)
21, boulevard du Petit Port
Nantes
Tel: 40-74-47-94

Camp Municipal La Colleterie
(3 star)
St-Etienne-de-Montluc
Tel: 40-86-97-44

Camp Le Plan d'Eau du Chêne
(2 star)
Road D37
St-Julien-de-Concelles
Tel: 40-54-12-00

Camp Municipal de La Grève
(2 star)
CD 119 boulevard des Pas
Enchantés
St-Sebastien-sur-Loire
Tel: 40-80-01-79

Camp Municipal de La Papinière
(2 star)
Road D37
Sucé-sur-Erdre
Tel: 40-77-75-54

Orléans
Camping Municipal (2 star)
rue du Pont Bouchet
Olivet
Tel: 38-63-53-94

Camping Municipal du Château
(3 star)
rue des Grèves
La Chapelle-Saint-Mesmin
Tel: 38-43-60-46

Camping Municipal (2 star)
Bord de Loire
Sully-sur-Loire
Tel: 38-36-23-93

Camping Touristique (2 star)
quai de Sully
Gien
Tel: 38-67-12-50 and 38-67-25-28

Camping Caravanage Les Bois du
Bardelet (4 star, recommended)
Poilly-les-Gien
Tel: 38-67-47-39

Camping Municipal
(2 star)
Bord de Loire
Beaugency
Tel: 38-44-50-39

Camping Caravanage du
Domaine de la Grenouillère
(4 star)
Suèvres
Tel: 54-87-80-37 (about 15km—
(9 miles—downstream on the
N152 towards Blois; highly
recommended)

Saumur
Camping Caravanning Ile
d'Offard (3 star)
avenue de Verden
Tel: 41-67-45-00

Castel Camping Etang de la
Brèche (4 star)
Varennes-sur-Loire
Tel: 41-51-22-92. Highly
recommended (5 km—3 miles—
upstream from Saumur).

Tours
Camping Caravanage Municipal
Eduard Péron
place Eduard-Péron (2 star)
Tours
Tel: 47-54-11-11

Other sites within 6km (3½ miles) of
the city centre are:

Camping Caravanage de la
Mignardière (4 star)
Ballan-Miré
Joué-lès-Tours
Tel: 47-53-26-49

Camping Municipal des Rives du
Cher (3 star)
62, rue de Rochepinard
St Avertin
Chambray-lès-Tours
Tel: 47-27-27-60

Camping Municipal Les Acacias
(2 star)
rue Berthe Morizot
La Ville-aux-Dames
St-Pierre-des-Corps
Tel: 47-44-08-16

Camping Municipal (2 star)
Ile Auger
Chinon
Tel: 47-93-08-35

Camping Municipal (1 star)
rue Quintefol
Loches
Tel: 47-59-05-91

Camping Municipal (2 star)
Route de Châtellerault
Richelieu
Tel: 47-58-10-13

Valley of Le Loir
Camping Municipal du Moulin à
Tan (2 star)
rue de Chollet
28200 Châteaudun
Tel: 37-45-05-34 and 37-45-11-91

Camping Municipal des Grands
  Prés (3 star)
rue Geoffroy Martel
Vendôme
Tel: 54-77-00-27

Camping Municipal
  (3 star)
Route du Mans
Le Lude
Tel: 43-94-67-60

Camping de la Route d'Or
  (3 star)
La Flèche
Tel: 43-94-55-90

Youth Hostels

LFAJ
Centre Charles Péguy
1, rue Commir Entrepont
Amboise
Tel: 47-57-06-36

FUAJ
Centre d'Acceuil du Lac de Maine
Route de Pruniers
Angers
Tel: 41-48-57-01

FUAJ
152, route de Châteaudun
Vernon
Beaugency
Tel: 38-44-61-31

FUAJ
18, rue de l'Hôtel Pasquier
Les Grouets
Blois.
Tel: 54-28-27-21 (simple)

FUAJ
22, rue Henri Sellier
Bourges
Tel: 48-24-58-09

FUAJ
23, avenue Neigre
28000 Chartres
Tel: 37-34-27-64

FUAJ
2, place de la Manue
Nantes
Tel: 40-20-57-25

LFAJ
14 rue du Faubourg Madeleine
Orléans
Tel: 38-62-45-75

FUAJ
Centre International de séjour
rue de Verden
Ile d'Offard
Saumur
Tel: 41-67-45-00

FUAJ
Avenue d'Arsonval
Parc de Grandmont
Tours
Tel: 47-25-14-45

FUAJ
place de la République
Vierzon
Tel: 48-75-30-62

The Right Place at the Right Price

Whichever town you visit in the Loire valley there will be a good range of hotels from which to choose, with several dozen in each of the larger towns and cities. The Ministry of Tourism classifies hotels from one- to four-star on the basis of their facilities, but below we have given an indication of price per room. French hotels normally charge per room which gives good value for couples. In the more expensive hotels most rooms will come with an adjoining bathroom.

The hotels listed below have been classified with regard price as follows:

I	up to 350F;
II	350–600F;
III	over 600F.

This is the cost per night for a room. Breakfast is usually charged as an extra. These price ranges should only be viewed as guides as hotels may have some rooms available that fall into the price band above or below the one in which they have been placed, and prices vary from season to season.

There are plenty of restaurants to tempt the palette in the region. Many hotels have their own restaurant and if this is the case it is indicated in the main hotel list. Each regional tourist board produces its own list of local restaurants which is updated annually. As restaurants rapidly come and go we have not attempted to produce a list here which would be quickly out of date. Instead we advise the visitor to obtain a local restaurant list from the nearest tourist office to where they are staying.

Amboise

Château de Pray　II
F-37400
Tel: 47-57-23-67
3 km from station and 1.5 km from Amboise. A converted 13th-century castle high above the Loire. Dining room. 16 rooms. Furnished traditionally with antiques. 1 January to 15 February.

Le Choiseul　III
36, quai Charles Guinot
F-37400
Tel: 47-30-45-45
Two hours from Orly International airport and 30 minutes from the station on the banks of the Loire. Dine in the garden in summer. 32 rooms. Terraced gardens and outdoor pool.

Novotel　II
17, rue des Sablonnières
F-37400
Tel: 47-57-42-07
2 km from city centre overlooking the Loire. 121 rooms. Swimming pool, tennis courts and minigolf.

La Brèche　I
26, rue Jules-Ferry
Tel: 47-57-00-79

Auberge le Chaptal　I
13, rue Chaptal
Tel: 47-57-14-46

These hotels all have restaurants but there are other hotels with or without restaurants in the town or immediate neighbourhood.

Angers

Anjou　II
1, boulevard Maréchal-Foch
F-49100
Tel: 41-88-24-82
4 km from Angers Airport and 800 m from the station. Restaurant and bar. 51 rooms. Summer terrace, swimming pool, gym and sauna.

341

Concorde ❙❙
18, boulevard Foch
F-49100
Tel: 41-87-49-54
9 km from Nantes Airport and 1 km from the station in the centre of town. Restaurant, bar and street café. 75 rooms.

France ❙❙
8, place de la Gare
F-49100
Tel: 41-88-49-42
A five-storey building close to the station. Bar. 57 rooms.

Ibis ❙
rue de la Poissonnerie
Tel: 41-86-15-15

Jeanne de Laval ❙
34, boulevard du Roi-René
Tel: 41-88-51-95

Saint-Jacques ❙
83–85, rue Saint-Jacques
Tel: 41-48-51-05
On the north bank, near the monastery.

Auberge de Belle-Rive ❙
25 bis, rue Haute-Reculée
Tel: 41-48-18-70
On the north bank, near the hospital.

Centre ❙
12, rue Saint-Laud
Tel: 41-87-45-07

Les Lices ❙
25, rue des Lices
Tel: 41-87-44-10

There are a lot of hotels in Angers, and the tourist office can supply a full list. A selection are included here, all of which have a restaurant, and which are in easy reach of the city centre.

Blois

Campanile ❙
rue de la Vallée Maillard
Tel: 54-74-44-66

Domaine de Seillac ❙❙
Seillac
F-41150
Tel: 54-20-72-11
An 18th-century castle in a 45 acre wooded estate 15 km from the station. Grill in summer. 87 rooms. Complimentary breakfast. Outdoor swimming pool and tennis courts. Cottages available.

Ibis Hotel ❙
15 Rue de la Vallée-Maillard
F-41000
Tel: 54-74-60-60
3 km from station on the outskirts of the city. 61 rooms.

L'Horset Lavallière ❙❙
26, avenue Maunoury
F-41000
Tel: 54-74-19-00
50 km from Tours Airport, central and within walking distance of Château Blois. 78 rooms. Golf and tennis are nearby.

Le Monarche ❙
61, rue Porte Chartraine
Tel: 54-78-02-35

Novotel Blois ❙❙
1, rue de l'Almandin
La Chaussée Saint Victor
F-41260
Tel: 54-78-33-57
5 km from station and 3 km from city centre. Grill restaurant and bar. 116 rooms. Wheelchair accessibility and outdoor pool.

Viennois ❙
5, quai Amédée Coutant
Tel: 54-74-12-80

A la Ville de Tours ❙
2, place de la Grève.
Tel: 54-78-07-86

All the above hotels have restaurants. Novotel is in a suburb to the east, off the N152 Orléans road, and Viennois is on the south bank of the river near the Gabriel bridge. The others are within easy reach of the centre. There are many other hotels in and near the city, with or without restaurants.

Bourges and the Surrounding Areas

Bourges
Hôtel d'Angleterre ❙❙
1, place des Quatre Piliers
Tel: 48-24-68-51

Hôtel d'Artagnan ❙
19, place Séraucourt
Tel: 48-21-51-51

Hôtel le Berry ❙
3, place du Général Leclerc
Tel: 48-65-99-30

Hôtel l'Hostellerie du Grand ❙
Argentier
9, rue Parerie
Tel: 48-70-84-31

Hôtel Le Rocher ❙
43, rue de Sarrebourg

All the above hotels have a restaurant and are within easy reach of Bourges city centre. There are several chain hotels including Campanile and Confortel Louisiane on the outskirts of the city. There are also various small Logis de France in villages not far away. One of these, Hôtel l'Echalier at Fussy, on the D940 road to the north of Bourges, has comfortable motel-style rooms in the garden, and the dining room offers a very good menu.

Surrounding Areas
Hôtel le Lion d'Or ❙
2, Marcel Bailly
Mennetou-sur-Cher
Tel: 54-98-01-13

Arche Hôtel ❙
place de la République
Vierzon
Tel: 48-71-93-10

Hôtel Berry-Nord ❙
21, rue du Docteur-Roux
Vierzon
Tel: 48-75-03-96

Hôtel le Lion d'Or ❙
place du Marché Valençay
Tel: 54-00-00-87

These hotels all have restaurants.

Chartres
Hôtel du Bœf Couronné ❙
15, place Châtelet
Tel: 37-21-11-26

Hôtel Mercure Châtelet ❙❙
6–8 avenue Jehan de Beauce
Tel: 37-21-78-00

Château d'Esclimont ❙❙❙
St Symphorien-le-Château
F-28700
Tel: 37-31-15-15
15 km from Chartres cathedral. 55 rooms. Set in 150 acre park, surrounded by moats, stone bridges and towers. Tennis, outdoor pool.

Hôtel l'Ecu I
28–30 rue du Grand Faubourg
Tel: 37-21-34-59

Le Grand Monarque III
22, place des Epars
PO Box 247
F-28005
Tel: 37-21-00-72
54 rooms. Dates from 1700, renovations in 1987.

Novotel-Chartres II
Av Marcel Proust
F-28000
Tel: 37-34-80-30
78 rooms. Outdoor pool.

Hôtel la Poste I
3, rue du Général Koenig
Tel: 37-21-04-27

All the above hotels have a restaurant and are centrally situated. Visitors who prefer a quieter location might prefer to stay outside Chartres. A suggestion is the Logis de France (2 star) or Hôtel au Quai Fleuri at Voves (2 star), some 15 km (9 miles) south of the city. Information on other hotels may be obtained from the tourist office.

Châteaudun

Hôtel de la Rose I
12, rue Lambert Licors
28200 Châteaudun
Tel: 37-45-21-83
4-star restaurant.

Chinon

Château de Marcay IIII
F-37500
Tel: 47-93-03-47
15th-century castle converted to a hotel in 1971, in beautiful park setting. 6 km from station. 38 rooms. Restaurant. Outdoor heated swimming pool.

Chéops Hotel I
Center St Jacques
F-37500
Tel: 47-98-46-46
Modern hotel in quiet area overlooking Chinon castle, 1 km from station. Restaurant. 55 rooms. Wheelchair accessibility.

La Flèche

Hôtel de l'Image I
50, rue Grollier
Tel: 43-94-00-50

Hôtel du Vert Galant I
70, Grande Rue
Tel: 43-94-00-51
Has an excellent restaurant and can be recommended.

Le Mans

Arcade I
rue du Vert Galant
Tel: 43-24-47-24

Campanile I
23 boulevard Pablo Neruda
Tel: 43-72-18-72

Concorde II
16 avenue Général Leclerc
F-72000
Tel: 43-24-12-30

Moderne II
14 rue du Bourg Belé
Tel: 43-24-79-20

Les Relais Bleus II
8 boulevard Alexandre Oyon
Tel: 43-85-49-00

With the exception of the Campanile hotel, which is to the east of the city, all hotels are reasonably central, and all have restaurants. There are at least 15 other hotels with restaurants, and a similar number without restaurants, in and around the city.

Novotel Le Mans Est I
Zac les Sablons
Blvd Robert Schumann
F-72000
Tel: 43-85-26-80
3 km from station. Grill restaurant. 94 rooms. Wheelchair accessibility, outdoor pool.

Nantes

Abbaye de Villeneuve Hotel IIII
Rte des Sables d'Olonne
Les Sorinières
F-44840
Tel: 40-04-40-25
An 18th-century Cistercian abbey 10 km from Nantes airport. 20 rooms. Parking and outdoor pool.

Albatros I
27, rue de la Montagne
Tel: 40-73-66-09

Altea Carquefou Hotel II
Rue de l'Hotellière
RN 23
Carquefou
F-44470
Tel: 40-30-29-24
In park 7 km from centre of Nantes. Restaurant and bar. 77 rooms. Tennis court. Golf nearby.

Arcade I
19, rue Jean Jaurès
Tel: 40-35-39-00

Arcotel-Centre Routier I
la Haluchère
Route de Paris
Tel: 40-49-27-87

le Domaine d'Orvault II
Chemin des Marais-du-Cens
Orvault
F-44700
Tel: 40-76-84-02
A country inn 18 km from the airport and 7 km from the station. 30 rooms. Tennis court. Golf nearby.

France II
24, rue Crébillon
F-44000
Tel: 40-73-57-91
6 km from airport and 1 km from station opposite the opera house. Restaurant, grill and bar. 76 rooms. TV lounge.

Ibis-Nantes Centre I
3, Allée Baco
Tel: 40-20-21-20

Novotel Nantes-Carquefou II
Allée des Sapins
Carquefou
F-44470
Tel: 40-52-64-64
25 km from Nantes-Atlantique Airport and 12 km from the station. Grill and bar. 98 rooms. Outdoor swimming pool.

Otelinn I
50–52, rue de l'Ouche-Buron
Tel: 40-50-07-07

Pullman Beaulieu Hotel II
3 Rue Dr Zamenhof
Beaulieu
F-44200
Tel: 40-47-10-58
An eight-storey hotel 10 km from Nantes Airport and 1.5 km from the station. Restaurant and bar. 149 room., Garage.

Sofitel ▮▮
15 boulevard Alexandre Millerand
F-44000
Tel: 40-47-61-03
2.5 km from station and town centre.
Restaurant, café and bars. 100
rooms. Sound-proof, air-conditioned
rooms, some non smoking. Car park,
tennis court and heated outdoor
swimming pool with bar and terrace.

La Terrasse ▮
25, boulevard Stalingrad
Tel: 40-74-16-48

Trois Marchands ▮
26, rue Armand Brossard
Tel: 40-47-62-00

The city and suburbs of Nantes are
well provided with hotels in all cat-
egories and the Tourist Office can
supply up-to-date information. Above
are a selection of hotels with restau-
rants within easy reach of the city
centre, most of which also have their
own parking.

Orléans and Surrounding Areas
There are many hotels in Orléans,
and a good number in the surround-
ing area, including several chain
hotels.

Orléans
Hôtel Bannier ▮
13, rue du Faubourg Bannier
Tel: 38-53-25-86
2-star restaurant.

Hôtel le Bec Fin ▮
26, boulevard Aristide Briand
Tel: 38-62-43-55
3-star restaurant.

Hôtel Chéops ▮▮
place de l'Europe (rue des
    Charrières)
F-45000
Tel: 38-43-92-92
2 km from station and one hour
from Orly International Airport on
the Loire. 111 rooms.

Novotel Orléans la Source ▮▮
2 Rue Honoré de Balzac
F-45100
Tel: 38-63-04-28
Opposite Floral Park. Grill room and
bar. 119 rooms. Outdoor pool. Ten-
nis and golf nearby.

Sofitel ▮▮
44–46, quai Barentin
F-45000
Tel: 38-62-17-39
1.5 km from station, in the centre of
town on the Loire. 110 rooms. A
multi-storey hotel with sound-proof,
air-conditioned rooms. Outdoor pool
and garage.

All the above Orléans hotels have
restaurants.

Hôtel d'Arc ▮▮
37, rue de la République
Tel: 38-53-10-94

Hôtel Jackotel ▮
18, cloître Saint-Aignan
Tel: 38-54-48-48

Hôtel Sanotel ▮
16, quai Saint-Laurent
Tel: 38-54-47-65

The above three hotels do not have
restaurants. A full list of hotels and
restaurants is available from the
Maison du Tourisme in Orléans.

Surrounding Areas
Hôtel les Cèdres ▮▮
17, rue Maréchal Foch
F-45000
Beaugency
Tel: 38-62-22-92
10 minutes from town centre. No
restaurant. 36 rooms. Quiet location.

Hôtel le Concorde ▮
1, rue Porte de Sologne
Sully-sur-Loire
Tel: 38-36-24-44

Hôtel l'Ecu de Bretagne ▮
3,5,7, rue de la Maille d'Or
Beaugency
Tel: 38-44-67-60

Hôtel Hostellerie le Canal ▮
19, rue du Pont-Canal
Briare
Tel: 38-31-22-54

Nouvel Hôtel du Loiret ▮
place Aristide Briand
Châteauneuf-sur-Loire
Tel: 38-58-42-28

Hôtel le Rivage ▮▮
1, quai de Nice
Gien
Tel: 38-67-20-53

Hôtel La Tonnellerie ▮▮▮
12, rue des Eaux Bleues
Tavers
F-45190
Situated in a small village in the
heart of the Châteaux de la Loire re-
gion, 3 km from Beaugency station.
Restaurant with open-air dining. 20
rooms. Outdoor swimming pool, golf
and tennis nearby. Open 24 April to
13 October. This hotel is highly rec-
ommended.

All the above hotels in the vicinity
of Orléans have restaurants.

Saumur and Surrounding Areas
Hôtel Anne d'Anjou ▮▮
32–33 quai Mayaud
Tel: 41-67-51-00

La Bascule ▮
1, place Kléber
Tel: 41-51-30-83

Campanile ▮
rond Point de Bourman
Bagneux
Tel: 41-50-14-40

Loire Hôtel ▮▮
rue du Vieux-Pont
Tel: 41-67-22-42

Le Prieure Hotel ▮▮▮
Chenehutte-les-Tuffeaux
Gennes
F-49350
Tel: 41-67-90-14
100 km from Tours Airport and 10
km from station on banks of Loire.
35 rooms. Heated outdoor swimming
pool, tennis, minigolf and fishing.
Open March to December.

Hôtel du Roi René ▮
94, avenue Général de Gaulle
Tel: 41-67-31-01

L'Ecuye ▮▮
14, avenue David d'Angers
Tel: 41-67-39-96

There are plenty of hotels in Saumur,
and the tourist office can supply a list
on request. A selection is given here.
All the above have a restaurant.
The Campanile hotel is situated
about 3½ km (2 miles) to the south;
the Loire Hôtel and Hôtel du Roi
René are on Ile d'Offard. L'Ecuyer
is on the north side of the river, near
the railway station.

Tours

Hôtel Akilène I
22, rue du Grand Marché
Tel: 47-61-46-04

Hôtel Alliance II
292, avenue de Grammont
F-37200
Tel: 47-28-00-80
3 km from station on the outskirts of Tours. 125 rooms. Nightclub, outdoor swimming pool, tennis court and games room. Golf and hunting grounds nearby.

Le Bordeaux II
3, place du Maréchal Leclerc
Tel: 47-05-40-32

Château d'Artigny III
Rte d'Azay-le-Rideau
Montbazon
F-37250
Tel: 47-26--24-24
25 km from Blagnac airport,19 km south of Tours. Restaurants, bar and lounges. 57 rooms. Library, outdoor swimming pool and tennis courts. Open 9 January to 30 November.

Chéops Saint-Avertin I
8 rue du Pont de L'Arche
Saint Avertin
F-37550
Tel: 47-27-56-56
10 km from Symphorien Airport and 2 km from station. 56 rooms. Nearby watersports.

Domaine de la Tortinière II
Veigne
Montbazon
F-37250
Tel: 47-26-00-19
A manor overlooking the Indre river 15 km from Tours airport and 12 km from Tours station. Restaurant and bar. 21 rooms. Outdoor pool and tennis court. Open March to December.

Fimotel I
247, rue Giraudeau
Tel: 47-37-00-36

Le Grand Hotel II
9 Place Maréchal-Leclerc
F-37000
Tel: 47-05-35-31
6 km from Symphorien Airport in city centre. Bar. 118 rooms. Sauna.

Hotel Jean Barclet III
57 Rue Groison
F-37100
Tel: 47-41-41-11
10 km from Tours airport and 1 km from town. 15 rooms. Outdoor swimming pool and water sports nearby.

Hôtel du Musée I
2, place François Sicard
Tel: 47-66-63-81

Le Parc de Belmont III
57, rue Groison
Tel: 47-41-41-11

Le Relais I
178, quai Paul Bert
Tel: 47-51-28-45

de l'Univers Hotel II
5 Blvd Heurteloup
F-37000
Close to station. 89 rooms. Bar. Garages.

Tours is very well provided with good hotels, with or without restaurants, both in the city and in the suburbs. Most of the hotel chains have establishments in the suburbs. The above are a selection, all with restaurants.

Vendôme

Hôtel la Bonne Etoile I
La Croix Ouest
route de Blois
Tel: 54-72-28-38

Hôtel du Château I
place du Château
Tel: 54-77-20-98

Hôtel Vendôme II
15, Faubourg Chartrain
Tel: 54-77-02-88

All three Vendôme hotels have a restaurant.

Index